THE GLOBAL EDGE

HOW YOUR COMPANY CAN WIN IN THE INTERNATIONAL MARKETPLACE

Sondra Snowdon

Simon and Schuster New York

Copyright © 1986 by Sondra Snowdon
All rights reserved
including the right of reproduction
in whole or in part in any form
Published by Simon and Schuster
A Division of Simon & Schuster, Inc.
Simon & Schuster Building
Rockefeller Center
1230 Avenue of the Americas
New York, New York 10020
SIMON AND SCHUSTER and colophon are registered trademarks
of Simon & Schuster, Inc.
Designed by Irving Perkins Associates
Manufactured in the United States of America
10 9 8 7 6 5 4 3 2 1
Library of Congress Cataloging in Publication Data
Snowdon, Sondra.
    The global edge.

    Includes index.
    1. Business etiquette.   2. Negotiation in business.
3. Export marketing.   I. Title.
HF5387.S59 1986   395'.22   86-3990
ISBN 0-671-60122-9

*This book is dedicated to
the global executive who believes
that through world trade nations
can and will build bridges for
greater peace and understanding.*

CONTENTS

8   Contents

FOREWORD

"The business of America is business," said Calvin Coolidge, a man of few words. Business, as America saw it in Coolidge's time, was indeed substantially an all-American affair. Our continental closed-circuit "common market" provided sufficient scope for the imagination, drive, and commercial genius of American enterprise. Of course, continental marketing required getting to know ourselves—at least well enough to sell suits, soaps, and sundries with equal ease in New York, Alabama, Minnesota, and California, to name a few disparate cultures. Thus arose the image—or caricature, if you will—of the American traveling salesman, at best comically out of tune with heartland values and lifestyles, at worst an unprincipled adventurer with whom no dollar or daughter was safe. But the best of the traveling salesmen knew their "territory."

Indeed, a country as culturally diverse as our own has provided a unique and valuable crucible for the development of cross-cultural marketing skills. Today's challenge is to extend that competency in order to meet and contain the growing power of world competition. For today, the business of the *world* is business. And the company or country that forgets or neglects that point will soon find itself in grave economic difficulty.

Moreover, the world is a quite different territory. Its population (which jointly and often severally dwarfs our own) looks to gods and glories that antedate the arrival of our founding fathers by many centuries. They descend from civilizations that rose and fell and now have risen again, with a kind of rhythmic inevitability. Sifting their ruins—and, when available, their literature—we sometimes learn why. More important, the surviving traits and values of the descendants of these civilizations are the living proof of both their resilience of spirit and their resistance to quick change. Not easily modified to accommodate to military or economic conquest, they are, for all practical purposes, and within all conceivable "corporate lifetimes," here to stay.

Peace, concord, and mutually beneficial trade with such a diverse array of societies will require a new breed of Americans, a generation less deserving of George Bernard Shaw's acerbic appraisal: "I have

9

defined the hundred percent American as ninety-nine percent an idiot." We no longer have a lock on world markets. The advent of new production technology in nations which already enjoy the advantage of low labor costs renders them that much more competitive, not only within their domestic markets, but within ours as well. This is an additional reason, and should be a considerable incentive, to ensure that every contact with a potential foreign customer is a positive one.

It can be so, and will be so, when that customer's cultural preferences and sensitivities are known in advance, and are properly recognized throughout the business relationship. Ordinary human courtesy may prove enough. Chances are, however, that some conscious suppression of a typical American impulse will be necessary. In some countries, for example, women do not enjoy the degree of freedom and equality they do in the United States. Whatever an American businessman may think of that, he will be wise to remember that his opposite number overseas is seldom comforted by such casual and innocent pleasantries as, "Please remember me to your wife"—never mind, "How's the little woman?"

Much has been written about the wide variances in proper timing for getting down to business in different countries. Read it all. Learn the pitfalls, but also try to be a bit creative with that "nonproductive" time. Today's executive is dealing with individuals, not clones of a monolithic culture. The Office of Protocol, before the arrival of each dignitary, briefs itself at some length not only on the distinguished guest's personal history but also on preferences in matters of dining, recreation, literary or cultural interests, family situation, hobbies, and pastimes as well. That information proves valuable to a president, a first lady, and all others likely to find themselves conversing with a prominent visitor. The latter's delight at having a recent article, golf score, or child's achievement recognized by the host, augurs well for the ensuing discussions.

Indeed, "protocol" is not simply what to *avoid* doing, but what to *do*. This might be the moment to reflect on the meaning of protocol, a question that has intrigued generations of puzzled reporters. I would define protocol as "the art of creating an environment for meetings so that they may be conducted and concluded with a minimum of misunderstanding, and maximum mutual satisfaction." These same principles apply whether the negotiations involve governments or the business community.

Remember, however, that in the international business community, the requirements of protocol do not begin and end at the doorstep of the business contact. They are a twenty-four-hour-a-day obligation, one that binds the businessperson no less firmly than the diplomat. Sondra Snowdon's book recognizes that point. She has defined the principles of business protocol and has provided the guidelines necessary to understand and employ them in today's expanding international markets to ensure successful competition. It is must reading.

JAMES W. SYMINGTON
Former U.S. Chief of Protocol

Introduction

HOW THIS BOOK CAN HELP YOU WIN IN WORLD MARKETS

The personal and professional demands placed upon the American business executive in today's international marketplace surpass any experienced in the past. How does one explore the potential of foreign markets, initiate contacts, secure representation, conduct complex negotiations in languages that he or she may not speak, in cultures very different from one's own, and finally outdistance the competition to conclude a successful deal?

Many large American corporations have set up special departments within their organizations to advise their executives on the techniques and strategies of doing business abroad. Many other companies, both large and small, have turned for advice to my own firm, Snowdon International, which was created specifically to provide American executives with the expertise necessary to conduct themselves and the process of negotiations with maximum effectiveness. But what of the ever increasing number of companies now entering the international marketplace? Or the individual entrepreneurs who seek to explore foreign markets or to introduce foreign investments, products, and services into the American market? Where do they turn?

There was a need, I felt, for a book that addressed the complete range of opportunities—and pitfalls—of doing business abroad for both the executives of multinational corporations and individual entrepreneurs. The global executive is not a tourist. One week this individual may be conducting business negotiations in Buenos Aires, the next in Beijing. For that reason, I resolved to go well beyond the conventional wisdom and the obvious generalities of protocol familiar to most international travelers. My emphasis throughout the discussion of the principles of business protocol and the descriptions of the 25 countries that represent the world's most important markets has been on the unusual and the unexpected. The information has been derived not only from my own experience, but also from interviews with over three hundred diplomats, consular officials, State Department negotiators, and American executives who have conducted international business for many years. My goal has been to provide the most practical and up-to-date guidelines with the comprehensiveness and depth that could come only from a broad spectrum of experts in this challenging field.

When football coach Vince Lombardi was asked why he had so many successful teams, he answered that the secret was in "mastering the fundamentals" of the game—running plays correctly, tackling and blocking effectively. His contention was that if these fundamentals were perfected, the successful plays and touchdowns would come more routinely. And they did. The same principle applies to the infinitely more complex game of international business. The fundamentals are, of course, a complete mastery of the subtleties of international business and of the variations in cultural attitudes that influence every business negotiation. Here, then, is your winning game plan for achieving *The Global Edge.*

PART I

ACHIEVING THE GLOBAL EDGE

STRATEGIC ISSUES IN INTERNATIONAL BUSINESS

The strategies and tactics appropriate for today's complex and ever changing international business environment often have little to do with the strategies and tactics of ten or fifteen years ago. Fundamental changes have occurred in the world economy. There is now increased competition and a greater need for close working relationships between individuals, companies, and governments.

The inability or unwillingness of many companies and individuals to become fully educated to the requirements of doing business internationally is a major obstacle to achieving success. Far too few take the time or make the effort to understand international business negotiating strategies or to adapt themselves to the realities of doing business in different countries, cultures, and languages. To illustrate this, consider the following question posed by a reader who wrote to me in the Career section of a recent edition of *Savvy* magazine:

> I am starting a new job in international sales where I will travel far and frequently—to Asia, Latin America, and Europe. I've heard all the stories about the importance of protocol—don't show the sole of your shoe to an Arab, don't open a gift from a Japanese associate in his presence, and so forth. Of course, I'm anxious to make a good impression and to make a sale, but isn't the importance of protocol exaggerated? I'm sure my clients will have a global outlook and be intelligent enough to realize that an American's customs and manners are different from theirs. How far must I bend to adapt to their ways in this day and age?

Further consider a recent letter to the editor of *Time* magazine written by Jeffrey T. Long of Long & Associates Architects, AIA, in Honolulu, Hawaii:

> I find it fascinating to learn more of the Japanese culture and traditions as my parents have recently returned from Japan bringing back a sampling of their heritage. My concern here, though, is our country's apparent preoccupation with the "Zen in Business Protocol," to the point where my associates question my "American"

17

directness when dealing with our Japanese clients. My explanation is: We are the leading business and financial country we are today because of our style and honesty in negotiations, our direct statement of purpose and the desire for swift results.

If we are indeed looking for equal advancement into the Japanese economy, the "Art of Silence" and protracted negotiations will only serve to camouflage our already delayed invitation into the Japanese market. We must maintain our identity and style and deal with our competition on an equal level, for the price of mimicking them will be a *defensive* negotiating position for ourselves.

I'll look forward to my first visit to Japan with the hopes of sharing in their rich culture and just possibly sharing, with them, the rich benefits of mine.

How far must we bend to negotiate effectively in the global marketplace? Or must we bend at all? The answer to that question is quite simple—and universal. The appropriate strategies and tactics will always depend upon the nature of the business relationship itself. In particular—Who is the buyer and who is the seller?

That distinction, however, is not the only consideration. Unfortunately, many business representatives make money together with little or no concern for each other as people. They are cordial and tolerant, but they enter into, negotiate, and conclude a deal, and then leave, often without any understanding of or deference for one another. In some cases, they may not even speak each other's language or have any knowledge of each other's customs. Those businesses that *do* show interest in the people with whom they are dealing have found that it will eventually lead to additional business. They have also found that if the global executive is going to be effective as a communicator and as a businessperson, he or she must be able to adapt to the different protocols each nation has as part of its tradition and heritage. Executive savoir-faire will not be enough to close the deal. With each diverse culture, a new and global perception must take place. In short, we must understand and employ all of the appropriate business diplomacy procedures and protocols if we are to be successful.

To quote Lundy Gordon, senior vice president, International, Shearson Lehman/American Express, Inc., "The bottom line is often considered to be the only measurement. However, without doing the homework and preparation on the *top* lines, and utilizing all the faculties and expertise available to you, there will be no bottom line."

Even beyond the bottom line, all of us involved in the international business community should ask: Are we to be mere ambassadors for profit, or look more to the future of the world in which we are dealing so that we will be ambassadors for *both* greater profits *and* better understanding?

International commerce is becoming more important every day. Businesses are affected by industrial, financial, and technological developments around the world. While the United States and Europe have hundreds of companies that receive over half their revenue from abroad and therefore have a high level of sensitivity to the new global economy, nationalistic attitudes are still operative in the majority of firms. The global business environment, however, encompasses many national cultures. While general business considerations are essentially the same the world over, the increasingly competitive environment calls for a specifically designed approach to each national market. This approach includes overall business objectives and goals, planning and negotiating strategy, and the subtleties of business and social protocol. While the attractiveness of a business proposal is determined by various factors, doing business overseas, or with a foreigner in our country, requires an understanding of the attitudes and customs of all participants.

The lesson for businesses, large and small, is that inasmuch as the global economy impacts on all businesses, whether directly via new competitors, or indirectly via fluctuating exchange rates and government policies, defensive strategies that insist there is only one way to do business—*your* way—are increasingly obsolete and dangerous. In the new global economy, managers and entrepreneurs must take an *offensive approach;* they must adapt themselves to other ways of doing business. It is the only way to compete successfully.

The recent emergence of international corporate giants has heightened the intensity of competition in both developing regions and in the developed world. An indicator of the increasingly competitive business environment is the number of new international partnerships, alliances, and mergers in which companies are participating. The new global economy is characterized by increasing numbers of joint ventures of all types uniting companies and institutions from opposite parts of the world in developing new technologies, products, services, and markets.

The "go-it-alone" strategy that fit the economic realities of the 1960s and 1970s is no longer the optimal strategy in all cases. Insider status in new markets and expertise in new technologies and processes are only a few of the potential advantages of avoiding the go-it-alone strategy. Developing a network of friends, partners, and associates helps both in good times *and* bad. As a result, today's executive will find that business associates may come from different cultures in many diverse parts of the world. Those above and below in the executive hierarchy may be of different nationalities. And last, but by no means least, the customers and clients may also be of different nationalities.

For some, the internationalization of business has proved to be a roadblock. For others, opportunities are increasing at an exponential rate. Predictability, however, cannot always apply to the global business setting. It is widely acknowledged that global pressures and tides affect almost all businesses, large or small, multinational or domestic. The requirement for greater attention and sensitivity to the global economics, trade, and investment environment are greater now than in the past, and will be greater still in the future. So, too, the requirements for greater attention and sensitivity to the principles of business protocol.

THE PRINCIPLES OF INTERNATIONAL BUSINESS PROTOCOL

The term *diplomat* originated in early history when it was customary to send messages on parchment from one leader, or king, to another. The parchment was known as a diploma, and the individual who presented the diploma to the leader came in time to be known as a diplomat. Today's international business executive plays much the same role, representing the corporation, and jetting across borders with an attaché case filled with contracts to be negotiated. Hence, the global executive is today's business diplomat.

In the early 1800s, a treaty was signed, known as the Vienna Convention, which outlined the protocol procedures that countries and their diplomatic representatives would adhere to. Prior to that time, there were incidents involving altercations, as diplomats sometimes literally fought to obtain seating positions at meetings or banquets in concert with their rank and status. The Vienna Convention established diplomatic precedence, based upon the chronology of the diplomat's presentation of credentials.

The Honorable True Davis, former U.S. ambassador to Switzerland, recalls a story about Adlai Stevenson. "I remember one time when Adlai Stevenson was ambassador to the UN and our relations with France were certainly not at their best; and he was intentionally slighted by the French ambassador to the UN, at a dinner party, by being given an inferior place at the table. He should have been up the scale, let's say, three or four seats. Adlai came in, looked at the seating arrangement, and left. It was the proper thing to do because that's an insult to your nation."

Recently, while having lunch with a consul general friend of mine, I learned that he had had a similar experience. He had been invited to a dinner party at the home of a bank president who lived in Connecticut, and he was gravely offended because he was seated in a position of lesser rank at the dinner table than many businesspeople in attendance. The bank president's lack of sensitivity to the correct protocol in the situation created unnecessary and undue displeasure. His attempt to entertain the consul general and his wife backfired. I asked my friend how he would arrange the table if the situation were now reversed, and he said, laughingly, that he would consider the rank and status of his banking guests, and then proceed to seat the banker representing the most money next to himself.

These two situations represent a relatively small indication of the much greater need to establish guidelines for dealing with the sensitivities which must be recognized in the overall building of social and business relationships by the global executive. It is imperative that we become more knowledgeable of the cultural and societal influences that impact on international business negotiations.

The following list of principles of international business protocol is designed to provide management and the individual executive with the insights necessary to conduct business on a global scale and to meet ably the competitive challenges that lie ahead.

PRINCIPLE ONE
DO YOUR HOMEWORK

The success of your venture anywhere and any time is largely dependent upon your preparation for participation—in other words, you must do your homework beforehand.

In the world of international business, the marketing and management skills employed today are much different from those utilized by American corporations domestically. Our style of initiating contacts, making presentations, negotiating agreements, and composing contracts is not universally accepted. Yet we still send our executives to negotiate with little or no understanding of the culture and customs of the countries where they are doing business. And we expect them to bring home the deal. Sadly, this seldom happens, so the number of deals that have been and are being lost through ignorance is staggering. The solution: adequate preparation.

We must expand our ability to be effective in dealing with foreign businesspeople. An understanding and an appreciation of the differences in business practices and attitudes of our foreign counterparts are essential in order to consummate successful negotiations. The absence of this understanding will result in the business going elsewhere. We are no longer the only game in town. Foreign firms are waiting to pick up the business whenever and wherever we slip up.

Before undertaking a foreign business transaction, the executive involved should take the time to learn something of the country in which he or she expects to do business: its history, its geography, its people, and its politics. One should be cognizant of the subjects of discussion that are welcome, and those that would be better to avoid. For example, the subject of politics is looked at differently in various countries. In some, the topic is extremely sensitive, while in others, it is almost a ritual game in conversation, playing a part in every discussion. Sports are a great topic to introduce. Nearly everyone likes to take a position on this subject. And what is more pleasant for someone to hear from a visitor than an account of the many attributes of his or her country, its beauty and its history? The fact that you care enough to have learned something about the country will be very meaningful to your foreign business associate.

Initiating Contacts

There are two myths associated with initiating contacts to do business: one is that your bank will introduce you to opportunities; the other is that the government agencies or Chambers of Commerce will actively lend a hand. While these sources in many cases may be somewhat useful, only in very special situations will they extend any real assistance. Certainly, if you are one of the bank's most valued clients, and represent millions of dollars in both your corporate and personal accounts, your bank will want to be involved. But for the smaller company or individual exporter, the service or attention you receive will be in direct proportion to the bottom line reflected on your last bank statement.

A second resource to consider in initiating contacts are the many international Chambers of Commerce. However, these organizations appear to have little or no social intercourse with each other. Seemingly, they operate independently and should be contacted on an individual basis. Each has its own market to promote and concentrates its efforts accordingly. Be conscious of this.

A more useful step in establishing business contacts would be your application for membership in the World Trade Center Organization located in the city in which you are endeavoring to do business. In many instances, these local centers hold membership in the larger international World Trade Association headquartered in New York City. Their clubs offer an interchange for members, and international business trips are organized for members to undertake together. World market trends and statistics are recorded and disseminated among the membership. For additional information about becoming a member of the World Trade Association, you may contact Mr. Guy F. Tozzoli, Executive Director, 1 World Trade Center, New York, N.Y. 10048.

You must be very cautious in dealing with other sources of introduction or with agency representation. Frequently, such contacts are unsavory, and should you become involved with this kind of representation, the reputation of your firm might be jeopardized. An investigation of the credentials of anyone employed to represent you should be done with great scrutiny and caution. Too much is at stake to be careless.

Your money will be well spent if you take a trip to the country in which you wish to do business and investigate, to the greatest extent possible, the avenues available to you in arranging representation. It is conceivable that your appearance in person may precipitate an interest on the part of a bank or another trade authority to assist you in your endeavors.

International Market Considerations

These suggestions will be helpful to you:

- Do a market research first. Is this the right market for you?
- Investigate thoroughly the risks involved. Bankruptcy is not legal in some places, and you could lose your passport and be detained until full reparation has been accorded, in the event your business fails.
- Know when legal counsel is necessary. Lawyers are considered unnecessary in some countries, and their presence initially can convey mistrust.
- Choose whether an advertising agency or a public relations firm would best serve your marketing activity.
- Above all, be sure that your own credentials are impeccable.

PRINCIPLE TWO
KNOW THAT FIRST IMPRESSIONS ARE LASTING

Forms of Greetings and Introductions

It is a universal truth that impressions, either positive or negative, are made by the first contact between two parties, whether that contact is written, oral, or in person.

In a letter, for example, the quality of your stationery, your use of titles, names, and addresses, the proper translation of your correspondence, and the overall appearance of your communication are most significant in creating a good—or bad—impression. Equally important are the forms of greeting and introduction used by you in first encounters. People frequently fail to recognize the favorable impression that one creates by employing the language of another in an initial greeting. When I recently interviewed the consul general of Italy,

Julio DeLorenzo, he said: "Italians are very touched by the fact that an American may speak some Italian. More so than if a Japanese did, or a Chinese, because they spend a great deal of time in preparation, and their own languages are very difficult. But we are touched, and we are in a way grateful, when we see an American, a man or a woman, who belongs to the most important country in the world, speak our language. The way to success in Italy is a knowledge of our language, even if it is only a few words. We appreciate it when other people come to us, not as superiors, but as equals."

The Japanese exchange traditional bows of respect in greeting one another. I have watched Americans attempt to emulate this custom while in the company of Japanese associates, merely feigning a knowledge of a very significant practice. Bowing is an art form, and in Japan the depth of the bow signifies the level of respect being accorded. An improper bow could be construed as a disrespectful gesture. The elderly are given the deepest and most respectful of bows.

I learned a lesson in greeting protocol while running the international protocol services for a major banking concern. I was given the responsibility to meet a plane on which a very important sheik, a client of the bank, was arriving. I was to greet him officially. We at the bank were unaware that by sending a woman to the airport, we were, in keeping with his custom, offering the company of the woman to him during his stay. We had a very unhappy customer to contend with when he learned this was not the case.

What's in a Name?

An obvious lack of sensitivity is evident when a person's name is used or pronounced incorrectly. We Americans have the reputation of being too presumptuous in calling others by their first names. This is not customary in many cultures, and is considered to be most insulting. Another insensitivity is not understanding the structure of names in other cultures. For example, a New York City bank spent considerable time, effort, and money courting Jorge Rojas Neto, who was a businessman of wealth and influence in Brazil. So it was perfectly understandable that, when he planned a trip to New York to discuss his account, the bank was pleased to handle many of the details, including his hotel arrangements. However, when Jorge Rojas Neto arrived at the hotel, there was no reservation in his name and other accommodations could not be easily found. This was a costly incident, since Jorge Rojas Neto decided to terminate his negotiations with the bank. He felt that if they couldn't handle a matter as simple as a hotel reservation, they weren't to be trusted with handling his money. Ironically, it was later learned that the reservation was actually in the hotel computer all along. The snafu had been caused by a misunderstanding of Portuguese and the structure of Brazilian names. "Neto" means grandson, and is used to indicate the "Third." Mr. Rojas III had an incorrectly placed reservation under the name "Neto."

As another example of the importance of one's name, an extremely wealthy sultan in Bahrein recently made overtures to investigate investment opportunities in the United States, stimulating a courting by several American firms dealing in real estate and securities. However, almost all of those who responded to his inquiries had their correspondence returned unopened and stamped "Breach of Protocol." Not one of those firms, on their first contact, had addressed him properly, and as a result none of their proposals got through. They simply did not know how to decipher and distinguish his name from the long lineage included in his title.

Business Dress

A consul general once told me that his friends said he was beginning to look more like a banker than a diplomat. His remark took me by surprise, since I had not paid that much attention to business dress before. I became very conscious of dress codes thereafter, particularly in those circles where it had definite importance. My observations were most interesting. In Great Britain, for example, men are often judged by a quick glance at their shoes. The famous Gucci loafer (a status symbol in the United States) is definitely out when doing business in conservative European circles. Loafers are thought of as bedroom slippers. Only proper lace shoes (not brown) are considered to be appropriate. The shoe should be sturdy and not appear to be new.

To solve that problem, I also learned, aristocratic families in Great Britain base part of their decision about the employment of a butler on whether he has the same shoe size as the master of the house. For it is one of the butler's duties to wear and break in any newly purchased shoes for nearly a year before the master will wear them out of the house.

This same attitude applies to a man's business suit. The quality of a suit is of great importance, of course. It should be able to last sometimes up to twenty years, and never lose its style. Suits that are slightly worn are considered to be very elegant and are recognized in Europe as an indication of wealth and distinction.

The Italians are extremely clothes-conscious and look first to see if a suit is hand-finished instead of purchased "off the rack." Even designer suits are less than acceptable to most. In South America the sight of a polyester suit is sometimes intolerable in business circles. One South American remarked that "polyester suits in business should be outlawed."

Dark suits are most preferred universally. Only on special occasions should one choose a sports jacket and slacks over a suit. Pin-striped suits are also universally favored, along with white or light blue shirts, French cuffs, and good gold cufflinks.

Men's socks should be only dark and high. According to one authority, "Women only should be allowed to show their ankles, not men." Ties are also important. In Great Britain, one should avoid striped ties as they may resemble the colors of a "club tie," which you are not allowed to wear. However, don't worry too much; the stripes of British ties go in the opposite direction from those woven in the United States. Designer ties are favored in Japan. Japanese businessmen sometimes wear their ties backward just to show off the "important label" inside! It is also necessary that a proper wardrobe be worn for hunting in Great Britain. While hunting in the United States is quite casual, in Britain it is a sport that requires a very proper attire.

Women must pay extra attention to their business wardrobe. The first challenge most women have is to be accepted as competent in negotiations or as representatives of their corporations. Any mode of attire out of place in a business context could easily cause a wrong impression. Tailored suits are always acceptable, however; but not suits with little bow ties which look masculine. In South America and Europe, this look is offensive; there they expect a woman to look like a woman, not like a male impersonator. In Japan, women should be careful of necklines on blouses or dresses, inasmuch as a woman's neck is considered the most sensuous part of her body. V-necklines could be distracting and should be avoided.

Part of your preparation for any business negotiation is a careful study and understanding of the preferences and customs of dress of the participants. Your dress could well be the key to your success!

Business Cards

Remember that, long after you have departed, your business card remains behind. It is your most important business and travel accessory; it represents you and your company.

Business card designs are as diverse as the many cultures in which they are exchanged. Corporate and personal impressions are conveyed by the size, colors, patterns, diagrams, lettering, and logos employed in their composition. Business cards are most effective vehicles for communicating correct language translations of one's identity, and for depicting the appropriate corporate image. When your business cards are translated, be sure that the translation correctly conveys your corresponding corporate rank in the culture in which you are distributing them; that is, that your rank is translated into a correct indication of your appropriate corporate authority. The European corporate name and address are both ordinarily printed in small letters, to impart an attitude of discretion, and with no disparity in size between the letters.

In Asia, particularly in China or Japan, business cards are exchanged with great formality and ceremony. They are special representations of each party, and are presented and accepted with considerable respect. In Japan, where an executive is likely to be associated with a single corporation during his entire life, the business card becomes a personal symbol of profound significance, expressing his dedication to his company of long relationship.

Business cards are used everywhere in the world. Make sure you have one that you are proud to present, and carry a large supply with you when you travel.

Business Accessories

Also conspicuous in the impression you create will be your personal effects and your business accessories, their quality and their expression of your taste. Your personal grooming should be meticulous: your hair, your beard, your nails, and the fit, appearance, and elegance of your apparel.

Sustained scrutiny will be imposed on your attention to detail: the type of luggage you carry, your cufflinks, your collar and tie pins, your wristwatch, jewelry, eyeglasses, briefcase, notebook, and personal computer, the pen and the stationery you use, to cite a partial list. You are measured by the propriety and quality all these project.

Be diligent in looking your personal best at all times. Carry yourself with the attitude and posture of confidence and use those accessories that will reinforce the standard of personal substance you wish to convey.

There are times, however, when a "status symbol" in one culture can be an insult in another. Such was the experience of a senior corporate officer of a firm with substantial Middle Eastern investments. While personally thanking me for the assistance I had been providing his junior officers in a Middle Eastern business briefing, he proceeded to pack his brand-new pigskin attaché case for a visit to a prominent sheikdom. While an impressive status symbol in the United States, it was the worst possible accessory he could carry to any destination in the Arab world, inasmuch as the pig has historically been considered unclean and a disease carrier in Semite cultures.

Again, the importance of these suggested preparatory precautions cannot be overvalued. They are vital to favorable, meaningful, and lasting impressions.

PRINCIPLE THREE
OPEN LINES OF COMMUNICATION

Establish a Relationship

Mr. Cedric Grant, vice president, Global Investment Banking, for Citibank, Geneva, Switzerland, tells a story that demonstrates the timing and patience required to open successful lines of communication, which vary markedly between cultures.

"There's an independent state, called Doha-Qatar (Qatar is the port), on the Arabian Gulf, down from Bahrein, and north of Saudi Arabia. It's a pretty wild and uncultured place. I took my boss there, an executive vice president, who was making his first trip to the Middle East. He was visiting because we seemed to be having trouble closing a deal with a very high-net-worth individual, who was a member of the ruling family. When we met with our prospect, I noticed that there were stuffed birds all over the place, and I asked him if he was a falconer, which, we learned, he was. For the next hour, all we discussed was falconry, much to the displeasure of my boss. I learned that there are times in the training of falcons when they just fly off with their prey. That can be quite a loss to an owner, inasmuch as these birds cost between $20,000 and $50,000. I mentioned to our prospect that there was a miniature electronic device that could be attached to a bird's leg and a receiver which could track its whereabouts for up to 12 kilometers, if one of his falcons did go off. I brought one set out to him, and he was ecstatic. He ordered five more for his friends, and they've all had great success with keeping their falcons from disappearing. I also had great success with a client whose business seems ever increasing. My boss, when we left the first meeting, said, Why didn't you talk about international investments? I said, He didn't want to hear about international investments. He wanted to talk about falconry."

In the Middle East, it is customary to arrange several meetings and have pleasantries exchanged before any business is ever discussed. This could take weeks, or several months. Only when the lines of communication are open—and that only comes with developing trust —can discussions begin.

It is extremely important that one understand the ingredient of timing involved in opening successful lines of communication. To say something must be done does not necessarily mean that it also must be done right now.

In order to open lines of communication, it is also important that you know your client. A story told to me by an architect friend demonstrates this clearly. A man came from Taipei, Taiwan, who wanted to build a house in this country. After looking over the property selected for the construction, the architect proceeded to prepare drawings in keeping with the suggestions of his client. At the time that the architect presented the drawings for final approval, the client indicated that he first wanted to take the drawings back to Taiwan to be examined by his friends and "some religious types." The architect said that he could understand showing one's house plans to friends, but was confused when his client said he wished to show them to religious individuals. The significance was lost on him, but only for a short time.

The client returned and advised that they could proceed with the building, but that certain modifications were necessary in keeping with the recommendations made by his Buddhist priest. The first modification dealt with the approach to the front door. In the Taoist philosophy, a direct approach to a main entry door, without some type of shield in front of it, is highly discouraged. This was finally accomplished by an interior circular stairway approaching the front door at an angle.

The house also had to face a southerly or easterly direction to enable it to be filled with morning sunlight, and away from a cold northerly exposure. The eldest family member receives the southeastern room where the best health elements of sun, energy, and warmth are believed to be.

Other factors, like the direction of the bed in the master bedroom, telephone numbers, and room measurements, were also significant. Even the house groundbreaking time had to take place at a specific hour on a specific day.

The influence of cultural sensitivity and tradition must be seriously considered in opening up and establishing lines of communication with your clients.

Nonverbal Communication

There are many forms of business and social communication of a nonverbal nature, such as facial expressions, the body's stance, posture or language, hand gestures, direct or indirect eye contact, or the grip of a handshake. Each action in its own way can signal either a positive or a negative emotional response to what you have conveyed.

In different cross-cultural situations these same movements may represent contrary intentions. For example, while direct eye contact is essential to establish credibility in the United States, in Japan it is considered to be a discourtesy, showing a lack of respect. In some countries, nodding the head in a vertical motion means "no." The firm handshake of the American is not used around the globe; in some countries a limp, single pump motion projects a warm greeting.

Pay close attention to these signs, and learn as much as you can about their significance. It is most important that you both give and receive the correct nonverbal messages.

PRINCIPLE FOUR
RECOGNIZE THE IMPORTANCE OF RANK AND STATUS

There is a story told about Mrs. Clare Booth Luce when she was first appointed as the American ambassador to Italy and invited to a state dinner at the Spanish Embassy. It is customary in Rome to dine at a relatively late hour, and customary for the Spaniards to dine even later. Dinner was served at 10:00 P.M. and, at its conclusion, the guests engaged in conversation. Mrs. Luce, wondering at what time she could leave, decided to follow the instruction she had been given that no one should depart before the dinner's guest of honor who, she assumed, was the British ambassador, the most senior member of Rome's diplomatic community. The evening wore on until past 1:00 A.M. and Ambassador Luce began to tire. In desperation, she asked the wife of the Spanish ambassador the time when the British ambassador usually left. The lady responded quite angrily, "After the guest of honor!" Mrs. Luce asked, "Who is the guest of honor?" The hostess responded, "You are!" Mrs. Luce said her appropriate good-byes and departed immediately. She learned later that as she was the only woman ambassador in the diplomatic corps there, she was seated, as per custom, to the right of her host and, accordingly, considered to be the guest of honor at each affair.

This story is an illustration of the embarrassing situations that can occur when someone is unaware of his or her own relative rank and status. One's rank and status are of immeasurable importance in many cross-cultural negotiating situations, particularly when at the first meeting of the participants, the most senior officers attend, showing their desire to pursue the deal.

Recently, a major international bank learned that it was not achieving the market share of Asian banking business that had been anticipated. An investigation revealed the reason why: there was a significant disparity between the ages of their younger traveling representatives and the more senior Asian officers on whom they were calling. In the Orient, the more elderly are accorded the highest rank and status. Since the younger bank representatives were not held in the same regard in a culture that venerated maturity, they were unable to close deals as effectively as a more senior executive might. As a result, this bank's Asian marketing officers are now predominantly grey-haired men over 60 years of age.

Rank and status are not always associated with age. In some cultures rank emanates from wealth or title or heritage. But in every culture or country it is an element that cannot be disregarded. Know the relative rank and status of all with whom you come in contact. The unwitting slight of someone could cost you the deal.

PRINCIPLE FIVE
BE COGNIZANT OF YOUR ROLE

"Know thyself" is an ancient Delphic precept that has special significance in foreign business. Unless you know yourself well, you will not be able to deal with others of a different heritage in a manner that will lead to improved understanding. In business negotiating, the questions "Am I properly prepared?", "Am I right for this assignment?", and "How am I viewed by my counterparts?" are all important considerations.

How you answer those questions will determine your negotiating effectiveness. Walk before you run. Examine with caution the situation in which you find yourself. Observe fully all around you. Remember that all eyes are upon you, and that how you conduct yourself will be a reflection on you, your corporation, and your country. Knowledge is the key to understanding.

Despite all the preparations you make before entering the global market, you will be sorely tested. International trade is looked upon as a glamorous field, but it is hardly that. It is a tough arena, demanding strenuous participation. The executive who has the best chance of succeeding is the one who possesses self-knowledge, self-confidence, and an understanding and appreciation of the relative situation of his or her counterpart across the table.

The Exchange of Gifts

In your role as a corporate negotiator, you will be confronted with situations involving the exchange of gifts. Be careful that they are not construed as bribes. Gift-giving is usually associated with pleasant occasions, but such is not always the case. Few people in business consider gift-giving and gift-receiving as comfortable activities. And gift-giving is an even more difficult task in global markets. Some of the people with whom you will do business expect to be given gifts;

others will consider a gift insulting. There are gifts that are well received, and there are those that are outright offensive. Knowing what is appropriate is the secret of successful gift-giving. Check into this carefully.

During the American presidency of Thomas Jefferson, it is recorded that the local viceroy representing the ruling sultan of Morocco offered the American consul a pair of lions as a gift in honor of the great regard in which they held the United States. The gift was rejected because of prohibitions in the bylaws of the U.S. Constitution. When a letter later arrived from Washington confirming the rejection, the viceroy advised the American consul that it was most regrettable on two grounds: one, that there would be no further relationship between their two governments; but even more regrettable, that he, the viceroy, would lose his head. An exception was quickly made and the two lions were brought to Virginia, where they reportedly lived to an old age.

Gifts can represent an expression of appreciation, the acknowledgment of an occasion, or just plain thoughtfulness on the part of the giver. Their recipient, on the other hand, may feel very good about receiving a gift, or guilty, if the cost of the gift is obviously in disproportion to the occasion.

A gift can be construed as a bribe, again if the cost is excessive, and if the timing is incorrect. For example, while the giving of the gift may be entirely correct at the conclusion of a negotiation or entertainment activity, presenting the gift before completion of the deal may carry a different connotation. The difference between a gift and a bribe is also determined by the relationship between the giver and the recipient. Bribery brings heavy penalties. Be extremely careful of any misinterpretation.

PRINCIPLE SIX
WIN WITH PERSUASION

Developing a proficiency in the art of persuasion is critical in any negotiation, but even more so in those involving negotiating parties from diverse international backgrounds. We asked Dr. Kathleen K. Reardon, professor of communication sciences, University of Connecticut, an authority on the technique of persuasion, to contribute her thoughts.

Persuasion is something you do *with* someone, rather than *to* someone, according to Dr. Reardon. Persons who do not want to be persuaded usually are not persuaded. Your first task is to establish a "common ground" with your business counterpart. This means discussing ideas on which you are in agreement. Establish a rapport. Your second task is to put yourself in the other person's position. You might even say, "I suppose if I were you I would be concerned about a, b, or c." If the person agrees that you are correct, proceed to respond to each of his or her concerns. By approaching them this way you are helping them reason through the issue from their own, rather than from your, perspective. With your guidance they will persuade themselves. Of course, you both know that you have much to gain from what is being proposed. You should be direct in your recognition of this. Let them know how your plan benefits *both* of you.

Many times our efforts to persuade people fail. Dr. Reardon emphasizes, because we forget that people do not like to change. The status quo is often secure even if inefficient or inappropriate. People resist since change often means uncertainty and risk. It is no wonder that successful persuasion is not a one-shot effort. There is a marketing persuasion technique known as the "foot-in-the-door" method. It means that before you can even begin to attempt to change someone, you must get their attention. Moreover, they must trust you if your proposed plan requires substantial risk on their part.

To be successful at persuasion you must be patient. Instead of trying to accomplish everything you want in one meeting, set up goals for each meeting. The first meeting might involve discussion of the issues. The second meeting might center around a discussion of proposed solutions. And so on. There are few important changes that can be made in a day. Sometimes we are lucky, but it is wise to plan on being patient.

Empathy is a word that should not be foreign to businesspersons. Without empathy, Dr. Reardon points out, persuasion attempts often go awry. The old phrase "You can't know a man until you have walked a mile in his shoes" is a good one to remember when attempting to persuade someone in a foreign culture. Find out how he or she thinks and feels about your plan. Don't be evaluative. Express an understanding of his or her views and a willingness to find a solution that will meet most of his or her concerns. Remember that all of us are ego-involved in our ideas and one sure way to lose an argument is to imply that someone else's views are ridiculous or misguided. If part of persuasion is establishing a "common ground," empathy can be a very important skill. You can't define a common ground until you understand the other person's position.

Persuasion involves good listening skills. You cannot establish a common ground during negotiations, Dr. Reardon adds, until you find out how he or she thinks. Then you can use the perspective to support your own. Statements such as "As you just mentioned" or "I share your concern about" can be used as lead-ins to your own arguments. This strategy bridges your two positions with similar reasoning.

Listening is a difficult skill to perfect because most of us would rather listen to ourselves than to someone else. It is, however, one of the most important persuasion skills. By determining how the other person thinks about an issue, you are in a better position to select your persuasion strategy.

After negotiations have been completed, Dr. Reardon concludes, be sure to avoid the pitfall of assuming that you and the other person agreed to the same thing. Take a few minutes to review what you have agreed upon. Many businesspersons return home only to discover that what they assumed to have been accomplished was not accomplished. Save yourself frustration by checking your perceptions of what occurred during negotiations with the other person at the end of each session. Upon your return home, follow up with a letter to your counterpart, reviewing the negotiations and expressing your pleasure at having worked together.

PRINCIPLE SEVEN
MASTER NEGOTIATING TECHNIQUES

Robert T. Moran, Ph.D., noted author, psychologist, and currently the director of the program in cross-cultural communication at the American Graduate School of International Management, Glendale, Arizona, offers this observation: "A successful negotiation is a 'win-win situation' in which both parties gain. Many factors affect its outcome, such as how consistent the negotiator's acts are with the other party's values, the approach he uses, his attitude, the negotiating methods he employs, and the concern he exhibits for the other side's feelings and needs. Negotiation comprises all of these factors. The manner in which a negotiator goes about trying to achieve his objectives may, by itself, meet some of the other party's needs and lead the way to agreement on the issues which brought the negotiators together."

The nature of the negotiating process differs vastly with diverse cultures. What is customary and appropriate conduct in one may be quite offensive in another. Americans, for example, have a rather predictable way of approaching international negotiating sessions. We are invariably informal, individually independent, and frequently impatient. We are also generally trusting, direct, and eager to do business, and we expect others to respond to us in like fashion. Our lack of knowledge concerning foreign business practices and our inability to speak languages other than our own are well known, and a topic of amusement in many international circles. In some quarters we are looked upon as being inconsiderate, naive, insensitive, and devoid of the global sophistication required to negotiate effectively.

Such criticisms can be overcome only by a thorough understanding of the inherent differences brought to an international business transaction. To illustrate a few, in many cultures, flexibility or "running room" is not even considered in the business proposals that are presented; the offer on the table is the one and only position. In others, the exchange of proposals and counterproposals represents the accepted and expected procedure.

The method of choosing negotiators also varies culturally. While American selections are usually predicated upon the experience and technical proficiency of an individual, foreign negotiators are often chosen because of the personal wealth, position, or authority they possess, regardless of professional competency.

Cultural differences influence how decisions are made, whether from the top down, or from input below, as by team consensus and the joint solution of problems. Consider the disparity between authority in an autocratic society compared to a socialist society as evidence of this.

Whatever the differences, however, they are many, and they impact measurably on negotiating situations. Make sure you prepare yourself by studying those peculiar to the parties with whom you are dealing. If it is with the Japanese, for example, do not interpret their silence as a request for an additional concession from you, and remember their discomfort with any disagreement. If your counterparts are

French, understand their innate initial mistrust, as they await your proof of your integrity. Be aware of all you can about your negotiating environment and the techniques, customs, idiosyncrasies, and characteristics of the parties opposite you. Your most effective negotiating tool will be your own knowledge. It will add to your confidence and ability to make the right decisions.

Ask yourself the following questions prior to entering a negotiation in a different cultural atmosphere:

• Do I know all I can about the culture of my counterparts, and what mannerisms and behavioral traits are customary with them?
• Am I adequately briefed in the verbal and nonverbal communication skills necessary to pursue and accomplish a successful resolution of the negotiation? Have I arranged to employ my own interpreter?
• Will I require at the negotiations the presence of the third-party intermediary who initiated and arranged my introductory contacts?
• Have I explored the appropriate time to introduce attorneys to the discussion, recognizing the mistrust that they convey between negotiating parties in certain cultures?
• Have I made any effort at all to acquire some understanding or speaking ability in the language of the culture in which I am trying to do business?
• What is the normal decision-making process employed by my counterparts, or in their culture?
• How does the age, education, training, and experience of my counterpart compare with my own? What effect will that have?
• What strategies or peculiarities of mine might be irritating to my counterparts?
• Am I in control of my demeanor and my appearance? Do I have a grasp of my objectives in the negotiation, and what fall-back position, if any, am I prepared to accept?
• Have I learned to express my own position in a framework that will meet the anticipations and preferences, and avoid the displeasure, of those with whom I am trying to communicate and negotiate?
• Finally, am I negotiating for long-term or short-term objectives? What are the consequences of my performance?

PRINCIPLE EIGHT
ENTERTAIN EFFECTIVELY

The entertainment of clients has long been employed as an important marketing tool in business. In the United States we have business breakfasts, luncheons, and dinners. We entertain at cocktail parties, on golf courses, at hunting lodges, on fishing boats, at sporting events, and in countless other ways. Business entertainment is, in fact, prevalent throughout the world and is considered to be an integral part of establishing good relationships.

How to entertain, when to entertain, where to entertain—all of these involve whom to entertain. On a business trip, it is essential to have a game plan to deal with your entertainment responsibilities. You will certainly have them, and it is extremely important that you handle them well.

In a corporation where a protocol officer is available for consultation, this person's advice will prove invaluable. Without such advice, however, the business traveler must become thoroughly familiar with the customs and protocols of entertaining in the country of destination and should personally investigate which restaurants are correct for his or her needs and purposes, or determine if reciprocity exists between his or her own private club and those abroad.

As important as learning whom, how, where, and when to entertain is knowing how to *be* entertained. In Korea, for example, there is a custom whereby each guest gives the guest of honor his own glass, and the guest of honor partakes to symbolize the friendship he shares with that person. This is a very warm custom, but one can get smashed very quickly with twelve people at the table. In Switzerland, the day after attending a business dinner at a private home, an American executive was reminded that he had overlooked leaving a tip under his dinner plate for those serving the meal, and that he had also forgotten to tip the maid and the butler who were at the front door of the home, as he departed. These gratuities are customary and expected in Switzerland, even in private homes.

Here are some guidelines for entertaining:

• Do prestigious entertaining at private clubs or in private corporate executive meeting rooms.

• Select restaurants with proper table spacing to permit private discourse.
• Be well advised as to the dining and drinking customs of the guests you are entertaining.
• Know the proper toasts and protocols of the environment in which you are entertaining or being entertained.
• Be aware that women should arrange, when hosting, to have the check *not* presented at the table. In many cultures it is considered an affront for a woman to pay.
• Pay serious attention to seating arrangement, invitations, and table place cards.
• Be cognizant of correct attire at all times.
• Always be sure that the establishment at which you are entertaining can accommodate additional last-minute guests that you might invite. Some cannot do so.
• Make sure, if you are hosting in an establishment new to you, that you take the time before your guests arrive to familiarize yourself with the restaurant and wine list, and introduce yourself to the maître d'. These advance details are as important to a successful gathering as are the food and the ambience.
• If possible, find out in advance the nutritional tastes or requirements of your guests. It is thoughtful to consider beforehand the dietary idiosyncrasies of one's guests.
• Be aware that the amount of tipping varies, depending on the status of the restaurant or the country. Avoid embarrassment by checking on this custom beforehand.

When I interviewed Sheldon Tannen of New York's internationally famous "21" Club, and one of the world's outstanding restaurateurs, as to why his club enjoys the extraordinary reputation that it does, he attributed its success to the fact that, while it is a public restaurant, every effort is made to provide the atmosphere of a private club. Tannen suggested that executives involved in business entertaining bring their guests to a restaurant in which they are recognized and in which they know they will be well received. Surroundings are of equally high importance and a restaurant offering an ambience of relaxation and a "private club" feeling, together with the individual attention associated with that type of establishment, will, indeed, be extremely successful.

PRINCIPLE NINE
BE ON GUARD

One of the most serious issues confronting every business traveler is that of security. In today's world of hijackings, terrorist attacks, kidnappings, and bomb threats, the old adage "To be forewarned is to be forearmed" has never been more meaningful. Few corporations want to add any more stress to a traveling executive's already exhausting itinerary, but it is extremely important that he or she be as fully briefed as possible on security precautions.

Surprisingly little information of this sort, however, has been made available to corporate travelers. One investment banker friend told me that he has been traveling in what have been considered volatile areas for years, without ever receiving any advice on security measures from his management. He is not an exception. This is a situation that must be improved, and quickly, as we expand our executive exposure in the international marketplace.

Executive Security

I had the opportunity to interview Mr. Vernon E. Bishop, executive secretary, who heads the recently formed government and industry committee on terrorism, the Overseas Security Advisory Council, and he offered the following brief security advice to traveling executives:

• *Change Your Attitude*. Don't believe it can't happen to you. It can. A careless attitude will lead to dangerous behavior in a crisis situation.
• *Be Informed*. Know where you are, and the circumstances and environment in which you are moving at all times.
• *Stay Alert*. Alertness is the key ingredient to a safe trip, and its importance must be emphasized. You must be constantly alert, especially in surroundings which are unfamiliar. Be attuned to the extraordinary.

Do not become paranoid, Bishop added. Just be prepared.

I surveyed several other officers from major firms on the subject of security, and they recommended the following:

• *Keep a Low Profile*. Never flash the "gold" card while traveling. The most inconspicuous credit card should be used. Unless a "status profile" is necessary to enhance negotiations, stay in a modest hotel; or, if in a first-class hotel, check into a standard room accommodation. The less attention you attract, the better. Never mention your firm's name, or your full name, to strangers you casually meet in hotel bars or local restaurants.

• *Know Your Hotel*. Many prestigious hotels may not suit your needs. Carefully check that your hotel has a telephone with a direct dial. Often, hotels with operators have "tuned in" to your itinerary. Operators have also been known to "sell" telephone numbers of calls placed from their switchboard to "your competitors."

• *Vary Your Travel Patterns*. Never establish a pattern in cities you travel to, such as using the same hotel, restaurants, and mode of transportation. Do not speak in front of strangers about your travel itinerary. Make sure your secretary, associates, or family do not give out information freely to callers while you are away.

One seldom-used precaution is the purchase of an alternate set of reserved airline tickets for a departure flight from another nearby airport, in the event the airport you are planning to leave from is closed down because of terrorist activity. Be sure the tickets are in hand, not just reserved.

When carrying a list of your clients and prospects, record them on plain paper, not on a corporate letterhead. List the names on one piece of paper, and the telephone and addresses on the other; and remember to keep them in separate places. You should never carry computer lists or portfolios with any names identifying them; only the person's telephone number. All records should be unidentifiable. All countries should be recorded in code.

The State Department strongly recommends that business travelers who plan to remain in a city longer than twenty-four hours go to the U.S. Embassy and register. This way, in case of an emergency, the Embassy will be advised of your whereabouts, and will also be able to track you down in case your office or family reports you are missing.

The State Department also offers a very useful service: the issuance of up-to-date travel advisories reporting on just about anything that affects the safety of American travelers, from critical hotel overcrowding to street riots, and everything in between. Contact the Citizens Emergency Center at the Department of State, (202) 632-5225.

Your passport is a much-sought-after prize by the black market in various countries and therefore must be judiciously guarded at all times. Immediately upon arrival, place it in the hotel's safe deposit for safekeeping. There is much red tape involved in replacing a lost or stolen passport, so hold on tightly to the one you have.

Mr. James M. Ziede, presently security advisor to the League of Arab States, is a twenty-one-year veteran of the New York City police force and holder of the Medal of Honor for Valor for saving the life of Chiang Ching-Kuo, premier of Taiwan, in an assassination attempt in April of 1970. He offered the following additional suggestions for travel security:

- Keep your travel plans confidential. Avoid announcing any intention of taking a trip, or of any precise arrival or departure times.
- Place hotel reservations discreetly, not for attention-getting. Your rank, title, or position should not be revealed in the reservation.
- Select alternative travel routes from each location to another, and brief anyone responsible for your security of these alternative routes, and the travel time required.
- Purchase your flight tickets at the airport.
- Reserve adjacent accommodations at hotels, when traveling with others. Have your quarters as close together as possible.
- Know the chauffeur, or business associate, who is to meet you upon your arrival.
- Avoid remote areas of the city you are visiting. Avoid darkness and isolation.
- Direct your drivers not to deviate from a chosen road. Do not let your children travel unaccompanied either in a taxi or in any public transportation.
- Be wary of taxis that are readily available when you emerge from an office building or your hotel.
- Be unpredictable.

Mr. Michael J. McNulty, Rockefeller Center's security chief, offered some suggestions as to vehicular use in foreign countries:

- Use vehicles common to the locale, and in ordinary colors.
- Use license plates that blend in with those used by local citizens, nothing conspicuous.
- Place locks on gas caps and hood, and check them along with fender wells before entering a parked car.
- Interchange company vehicles if you are an executive.
- Keep garage vehicles only in secured locations.
- Equip vehicles with two-way radios for emergencies.
- Never drive with less than half a tankful of gas.
- Install curtains in the rear window, and always install side-view mirrors.
- Do not park in the street overnight.
- Keep doors and windows locked while driving.
- Do not pick up hitchhikers, or slow down for street disturbances.
- Be alert, observe traffic around you, particularly to the rear.
- Be alert regarding motorcycles and bicycles in traffic.
- Separate your ignition key from all other keys.
- Keep your vehicle well maintained at all times, to avoid breakdowns.
- Know the location of the police stations, and learn to recognize local police uniforms.
- If you believe you are being followed, try to get a license number, and head for the nearest police station.
- Be especially alert in underground garages.
- Have a prearranged signal to be used by your driver if he is under duress, to warn you against entering the car.
- Keep your home and office advised of your whereabouts at all times.

And some notes on executive kidnapping:

Kidnap victims are usually selected from a large list of eligibles, all of whom would command high ransoms or other concessions. Before a successful kidnapping can take place, the potential abductor must engage in surveillance, intelligence gathering, and planning. During this time, the alert executive has an opportunity to observe warning signs of an impending kidnap attempt. Analysis of hundreds of cases reveals that 95 percent of all kidnappings take place between the residence and the office; most attacks occur just after the victim has left his residence or within several blocks of it; and 80 percent of all kidnappings involve blockage of an automobile carrying the victim.

An executive, by altering his or her route to work and other daily routines, can frustrate attempts at kidnapping. By making one's movements random and unpredictable, the executive reduces the possibility of becoming a target of kidnappers, for they rely on routine behavior to plan their attack. However, one must always prepare for a possible kidnapping. Following are some suggestions for the person who becomes the victim of a kidnapping.

- Suppress your initial panic. Stay as calm as possible; attempt to appear calm (but not indifferent). Be alert to situations that you can exploit to your advantage. Keep in mind that people are actively working for your safe return.
- Do not become depressed if negotiations take time. Time is on your side. The more time that passes, the better your chances are for release.
- Attempt to get on a name basis with your captors. If they think of you as a person rather than as an object, things may go easier for you.
- Do not become sympathetic or feign allegiance to the kidnappers' cause. You may be placed in a more dangerous position should they decide to exploit your professed sympathies.
- Remember that you could be dealing with a bright, clever (and possibly ruthless) criminal. Treat the person's mind with respect while using your business acumen and negotiating skill.
- Do not fight back or struggle physically unless you are fairly certain of success. No matter how reasonable your captors may appear to be on the surface, they cannot be trusted to behave normally and their actions may be unpredictable.
- Comply with the instructions of your abductors as well as you can.
- Object to life-threatening procedures. Hostages stuffed into car trunks have been killed. If you can, offer alternatives which will minimize the hazards but still assure protection of you, "their

merchandise." Appear to have a genuine concern for the outcome of their predicament.

• Do not reveal that you recognize your abductors if they are attempting to conceal their identity, and you recognize one of them.

• Do not discuss what action may be taken by your family, friends, or employer. Claim you do not know.

• Make a mental note of all movements, including times in transit, direction, distances, speeds, landmarks along the way, special odors and sounds like transportation, bells, construction, and so on.

• Whenever possible, take note of the characteristics of your abductors, their habits, surroundings, speech, mannerisms, what contacts they make, their physical descriptions, names used, and so on. Such information can be of great value in their apprehension.

• Escape, unless attempted during the initial abduction stage, should be attempted only as a last resort. Generally, you cannot expect to have a good opportunity to escape, and any attempt to escape should not be made unless it has been carefully calculated to ensure the best possible odds for success.

• Avoid making provocative remarks to your abductors. Do not be belligerent. As noted, they may be unstable individuals who react violently to provocations made by you.

• Request special medicines or medical attention immediately if you have a disease or physical condition which requires treatment.

• Be prepared to get out of the way should a confrontation become imminent between the kidnappers and law enforcement officials.

On Surviving Terrorism

American citizens and property have become the prime target of international terrorist attacks. In 1985, 35 percent of all such incidents were directed against Americans. Between 1979 and 1983, there were 945 international attacks on American persons and property, involving bombings, shootings, kidnappings, arson, and hijackings. In 1985, 17 Americans died and 154 were wounded.

These are sobering statistics. They emphasize the need for your awareness. Instructors in antiterrorism stress that "what you do is probably the primary factor in your security." Keep in mind these additional State Department precautions for coping with terrorism:

- Don't wear flashy jewelry.
- Don't resist attackers; give up valuables.
- Don't use short cuts that take you off well-lit main thorough-fares.
- Be alert for possible surveillance on you.
- Become familiar with safe havens—hospitals, restaurants, and police stations.
- Yell "fire" or "accident" if attacked; it is more effective than yelling "help."
- Install physical fortifications, such as locks, peepholes, yard lighting, and grilles on windows and doors.
- Do not accept unmarked packages.
- Establish a "safe haven" room with steel door and radio. In high-threat posts the State Department will often offer counsel and help.
- Don't place your desk in front of large windows; consider safety before the view.
- Don't rush to the windows if you hear gunfire or bombings; take cover instead.
- Install sirens and smoke alarms.
- Prepare children and servants not to give away even casual information to strangers.

PRINCIPLE TEN
THE BEGINNING IS AT THE END

When the negotiations have been completed, the deal has been agreed to, the documents have been prepared and executed, and the hand-shakes exchanged—that is the time when the business relationship actually begins. Everything accomplished before was merely prelimi-nary. The association between the negotiating parties must now take a foothold.

This new association can either be a one-shot business arrangement, or the initiation of a long and pleasant relationship, built on mutual confidence and trust. How each party performs in fulfilling the requirements of the contractual obligations they have accepted will determine whether there will be any future ventures together. This performance measurement will also be the gauge of the duration of any business in the future, and of the degree of cooperation and dedication each party might anticipate.

In most parts of the world, business executives in other cultures strive to develop long-term relationships. Such an association cultivates a comfortable atmosphere of trust and dependability between business counterparts, and obviates the need for endless renegotiations. Americans in general, however, do not always emphasize establishing more permanent business associations. In our somewhat mad pace to make a deal and then move on, we often fail to cement a relationship with today's foreign business counterpart that could eventually result in a sizeable amount of recurring business tomorrow. In part, this might be attributed to the mobile nature of the American business executive. Nowhere in today's business world do executives bounce so often from one corporation to another. Although this upward corporate mobility is quite acceptable in our business community, it is not necessarily well received in other cultures. An extreme contrast to ours, of course, would be the Japanese, whose executives enlist in their corporation for life and are accustomed to developing their game plans for the long term.

The American executive competing in the international business arena would be well advised to keep an eye on tomorrow. The deal that is concluded today will have a marked effect on the success of future ventures.

SUMMARY

Let's take a moment now to quickly review all ten of the principles of international business protocol:

Principle One, *Do Your Homework*. Learn everything you can about the culture of the people with whom you plan to do business, the steps necessary to initiate contacts, and the market considerations that could affect your objectives.

Principle Two, *Know that First Impressions Are Lasting*. Make a positive and pleasing impression by your knowledge of the proper forms of address, what constitutes appropriate business dress and accessories, and the most effective form and use of business cards.

Principle Three, *Open Lines of Communication*. Understand the steps required to establish close relationships with your business counterparts by recognizing the cultural differences in both verbal and nonverbal communication.

Principle Four, *Recognize the Importance of Rank and Status*. Be sensitive to the cultural differences that signal rank and status and how they affect business negotiations.

Principle Five, *Be Cognizant of Your Role*. Know yourself in order to deal effectively with others.

Principle Six, *Win with Persuasion*. Learn and use the skills of persuasion to obtain your business objectives.

Principle Seven, *Master Negotiating Techniques*. Be familiar with varieties in the nature of the negotiating process in different cultures and use them to your advantage.

Principle Eight, *Entertain Effectively*. Learn when, where, and whom to entertain, and how to *be* entertained.

Principle Nine, *Be on Guard*. Follow the security measures recommended for your personal safety when traveling on business abroad.

Principle Ten, *The Beginning Is at the End*. Negotiate both for the present and the future benefit of all the participants in a business transaction.

PART II

INTERNATIONAL BUSINESS BRIEFS

GUIDELINES FOR COMPETING SUCCESSFULLY IN GLOBAL MAJOR MARKETS

Although the global executive may be concerned with negotiating agreements that pertain to a single product or service, every target in the world marketplace is unique. Techniques and strategies that will prove successful in the Middle East may be totally incomprehensible to the Asian businessperson. In China and the Soviet Union, you will be dealing not only with individual business people but with government representatives as well. The cultural differences between even neighboring European countries, like France and Italy, are vast.

In the following brief sections, you will find all the information necessary to conduct business in the world's 25 major markets. For ease of reference and quick comprehension, this information is arranged as follows:

Cultural Overview

Business Opportunities

Initiating Contact

Business Protocol and Procedures

> Business environment
> Rank and status
> Forms of address
> Business cards
> Business dress
> Gift-giving
> Communication styles

Negotiating Techniques

Business Entertaining

General Tips

Executive Travel

> Documents
> Inoculations

53

Airport(s)
Customs
U.S. Embassy
Transportation
Tipping
Hotels
Restaurants
Travel tips

ASIA

CHINA

Cultural Overview

The People's Republic of China, a vast nation larger in area than the United States but smaller that the Soviet Union and Canada, contains fully 22 percent of the world's population. Located in eastern Asia, its terrain is varied, with mountains, deserts, rivers, and plains.

The Chinese Communist party (CCP) is the major political force in China, and is governed through the Politburo of the CCP Central Committee. The highest state authority is the National People's Congress, which is composed of deputies from all over the country who meet annually. These legislators, elected for five years, can enact laws and amend the constitution. The state council holds executive power and governs through a premier, several vice premiers, heads of ministries, commissions, and special agencies. Judicial power is invested in the Supreme People's Court.

The Communists gained power in 1949, and began to improve China's technologically backward society. Today, China's natural resources, communication networks, industries, commerce and trade, transportation systems, urban public utilities, and other major economic sectors are all publicly owned. Planning programs have been the key to controlling investment, production, and redistribution of wealth.

The goal of the "Four Modernizations" program is to quadruple GNP in the last twenty years of this century. To accomplish this, there are a series of five-year plans and targets for each sector of the economy. Capitalist approaches have also been apparent in China, especially since the economic reforms that were announced in late 1984. It appears that the nation is moving away from a rigid, centralized, and planned economy to a more mixed one. China calls this "one-country, two systems." In effect, China can be viewed as a giant cooperative with strong leanings toward adoption of capitalist incentives.

China leads world markets in the production of rice, tobacco, and pork, and is second in corn, barley, soy, and peanuts production. As agriculture is the foundation of the economy, it remains a top priority, along with light industry, energy and transportation. China is a major industrial power because of its coal, oil, tungsten, steel, and energy resources.

Although China's GNP is the sixth largest in the world, it has one of the lowest per capita incomes: about $300 annually. This is because China is the most populous country in the world, with more than 1 billion people. Every fourth person in the world is Chinese. More than 90 percent of the Chinese people live on one-sixth of the land, around the deltas of the Yellow (Huang) and Yangtze (Ch'ang Chiang) rivers. At least 56 different ethnic groups are found in China; the major one is the Han, who comprise 93 percent of the total population.

Beijing (formerly called Peking) is the capital of China, and, like Washington, D.C., it is an autonomous goverment independent of a province (or state). As does the United States, China has a varied continental climate, although its summers tend to be hotter and its winters colder. Beijing's climate is similar to Philadelphia's, and Shanghai's is much like northern Florida's. Guangzhou (Canton) has weather similar to New Orleans.

Devotion to the family is strong in China. Family life takes precedence over loyalty to the state. However, material incentives from the government, such as money to rear the child or assistance in finding a nursery, are given to couples who have just one child, in order to stabilize the birth rate. Having a second child is strongly discouraged by the government and education in family planning is a "must" priority. The divorce rate is low and family disputes are arbitrated by local governing units. Dating and premarital sex are discouraged, and pressure is exerted to marry late. Chinese women have a considerable degree of equality, and do not take their husbands' names at marriage. All the remnants of Mandarin subservience now appear to be gone.

Human relationships are very important to the Chinese, and they respect feelings. Because the group is more important that the individual, they will say "we" rather that "I." A person's reputation and standing in the social structure means much, and because of a network of social relationships, the Chinese are resourceful and able to get things done. They also value honesty, hospitality, morality, and tradition, believing that "the past is to be used as a means to serve the present better."

Although atheism is officially endorsed by the constitution and the government, many Chinese continue to adhere to Confucianism, Buddhism, Taoism, Islam and Christianity.

The Chinese place great emphasis on education, particularly in the sciences, because of the need for technicians and research workers. Since 60 percent of its population is under 25, the task of education is immense. Some Chinese students study in the United States. The literacy rate is 60 percent. The official language is Mandarin Chinese, the dialect of Beijing and northern China; it is spoken by 75 percent of the people. Many Chinese also speak their native dialect. Cantonese, particularly, is prominent in the southern part of the country. The written language is based on a system of several thousand characters, or ideograms, that represent an idea or object.

Business Opportunities

Since normalization of relations between China and the United States in 1979, the atmosphere for doing business has vastly improved. The Chinese government is committed to obtaining Western technology and to promoting economic relations and trade with the United States. It ranks twentieth in the export markets for the United States, primarily in agricultural products. The United States also imports clothing, accessories, and petroleum products from China.

For purposes of trade, economic cooperation, and technical exchanges with other nations, China has designated certain areas in the cities of Shenzhen, Shuhai, and Shantou in Guangdong Province, and Xiamen in the Fujian Province as Special Economic Zones (SEZs). Foreign companies are encouraged to invest in the SEZs by setting up solely-owned enterprises or initiating joint ventures. The government has directed the SEZs to give preferential treatment to executives who invest in them. China particularly needs advanced technology projects. There is also a new consumer trend for high-grade products: TV sets, cassette recorders, washing machines, refrigerators, and electric fans.

Initiating Contact

There are several ways of making initial contact. You must first receive an invitation to visit China for business purposes in order to obtain an entry visa. Contact any of the following organizations or try the following strategies for initial assistance in getting an invitation:

- The National Council for U.S.–China Trade in Washington, D.C., provides background information, helps you with proposals and covering letters (it is a gesture of respect to send the letter in Chinese), and often sets up contact with one of the more than fifty Chinese Foreign Trade Corporations and Commissions (FTCs). An FTC can extend an invitation, be your host, and make business appointments and arrangements for you. You can submit an application directly to an FTC or government agency. But this could take up to a year.
- You can become part of a trade delegation to the Chinese Export Commodities Fair (CECF), held twice a year at Guangzhou (Canton), where 30 percent of China's foreign trade is arranged. Other trade fairs are held in Hong Kong. The U.S. information source for these activities is the International Trade Division of the U.S. Department of Commerce.
- You can arrange a technical seminar in China.

Most business and all marketing trips to this country begin with an invitation to participate in a technical seminar or *jishu jiaoiu* (technical exchange). This is a comprehensive review of a product, a technology, or a service. The Chinese use the occasion to evaluate your firm's capabilities, to question your technical expertise, and to determine whether to enter into a contract with you. It is an important way for the Chinese to acquire knowledge about a new technology, whether a contract is reached or not. Some U.S. and Japanese firms have resisted such presentations before securing a contract because of fears of creating a new market rival and inadvertently strengthening China's military capabilities.

The technical seminar has many elements common to a formal presentation on the product or technology, but should go beyond that to include:

- the position of your company within the industry;
- the distinguishing technical or service features of your product;
- a list of published experts who have contributed to the prestige of your firm.

You should also have available technical articles commenting on the product, in addition to catalogs, brochures, and your annual report.

The Chinese welcome descriptive material sent ahead, if it can be distributed right away. But they will not store it. You can ship material to be used at the technical seminar by air freight; it will be left at the airport for pickup. The safer but more expensive way is to bring in the brochures with you as excess baggage.

The Chinese consul with offices in New York, San Francisco, and Houston can issue a business visa and assist you on general information on how to do business in China.

Other sources to contact are:

United States Department of State
Desk Officer for the PRC
Washington, D.C. 20230
Phone: (202) 632-1436

National Council for U.S.–China Trade
1818 N Street NW
Washington, D.C. 20036
Phone: (202) 429-0340

Preparatory Office of Shanghai World Trade Center
c/o CCPIT Shanghai Sub-Council
33 Zhong Shan Dong Yi Lu
Shanghai, PRC.
Phone: 232348   Telex: 33290 SCPIT CN

National Council for U.S.–China Trade
Beijing Hotel, Room 1136
Beijing, PRC
Phone: 552231 or 556531/Ext 1136

United States Commerce Department
Country Specialist for the PRC
14th Street and Constitution Avenue
Washington, D.C. 20230
Phone: (202) 377-3583

China Council for the Promotion of International Trade
4 Taipinggiao Street
Beijing, PRC
Phone: 662835

BUSINESS PROTOCOL AND PROCEDURES

Business Environment

It is usual for the Chinese delegation to meet your group at the airport
and escort you to the hotel. The coordinator will want to sit down and
organize timetables and agendas with a member of your group. This
person will know precisely how long it takes to reach your meeting
destination.

The business day in China runs from 8:30 A.M to 5:30 P.M. with an
hour for lunch. The day itself begins much earlier, with most Chinese
people turning out for group calisthenics at 4:30 or 5:00 A.M. At 7:00
A.M. the dining rooms in hotels open. You should expect phone calls
about negotiations as early as 7:30 A.M. Business meetings rarely begin
before 8:30 A.M.

It is important to be punctual for business meetings as well as other
engagements. Everything in China runs on time, and you are seldom
kept waiting. The Chinese are usually there in advance of the appointed time. Many business firms in China (both local and foreign)
have offices in hotel rooms. Hotels can offer cable machines, telexes,
and other communications services.

The Chinese chief negotiator may be near the entrance to greet you.
Or you may be guided to a reception room, where some or all of the
Chinese group are gathered. They will rise as your delegation enters
the room. The senior Chinese representative will always stand, and
therefore is the first to be greeted. The Chinese will assume that the
first person to enter the room is the top U.S. executive and negotiator.

The meeting-room table is usually rectangular. The Chinese executives will sit in the middle on the north side, facing the door. The
U.S. executives will be invited to sit opposite them on the other side

of the table. If it is a small group, there may be no table. Instead, you will be invited to sit in armchairs. The two senior executives from each country will sit next to each other. The chairs will be near the sides of the room. There will be a small table for tea.

Late arrival for a meeting is viewed as either careless business practice or as a lack of serious interest.

Casual, informal entry into a meeting room is bad form. Be sure your entire group enters one at a time, in order of rank.

When being introduced, a courteous gesture is to have each of your group remember the name of the Chinese executive who corresponds to him in the ranking order of introduction.

As a sign of hospitality, your Chinese hosts will offer you tea and cigarettes shortly after everyone is seated. Green tea is mildly flavored and served burning hot. Good manners dictate that you drink at least some of it. Blow the leaves away from the edge of the cup before sipping, or you may get leaves in your mouth. If you do, take them off your tongue with your fingers. Watch the Chinese and do what they do.

RANK AND STATUS

The Chinese are extremely status conscious. It is important to send a high-ranking executive to meet with the Chinese. This will indicate how sincere you are. They will have an official of similar rank to meet your delegation. You will need one person to act as chief spokesperson; the Chinese expect this. Choose a main representative, even if the executives from your company are of equal rank and have different interests. Decide this in advance, as it is usual for the Chinese group to meet your delegation at the airport, and escort you to the hotel.

FORMS OF ADDRESS

Regardless of whether the first introductions take place at the airport, hotel, or business office, the hierarchical leadership structure will be present. The ranking member of the Chinese group will introduce members of that team in order, and then turn to the visiting group for introductions. It is best to identify the spokesperson to the Chinese as soon as possible. Interpreters may also help by introducing their superiors in order of rank, and can guide the visitors through

the subtle distinctions of rank. It is incorrect to have members introduce themselves.

Use last names when making introductions. And when speaking to
someone, use "Mr." or "Madame." In China, the one-syllable family
name precedes, followed by a two-syllable first name. Thus, Zhang
Chan is addressed as Mr. Zhang, and Liu Minhui is addressed as
Madame Liu. If possible, use the Chinese for "Mr." (*Xiansheng*,
pronounced "shian-shay"), "Mrs.," "Madame" (*Taitai*, pronounced
"tie-tie"), or "Miss" (*Xiaojie*, pronounced "she-ow-jay"); thus,
Zhang Chao would be be Zhang *Xiansheng* and Liu Minhui would be
Liu *Taitai*. As a foreigner, you may be addressed as *peng you* (friend).
Feel free to use *tongzhi* (comrade) to address either man or woman.
The Chinese use surnames and titles in formal settings. Some titles
are:

- Minister: *Buzhang* ("boo-jahngg")
- Vice minister: *Fubuzhang* ("foo-boo-jahngg")
- Office director: *Chuzhang* ("choo-jahngg")
- Managing/deputy manager: *Jingli* ("ching-lee")
- Assistant manager: *Fujingli* ("foo-ching-lee")

Here, again, use the surname followed by the title in direct address
("Liu *Buzhang*," "Zhang *Jingli*"). You may want to give only your
last name to avoid confusion. Say, "I am Smith," or "My name is
Smith." The informal use of first names is considered disrespectful.

Shake hands firmly with a single handshake, a gesture that is replacing the traditional Chinese bow when U.S. executives are being
greeted. At a first meeting, say *"Xing hui"* (pronounced "shing
hwei"), meaning "I'm pleased to meet you." On subsequent meetings
a simple *"Ni hau"* or "hello," will do. It is a standard greeting, as is
"Ni hau ma" (How do you do?).

BUSINESS CARDS

Business cards are presented to each person with great respect at the
beginning of the meeting. Bilingual cards are most important with
Chinese printing on the side you offer. You company name will appear in the upper right-hand corner. The spokesperson or chief of the
visiting delegation should present his or her card first. Confirm last
(family) names orally. Also, leave your business card with the repre-

sentatives who made the appointment. Business cards are viewed as an extension of the person and are formally presented, not casually tossed across the table or used for taking notes.

BUSINESS DRESS

Dress conservatively in a suit, shirt, and tie. The Mao suit is worn by Chinese men for both business and formal occasions. The Chinese are less concerned with fashion and style than are people from other countries. During hot weather the hosts will suggest that jackets be removed. A businesswoman can wear suits, dresses, or pantsuits, since Chinese women wear Mao suits or slacks. The key is to be conservative, with no revealing necklines or short skirts. Minimal jewelry and makeup is advised. Personal adornments might be considered tasteless if they suggest luxury or wealth.

GIFT-GIVING

In China, giving gifts is not a standard practice because of government rules. The most acceptable gifts are reciprocal banquets. However, small inexpensive mementos may be given. For the host, a corporate gift that can be displayed is best, such as a book or calendar. The more utility it has, the better. Pen sets are popular. For interpreters, cassette tapes and books are welcome. Cigarettes, brandy, or cognac are considered quite acceptable, once a relationship has been established.

Gifts should not be exchanged until the close of negotiations. The appropriate time to present gifts between companies is at the time of the banquet you arrange for your Chinese counterparts. Do not present individual gifts in front of others, and offer your present with both hands.

Gift-giving should be related to rank and status, and should not suggest bribery in any manner.

Be careful to avoid giving certain items as gifts. The Chinese pronunciation of the word for clock, for example, is a homonym for "being at the deathbed of a loved one," or symbolizing a severing of ties. And flowers are used only for funerals. Do not wrap your gift in white paper, the color of death and mourning in China.

COMMUNICATION STYLES

Through the centuries, the Chinese have created, defined, and enforced acceptable behavior, which is characterized by geniality, courtesy, and cooperation. Thus, the atmosphere in a meeting will be jovial and the first minutes are spent in conversation not related to business. Talk is on the light side, and jokes are made.

The Chinese prefer to avoid answering "yes" or "no" to a direct question. Instead you will hear the words "maybe" and "perhaps." For instance, "Maybe I will come" means "I'm coming." And "It is not so convenient" means "It is not possible." In response to verbal requests, you may get an answer of "We'll study it," or "We'll give it our consideration." This generally reflects reality: regulations have to be followed, and permissions obtained.

Sensitivity to the concept of "face" is critical. Do not challenge the Chinese directly, or demand an answer to a specific question. They may have to consult superiors. Their remaining silent may make it appear that they have lost control of the situation, which is not necessarily so; they often become silent to collect their thoughts. The Chinese have an aversion to dispute, to contentiousness. To react in anger is not acceptable. In situations that appear troublesome, the Chinese usually act as if nothing has happened.

Most Chinese avoid direct eye contact since they believe it is disrespectful. While it may be appropriate to meet someone's eye, holding a stare is considered to be discourteous. Give the Chinese more physical space than you might require yourself. Remain more than an arm's length away, and refrain from touching the other person.

Negotiating in China

Business negotiations are complex and multifaceted, and can be trying since they are prolonged and more technically oriented than in the United States. The pace is slow because the Chinese prefer a business arrangement built on mutual trust and respect. In terms of future business dealings, developing a friendship is to your advantage because the Chinese favor suppliers with whom they have a solid personal rapport.

The first meeting is largely ceremonial, leaving matters of substance to subsequent meetings. It is designed to establish the boundaries of the relationship between the two organizations. No one speaks but the senior executives, who read statements of purpose.

The Chinese representatives will be well prepared and organized. They may ask detailed questions, and will expect responses from highly qualified people who are also well prepared. They like to study detailed and technical literature. Your first step may be to convince the Chinese that your firm has developed a special niche that would be difficult for them to explore on their own. Although defining technical capabilities is essential, the Chinese do not like exaggeration or evasiveness.

When doing business in China, you will be dealing with some part of the government, and it is much like dealing with a decentralized government department in the United States. You will find quite a lot of bureaucracy. The latest decentralization had led to initiative among officials, who compete with each other and with other departments to do business.

The Chinese are astute negotiators and may try to get premium discounts from your firm, knowing full well your desire to penetrate such a huge market. Decide in advance how much you are willing to concede to enter this market. Also, decide how much technical and commercial information you can divulge, and at what stage. The Chinese are tough negotiators and skilled bargainers.

The Chinese expect that one person will speak and that others will not contradict the delegation line. Control your enthusiasm, and do not speak out of turn. Individualistic Westerners may find this difficult, but if you want to get something accomplished, make sure you exercise restraint.

The basic method of negotiating price and finance in China is the time-honored haggle. The seller will offer a price and the Chinese will respond with a counteroffer. Another quote is given, and the Chinese improve their offer, continuing the process until agreement is reached. You will see new faces during this phase because the Chinese bring in people who are experts in haggling, sometimes FTC members themselves. At this time it may be necessary to review much of what went on at earlier meetings. The new officials may be aware of what was done earlier, but they are taking one more opportunity to sound out prospective partners.

It also takes a long time for the Chinese to arrive at their group decisions. Indeed, lines of decision-making authority are far from clear. It is difficult to sort out the exact role played by each Chinese executive you meet. It is wise to discount no one, because only time will reveal the true position of an official. It is common to be ready to leave when last-minute bargaining takes place. Also, after a final price has been agreed on, the Chinese may ask for a further "good-faith" discount—as much as 10 percent.

In China, a contract is a document that defines the desired outcome, not the strict rights and responsibilities. It is a less legalistic country than the United States, relying more on trust than on the law. Chinese contracts are short and printed in English (although copies in Chinese are also prepared). A standard contract is used and the Chinese feel free to make revisions in it; it includes a *force majeure* (act of God) clause that is hard to define. Large-volume transactions and those involving unusual commodities will require special contracts.

Some more suggestions:

• Keep all previous correspondence handy for reference during negotiating talks.
• Take precise and plentiful notes about any agreement. Such data will be useful if minor disputes arise at contract time.
• Understand that it is difficult to negotiate and present technical details in Chinese. A person who can explain matters skillfully is extremely valuable. The central points should be presented first in a straightforward manner, then clarified by showing what is not represented.
• Be aware that high-pressure sales techniques may be counter-productive and offensive to the Chinese.
• Know that in the first meeting, the Chinese will only discuss their organization in general terms. They will not be prepared to go into specifics, so refrain from asking questions.
• Understand that the Chinese may have unusual requests. You may reach an agreement for the Chinese to buy equipment, for example, but they may also expect you to supply parts and services for years.
• Be patient as negotiations enter the financing phase, even if you are dealing with new people. Answer questions politely and consistently. Emphasize the value of your product to the PRC.
• Present a technical seminar to establish your credentials and credibility. It should focus on your firm's desire to help China in its modernization program. Play up your expertise, but play down the benefits to your firm.

• Convey the impression that your firm is eager to enter into the role of advisor and is capable of helping China progress technologically; this is essential. If you approach the Chinese with a genuine desire to share and assist, your efforts to strike a mutually advantageous contract will be fortified.
• Know that many firms leave the seminar materials behind as a gift, and the Chinese have begun to expect this.
• Be prepared for barter offers. For instance, if you are a seller of textile machinery, you may be offered the finished product as partial payment.
• When speaking through an interpreter, look at the person who is being addressed, not at the interpreter. The same principle applies when listening.
• Speak slowly, audibly, and clearly, even if your host understands English. Others in attendance may not understand the language. Use simple words, not colloquialisms.
• Be patient if the conversation is being conducted in English, and compliment your hosts on their use of the language.

Business Entertaining

One of the most important ways to open lines of communication and develop a close working relationship in China is through the Chinese banquet. These banquets must not be looked upon only as a form of business entertainment, but more importantly they must be viewed as a vital prelude to negotiations.

The banquet is a time to build friendship and trust between each other. Business is customarily not discussed. The banquet will be both ceremonial and formal, conducted with precise rules of etiquette. The visiting delegation should be well briefed in advance and confident in the roles of both guest and host for this occasion.

The Chinese will often be first to extend the visiting delegation an invitation to a banquet. It is imperative that the visiting delegation not only accept this invitation but also reciprocate by giving a banquet to honor the Chinese delegation prior to departure.

Most banquets take place in a public hall or restaurant. There is still an official policy about limiting contacts between Chinese and Westerners. You will not be invited to a Chinese home unless you develop a close personal friendship with your Chinese host, and it is considered politically feasible.

Usually, the banquet takes place at a round table that seats ten people. Spouses of Chinese officials and businesspersons do not normally attend, and it is not necessary to invite them to your banquet. If you do extend an invitation, they may not attend. If you are traveling with your spouse, it is appropriate that you both attend the banquet that the U.S. negotiators host.

Be prompt for dinner, which is usually at 6:30 or 7:00 P.M. Banquets usually last about two hours, until 8:30 or 9:00 P.M. You will be greeted and offered a cup of green tea before dinner begins in the formal dining room. Light snacks may accompany the tea—though not usually. When you are ushered into the banquet hall, your host will give you the seat of honor to the right, facing the door, in the middle of the table, and not at the end.

Your host will serve you. Begin eating when your host picks up chopsticks and urges everyone to eat. If he speaks English or has an interpreter, the signal to start may be, "Please begin." Chopsticks are normally used in China, but do not be embarrassed to ask for a knife and fork if you do not know how to use chopsticks. If you want to try, your hosts will help you. It can be mastered quickly.

The banquet may have 12 or more courses, so pace your eating. The more interesting dishes come as the meal progresses, and it is polite to taste everything. If you do not like a particular dish, simply leave it untouched; the plate will be removed, and a clean one provided for the next course.

Several assorted cold dishes are served first, followed by stir-fried, stewed, or deep-fried foods. The first of the major dishes is usually an exotic soup such as shark's fin or bird's nest. Two popular entrees are "Peking" duck and Hunan ham. A clear soup is served either at the beginning or toward the end of a meal. A steamed fish is usually the last major item before dessert. Leave a little fish on your plate. (Fish in Chinese means "a little extra.") The last course is fruit and tea. Hot towels are offered so you can cleanse your face and hands.

The evening's entertainment is over after the meal is finished. Discussions should not be prolonged after this. The guest usually makes the first sign to leave, as a general rule of thumb, about ten minutes after the towels appear. The host might say *"Xie xie nimen lai"* (thank you for coming) to conclude the meal.

When you are the host, tell the maître d' of a restaurant or public hall how much you wish to spend per person, and the meal will be arranged accordingly. Make certain that the banquet you give does not cost more than the banquet given for you. This will cause the Chinese to "lose face" and back off from the relationship. As host, you will start the meal by using the extra chopsticks near your place to put food on the plates of the guests next to you. It is not hygienic to use your own chopsticks to do this. Your Chinese guests will appreciate the more exotic and expensive delicacies such as *haisen* (sea slugs) and *yuchi* (shark's fin). Make arrangements to pay after your guests have left. Tipping is considered an insult.

It is considered impolite to drink alone. Your host will be first to toast you by simply raising his glass and saying *"chin-chin."* Whenever you raise your glass make sure you catch the eye of other guests at the table and also say *"chin-chin"* before drinking. Wait until others raise their glasses to drink with you. Toasting will continue throughout the meal. However, drunkenness is frowned upon.

The banquet is used to build friendship and trust. Business is not discussed; concentrate on building the relationship.

General Tips

• Economic and social accomplishments are a source of pride to the Chinese. They provide excellent topics for conversation at first meetings. Still, while everybody is interested in the responsibilities and obligations that go with the new society of China, you should approach this subject with a light touch.
• The Chinese prefer their country to be called China, The People's Republic, or The People's Republic of China. It is best not to call the nation Red China, Communist China, or Mainland China.
• The Chinese are the world's oldest continuous civilization and are proud of this, and of their tremendous cultural influence on surrounding countries.
• You will please your host if you show keen interest in China's modern-day progress. But remember that the period of Western domination remains a sensitive subject.
• You may ask questions about politics, sex, the Cultural Revolution, the "Gang of Four," or Taiwan. But if your Chinese hosts seem reluctant to answer, do not pressure them or embarrass them, or cause them to lose face in any way.

EXECUTIVE TRAVEL TO CHINA   •

DOCUMENTS

All U.S. citizens must have valid passports, visas, and proper health certificates. Business visas are obtained only through the submission of a business firm's proposal, and a responding invitation from the PRC (People's Republic of China), whose official agency will advise you of all entry requirements.

INOCULATIONS

Smallpox vaccination is not required, but a cholera inoculation may be required if traveling to China from tropical areas. Gamma globulin and typhoid inoculations are recommended.

AIRPORTS

Direct flights are available to Beijing or Shanghai. Business people en route to Guangzhou usually fly to Hong Kong and the CITS office will make arrangements to complete the trip. The Shanghai airport is about 13 miles from the downtown area and the distance is 16 miles from the Beijing airport to the center of the city, each about a 30-minute trip.

CUSTOMS

You are required to fill out a Baggage Declaration Form before arrival, itemizing valuables you are bringing in. You are permitted four bottles of liquor for personal use, two cartons of cigarettes, and most personal effects. Books or games that might offend the morals, culture, or politics of the Chinese people are prohibited.

U. S. EMBASSY

17 Guang Hua Road, Beijing
Phone: 552-033

TRANSPORTATION

Taxis can be hired for an entire day, but it is advisable to hire a car and a driver/translator for the length of your stay.

TIPPING

Do not tip in China *under any circumstances*.

HOTELS

BEIJING *(Peking)*

(All accommodations are arranged through CITS but you are free
to state a preference.)

Diao Yu Tai State Guest House
San Li He Lu
Phone: 867129 or 866250

Great Wall Hotel
North Donghuan Road
Phone: 483831   Telex: 20045

Jainguo Hotel (Build the Nation)
Jainguo Men Wai Avenue
Phone: 595261   Telex: 22439

Peking Hotel
Chang An Boulevard
Phone: 556551 or 552231

Xin Quiao
2 Fan di Lu, Chung Wen Men
Phone: 557731

GUANGZHOU *(Canton)*

White Swan Hotel
Shamian Island (1 South Street)
Phone: 86968   Telex: 44149 WSH

SHANGHAI

Peace Hotel (Heping)
On the Bund
Phone: 211244

RESTAURANTS

BEIJING *(Peking)*

Beijing Kao Yan Dian 13 Wang Fu Jing Phone: 553310	*Peking duck*
Fang Shan Bei Hai Park Phone: 442573	*Classical imperial*
Qianmen Roast Duck Restaurant 24 Quianmen St. Phone: 751379	*Peking duck*
Sichuan 51 Rong Xiang Hutong Phone: 336356	*Szechwan*
Ting Li Guan Summer Palace Phone: 281936	*Seafood*

GUANGZHOU *(Canton)*

Beiyuan Restaurant 439 Dengfeng Road Phone: 33365	*Cantonese*

SHANGHAI

Old Town Restaurant (Lao Fandian) 242 Fuyou Road Phone: 282782	*Chinese*

TRAVEL TIPS

• Most hotel rooms do not have locks and keys. The incidence of theft is rare, but it is best to use good judgment as to valuables.
• Most of these hotels also have twenty-four-hour English-speaking operators. For overseas calls, it is wise to book your call a day in advance.
• Like your hotel arrangements, an itinerary of tours, sightseeing, and so on will probably be arranged for you by CITS and/or

the FTCs with which you are conducting business, and they will provide appropriate bilingual guides or escorts and transportation.
• If your schedule allows, you may also travel and sightsee with freedom on your own, to and within any of 29 "open cities" in China. Simply let CITS know of your plans and they will provide whatever assistance or authority you need.
• Be sure to visit the department stores, specialty stores, and Friendship Stores reserved exclusively for foreign visitors. Seek out values in silk, cashmere, carpets, and Chinese objets d'art.
• Tickets for such events as the Peking Opera (as well as regional operas), folk dances, circuses, puppet shows, musical theatre, and sporting events can be obtained through CITS at your hotel. Remember that polite audience behavior at these events is restrained.
• Business executives who plan to work in their hotel rooms should bring along high-wattage bulbs, as the lighting in the room is usually inadequate. A calculator or portable typewriter may be hard to come by, so you may want to bring them along with you.
• Mandarin is spoken in most of China, with Cantonese spoken in the city of Canton.

HONG KONG

Cultural Overview

A British Crown Colony since the middle of the nineteenth century, Hong Kong is actually 236 islands and a part of the southern Chinese mainland. Commercial and government activity is centered on Hong Kong Island, a bustling international city. In 1997, sovereignty will pass to the People's Republic of China (PRC), but free enterprise, the right to private property, and a form of self-government will remain. People appear to be preparing for the transfer of power with confidence and optimism.

In Hong Kong, traditional Chinese values have been modified by the strong entrepreneurial spirit that has made this city a major international center of trade. Family loyalty and group solidarity remain

fundamental, and politeness, modesty, and "face-saving" are still primary values. Hong Kong businesspeople, however, are likely to get
to the business point more directly than other Asian executives, although they are not as direct as Americans. Hong Kong's heroes are
those who have founded the great shipping, trading, and banking
organizations.

Until the transfer of sovereignty in 1997, Hong Kong will continue
to be governed by British and Chinese civil servants. A British governor has top military and civil authority. An executive council and a
legislative council, composed of top government officials and representatives appointed from community groups, help formulate policy
and local laws. Hong Kong–born Chinese will be taking more active
roles in the government over the coming years, as the British civil
service prepares to leave. The PRC appears to have no plans to change
Hong Kong's basic nature, since the city has a major role to play in
the mainland's push for modernization.

Hong Kong's economy is perhaps the freest in the world. There are
no import duties or export levies and no currency controls. The economy has been growing rapidly over the past several years, with a
growth rate of approximately 10 percent.

As a major international banking and finance center, Hong Kong
has over 130 foreign banks and four stock exchanges which are being
consolidated into one. The absence of foreign currency controls has
been a key factor in making Hong Kong a world financial center.

A plentiful supply of good, low-cost labor for many years made
Hong Kong a manufacturing center for clothing and textiles, time-
pieces, toys, electronic equipment, and electrical machinery. Recent
competition from other Asian countries, however, has made Hong
Kong manufacturers turn to the production of higher quality, higher
priced goods in the textile and electronics markets.

Chinese society does not limit a person to one religious belief, and
Buddhism, Taoism, and Hinduism are widely practiced in various
forms and degrees. About 12 percent of the people are Christian.

As in most Chinese communities, education is highly valued. Primary school is compulsory and free; secondary schools are neither.
Competition is increasing for high school admissions and acceptance
at the government-run universities. Many students from Hong Kong
attend school in the United States or Great Britain.

Marriage and the family in Hong Kong still reflect traditional

Chinese values. Family loyalty is extremely strong, and the senior members have great power and influence. The basic belief that the prestige, education, wealth, or reputation of any one family member reflects on all the others still prevails.

Although older women assume the traditional roles of wife and mother, younger women are increasingly entering the workplace. The majority of working women still hold low-paying factory jobs, but women are also represented in the professions, government, and such businesses as advertising and public relations. There are also women in entrepreneurial roles, although they are a small minority. There is little resistance to foreign businesswomen in Hong Kong.

Although Hong Kong is composed of many islands and part of the mainland, activity is concentrated along the coastline of Hong Kong Island, which has an area of 52 square miles. Its climate is semitropical, with hot, wet, humid summers between May and October. The rest of the year is mild, with a few colder weeks in January and February.

Hong Kong has close to six million people, the vast majority of them Chinese. In recent years, illegal immigration from the PRC has contributed to a high rate of growth, but recent legislation has slowed the influx.

English is the official language of business and government. The major Chinese dialect is Cantonese.

Business Opportunities

Prospects for doing business with Hong Kong are better than ever before. There are particularly good markets for electronic components, textiles, fabrics, consumer goods, computers and other sophisticated business equipment, packaging equipment, and processed food.

Hong Kong's focal position in trading with the PRC is increasing its already great importance as a commercial center. Almost a quarter of the PRC's foreign trade goes through Hong Kong. In addition, Hong Kong's domestic exports have been increasing dramatically, to well over $1 billion annually, and the reexport business has been booming.

Initiating Contact

Banking contacts are extremely useful in exploring business opportunities in Hong Kong. U.S. banks can set up meetings for you with likely prospects and also give advice on doing business in Hong Kong.

Another very important source for U.S. businesspeople is the Hong Kong Trade Development Council. This organization has a computerized roster of Hong Kong businesses interested in pursuing international contacts, and also provides information on potential markets. The council has offices in several cities, including New York, Dallas, Chicago, and Los Angeles.

Initial contact with Hong Kong firms should be through a personal letter from a senior executive. If the U.S. company has an international department, the executive in charge should initiate the contact. In smaller firms, the president or next senior executive should write the letter, which is addressed to important managers at larger companies, senior executives at smaller enterprises. Letters should be written in English, and a small amount of product literature may be included.

A first trip should be regarded as a fact-finding mission and a time to get to know the Hong Kong firm. It is acceptable for just one executive to make this first visit, and, in fact, a large party might seem strange for an initial meeting.

For further information, contact:

World Trade Centre Hong Kong
% World Trade Centre Club Hong Kong
2/M & 3/F World Trade Centre
Causeway Bay, Hong Kong
Phone: 5-779528   Telex: 71729 WTCEN HX

American Chamber of Commerce
Swire House, 10/F, Hong Kong
Phone: (5) 260165   Telex: 83664

U.S. State Department
Desk Officer for Hong Kong
Washington, D.C. 20025
Phone: (202) 632-1436

Commissioner for Hong Kong Affairs
126 East 56th Street
Tower 56, 17th floor
New York, N.Y. 10022
Phone: (212) 355-4060   Telex: 961075

Hong Kong Trade Development Council
Connaught Central, 3/F, Hong Kong
Phone: 5-8334333   Telex: 73595
(U.S. offices in Chicago, Dallas, Los Angeles, Miami, and New
  York.)

Business Protocol and Procedures

BUSINESS ENVIRONMENT

Meetings are usually held at the Hong Kong executive's offices. Business hours are generally 9:00 A.M. to 5:00 P.M., Monday through Friday, with lunch from 1:00 to 2:00 P.M. On Saturdays, businesses are open from 9:00 A.M. to 1:00 P.M.

When you arrive for your meeting, a secretary will probably escort you to the appropriate office. Your host will seat you in the most favorable place in the office, with a view of the harbor if possible.

The discussion may begin with tea and a little small talk. In contrast to the custom in many foreign business centers, however, in Hong Kong this initial conversation is not expected to last very long. The executive with whom you are meeting is likely to be very busy and to appreciate your getting to the point quickly.

Because English is spoken so widely in Hong Kong, interpreters are not usually necessary. The chances of your doing business with a non-English-speaking executive are quite remote.

RANK AND STATUS

Confucian teachings on the necessity of honoring and obeying one's superiors and elders underlie the structure of at least Chinese-run Hong Kong organizations. Ninety percent of all private enterprises are family owned and operated. The senior executive is the head of the family, usually the oldest man. Decision making is a top-down process, and what the firm's head decides (perhaps with the advice of a few other high-ranking family members) is what gets done.

Business titles in this situation are not always clearly defined. Usually, the senior executive in a family-owned organization is the chairman. Below this executive, the table of organization is likely to be difficult to discern. Executive directors generally report to the chairperson and have operating responsibilities for specific areas of the business.

FORMS OF ADDRESS

When entering an office, you are expected to greet people individually, shaking hands with everyone. English greetings are acceptable, and you are not expected to try Chinese phrases. Businessmen should be addressed as Mr. ———. In traditional Chinese names, the family name comes first, so Mr. Cheung Yu-tang would be addressed as Mr. Cheung. Women are addressed as "Mrs." if married and "Miss" if single; last names are used. Younger executives who may have been educated in Great Britain or the United States might reverse this traditional order. With the younger businesspeople, too, you may be able to use first names.

BUSINESS CARDS

Once introductions have been completed, business cards are exchanged. Cards should be bilingual, English on one side and Chinese on the other. They should be presented with the right hand, the Chinese side up. If you do not have cards or run out, the top international hotels can usually arrange to have them printed within twenty-four hours.

BUSINESS DRESS

Acceptable dress is conservative business attire, adapted as much as possible to the warm climate. Blue or gray suits, white or light blue shirts, and subdued ties are appropriate for men, tailored suits and simple jewelry for women.

GIFT-GIVING

Gifts from foreign executives are not expected, but gift-giving is traditional in Hong Kong, and still much appreciated. Gifts, regardless of their intrinsic value, communicate respect and appreciation for friendship. They can be exchanged at the end of an initial visit and upon each subsequent trip. A gift of expensive French cognac is very much appreciated. Scotch, usually a prized gift in international business centers, is not special in Hong Kong.

The government and most of the major companies do not look kindly upon executive gift-giving; it is viewed as a genteel form of business corruption. Business entertainment (luncheons, receptions, and dinners) is widespread, however, and can be most exhausting.

COMMUNICATION STYLES

The style of business communication in Hong Kong combines traditional Chinese values with modern Western practices. Politeness, personal relationships, and modest, quiet conduct are the norm. Raising one's voice in anger is not acceptable to the Chinese. Saving face is another key concern, which means that one must avoid calling attention to another's error, failure to understand something, or ignorance of something he or she should have known.

The Chinese also do not like to say no or to express disagreement, and this can confuse a Western executive. It is important to test apparent statements of agreement, since they may in fact be masking concerns or even downright disagreement.

Despite tendencies toward traditional behavior, most Hong Kong executives are more direct than other Asians. The business transaction is a primary concern, and your Hong Kong counterparts are likely to get to the point quickly and make an agreement based more on the particulars than on personalities. Nonverbal communication in Hong Kong is more like that in the West, although it depends on the type of company with which you are dealing. Companies with international experience are more Western in approach and expectations than smaller, family-run firms doing local business. Formal behavior and politeness are trademarks of dealing with these firms. Eye contact is expected.

Negotiating in Hong Kong

The purpose of a first visit is usually not to conduct hard negotiations but to get to know your counterpart. Personal relationships between business partners, while less important in Hong Kong than in many other Asian centers, still count considerably. During this visit, you can learn about the business, its major competitors, and its operations and needs.

It is important to know who will be making the final decisions when you are negotiating. In the family-owned enterprises—which the vast majority are—the head of the family will have absolute authority. In some cases the head person will designate another to participate in negotiations, often the eldest son. When this is the case, the final decision will not be made at the meeting, but later, by the head executive.

Lawyers are not included in negotiations until final contracts are being drawn up and signed. At the first meetings, they would be inappropriate.

The Hong Kong market is an important one for U.S. suppliers and will become even more attractive as trade with the PRC grows. U.S. businesspeople should keep a long-term perspective when negotiating with Hong Kong firms and bear in mind that their executives are interested in developing stable commercial relationships. The more confidence the Hong Kong executive has that a business relationship will last, the greater the chances for successfully closing a deal will be.

Hong Kong's distance from the United States makes businesses particularly concerned about the reliability of the product, shipping, and service. This applies to industries such as electronics, in which down time costs the buyer money and can hurt his reputation. Having a competent representative in the city, therefore, is a crucial element in negotiating sales to the Hong Kong market. Finding a good representative might be difficult, given the competitiveness of the situation in Hong Kong, but a capable agent is critically necessary.

The fierce competition for Hong Kong's business has made price another key element in negotiations. Many transactions are closed on price alone, but other considerations can balance the price issue. All elements of a total package are important, and if the long-term agreement, service guarantees, and perhaps financing issues are attractive enough, the price issue may be outweighed.

Business Entertaining

Getting to know your Hong Kong counterparts in a social setting is important. Dinner is the usual entertainment, and, at least once in your trip, your host will probably stage an elaborate banquet.

At a restaurant, the guest of honor sits with his or her back to the wall, facing the kitchen. The person sitting nearest the guest will keep serving what might seem to be a great deal of food. In such circumstances, it is polite to eat as much as possible.

Toasting is an important part of Chinese dinners. Toasts should not be overly elaborate or lengthy. It is correct to give a simple, polite toast to friendship, cooperation, and hope for future success. Glasses are held in one hand.

Using chopsticks is appreciated as a sign that you are willing to adapt to local practices. If you do not know how to use them, it would be a good idea to try to learn before your trip.

When you have finished eating it is polite to lay the chopsticks on the chopstick rest, which is usually part of the place setting—never leave them on a plate or in food.

Smoking at the table is *not* impolite, but it is courteous to ask permission before lighting up.

General Tips

• When engaging in small talk, the Chinese consider talking about family issues to be in poor taste.
• The subject of Hong Kong's future was a worrisome issue until 1984, when the agreement between Great Britain and the PRC was reached. Its terms have allayed many fears, but the coming transfer is still a touchy issue. It is best to approach the topic, if at all, with great caution and politeness, and only when alone with a person with whom you have already established a good personal relationship.
• The Chinese consider calling attention to oneself ill-mannered, since they feel that personal achievements should be coordinated with the good of the group. Thus, if you compliment a Chinese person, he or she may be pleased but will still decline the compliment. You, too, are expected to be humble and modest in receiving a compliment.
• Remember that the Chinese do not like to say no directly. Statements of agreement may not really be accurate, and you may need to check them carefully. Of course, this requires considerable tact if you are to avoid making your counterpart lose face.

EXECUTIVE TRAVEL TO HONG KONG   •

DOCUMENTS

U.S. citizens holding valid passports may visit for one month without a visa, provided they have a return or onward ticket. Extensions are granted easily.

INOCULATIONS

None required when traveling from the United States. Cholera and yellow fever inoculations may be recommended—check with your doctor.

AIRPORT

Kai Tak Airport is in Kowloon, across the harbor from the center of Victoria (about 4½ miles).

CUSTOMS

You are allowed to bring in one quart of liquor and 200 cigarettes (or 50 cigars or ½ pound of tobacco). There are no restrictions on goods taken out of the country except for works of art. Check with the Hong Kong tourist board for more details.

U.S. EMBASSY

26 Garden Road, Central Hong Kong
Phone: 5-239-0111

TRANSPORTATION

A new metro opened in 1980 links Hong Kong to Kowloon. It is suggested that the business traveler arrange for a car with driver/translator for the period you will be in Hong Kong.

TIPPING

Service charges are usually added to the bill at hotels, restaurants, and taxis. An additional 10 percent is welcomed for special services.

HOTELS

The Mandarin
5 Connaught Road, Hong Kong
Phone: 5220111   Telex: 73653

The Peninsula
Salisbury Road, Kowloon
Phone: 3666251   Telex: 73821

The Regent
18 Salisbury Road, Kowloon
Phone: 3721121   Telex 37134

The Shangri-la
64 Mody Road, Kowloon
Phone: 3721211   Telex: 36718

RESTAURANTS

Gaddi's   *International*
Peninsula Hotel, Salisbury Road
Kowloon
Phone: 3666251

Man Wah   *Chinese*
Mandarin Hotel, 5 Connaught Road
Hong Kong
Phone: 5220111

Fook Lam Moon   *Cantonese*
459 Lockhart Road, Causeway Bay
Phone: 5772567

Pak Lok Chiu Chow   *Chiu Chow*
23–25 Hysan Avenue, Causeway Bay
Phone: 5768886

Pierrot   *French*
Mandarin Hotel, 5 Connaught Road
Hong Kong
Phone: 5220111

World Trade Center Club   *International*
Excelsior Hotel, Causeway Bay (private
   membership club)
Phone: 5767365

TRAVEL TIPS

• International communications are excellent. Telephone, telex, and cable links are reliable.

• Personal safety and health compare fully with the West. There are several modern pharmacies and private hospitals. Clinics for minor injuries and illnesses are found on both Hong Kong Island and Kowloon peninsula.

• As a duty-free port, Hong Kong has advantages over other cities. No duties are levied on imported or locally manufactured goods.

• The golden rule for shopping in Hong Kong is to compare prices, especially if buying an expensive item. Bargaining is a tradition in Hong Kong; this practice is only done in small shops, stalls, and markets. Offering one-half the stated price is a good place to start.

• Hong Kong's entertainment is world renowned, especially its nightlife. After-hours entertainment centers around Hong Kong's over four thousand restaurants, clubs, discos, bars, and musical revues. Gambling is available a short hydrofoil trip away in Macao, the Portuguese colony.

• Horseracing is the nearest thing Hong Kong has to a national sport. The season is from September through May. Two tracks operate, the modern Shatin and the traditional Happy Valley.

• There is a fifteen-hundred-seat concert hall, more than eighty movie houses, and a philharmonic orchestra. Be sure to check the schedule of events at the newly opened Hong Kong Arts Center located on a waterfront site in Wanchai.

• Cantonese is the dialect spoken in Hong Kong, for the most part.

INDIA

Cultural Overview

The vast subcontinent of India has intrigued Western imaginations for centuries. Ancient temples, Victorian monuments, and modern skyscrapers coexist in her cities, as do beggars, bejeweled matrons in bright saris, and prosperous businesspeople in conservative suits. Still a developing nation, India has enormous potential for growth and position as a world leader.

The ancient land of India is quite new as a modern nation, having gained independence from Great Britain only in 1947. Based on the British parliamentary system, the government has a bicameral legislature and executive and judicial branches.

A member of the British Commonwealth of Nations, India is nominally headed by a president, who appoints the prime minister, the leader of the majority party in parliament or of a coalition of parties. The actual power, however, rests with the Council of Ministers, or cabinet; and with the prime minister, its chief executive officer.

India's centrally planned economy has been directed, since 1950, by a series of Five-Year Plans that set goals and allocate resources. Although a vigorous private sector exists, the government owns and runs many enterprises, including the airlines, railroads, insurance industry, power facilities, and irrigation projects. The government also predominates in many other industries, including the production of steel, metals, chemicals, and engineering equipment. Eighty-five percent of the nation's banking assets are government controlled.

India's economy has been growing at a creditable pace, the GNP has been rising steadily for several years, and inflation has remained relatively low. One of the world's top ten industrial producers, India has a very large pool of technical and scientific workers, established domestic capital markets, competent management personnel, and low labor costs. The economy possesses a mature infrastructure of facilities, and no major debt obligations currently exist.

In recent years, the climate for private industry and international trade has been improving. Taxes have been lowered, some licensing restrictions have been removed, and the importation of capital goods has been liberalized. Industrial growth is being encouraged, but serious economic problems remain. India is the second most populous country in the world, and chronic unemployment and severe poverty continue to be widespread.

Agriculture accounts for about 40 percent of the GNP and employs about 75 percent of the workforce. Major mineral resources include iron ore, coal, manganese, and mica. The country is oil-rich and, with recent efforts to develop its reserves, India is expected to produce 90 percent of its own requirements by 1990. The United States is India's leading trading partner, accounting for approximately 25 percent of all Indian exports.

India's culture is ancient and complex; it embraces many religious and diverse peoples. The rigid caste system is dying out, but a hierarchical prejudice still survives. In addition to Hindus, India has Muslims, Buddhists, Sikhs, Parsees, Jains, Christians, and Jews. Whatever their specific belief, Indians tend to be very devout, or at least spiritual in orientation. Social harmony, humility, and self-denial are primary virtues. Change is not valued for its own sake, and comes slowly. However, a new dimension has been given under the youthful Prime Minister Rajiv Gandhi. Such attitudes will influence business dealings, and the foreign executive should be aware of them and accord them respect.

The exended family is the main unit of society, with all members living under one roof, under the authority of the oldest male, or a widowed matriarch. Women are not submissive, although the family has been the traditional place for them. Women are increasing in numbers and power in the workforce, especially in the professions and in government.

In an area roughly one-third the size of the United States, India has 15 different dialects, with Hindi being the official language of the union. English, however, is used officially as well for commerce, and you will be able to get along with it in general, at least in the major cities. India's topography varies widely, and half the land is cultivated. Most of the country has a tropical monsoon climate, with almost daily rains from June to September in many areas. October to February is the best time, weather-wise, to visit.

The major business centers are the cities of Bombay; New Delhi, the capital; Calcutta, center of the jute and steel industries; and Madras, the leading industrial city in the south. Poona, two hours by train from Bombay, and Bangalore, in central India, have the major share of India's defense and electronics industries. The majority of India's people, however, live in the rural areas.

Education is free and compulsory to the age of 14, but only about one-third of the population is literate.

Business Opportunities

India's climate for foreign business appears to be improving as trade barriers drop and the bureaucratic structure becomes simpler. Nevertheless, this country remains highly selective about those areas in which foreign business can be involved.

Foreigners can share in India's economy in three major ways: through investment, usually in a joint venture; through trade; and in collaboration, through the transfer of technology. Not regarded as crucial for India's capital requirements, foreign equity is seen primarily as a means of facilitating the acquisition of needed technology and of boosting exports. Opportunities for U.S. firms exist in supplying raw materials, high-tech equipment, capital goods for Indian projects in mining and excavation, food processing, shipbuilding, pollution and industrial controls, chemical and petrochemical production, and oil and gas exploration and refining.

Investment proposals are evaluated on an individual basis. Approval depends on many factors, including how the proposal supports development plan objectives and the level of foreign exchange costs met by the investor. The key to approval is convincing the Indian government that the technology involved is up to date, will not soon become obsolete, and is suitable to be needs of the country. Supporting documents must be provided that indicate product specifications, experience in other collaborations, and evidence of a proven business track record.

To protect against loss of investment because of a variety of contingencies, a company can get insurance from the U.S. government–run Overseas Private Investment Corporation. The address is: Finance Officer, Asia Division, OPIC, 1129 20th Street N.W., Washington, D.C. 20527. Phone: (202) 653-0920.

In the area of trade, India enforces a strict import/export licensing policy to conserve foreign exchange. Licenses are issued on a CIF (cost-insurance-freight) basis, and normally do not permit any variation in the quantity. They are usually valid for two years. For most goods, no letters of credit or any payment are allowed without a license.

U.S. companies interested in collaborating with Indian firms on technical projects should be aware that payments are in the form of royalties. These payments cannot exceed 5 percent of the factory price of the product and can extend for a period of no more than ten years. For the sale of technical knowledge, royalties may be as high as 8 percent if the technology is important to government objectives.

For specifics regarding product standards, contact Indian Standards Institution, Manak Bhavan, 9 Bahadur Shah Marg, New Delhi 1, India.

Initiating Contact

Finding a good Indian agent is generally crucial for doing business. Only a registered agent can enter into an agreement on behalf of a foreign principal, and one is necessary for establishing good personal and government contacts, answering questions firsthand, and otherwise facilitating the complicated process of doing business in India. Agents will also know the needs of the market and how to make bids more attractive to local conditions. Government purchasing offices maintain lists of approved agents and must verify that an agent is authorized to act on behalf of a foreign firm.

An agent should be able to cover all the major industrial areas and have offices in the principal business centers, especially New Delhi. The Indian Investment Center, herein listed, can assist U.S. investors in locating qualified agents.

Additional information about trade and investment can be gained from the following:

Indian Chamber of Commerce of America, Inc.
445 Park Avenue
New York, N.Y. 10022
Phone: (212) 755-7181

Trade Development Authority
Bank of Baroda Building
16, Sansad Marg
P.O. Box 767
New Delhi 110001, India
Phone: 312819   Telex: 2735

World Trade Center, Bombay
M. Visvesvaraya Industrial Research & Development Centre
Cuffe Parade
Colaba, Bombay 5, India
Phone: 214434   Telex: 011-6846

U.S. Commerce Department
Country Specialist/India

14th Street and Constitution Avenue
Washington, D.C. 20230
Phone: (202) 377-2994

Consulate General of India
3 East 64th Street
New York, N.Y. 10021
Phone: (212) 879-7800
(Also offices in San Francisco and Chicago.)

Business Protocol and Procedures

BUSINESS ENVIRONMENT

In India, you will find modern facilities and astute, well-trained Indian executives, knowledgeable about international affairs and the West. Foreigners who reveal an ignorance of Indian affairs are presumed to be looking down on the country, so some advance study is highly recommended.

The business day generally starts between 9:00 A.M. and 10:00 A.M. and ends between 5:30 P.M. and 6:00 P.M. Many companies are open for half a day on Saturdays. Lunch is usually at about 1:00 P.M. Government offices operate from 10:00 A.M. to 5:00 P.M., Monday through Friday.

The concept of time in India differs from that in the West. It would be offensive for you to be late for business appointments, but you may be kept waiting by your Indian host. The pace, in general, is considerably slower in this nation.

When you arrive for an appointment, present your business card to the receptionist. In all circumstances, you should wait for an invitation before entering a room, sitting down, or lighting a cigarette.

The normal business greeting is a firm handshake, but Indians do *not* shake hands with women, or even touch them. Educated Indian women, however, will offer a handshake to Westerners, which it is appropriate to accept. Your Indian host will probably offer tea, coffee, or a cold drink when you arrive, which should be accepted.

All public or private Indian corporations are governed by boards of directors. At board meetings, the chairperson, the founding family member of the company, or the chief operating officer will usually sit at the head of the table. The second-in-command usually sits to this person's right.

In general, Indians are friendly toward strangers and oriented toward forming relationships. Aloof behavior discourages them and American warmth and friendliness will create the right impression. Loudness, brashness, or backslapping are not appropriate. Whistling is considered impolite, and feet or shoes are never placed on a desk or table. If your feet or shoes touch someone, you should apologize.

RANK AND STATUS

Wealthy families control much of the industry; nepotism is an accepted practice, and each layer of society retains its "old boy" network. Education and democratic principles have altered dramatically the earlier institutions of colonialism and caste.

FORMS OF ADDRESS

It is proper and customary to call Indians by their last names and to use titles, such as "Dr." or "Professor." "Mr." or "Shri," which stands for "Mr.," should be used. The chairman of a company may be addressed as "Mr. Chairman." Adding the suffix "ji" after a family name shows respect.

BUSINESS CARDS

If the receptionist does not give your business card to your host, do so yourself once introductions have been completed. Indians put all their professional credentials, such as M.B.A., on their business cards, and you may find strings of initials unknown to you on your counterpart's card.

BUSINESS DRESS

Business attire in India is informal. The Indian men usually wear slacks and light-colored, short-sleeved shirts, open at the neck. Visiting executives, however, should wear suits and ties for at least the first meeting. Later, the visitor may dress more casually.

GIFT-GIVING

In a social context, gifts are considered a sign of friendship and also of appreciation. A bottle of imported liquor (especially scotch), perfume or cologne, a carton of cigarettes, or a fine pen are most welcome.

COMMUNICATION STYLES

The style of Indian business speech and correspondence is generally formal and indirect. It is considered impolite to say no directly, and Indians will say yes when they do not mean it. The purpose of a business letter may not become clear until the end of the first page.

Indians may avoid eye contact or bow their heads slightly when you are speaking. These actions signal respect, not lack of interest. Shaking the head from side to side means "yes," not "no," in India.

Negotiating in India

Negotiations in India take place, in general, in a friendly and low-key atmosphere. Patience will stand you in good stead, as will taking the time to develop good relationships with your counterparts, and to gain an understanding of Indian culture.

The first meetings will not produce tangible results, as a rule, and transactions can be especially drawn out with government entities. Taking time, however, can pay off extremely well, for business relationships have longevity in India.

Indians are clever businesspeople, and bargaining is a way of life. You should not put all your cards on the table at the start. You are expected to refuse the first offer.

Although you may meet with boards of directors, Indian business decisions are not made by committees. The managing director, or someone at that level, usually has the final authority. It is important to leave a strong, positive impression with the person in this position.

Being thoroughly knowledgeable about the Indian market for your goods or investments is very important. Keep in mind that India is still a developing country whose markets have not yet fully matured. Be ready to be flexible and to downgrade your initial expectations to accommodate the realities.

In negotiations, proposals do well that clearly address the country's needs. They should also stress relative price, the absolute limit of the initial investment, after-sales service if required, prompt delivery, and, above all, credit terms and availability. Prices should be stated on a firm basis. Of lesser interest to the Indians is savings on labor costs or issues of long-term efficiency.

A handshake at the end of negotiations does mean agreement—but it is not binding. India operates under a legal system based on British law, which states that contracts are not binding unless in writing, and signed.

Letters of intent, too, are only preliminary since most business transactions with foreigners must be approved by the Indian government.

Here are some useful ideas:

• Except for people introduced to you by the Indian Investment Center, it is a good idea to run an independent check on prospective Indian associates, to be sure those firms and individuals are reputable.
• In submitting bids, tender specifications should use the metric system. Tons should be designated as metric, long, or short.
• India follows the British practice that goods, once sold, are never taken back.

Business Entertaining

Business discussions often continue over lunch in India, which is usually at a restaurant or a private club. Your hotel bar or restaurant is also appropriate. Lunch starts about 1:00 P.M. and lasts approximately two hours. Your Indian counterpart will always offer to take the check, out of politeness, even if you issued the invitation. If you did, however, you must pick up the tab.

Invitations for dinner will come only after a comfortable relationship has been established. Spouses may be invited to join you for this meal, but if they are, business is not an appropriate topic of conversation.

Many Hindus eat no beef, and Muslims, no pork; vegetarianism is widespread. Approximately half the Indian businesspeople you meet will drink no alcohol and in fact, individual liquor permits may be required for consumption in certain areas. These are issued freely to foreigners but not to Indians, which could mean that you would be allowed to drink in a restaurant while your host would not be. This should not be embarrassing, but, depending on the circumstances, it may be polite for you to forego having alcohol with your meal.

You may be invited to your host's home for dinner, which will be a lavish occasion. Your host may send a car to pick you up at your hotel, and you will surely be urged to eat a great deal. You need not eat more than you wish, and it is not impolite to avoid some dishes that are too spicy or otherwise unappealing. Indians often eat with their hands, but you are not expected to if you do not wish to do so.

"Indian time" prevails for social occasions. If you invite someone for dinner at eight, the guest will probably not arrive until nine. If you are invited for cocktails at seven and arrive on time, your host will very likely not be ready to receive you.

If you stay with your Indian colleagues, you are expected to tip the servants before you leave.

General Tips

- Indians speak British English, and they use British slang such as loo for bathroom and fag for cigarette and British spelling, such as harbour, colour, centre, and cheque. When they write dates, the day comes first, not the month: that is, 3/12/86 means December 3, 1986.
- To show respect, Indians often engage in elaborate "after you" rituals. And they usually ask permission before taking leave of you.
- Women traveling in India should dress very modestly, which means keeping the upper arms, chest, and back covered.
- If you meet an Indian businesswoman, which does not happen very often, she is to be treated as a professional. It would be inappropriate to invite her to your room for drinks or a business discussion, but perfectly proper to meet her at your hotel bar.
- When drinking water from a communal cup, as may happen in a traditional Indian home, your lips must not touch the cup.

EXECUTIVE TRAVEL TO INDIA   •

DOCUMENTS

U.S. citizens visiting India for business require a valid U.S. passport, a business visa, and a round-trip ticket. The visa application, which is obtained from the office of the Indian Consulate, must include a passport-size photograph and a sponsoring letter from the applicant's firm stating the nature of the visit and guaranteeing financial and moral responsibility for the period of time in India.

INOCULATIONS

No special inoculations are required for U.S. citizens.

AIRPORTS

The airport in Bombay is located about 15 miles from the center of the downtown area and the New Delhi Airport is about 10 miles to the center of downtown. Travel time should be approximately 45 minutes.

CUSTOMS

Visitors are entitled to bring into India free of duty 200 cigarettes, 50 cigars or 250 grams of tobacco, up to a liter of liquor, reasonable amounts of perfumes and medicine, and a reasonable amount of personal property.

U.S. EMBASSY

> Shanti Path, Chanakyapuri 21, New Delhi
> Phone: (011) 690351   Telex 314589

TRANSPORTATION

Indian taxis are small and never air conditioned. It is recommended that you hire a driver/translator for the length of your stay.

TIPPING

A service charge of 10 to 15 percent is usually added to restaurant and hotel bills. Beyond this, tips to waiters and hotel attendants are voluntary.

HOTELS

BOMBAY

> Oberoi Towers
> Marine Drive, Nariman Point
> Phone: 234343   Telex: 114153

President Hotel
90 Cuffe Parade, Colaba
Phone: 219141   Telex: 114135

Taj Mahal Inter-Continental Hotel
Apollo Bunder
Phone: 2023366   Telex: 112442

New Delhi

Hyatt Regency
Cama Place, Ring Road
Phone: 624984   Telex 110066

Maurya Sheraton
Diplomatic Enclave
Phone: 61163   Telex: 0313247

Taj Mahal Hotel
1 Mansingh Road
Phone: 386162   Telex: 313604

Taj Palace Hotel
2 Sardar Petel Marg
Phone: 344900   Telex: 0315151

RESTAURANTS

Bombay

Café Royal   *French*
Oberoi Towers Hotel
Marine Drive, Nariman Point
Phone: 234343

Moghul Room   *Indian*
Oberoi Towers Hotel
Marine Drive, Nariman Point
Phone: 234343

Pasha Restaurant   *Mughlai*
Rusi villa, 9 Deshmukh Road
Phone: 368332

Rendezvous   *French*
Taj Mahal Inter-Continental Hotel
Apollo Bunder
Phone: 2023366

Tanjore   *Indian*
Taj Mahal Inter-Continental Hotel
Apollo Bunder
Phone: 2023366

NEW DELHI

Bokhara Restaurant   *Indian*
Maurya Sheraton Hotel
Diplomatic Enclave
Phone: 61163

Café Chendi   *Continental*
Oberoi Inter-Continental Hotel
Zakir Hussain Marg
Phone: 699571

Hande   *Indian*
Taj Palace Hotel
2 Sardar Petel Marg
Phone: 344900

House of Ming   *Chinese*
Taj Mahal Hotel
1 Mansingh Road
Phone: 386162

Taj   *Indian*
Oberoi Inter-Continental Hotel
Zakir Hussain Marg
Phone: 699571

TRAVEL TIPS

• Good medical care is available in the major cities. The doctors,
many Western-trained, speak English.
• The dental care in India is not what you are accustomed to, so
try to postpone dental visits.
• All of the top hotels provide secretarial services and communication centers for telex and cable. The phone system, however,

is unreliable and even local calls are difficult to place. You would do better to send a telex between Bombay and Delhi if the need arose. The postal system is excellent, with next-day delivery between the four major cities.

• India can be a shopper's paradise. Great bargains can be found in pottery, engraved copper items, brass figurines, tie-dyed textiles, leather accessories, and native hand work. Bargaining is allowed and expected.

• Some items are difficult to come by. A businessman should bring enough blades for his twin-blade cartridge razor and sufficient shaving foam, and carry a spare refill for his Cross or Parker pen.

• Expect to be stared at; the Indian people do not mean to be rude, but they are very interested in visitors from other lands.

• Arrange through your hotel for qualified guides, tour operators, driver/translators, or anyone else whose services you will require.

• Book well ahead for Bombay hotel accommodations, as space is limited—especially during the peak winter season.

• The Sea Rock Hotel in Bombay has a lovely rooftop nightclub. For more serious entertainment, the National Center for the Performing Arts offers modern dance and drama.

• Delhi's National Art Gallery and National Museum have outstanding examples of India's and Central Asia's artistic treasures.

JAPAN

Cultural Overview

Japan is the most industrialized nation in the Far East and one of the foremost traders in the global marketplace. Geographically, Japan is comprised of four large islands plus thousands of islets, roughly the size and shape of California. It has 120 million people, approximately half the current population of the United States. This density of population, and the fact that Japan is a racially and culturally homogeneous society, greatly influence its character.

Japan is a constitutional monarchy headed by an emperor, who is the symbol of the state. Its structure of government and constitution are similar to that of the United States. There are three branches of the national government. Executive power is vested in a prime minister, who is responsible to the Diet (parliament) and elected from its members. The Diet is elected by the people and composed of two houses: the House of Representatives (lower) and the House of Councillors (upper). The judicial branch is composed of a supreme court and lower courts. There are two main political parties. The conservative Liberal Democratic party (LDP) is the party of free enterprise, with links to the business community. The Socialist party has links with major trade and labor unions.

Even though it has few natural resources, Japan is the third leading industrial superpower after the United States and the U.S.S.R. Shipbuilding, car manufacturing, and steel production are major industries in Japan. It imports fossil fuels, wood products, metal ores, raw materials, machinery, and equipment from the United States, as well as food products, such as corn, wheat, sorghum, soybeans, and meat.

Japan has a free-enterprise economy but the government participates in and exercises control over planning committees and banks. The MITI (Ministry of International Trade and Industry) guides business and industry toward stated and specific goals. An important development is the government's stress on the formation of joint ventures with Japan's trading partners.

Since World War II, Japan has had great economic success. This has been attributed to an intelligent and diligent workforce, trade barriers that keep out imports, and allocation of less than 1 percent of the GNP for defense.

The largest of the Japanese islands is Honshu, which is also the seat of the major cities and of agricultural and manufacturing production. Tokyo is the second largest city in the world with 12 million people. Japan's overall climate is similar to the east coast of the United States, with seasonal changes. Tokyo's climate is similar to that of Washington, D.C. There is a rainy season from mid-June to mid-July.

Following tradition, marriages are more of a partnership than a romance in Japan. Sixty percent are still arranged, and people tend to marry late: men at 28 or 30, women at 26. Also, the Japanese family is small, with no more than two children. Abortion is common. While divorce is uncommon, it is increasing among couples whose children have reached adulthood.

Women have charge of the family, expenses, and the education of the children. This is important, as children are regarded as the country's treasures, and there is therefore great emphasis on education as a means of upward mobility. The mother is charged with the responsibility for the child's success, and the mother–son relationship is particularly important. It is not usual to find top-level female executives in Japan unless the business is privately owned. Women may have some managerial jobs in businesses such as interior decorating.

A person's status and position in Japanese society are linked to the university attended, and then to the corporation. Thus, children are under pressure to achieve scholastically, and there is a struggle to get into a university, particularly the top ten. The Japanese have one of the highest literacy rates—99 percent.

The Japanese are eclectic in their approach to religion. The major ones are Buddhism and Shintoism, but a Japanese person may be married with Shinto rites and buried with Buddhist ones. The religious celebrations and practices are more ceremonial and social than firmly based in spiritual conviction.

Japanese is the official language, and, since equal stress is given to each syllable, it is not difficult to speak it. Written Japanese, however, is quite complicated. It uses Chinese characters, called ideograms, and two phonetic alphabets. English is a widely used second language in Japan.

There is a great respect for age in Japan. Elders are still considered the children's responsibility. The Japanese also place high value on conformity and predictability, traits that are related to the density of population, and achievable because of the homogeneous society. Both a Korean minority and the aboriginal Ainu are excluded from the mainstream. Japanese children are taught to avoid behavior that could be rude, insulting, or hurtful. Overt displays of anger or impatience are construed as signs of a weak character. The Japanese also have a tradition of "face," which is the image that is shown to others. For this reason, there is much concern about what others in your group think of you.

Business Opportunities

Japan is one of the most difficult markets to penetrate, but it is a profitable one. In addition to food products and raw materials, other sales opportunities for U.S. businesses are office and personal computers and software, electronic components, telecommunications equipment, pharmaceuticals, building products, and medical and dental products. New emphasis is being placed on energy-conserving, high-tech industries.

Initiating Contact

Without a third-party introduction, it is difficult to do business in Japan. The third party should be of appropriate rank such as a representative of a bank, large trading company, or a member of an acknowledged trade association. The third party can also act as an intermediary during the negotiations. In this nation, banks and trading companies can join the business ventures they support. You need a local agent or distributor to sell your goods in Japan, whether it is a joint venture or a licensing arrangement. Most importing and exporting is done through trading companies. The nine largest comprise 90 percent of the trade: Mitsubishi, Mitsui, Marubeni, Kanematsu-Gosho, C. Itoh, Sumitomo, Nissho-Iwai, Tomen, and Nichimen. Most have offices in major cities of the world. There are also seven thousand smaller trading companies.

When sending written correspondence, it is helpful to know a specific department and person within the company. If you do not get an answer, it may be because of the Japanese preference for a third-party introduction, or face-to-face discussions. The letter should be translated into Japanese.

For further information and assistance, contact:

World Trade Center of Japan, Inc.
P.O. Box 57 World Trade Center Building
No. 4-1, 2-chome, Hamamatsu-cho
Minato-ku, Tokyo 105, Japan
Phone: (03) 435-5651   Telex 242 2661 WORLDT J

American Chamber of Commerce
701 Tosho Building
2-2 Marunounchi, 3-chome
Chiyodaku, Tokyo, Japan
Phone: (03) 433-5381   Telex: J23736 KYLE

JETRO (Japanese External Trade Organization)
2-5 Toranomon, 2-chome
Minato-Ku, Tokyo, Japan

Phone: (03) 582-5511   Telex: J24378
(Also, offices in New York, Chicago, Houston, Los Angeles, San
    Francisco, Toronto, and major cities throughout the world.)

U.S. Department of Commerce
International Trade Administration
Japan Desk
14th Street and Constitution Avenue
Washington, D.C. 20230
Phone: (202) 377-2425

Japan Chamber of Commerce of New York
145 West 57th Street
New York, N.Y. 10019
Phone: (212) 246-9774

Business Protocol and Procedures

BUSINESS ENVIRONMENT

Business meetings are held at the office of your Japanese hosts. Plan
to be prompt.

Business hours in Japan are from 9:00 A.M. to 5:00 P.M. on weekdays, with some offices open Saturdays from 9:00 to noon. Try to
avoid making business meetings during "Golden Week" in late April
or early May (when three holidays fall within a week of each other);
in August, the Japanese vacation season; or at the end of the year.

The first meeting will last for approximately an hour, and is largely
ceremonial. The Japanese want to establish trust, and determine
whether they wish to conduct business with you. If the atmosphere is
congenial, subsequent meetings will be held in the next few days.
Plan to stay in Japan at least two weeks. Your negotiations may take
longer than you expected.

Business meetings are held in the executive conference room, which
often has plush, cushioned chairs around a long rectangular table.
The senior manager will sit in the center, with his next ranking executive on his right and the second on the left, facing the door. The
U.S. team will sit opposite them on the other side of the table. An
interpreter sits close to the table. Middle-level executives may hold
meetings in a reception room, as there are few private offices.

It is acceptable to use the Japanese company interpreter in the first formal meeting. But once negotiations begin, you will need your own interpreter. It is useful to ask for an interpreter with experience in your field. The Japanese company usually uses an interpreter even when they understand or speak English quite well.

RANK AND STATUS

Status is very important to the Japanese; it is tied to their corporation and to their rank in this corporation. Even personal relationships are hierarchical. For example, older people have a higher status than younger ones. The same is true for men and women, and senior executives and junior executives. And, in the Japanese culture, there is a difference between a buyer and a seller; the buyer enjoys a higher status and is treated with deference and respect.

Your position in the United States will dictate whom you meet in Japan. A manager from the United States will meet a manager from the Japanese firm; a director, a director. You should be respectful to your Japanese hosts, especially to the older senior managers.

FORMS OF ADDRESS

The hosts usually start introductions with a junior manager introducing the senior staff. The senior member of the U.S. team does the honors, unless one of the U.S. executives has met the Japanese on a prior visit.

Most Japanese businesspersons simply shake hands with visiting executives. Or they may combine this with a slight bow. You should shake hands with a single, firm gesture. Say "How do you do" or "I'm pleased to meet you," which are considered more polite than just "Hello." If you feel comfortable, bow slightly and say something appropriate in Japanese. With each other, the Japanese bow from the waist. The depth of the bow indicates the level of respect accorded.

The traditional *ojigi* (oh-jee-gee) or bow is used both in greetings and farewells among the Japanese. Those who try to mimic this gesture should be made aware of its importance. Depending on the occasion, or the persons, the *ojigi* will determine the appropriateness of the respect accorded. There are three forms of bowing: the informal, the formal, and the *saikeirei* (sie-kay-ee-raye), which confers great honor. The informal bow, which is used between persons of all ranks, is done with the hands at the side and the body bent approximately 15 degrees forward. In the formal bow, the hands are together, palms down and touching the knees; the body is bent forward 30 degrees. This position is held for a few seconds. The recipient of this bow will do the same. However, if the recipient holds the bow for a longer period of time an exchange of several bows (2 or 3) may occur between the parties. The *saikeirei* bow is a slower and deeper bow, approximately 45 degrees.

For the traveling executive going to Japan—You may be greeted at *ryokan* (rio-kahn) inns or geisha houses by maids or geisha women who will bow to you while kneeling on the floor. To reciprocate this "bow" may take some practice!

It is correct to address someone by using his or her surname and the form "Mr." or "Mrs" when first meeting. The use of first names should always be avoided. If you are introduced, use only your surname. Do not try to make friends with the Japanese by saying, "Just call me Al"; they find such premature familiarity uncomfortable. Never use a nickname; as you become more familiar, the word "San" may be used only if initiated from the other side. "San" is used among friends. For example, Mr. Rodgers will become "Rodgers-San" and Mr. Suzuki will be addressed as "Suzuki-San."

Because company names are more important than personal names, it is not uncommon to hear, "I am from Honda. My name is Tanaka."

BUSINESS CARDS

In business circles the *meishi*, or business card, is one of your most important assets. Make sure when having your card translated that the format of translation as well as your title is taken into consideration. Your rank is of great importance and will be essential in determining who your negotiating counterpart will be. To avoid any confusion, your title should be matched with your counterpart's title. Beware though, that a manager in one culture may not have the same responsibility or position as in another.

When a Japanese extends his business card to you it is an important gesture. The Japanese, in most instances, work with a single company for life, so the business card is an extension of his life. Accept it graciously by bowing slightly as you take the *meishi* in your right hand. Study its contents and bow again as you read it. Never use a business card to write on or take notes; this is a serious affront, especially when attempting to establish a meaningful relationship.

Present your business card by holding it out with both hands,

Japanese print face up, so the card can be read easily. Present a card individually to each Japanese executive, and say your name. If you have exchanged *meishi* previously but have forgotten the meeting or a name, a Japanese person will be insulted.

Remember to keep a card file of the *meishi* you receive. Index it by company name, with the date and subsequent meetings on the back, along with impressions of the person.

Make sure that you have an ample supply of cards; keep them in your breast pocket so you do not have trouble finding them.

BUSINESS DRESS

Japanese men wear a blue or grey suit for business. Grey is preferred by older executives. White shirts, conservative ties, tie pins, and cuff links are worn. U.S. business executives should also adopt conservative attire for their appointments. A light blue or pinstriped shirt may be worn, although white is best. Women should dress modestly in suits or dresses with high necklines, since the Japanese feel a woman's exposed neck is erotic. The Japanese value good-quality clothes and brand names. Gold jewelry or designer scarves are good choices as accents. Shoes without laces are suggested since you have to remove your shoes in many places.

GIFT-GIVING

Gift-giving is an important part of the Japanese business and social world. It is reciprocal; a gift received requires a gift to be returned, favor for favor. Appropriate gifts are a leather office item, pen-and-pencil set, or regional souvenir, or a company tie or shirt. Logo gifts are highly appreciated. A gift can be given at the beginning or end of your first meeting.

Present the gift in a low-key manner right after you have been introduced while still standing or after you have taken your seat. You should give and receive a gift with both hands and a slight bow. It is not customary in Japan to open a gift in front of the person who gave it to you. Your gift will be accepted politely and put aside. Your host will reciprocate with a gift at the end of the meeting or on the last occasion you will be together, which gives them an opportunity to give a gift of equal worth. The Japanese apologize for their "poor" gift, even when it is costly.

On the second visit, a more personal gift is acceptable. Bring Johnnie Walker scotch, brandy, or cigarettes. Avoid giving a gift to an individual in front of others.

Two specific occasions for gift-giving are critical for the business relationship: at *"Chugen,"* or midsummer (June 15), and at *"Seib,"* year's end (January 1). Give pocket diaries and calendars or liquor and cured food items. Also, in Japan, gift-giving is an inducement for future services rather than an appreciation for past kindnesses. Basically, gifts are given to anyone whom you wish to owe you a favor in the future.

Avoid giving white flowers as these are traditionally for mourning. Also, do not give four of anything, or on the fourth day. Like thirteen in the Western world, it is considered bad luck.

Gifts should be wrapped attractively in paper. Ribbons and bows are not necessary. The Japanese like subdued colors or red, which means luck. Black and white packages are used for funerals.

Keep in mind the following:

• Let your Japanese counterpart initiate the gift-exchange unless he or she is visiting you or your gift is a reciprocation.
• Do not out-gift the Japanese. Gift-giving is part of their culture. Allow the Japanese to derive satisfaction from giving and avoid obligating them by giving a more expensive gift.
• The Japanese are very status-conscious. They greatly admire designer gifts, such as a leather desk set by some noted artist. They also like to receive logo gifts.
• Whenever possible, give a gift that shows that you did your homework. Get to know the recipient's personal preferences if you can.
• Flowers are well received when visiting a home. Fifteen-petal chrysanthemums are acceptable, but the 16 petal chrysanthemum is used in the Imperial Family Crest and should not be used commercially.

COMMUNICATION STYLES

In business discussions, the Japanese may respond with what they think you want to hear, rather than with a reflection of fact, and this may lead to misunderstanding. It is done because the Japanese wish to avoid saying no. They do not want to cause disappointment or to be impolite. In Japan, a question may be asked as a negative, so the answer can be affirmative, such as "Yes, it is not." If pressed for an answer when unwilling to give one, the Japanese person may chuckle, which is a sign of embarrassment, not amusement. He or she may also say, "It is very difficult," or "It is not so convenient." A nod usually means "I understand you," not "I agree with you."

A few hints on communication styles:

• Japanese businesspeople may not look you directly in the eye. This does not mean a lack of honesty or forthrightness. Direct eye contact is not their custom.
• Avoid beckoning with the second finger or with the palm up. Avoid the gesture common to the children's game "Who's got your nose." The thumb between the second and third finger is considered sexually suggestive.
• The Japanese in their reserve are not accustomed to physical forms of contact. Therefore a slap on the back or sometimes even a handshake may be uncomfortable for them. However, the handshake has become an accepted form of greeting. It is important to remember that while shaking hands you not be "so firm" and should avoid any "pumping" motions. A slightly firm "single pump" is most favored.

Negotiating in Japan

In general, the Japanese prefer a respectful and unhurried approach to business. Their goal is a long-lasting relationship. Even if you have a quality product and the price is right, it is not enough unless you have trust and respect. The Japanese value good rapport in relationships and loyalty to the company, with the group more important than any individual.

The Japanese way of doing business is a combination of state-of-the-art technology and centuries-old traditions, customs, practices, and attitudes. The key word in Japanese business is harmony, followed closely by politeness and patience. There is no word in the Japanese language for competition.

Until friendship and trust have been established, it is highly unlikely that any business will ever be seriously discussed, let alone consummated. The Japanese are much more concerned with a lasting and harmonious partnership characterized by mutual trust and esteem, than with immediate profit. Because the Japanese place greater importance on personal relationships than on the bottom line, you should not attempt to rush into business dealings. Trust and accord are not easy to attain, and the cultivation of a sound relationship may take considerable time. Patience could well be a virtue in this relationship. But once a mutual acceptance takes place, the commitment will be long-term. In establishing this relationship, communication is based on more than just spoken words; it will involve your attitude, your demeanor, and your sincerity.

The Japanese are very formal in comparison to Western ways. Formality and reserve are a part of their tradition, and carry substantial significance. Correct form and protocol are not only appreciated, but expected.

It is preferable to send a team of three or four people to negotiate rather than just one person. A team commands more respect and shows seriousness of purpose. Include persons with technical and marketing skills, and someone with the authority to complete the transaction. If a woman is part of your team, expect confusion at the beginning from the Japanese. One way to handle this is for male members of the group to defer to her when a question arises, establishing her competence and reliability. Eventually, a Western woman in a managerial position is accepted on the basis of her profession, not her sex. As the negotiations continue, and if they occur at intervals, it is best to send the same representatives. Otherwise, the acquaintanceship period has to be repeated.

In making your formal presentation, remember that the Japanese appreciate the printed word. Provide as much material as possible before negotiations begin. Company brochures, annual reports, and product information are good. The Japanese are technically oriented and like diagrams and blueprints. Dub films and slide shows into Japanese.

Begin by discussing common ground and what you hope the talks will accomplish. Put your position in writing as a sign of the importance you attach to negotiations. Save points of contention until firm groundwork has been laid. Begin each session with a review of the main points agreed to in the previous session.

In addition to the initial getting-acquainted stage, there are three other stages: the second is the exchange of information where you find out each other's needs and possibilities; the third stage is that of persuasion; and the fourth is final concessions and agreements, using various tactics of bargaining and compromise. The Japanese prefer a holistic approach, receiving all the input and then making a judgment. Since Japanese companies are motivated to long-term growth rather than short-term profits, what you want to do is match your resources to their needs.

The Japanese place great value on group cohesiveness, and business decisions are made by consensus. Decisions are made on the basis of what is good for the company. Do not single out a member of the team and press for an immediate answer. Although it may appear that nothing is happening, the elaborate, ritualized group decision-making process is proceeding behind the scenes. Once a decision is reached, implementation goes quickly as all levels of employees have been involved since the beginning.

A long delay can be a face-saving technique, or it may be because of government requirements for documentation. In Japan, the government is often a silent partner in negotiations between your company and the Japanese concern. And the businessperson can always say that the government did not permit the deal to go through.

Americans tend to set prices high to allow for compromising and splitting the difference. But the Japanese do not like to haggle over price. Their first offer is close to what they want to pay. Compromise to the Japanese implies that they have lost something. At least publicly there should be no compromise or loss of face.

The Japanese prefer oral agreements over contractual ones, and purposely leave subsequent documents general. Instead of a legally binding contract, the Japanese prefer it to be vague and flexible. They will alter contracts when conditions change. The tradition of oral contracts is one reason that the Japanese want a known intermediary to make introductions and act as a go-between.

Suggestions for negotiating:

• If you rush the discussions and try to push things through to a decision, the Japanese will judge you to be insincere.
• Avoid the use of slang.
• You may get good information by asking your interpreter for his or her assessment of the negotiations.
• Do not assume that the Japanese person who speaks English best is the most important member of the team. If you direct

comments to this person, you risk insulting more senior members.

• Be formal throughout the negotiations. Do not use first names and do not appear in shirt sleeves.

• If negotiations are stalled, try to find a third party with access to the Japanese team. This is why an intermediary is good. Ask him or her where to find out what can be done.

• It is important to be patient with government bureaucracy and the need for consensus.

• The "white envelope" can appear in business transactions in Japan as elsewhere. It is viewed as a commission, not bribery, and found at all levels.

• Silence during discussions may mean only that the Japanese are seriously considering your point. Try not to let it make you uncomfortable, or to compel you to fill the void with sounds.

• Speak slowly. The Japanese will not tell you if they have difficulty understanding your English. Use fairly simple words, and repeat what you say, rephrasing your message.

• If you get an evasive answer, figure out what the problem was, and find another way to ask the question.

• Avoid excessive praise of your product or service. Avoid self-praise or references to your "generous offer."

• Large numbers can be mistranslated. Keep them to a minimum and write them down.

• Japanese negotiators dislike power plays and individualism. They have a proverb—"The nail that stands out will get hammered down."

• The Japanese make decisions by consensus. This is referred to as the *ringi seido* and takes time.

• Observe protocol scrupulously as the negotiations proceed. This involves such issues as who sits where and what gift is to be presented to whom.

Business Entertaining

The Japanese have a saying "You get through to a man's soul at night." This is the time when most entertaining is done, and the time when the Japanese cultivate socially the personal relationships they wish to establish. Through social intercourse, friendships and mutual respect are permitted to develop, even before any business is ever transacted.

Your Japanese hosts will entertain you extensively. Expense accounts are part of the perks of employment in a large company. Japanese men spend several evenings a week dining out, which adds to the important network of business relationships. Department heads entertain subordinates to keep interpersonal friction to a minimum and to ensure loyalty.

You should accept an invitation to dine and not place limits on your time. The Japanese leave their wives at home and prefer that you do, too. Also, evenings out are not a time to continue business discussions. The purpose is to get to know each other better. It is best to go out with a section chief or higher level person, known as the expense-account class. An evening out can be very expensive. Your Japanese host will pick up the tab in his own country and expect you to do the same in the United States. Invitations to a Japanese home are rare. Most men commute to work.

You will dine at a hotel or traditional Japanese restaurant where a geisha may be invited to play the *samisen* (a three-stringed instrument), sing songs, and perform Japanese dances. She will also serve sake, a rice wine that is the national drink. The Japanese normally drink sake before a meal, although there are sake bars that also serve food. And there is a ritual to serving. Sake is poured into small ceramic cups, and drunk hot. It is polite to fill each other's cup, and to acknowledge with a thank you. The cup is held in your right hand and supported with the left hand.

After dinner, you will go to one of four types of drinking places: a cabaret, where a hostess is assigned to each guest; a nightclub, where a hostess is not assigned unless the customer wants one; a bar, which is a drinking place without hostesses or food; or a *karaoke* bar, with taped music in the background to which people sing. Middle-class Japanese businesspeople like to sing sentimental songs. Dinner hours are from 7:00 to 9:30 P.M., but an evening out could extend to 10:00 or 11:00 P.M.

The Japanese diet is composed of rice as the staple food, with side dishes of pickles, fish, or soup. Fish and seafood are prepared in a variety of ways, either raw as *sushi*, broiled, dried, boiled, pickled, or fried. Meat is expensive and not a big item in the diet. They prefer food in its natural or raw state as much as possible, and also eat foods normally not consumed in the United States, such as seaweed, squid, and eel. Attractiveness and appeal are just as important as taste to the Japanese.

When visiting a Japanese restaurant, remove your shoes and sit on the *tatami*, or straw mats, on the floor. You will sit around a low table. The senior Japanese will take the middle seat at the table, with the highest ranking guest to the right. If you are uncomfortable sitting on the floor for an extended time, ask for a backrest.

Your host may raise chopsticks and say *"Dozo,"* which means "Please have some." After this, you may begin eating. It is considered polite to let the oldest or most senior person begin. It is not difficult to learn to eat with chopsticks; it will make an impression on your hosts and avoid embarrassing them. Do not leave chopsticks in a crossed position on your plate or stand them up straight. Place them on the chopstick holder found on the table at the tip of your plate. Use the end of the chopsticks you have not eaten with to select food from the common plate. Place your hand under the chopsticks to keep food from falling.

It is polite to try every dish, but you need not finish everything on your plate. A polite way of refusing more food is to wave your open hand in a fanning motion in front of your face or chest with a slight shake of the head. Several other rules:

• Soup is sipped holding the cup in two hands with the chopsticks in your cup.
• Use a quick dip gesture to dip food in sauces.
• When using a toothpick, place the other hand in front of your face because the Japanese do not show the inside of the mouth.
• The slurping of noodles is considered a sign of appreciation.

The Japanese eat quickly, but there is no pressure to leave a restaurant. They will sit and linger after the meal is done, and drink tea, plum wine, or other alcoholic beverages.

To make a proper toast, raise your cup, make eye contact, say *"kampai,"* which means "cheers," and drink up with one gulp. The chanting of *"ekey, ekey,"* or "bottoms up," is not usually heard until the end of the evening. In your formal toast, acknowledge the Japanese host company and thank the people who have assisted you, particularly the corporate leaders. Toasts can also be made to the good relations between the United States and Japan.

Japanese businessmen consider it a sign of honor and respect to be invited for lunch or dinner at a private club. It could be extremely advantageous to obtain corporate or individual membership at one of the more prestigious clubs in the major Japanese cities.

Here are a few things to remember when enjoying the company of your Japanese hosts or guests:

- An invitation to one's home is usually considered to be a great honor. If you invite Japanese guests, avoid overwhelming them by inviting many friends or relatives in to meet them. Should you visit Japan, it is very unlikely that you will be invited to their home. Many Japanese homes are small and uncomfortable to visit. It is also not their custom to do so.
- The Japanese consider it important to know about the place where they are being entertained. Gather some facts, historical data, stories about the owner, and the building and its architecture, to add interest to the conversation while dining.
- When you are in Japan, you will very likely be entertained by your host at a banquet. This affair will be a meticulously prepared dinner with many designated courses and much toasting. Each element of this very formal activity carries a great deal of significance. In reciprocation, you will be advised to have a banquet also, which can be arranged with a Japanese restaurant.

Be extremely careful that your dinner does not in the slightest exceed the cost of the banquet given for you. This would be a serious affront to your Japanese host, and cause him to "lose face."

If you have trepidation about dealing with the extensive ceremony involved, or the protocols governing such entertaining, your best bet would be to entertain in either a French or American restaurant.

- Gifts are usually exchanged during a Japanese banquet. Be prepared to reciprocate. Remember that the gift you give and the wrapping of it has special significance, which should be investigated beforehand. Certain gifts and wrappings can be offensive.
- If a woman representative from your firm is part of your negotiating team, be sure that she does not find it insulting not to be

invited to a social function. Japanese entertaining generally does not include women.

General Tips

• It is important to present a proper image of yourself. Correctness in speech, attitude, dress, and behavior matters to the Japanese. Posture—the way you stand, sit, and walk—is considered an important part of the image. Learn to sit on the floor with your legs crossed, and to appear comfortable.

• The Japanese are avid golfers and rarely decline an invitation to play. More progress in negotiations may be made during an afternoon on the links than can be accomplished by spending an hour with the executive in his offices.

• Express sufficient thanks and appreciation even if it is awkward for you or appears to be ritualistic.

• "Face" is important; do not joke or embarrass someone in front of others. Avoid the U.S. game of one-upsmanship.

• The Japanese are sensitive about the economic rivalry and competition between the two countries, World War II, the bombings at Hiroshima and Nagasaki, and Japan's military budget. Avoid asking about *seppuku* (suicide) also.

• You may be asked your age, your salary, the cost of items, and religion—subjects that are not sensitive to the Japanese. Do not take offense.

• Japanese men seem to enjoy drinking, which is viewed as a legitimate outlet for pent-up emotions. Drunkenness is common and does not have a social stigma.

• The Japanese are fastidious about cleanliness, and have been known to ask a stranger to pick up discarded pipe ashes from the street.

• Show the proper respect at shrines and temples and remove your shoes before entering.

• Make an effort to be formal. Do not ask to call anyone by their first name, or if it would be permissible to take off your suit coat to relax. A casual approach projects insincerity.

• Go over specialized words with your interpreter.

• To establish a personal relationship with your Japanese hosts, find out their hobbies, interests, and family backgrounds.

• Avoid public displays of affection. Speak in a low voice. It is also best to keep laughter quiet and to cover your mouth with one hand when laughing.
• You will make a big hit if you are willing to sing a song in English in a *karaoke* bar.
• Japanese identify with their family, so that praising your own family appears to be self-praise. Boasting in public, even in jest, is inappropriate.
• The numbers 4 and 9 are considered unlucky inasmuch as they connote death and suffering, respectively, by phonetic resemblance in the Japanese language.
• Little or no tipping is customary in Japan.

EXECUTIVE TRAVEL TO JAPAN •

DOCUMENTS

Short-term business travelers (less than 90 days) must obtain a short-term commercial visa. Requirements for such are a valid passport, completed application, letter from an authorized officer of your company outlining details of your trip and accepting of financial and moral responsibility for you during your stay, and a business reference in Japan. Applications can be sent to the Japanese Consulate in New York City at 299 Park Avenue, New York, N.Y. 10017.

INOCULATIONS

None are required for U.S. citizens.

AIRPORT

Tokyo International Airport (Narita Airport) is 40 miles from the downtown area, about a 75- to 90-minute drive.

CUSTOMS

Visitors may bring in duty-free three bottles of liquor, 400 cigarettes or 100 cigars, and two watches.

U.S. EMBASSY

10-1 Akasaka 1-chome
Minato-Ku (107), Tokyo
Phone: 583-7141   Telex: 2422118

TRANSPORTATION

It is suggested that you arrange for a car and a driver/translator for your business trip, as the taxi situation is very inadequate.

TIPPING

This is not a common practice in Japan and in some instances might be taken as an insult. Service charges are automatically added to the bill at hotels and restaurants. Waiters, hotel porters, and taxi drivers do not expect tips. However, it is customary to tip the driver of a hired car.

HOTELS

Tokyo

Hotel Okura
10-4 Toranomon 2-chome, Minato-ku
Phone: (3) 582-0111   Telex: 22790

The Century Hyatt Tokyo
2-7-2 Nishi-Shinjuku, Shinjuku-ku
Phone: (3) 349-0111   Telex: 29411

Capitol Tokyo Hotel
10-3 Nagata-cho 2-chome, Chiyoda-ku
Phone: (3) 581-4511   Telex: 24290

Hotel New Otani & Tower
4-1 Kioi-cho, Chiyoda-ku
Phone: (3) 265 1111   Telex: 24719

Osaka

Osaka Nikko
7 Nishino-cho Daihojicho, Minami-ku
Phone: (6) 244-1111   Telex: 5227575
    (1) 800-221-4862 (toll-free)

Royal Hotel
5-3 Nakanoshima Kita-ku
Phone: (6) 448-1121   Telex: J63350

RESTAURANTS

TOKYO

Fuku-Zushi   *Sushi*
5-9-22 Roppongi, Minato-ku
Phone: 402-4116

Ten-Ichi   *Tempura*
Ginza 6-chome
Phone: 571-1949

Zakuro   *Shabu-shabu/sukiyaki*
TBS Kaikan Building BF
5-3 Akasaka, Minato-ku
Phone: 582-6841

OSAKA

Kitcho   *Tempura/sushi*
3023 Koraibashi, Higashi-ku
Phone: 231-1937

Nishijima   *Steakhouse*
50 Kinugasacho, Kita-ku
Phone: 364-8286

TRAVEL TIPS

• There is no personal safety problem in Tokyo, and you can move about the city freely without fear of theft or assault.
• Medical and dental facilities are plentiful, and many of the doctors and dentists speak English, having received their training in the United States or Europe.
• In Tokyo, the Meiji Shrine, Imperial Palace, Tokyo Tower, and So-ji Temple should be visited, as well as the beautiful parks such as Hibiya, Shiba, and Yeno.
• Department stores abound, as do one-stop shopping arcades such as the Handicraft Center, International Arcade, and JapanTax-free Center.
• Of cultural interest are the Kabukizi Theatre and the Fujiwara. Although the programs are in Japanese, it is a visual treat hearing the music and seeing the costumes. The set designs are outstanding.

• Traditional Japanese sports are *sumo* wrestling, kendo, judo, karate, and *aikido* (all forms of self-defense, and referred to as martial arts). Baseball is the most popular of Western sports. A businessman staying at a first-class hotel can make arrangements for golf, tennis, swimming, or any sport or recreation desired.

• Japan has the best communications system anywhere in Asia, and telephone, telex, and cable facilities are readily available. Language assistance operators are available by calling 502-1461 in Tokyo.

SINGAPORE

Cultural Overview

Strategically located on an island at the tip of the Malay peninsula, Singapore has been a crossroad of travel and trade with all of Southeast Asia for over 150 years. This city-state was a British colony until 1959, then a part of Malaysia until gaining independence in 1965. Today this dynamic international center combines Western attitudes and practices with Oriental traditions.

The Republic of Singapore has a parliamentary system of government, elected by full adult suffrage. The president is elected by the parliament for a four-year term. As the head of state, the president appoints a member of parliament as prime minister.

Singapore is the world's second busiest port, the major trading center for Southeast Asia, and an international financial center with over one hundred banks. Singapore is Asia's most highly developed nation after Japan. It has also become a center for those marketing to Southeast Asia, with the United States as its biggest investor. It has achieved these distinctions in the absence of significant natural resources except for its excellent harbor.

The government is now encouraging manufacturers to switch from labor-intensive industries to those requiring more skill and technology, in response to the competition from other Asian neighbors, where labor is more plentiful and less expensive. Chief industries now are refining petroleum and manufacturing petroleum products, shipbuilding and repair, manufacturing electrical and electronic products, processing foods and beverages, producing chemicals, and printing and publishing.

Over 75 percent of Singapore's nearly 3 million people are of Chinese descent; about 15 percent are Malay; and most of the rest are from south Asia, particularly from India. The values of this mixed culture are strongly influenced by Oriental beliefs in the primacy of family and the values of courtesy, face-saving, modesty, and respect for and obedience to authority.

Counterbalancing these values, however, are ideas and traditions formed by 140 years of British rule and the city's role as a center of trade. Economic achievement is very important, and successful entrepreneurs enjoy considerable prestige. Among some younger people, traditional respect for authority and obedience are giving way to more Western attitudes.

Although interracial marriages are becoming more common, and some people are voluntarily limiting the size of their families, the traditional Oriental family is still prevalent in much of the society. Most women still fill the established roles of wife and mother. More women today, however, are attaining academic, professional, and business status than ever before.

Education in Singapore is not compulsory, but it is free at the elementary level for all children. Parents bear some of the cost of secondary schooling. About 25 percent of the students go on to college.

Singapore has four languages. Malay is the popular everyday tongue, English the administrative language. The other two are Mandarin Chinese and Tamil. All are officially recognized, and Singaporeans are encouraged to be at least bilingual.

Religious faith reflects the varied population. Most Chinese practice Taoism, Buddhism, and Confucianism. About 16 percent of the people are Muslims, 10 percent are Christians, and 3.5 percent are Hindus.

Business Opportunities

Singapore's government has taken many steps to accommodate foreign investors and enterprises. There are no restrictions on the ownership of businesses; on foreign exchange, profit, or capital repatriation; on the importation of capital equipment, machinery, or raw materials; or on foreigners working in Singapore, as long as they are qualified for the job. The government and private businesses are corruption-free, and bribery, which is illegal, has no place in the business culture.

Singapore's future plans center on compensating for the fact that its only resource, other than its harbor, is its small, high-quality workforce. Attention is focusing on freeing unskilled labor through automation and retraining workers to take part in more sophisticated, high-tech industries. Any business proposal that takes advantage of Singapore's strategic location, requires skilled labor, brings new technology, or otherwise contributes to the nation's goal of becoming a financial, computer, information, and professional center for the region will have a good chance for success.

The United States is Singapore's most important trade partner. Major U.S. exports to Singapore are electronic components, aircraft engineering equipment, and machinery parts. Principal imports are electrical machinery, telecommunications equipment, crude rubber, and textile products.

Initiating Contact

Third-party introductions are generally required to start doing business in Singapore. Getting in touch with U.S. banks and corporations with offices in the city is an excellent approach. These organizations can also give advice on business conditions in general.

Imported goods are usually distributed through established trading companies with branches in Singapore and throughout Southeast Asia. In addition to handling sales, these companies also manage service, and can offer technical and engineering assistance. For U.S. firms selling to Singapore, obtaining the services of a reliable agent is extremely important, since customers in Singapore are understandably concerned about buying from a supplier so far away.

Valuable information about market conditions and potential agents, partners, and importers is available from the Singapore Trade Development Board, which has offices in New York, Los Angeles, and Houston. Since unsolicited letters or promotional material will probably be ignored by most Singaporean firms, this organization can help the supplier arrange the appropriate contacts with trading companies and end-users. The annual Trade and Industry Fair, held every summer in Singapore, also offers an opportunity for meeting other suppliers or potential customers, or for exhibiting products.

Once your first contact has been made, a personal letter and information about your company and products or services should be sent to a senior executive in the Singaporean firm. All correspondence can be conducted in English. The letter should be followed with a personal phone call.

For further information, contact:

World Trade Centre Singapore (R-O)
1 Maritime Square, No. 02-11
World Trade Centre, Singapore 0409
Phone: 2712211, ext. 2791

Ministry of Trade and Industry
Department of Trade, Suite 201
World Trade Centre
Telok Blangah Road, Singapore 0409
Phone: 2719388

Singapore Economic Development Board
1 Maritime Square, No. 10-40
World Trade Centre (Lobby D), Singapore 0409
Phone: 2710844   Telex: 26233

U.S. Commerce Department
Marketing Manager for Singapore
14th Street and Constitution Avenue
Washington, D.C. 20025
Phone: (202) 632-3276

Singapore Economic Development Board
745 Fifth Avenue, Suite 1601
New York, N.Y. 10151
Phone: (212) 421-2207
(Offices also in Los Angeles, Boston, Chicago, and Houston.)

Business Protocol and Procedures

BUSINESS ENVIRONMENT

Business hours in Singapore are generally 9:00 A.M. to 5:00 P.M. Monday through Friday and 9:00 A.M. to 1:00 P.M. on Saturdays.

Meetings are usually held at your host's offices, and punctuality is expected.

For the first meeting, a U.S. firm need only send one representative, a senior decision maker, since Singaporean culture does not demand an entourage for the sake of image. The Singaporean company will probably be represented by a senior executive and one junior manager or staffperson.

The senior Singaporean will direct the first part of the meeting. There may be a very short period for exchanging pleasantries or making more detailed introductions but business will get under way quickly.

Interpreters are not necessary, since English is spoken widely, especially in the business world.

RANK AND STATUS

Titles, power, and status vary widely among Singaporean firms and depend largely on how westernized an organization has become. Most banks and large corporations are organized on a structure like those in Great Britain or the United States, with hierarchical structures headed by chairpersons, presidents, or managing directors. In smaller, more traditional family-owned operations, the top executive is usually the oldest male and the family patriarch. Status in the city, in general, comes with entrepreneurial success.

FORMS OF ADDRESS

A handshake is a common greeting and should be accompanied by a smile, direct eye contact, and a simple hello. Singaporean men are addressed as "Mr.," women as "Miss" or "Mrs."

BUSINESS CARDS

Business cards are exchanged with all participants in a meeting, after introductions have been made. Your title and company name should be clear. Bilingual cards are appreciated.

BUSINESS DRESS

A tropical country, Singapore has a year-round average temperature of 85 degrees and high humidity. Lightweight wool suits are comfortable and acceptable. Conservative style is customary, with dark blue or grey suits, light dress shirts, and subdued ties for men, tailored suits and blouses for women.

GIFT-GIVING

Gift-giving is not routine with the larger banks and corporations in Singapore. Small tokens of friendship or thanks, however, are apt to be appreciated. Appropriate presents for a first trip are corporate gifts of high quality. A more personal gift may be in order on subsequent trips or at the end of a particularly successful business transaction. Books, music, or French or Italian ties would be appropriate. Since Singapore is a free port, imported liquor is not a special treat.

COMMUNICATION STYLES

Communication styles in Singapore depend to a large degree on how much international business a company does and, as a consequence, how westernized its people have become. A direct style focused on business issues is appropriate for the more sophisticated, westernized Singaporean executives, accustomed to conducting international business.

In smaller firms that are traditional and family run, which may do more local than international business, Oriental influences will obviously be stronger.

The visiting executive will have to pay attention to such factors as courtesy and face-saving; developing personal relationships will be more important in doing business.

In the larger, westernized organizations, nonverbal communication will be similar to that of the United States. In the more traditional local firms, nonverbal communication is more subtle, or at least unfamiliar to the Western executive. Excessive laughter or evasiveness indicate discomfort or disagreement, which is not polite to express. A nod of the head only indicates understanding of what has been said; it does not necessarily mean agreement.

Negotiating in Singapore

Negotiating in Singapore can be very much like doing business in the United States. The banks and larger corporations, especially those with international interests, are concerned with such fundamentals as marketing strategies, pricing, credit, after-purchase servicing, and attention to the "bottom line."

In such corporations, you will be dealing with businesspeople who are likely to have good managerial skills, be straightforward, and negotiate skillfully. Most commercial and merchant banks will be organized much like their counterparts in the United States, with many vice presidents and assistant vice presidents, having about the same decision-making power and responsibility as do people in similar positions elsewhere. The ultimate authority in these organizations rests with the chairpersons, presidents, or managing directors.

In some large banks and industrial companies, including those that are family owned and run, the board of directors may be the central decision-making group. Members of the board may hold substantial equity positions in the company and have senior executive posts. In such organizations, you may give presentations to the entire board rather than just to one or two executives.

In contrast to the banks and larger companies, the smaller firms are likely to be run like more traditional Oriental organizations. The top decision maker may be the director or president, perhaps the family head. Decision making in these firms usually rests with this one person.

Attention to practical business considerations will be important in any negotiations with Singaporean businesses. While it will be helpful to develop a good personal relationship with your counterpart, the ultimate decision will be based more on the attractiveness of the business proposition, its relevance to the Southeast Asian market, and its profit potential.

Business Entertaining

Entertaining is not so crucial in Singapore as it is in other Asian cities. Socializing is not usually elaborate, and its purpose is simply to facilitate the development of good relationships between the businesspeople involved. It will not be considered rude or unacceptable if you do not initiate some business entertainment, although it would be to your benefit to arrange at least a small dinner for your host.

Business lunches, at hotels or restaurants, are appropriate times for business discussions. Discussing business at a dinner considered a social occasion, however, is not encouraged. Wives are invited to dinners, which start between 7:00 P.M. and 8:00 P.M. and last about two hours. These dinners can be informal, or they can be formal banquet-style affairs at a traditional round table. At these meals, the guest of honor serves himself or herself first. The host sits opposite the guest of honor. Chopsticks should be used at formal meals, and you might try to learn to use them before your trip if you have not already mastered the art. When tea is served, the dinner is over.

General Tips

• Singapore is known as a serious city, and the Singaporeans are serious about their work. They think of Singapore as a city/country that works, and they respect authority. Sober business analysis and decision making are expected.

• Building personal relationships is part of doing business in Singapore. But this is not a "backslapping" society, and such familiarity is not characteristic.

• Issues of cash and credit are usually of lower priority for Singaporean firms than for many others, thanks to the healthy financial climate. More appealing to Singaporean businesses, however, will be proposals that take into consideration Singapore's unique environment and that are designed to bring a high, value-added component to the economy.

• Having detailed financial analyses augmented with graphics or computer printouts will enhance the impact of your presentation.

• Personal appearance and conduct are very important in Singapore. Behavior that suggests respect and courtesy, along with conservative attire, will project the proper image.

• Acceptable subjects for small talk and conversation vary in Singapore. For most Singaporeans, the Oriental stricture against discussing family issues with casual acquaintances still obtains. With more westernized Singaporeans, almost any topic is acceptable if approached with tact and sensitivity. Singaporeans are proud of their country, and any question about it and its development is likely to be welcome.

EXECUTIVE TRAVEL TO SINGAPORE   •

DOCUMENTS

A valid passport and proof of onward or return transportation is required of all visitors. Visas are not required for U.S. citizens for stays of up to two weeks or less for either business or pleasure.

INOCULATIONS

No inoculations or vaccinations are required for U.S. citizens unless a prior stop has been made in an infected area.

AIRPORT

Changi International is approximately a half hour's drive by expressway to downtown by airport taxi.

CUSTOMS

Customs regulations permit the duty-free import of one bottle of wine and liquor, 200 cigarettes, and personal possessions.

U.S. EMBASSY

300 Hill Street, Singapore
Phone: 30251

TRANSPORTATION

The road system is excellent and travel moves on the left, British style. Taxis are plentiful and reasonable in cost. It is recommended that you hire a driver/translator for the length of your stay.

TIPPING

Most hotels and restaurants add a 10 percent service charge to the bill, in which case tipping is not necessary. In other places, a tip of 10 percent is customary.

HOTELS

Goodwood Park Hotel
22 Scotts Road
Phone: 7377411   Telex: 24377

The Mandarin
333 Orchard Road
Phone: 7374411   Telex: 21528

The Marco Polo Singapore
247 Tanglin Road
Phone: 4747141   Telex: 21476

The Shangri-La
22 Orange Grove Road
Phone: 7373644   Telex: 21505

RESTAURANTS

Belvedere   *Chinese*
Mandarin Hotel
333 Orchard Road
Phone: 7374411

The Harbour Grill   *French*
Hilton Hotel
Orchard Road
Phone: 7372233

The Marco Polo   *Steakhouse*
Marco Polo Singapore
247 Tanglin Road
Phone: 4747141

The Mayflower   *Cantonese*
DBS Building
Phone: 2303133

Rendez-Vous   *Malay*
4-5 Bras Basah Road
Phone: 3376619

TRAVEL TIPS

• The streets are safe at any time; take note that there is a fine for jaywalking as well as for littering.
• Singapore offers a great variety of goods. Among the bargains are cameras, watches, electronic, audio, and video equipment (duty-free), Persian carpets, batiks, jade jewelry, gold, silver, and pearls.

• The climate is tropical with high humidity year round, so dress accordingly.
• Nighttime entertainment is limited to cabarets and nightclubs.
• Medical facilities are excellent, and there are many English-speaking doctors available.
• The unit of currency is the Singapore dollar and there is no limit on the amount of foreign currency which may be brought in or taken out.
• Sightseeing offers a harbor cruise by Chinese junk, a visit to the National Museum, as well as tours of an assortment of parks, temples, and botanical gardens.
• Sporting facilities include, golf, squash, tennis, swimming, sailing, scuba diving, and bowling.
• Services available at most major hotels include international direct dialing phones, telex and cable, air conditioning, twenty-four-hour room service, and television.

SOUTH KOREA

Cultural Overview

The Republic of Korea (South Korea's official name) is a highly civilized nation that was little known to the world until the Korean War in the 1950s. Since then, it has enjoyed rapid and dynamic economic growth, thanks to its hard-working people and government support of development.

In theory, South Korea is a constitutional democracy. The president, who is elected by the National Conference of Unification, serves for one year. Two-thirds of the sole legislative chamber, the National Assembly, are elected by direct popular vote, and the rest by the national Conference for Unification. A supreme court is the highest tribunal in the judiciary branch, and the chief justice is appointed by the president with the consent of the National Assembly. In practice, however, Korea is an authoritarian regime, with the president having supreme power to make decisions, including military decisions, that the National Assembly then routinely approves.

The government has guided South Korea's economic development with a series of five-year economic plans, specific industry expansion programs, and price controls. Korea's economy was initially based on the manufacture and export of low-quality, low-price textiles and consumer goods, but now it has a much broader base. South Korea is the world's second largest shipbuilder. It ranks tenth in producing electronic goods and fifteenth in iron and steel production. With the help of the United States, Korea is expanding automobile production.

The government owns part or all of about thirty companies that are organized as private concerns with independent management. Among these are Agricultural Development Corporation, Korea Oil Corporation, Korea Electric Power Corporation, Korea Housing Corporation, the Korean Telecommunication Authority, and Pohang Iron and Steel Corporation.

South Korea's terrain is mostly mountainous and the country's thirty-eight thousand square miles of territory are situated in the southern half of the Korean peninsula. (Korea was divided along the 38th parallel after World War II so the disarmament of the defeated Japanese forces there would be easier for the United States and Russia to control. Three years later a UN commission failed in an attempt to reunify the country.) South Korea's climate ranges from very dry, cold winters to hot, humid summers. The rainy season extends from June to August. The west coast has many natural harbors. The best seasons for visiting Korea are spring and fall.

The Koreans are an urban people, with 70 percent living in the larger cities. Approximately 9 million live in Seoul, the capital, which is the center of government, industry, education, and culture. Of the 39.3 million South Koreans, 60 percent are under age 25. The official language is Korean and is written with phonetic characters (*hangul*). It is the Asian language that is easiest to master, as it has only ten vowels, 14 consonants, and 24 characters. It isn't necessary to learn Korean, however, since most executives will speak English to some degree. Many older Koreans speak Japanese, a result of the colonization of Korea (1910–1945) by that country.

The oldest religious tradition in Korea is shamanism, which holds that nature, the earth, mountains, and rivers are sacred. Its influence is imposing, with 26 percent of the people adhering to its beliefs.

The fastest growing religion is Chirstianity, which 31 percent of the Korean people now practice. Sixteen percent of the population are Buddhist, while Confucianism remains a pervasive force in the Korean culture.

By reason of their Confucian heritage, Koreans value education highly and have a strong sense of family loyalty. Education offers the road to elevated status, wealth, and success.

South Korea's literacy rate is high—over 90 percent. School attendance is mandatory for children age 6 to 16. Secondary schools have full enrollment and are very competitive. Due to the limited space in the university-level institutions, many Koreans, especially those in technical areas, matriculate in the United States.

The family is the foundation of Korean life, bound by a powerful sense of duty and obligation. The average family size is 4.5 people. Although arranged marriages are still customary, families now tend just to introduce the couple, leaving the courting up to them. Koreans marry relatively late—men by age 27, women by 24.

As a result of their upbringing and tradition, Korean women are generally shy. They do not engage in business and certainly not in any managerial position where they would be dealing with executives from other countries. Korean women usually have low-ranking jobs.

Koreans are quite independent and individualistic compared with other Asians. They are self-reliant and proud of their progress in the last thirty years. Openly competitive, they respect a person who succeeds through individual effort. Still, despite Western influences, Koreans retain some of the ancient Confucian feelings about group spirit and national unity.

Business Opportunities

South Korea is the seventh most important trading partner of the United States. Korea has traditionally been a large importer of American agricultural commodities and industrial raw materials. Other Korean markets where U.S. companies can compete are in the fields of medical equipment, telecommunications devices, special-purpose computers and peripherals, machine tools, and food processing and packaging equipment. The Koreans are interested in proposals providing advanced technology and trouble-free, finished products. Modern inventions, new trend-setting ideas, and totally new fields of endeavor are welcome.

Initiating Contact

It is preferable to make the first contact with a Korean firm through an introduction from a mutually respected third person. Koreans living in the United States can open doors in their native land, because the international Korean business community is relatively small; most influential people know or are known to each other.

Although approaching via an intermediary is the preferred procedure, you can initiate business in South Korea without a formal introduction. Several suggestions are as follows:

• Send a letter with a proposal and a description of its attributes to a potential Korean business partner; follow up with a telephone call, asking for a personal appointment to pursue discussions.

• If you are planning to sell your product in Korea, you might attend the Seoul Trade Shows in mid-June and mid-October. To market products in Korea, you must have either a registered local offer agent or a trading firm act as your representative. About five thousand general trading companies (GTCs) are registered as official import–export agents. Nine of these have strong foreign trade capabilities, and due to the large size of their operations receive preferential incentive treatment from the government. These companies are authorized to import and export for their own accounts. The more than two thousand registered offer agents in Korea charge a commission to represent you. They cannot import on their own.

• Some companies are exempt from the agency system, and can import directly. These are generally subsidiaries of foreign companies, producers of certain raw materials converters, and government purchasers. You will need the services of a local representative to bid sucessfully with the government purchasing Office of Supply (OSROK).

• If you are a buyer of Korean products, you will find associations easy to establish. A first step would be to contact any of the Korean Trade Promotion Center (KOTRA) offices found all over the globe. Other sources are the offices of GTCs located in business centers worldwide.

Additional assistance can be obtained from:

World Trade Center Korea
Korean Traders Association
10-1, 2-Ka Hoehyon-Dong, Chung-Ku
C.P.O. Box 1117, Seoul, Korea
Phone: 771-41   Telex: K24265

U.S. Department of Commerce
Marketing Manager for Korea
14th Street and Constitution Avenue
Room 2310
Washington, D.C. 20230
Phone: (202) 377-4399

American Chamber of Commerce in Korea
Room 307, The Westin Chosun
87, Song-Dong, Chung-Ku
Seoul, Korea
Phone: 752-3061   Telex: Chosun K28432

Korea Chamber of Commerce and Industry
111, Sokong-Dong, Chung-Ku
Seoul, Korea
Phone: 777-8031/42

Korean Trade Promotion Center (KOTRA)
460 Park Avenue
New York, N.Y. 10022
Phone: (212) 826-0900
(Offices in Chicago, Dallas, Atlanta, Miami, Los Angeles, Seattle,
    San Francisco, and San Juan.)

Business Protocol and Procedures

BUSINESS ENVIRONMENT

The first appointment should be made at the senior executive level. If
you have a local agent, he or she will confirm your appointment.

Formal office hours are from 9:00 A.M. to 5:00 P.M. weekdays, and
on Saturdays from 9:00 A.M. to 1:00 P.M. However, a 52-hour work-
week is average for hard-working Koreans. It is a common practice to

conduct business in your hotel before the office meeting, and after closing hours of the office. Successful Korean executives take pride in 16-hour workdays.

You should arrive at your host's office on time, although you may have to wait as long as half an hour. This is not a sign of gamesmanship, but reflects the pressure of time on senior Korean executives, and the belief that a new engagement is less pressing than an ongoing one.

The meeting may take place on neutral ground, in a special meeting room rather than in the executive's office. Often, you will be escorted by the executive's secretary, or a member of the staff. Rarely will the executive come out to greet you.

You will be offered coffee or tea, and it is good manners to accept this sign of hospitality, at least the first time. Younger managers may not offer, or will not be offended at a rejection of, this gesture of hospitality.

If you feel ill at ease or think language will be a barrier to understanding, you can get an interpreter. Most executives do speak English. Larger Korean enterprises have in-house interpreters.

RANK AND STATUS

Koreans do not have the same concept of equality in personal relationships as Americans do. Rather, the opposite is true. Each person is in a relatively higher or lower position. You must show respect to your superiors and elders. If you do not, the higher status person might withdraw on any pretext and avoid future contact with the one who made the blunder. It is important to realize that a respected Korean may be humble and self-effacing in social relationships; this manner does not indicate low status, as Americans might assume. And even if an older person has no power in the company, age allows him or her to be influential in shaping the opinion of others.

As a general rule, you must send a senior-level executive from your country to meet with senior-level Koreans. Most large corporations have a chairperson and a president, who are often members of the family that controls the firm. The vice president, or executive managing director, are equivalent to U.S. executive vice presidents. Directors and managers on the next level are involved in the day-to-day operations, and have little responsibility beyond their own units. You should not negotiate with anyone below this level.

FORMS OF ADDRESS

The traditional Korean way of greeting is bowing, but it is a complex practice, and not necessary to use in business. The common way to greet a Korean executive is to shake hands (but not firmly) or give a slight nod of the head. Some U.S. executives have learned to combine a handshake with a slight bow. Koreans bow deeply to elderly people to show respect.

Since social relationships between men and women in Korea are highly structured, even a simple greeting can be difficult. A man should not shake a Korean woman's hand unless she offers it. It is best simply to nod your head. Likewise, a woman executive from the United States must first extend her hand to the Korean executive, so that he will not be confused about how to greet her.

It is important to greet your host by the family name. When doing business, even Koreans use each other's family name. The most polite way of addressing someone is by his or her position, title, trade, or profession, such as, "Good morning, teacher." However, last names will suffice in business dealings.

BUSINESS CARDS

Before negotiations begin, present your business card, and with dignity—Koreans view it as an extension of yourself. The only proper way to present it is with your right hand. Using bilingual cards is a decided plus.

The sequence of names on the Korean card can be confusing, but family names in South Korea are often common and recognizable.

BUSINESS DRESS

Korea has four seasons similar to those in the United States. Winter can be cold, with snow. Regardless of the season, Korean businessmen wear conservative suits. You should also. Solids or a pinstripe grey or blue are commonly worn, with white or light blue shirts, and ties of a traditional pattern. American women executives in Korea should dress conservatively and modestly.

GIFT-GIVING

Koreans are gift-givers, but it is best if you wait to present one until your Korean counterpart first gives you a gift, which may even be at the first meeting. A common gift from a Korean is ginseng tea, or a local craft. You can then reciprocate, but with a modest offering such as an impersonal logo gift, something practical for the office, a pen set or ashtray, or a good bottle of scotch. Be sure your company's logo gifts do not come from Korea. Avoid food gifts. Many Koreans like gifts that come from your own region of the United States, such as a Western-style belt.

The proper presentation of a gift requires both hands. The correct acceptance includes taking the present with both hands.

COMMUNICATION STYLES

Hospitality is central to Korean culture, and your host will be accommodating and friendly. The overall atmosphere is usually warm, although younger Koreans may be more distant and cool.

Koreans have a direct business style that can be aggressive at times. This stems from the country's rapid development and their strong desire to succeed. The executive may even be straightforward, saying what is on his mind, and answering your questions. He may tell you no, and sometimes argue or interrupt you in midsentence. Moreover, a westernized Korean will often get to the point without a preliminary get-acquainted period.

This is not to say that Koreans have disregarded tradition. Underlying all discussion is a feel for *kibun*, a word that means inner feelings. The closest English word is "mood," which does not capture the essence of *kibun*. Good *kibun* is vital to a person's conduct and relationship to others. The first priority for most Koreans is to keep *kibun* in order. An executive strives to work in a way that will enhance the *kibun* of all the people in the discussions. If *kibun* is damaged, the relationship may end.

Koreans are highly sensitive to feelings, and expect you to be aware also. The meeting tone—what you see and feel—may be just as important as what you hear.

Eye contact is important as it shows attention and sincerity, and forms a subtle bond of communication.

Some Koreans, especially older ones, may avoid a definite answer. Instead of saying yes or no, they may squint, or lean back in their chairs, or crook their heads, which may indicate an impasse. In effect, they are skipping their turn to speak, and want you to continue. If this happens, make the same point from a different perspective. Koreans indicate interest by leaning forward, with hands clasping their knees. If a Korean holds his cigarette in the Northern European fashion, with thumb and fingertips, this may be a natural motion, or it could be a conscious tactic. Many will let the smoke rise slowly and drift, giving them the air of being deep in thought. With this tactic, they are symbolically trying to stay in command of the situation.

Negotiating in South Korea

South Korea is unique in Asia in that the industrial elite are either in their fifties and sixties, or much younger, such as in their mid-thirties. The younger postwar managers are often descendants of the founders. A youthful Korean negotiator is likely to be competent, dedicated, educated, trained, and powerful. Discussions with younger men may be easier, as they may be westernized. Discussions with the older power group are likely to follow more traditional patterns.

You may negotiate with an individual or only a few people rather than a large group. The larger Korean firms may have executives with Western educations. Korean male executives are not accustomed to dealing with women executives. Sending a woman to negotiate must be considered in this light.

During the first meeting, a fairly heavy impact is important, and you might want to use graphic presentations. Be assertive. When Koreans show curiosity about a point you are making, they mean it. Seize the chance and develop it. On the other hand, if not interested, the Korean executive may abruptly change the conversation and you may not be able to regain control.

Those with decision-making power are at the senior levels of organizations. But it will not take as long to get a decision as in Japan, because it is not as essential to get a consensus. Korean managers ordinarily need approval from superiors, but some are willing to take risks.

Here are some suggestions for negotiating:

• Begin with a brief introduction. Be concise and summarize the issues you will discuss.
• Avoid the hard sell, but do not be too roundabout and vague in making your presentation. Explain facts objectively.

• Recognize that, if you are greeted with silence, your Korean hosts may not have understood. Do not ask this directly. This is where "face" comes in. Even Koreans who understand English may have difficulty following you, because of rapid speech or a regional accent. Ask instead, "Would you like to have any further information?"

• Again, avoid politics, a very sensitive subject. Interesting and relevant topics for discussion include global economic and business developments, and sports, cultural, and historical issues.

Business Entertaining

South Koreans are sociable, believing that mixing with others will give them a chance to learn new things, enabling them to make progress. Evening entertaining plays a key role in business in South Korea. However, only the negotiating team is usually invited—not spouses. Koreans want to entertain you, but you should also let them know that you prefer cabaret to opera, or vice versa.

If you are staying only a few days, your host will probably invite you to lunch or drinks. Try to reciprocate before you leave. Businessmen are likely to be invited to a *kisaeng* (key-san) house, a traditional restaurant or bar formerly for men only. Very few visitors will be invited to a Korean home, and then only after a relationship is well established.

Koreans often assume Americans dislike Korean food, which means that dinner will be at a continental restaurant. If you do want to sample a traditional meal, speak up, and your host will take you to a *kisaeng* house or a nightclub.

The traditional meal is served in one elaborate course and consists of many small dishes, some highly spiced. The basis of the meal is rice with meat, poultry, and fish, and vegetables added. The national dish, *kimchi*, a vegetable pickle seasoned with garlic, red pepper, and ginger, is always served. You can help yourself to an assortment, and do not have to wait to be served.

Traditional drinks include *soju*, a clear fermented liquor; *jungjong*, similar to sake, the Japanese rice wine; *ginseng* wine, which is strong and sweet; *takju*, more potent than beer; and beer.

No matter where you dine, you will finish the evening at a *kisaeng* house. The favorite drink is scotch. Hostesses, whose relationship with guests is platonic, will join you at the table. Everyone takes turns singing songs. The cost of the evening can be several hundred dollars. American women executives are now invited to these *kisaeng* houses.

Reciprocate with a restaurant meal at your hotel.

In South Korea, a glass will not be refilled if there is still some liquid left in it. Koreans keep a watchful eye on the glass and, when it is completely empty, they will promptly refill it. If you are pouring, remember that it is bad manners to replenish a glass not entirely drained.

If you are the guest of honor being hosted by a group of Korean traditionalists, everyone may want to exchange glasses with you. The host will shake out the few drops that remain in his glass, presenting it to you with two hands, and refilling it with a bottle held in both hands. The proper response is to finish your glass and shake it out, present it to the host, who gave you his glass, then refill it using both hands. This, of course, may go on and on, leading to much drinking. It is not necessary to drink everything you are offered; do what you can to drink moderately.

General Tips

• Koreans tend to be good-humored and sentimental. They love singing and telling stories, especially sad, nostalgic tales. They love to tease, and can laugh at themselves.

• Avoid talking shop at meals and *kisaeng* parties, if you have had a lot to drink. Koreans will hold you to your promises, whether or not you were sober when you made them.

• Do not talk about local politics. It's forbidden by the government for reasons of national security, and can get Koreans in trouble. Talk about Korea's remarkable accomplishments—including movable metal type, ironclad warships, and encyclopedias—in their five-thousand year history.

• The Korean national anthem is played at various times, and in various places. If you are in the underground arcades or at shopping malls, stand at attention when it is played.

• Inquiries into your host's family life are considered taboo, except for the best of friends. Do ask about his hobbies, interests, and philosophical beliefs.

• Shoes should always be removed when entering a Korean home or temple. When putting your shoes back on at the temple, do not sit on the steps with your back to the site of worship.
• Koreans consider it a personal affront to be touched, except by a relative or close friend.
• It is best not to write a living person's name in red. This color indicates a deceased person.
• If you want to practice the traditional Korean greeting, it is a bow from the waist in a slow flowing motion, keeping the back straight, the chin tucked in, and the palm on the hips. You do not need to do this however, unless you feel comfortable doing so.
• When dealing with an older Korean, it is polite to pass and accept documents, food, and other items with the right hand, not the left.
• Be softspoken rather than loud. Koreans dislike noisy laughter, exaggerated gestures, and overly convivial behavior.

EXECUTIVE TRAVEL TO SOUTH KOREA   •

DOCUMENTS

Valid passport, visa, and onward travel reservation required for U.S. travelers to enter and leave Korea, for a period not to exceed 15 days.

INOCULATIONS

None required for U.S. travelers. However, malaria precautions are advisable.

AIRPORT

Seoul's international airport is Kimpo, located about 20 miles from downtown Seoul.

CUSTOMS

Visitors may import duty-free 400 cigarettes, 50 cigars, two bottles (750cc.) of liquor, and a reasonable amount of perfume for personal use.

U.S. EMBASSY

82 Sejong-Ro, Congro-Sku, Seoul
Phone: 722601

TRANSPORTATION

Taxi drivers understand enough English so that basic instructions about hotel and restaurant destinations will be understood. Tipping drivers is not standard practice. It is advisable to hire a car and a driver/translator during your stay.

TIPPING

Tipping is not a common practice in Korea. Service charges are automatically added to bills at hotels and restaurants.

HOTELS

SEOUL

Hyatt Regency Seoul
747-7 Hanam-Dong, Yongsan-Ku
Phone: 795-0141   Telex: 24136

Seoul Hilton International
411, 5-ka Namdaemun-ro Jung Ku
Phone: 753-4514   Telex: 26695

Shilla Hotel
202, 2-ga, Jangchung-Dong, Chung-Ku
Phone: 295-3111   Telex: 24160

The Westin Chosun
87 Sokong-Dong, Chung-Ku
Phone: 771-0500   Telex: 24256

RESTAURANTS

SEOUL

Akasaka   *Japanese*
Hyatt House 747-7 Hanam-Dong
Phone: 795-0141

Chunghkukkwan Sheraton Hotel San 21 Kwangjang-Dong Phone: 445-0181	*Chinese*
Hanil Kwan 119-1 Chonjin-Dong Phone: 776-3388	*Korean*
Maxim Lotte Hotel, 1 Sogong-Dong, Jung-Ku Phone: 771-1000	*French*
Myong Wol Kwan Walker Hill Phone: 445-0181	*Korean*

TRAVEL TIPS

• For the shopper, a wide range of typical Korean handicrafts, custom-made clothing, and electronic goods are available at reasonable prices.

• Personal safety is not a factor and the streets are safe for visitors to walk. The Korean people are friendly and eager to help strangers.

• Medical facilities can be located by calling the American Embassy (72-2601).

• There is plentiful nighttime entertainment in Seoul. Your Korean hosts will no doubt show you around, but you should know the choices available. There are various nightclubs and discos (restricted to hotels); *fabang* (tearooms); and for a single, flat fee, theatre-restaurants will provide a dinner with drinks and a musical revue of either domestic or foreign origin.

• The Sheraton Walker Hill in Seoul has a large casino for those inclined to gamble.

• The sportsperson may attend basketball games, and tennis and soccer matches, as well as traditional martial arts. Fishing is a major activity, including both fresh and ocean fishing. There are 15 private golf courses; it is relatively easy for visitors to use the facilities as guests. There are now three major ski resorts, all easily reached from Seoul.

- International telephone service via satellite is available. The best time to call the United States is in the evening. Telex service is also available.
- The visitor can see many museums, palaces, and fortresses which represent various styles of Korea's over-five-thousand-year-old civilization. Seoul was selected as the royal capital of the Yi Dynasty and has preserved much of its rich past, displayed in the Kyongbokkung Palace, the National Museum, and the Folk Museum. The Korean Folk Village, which is a living-functioning community, includes 68 exhibitions of Yi Dynasty lifestyle, including blacksmiths, potters, millers, brass workers, and carpenters.

TAIWAN

Cultural Overview

Remarkable economic growth has characterized Taiwan for the past thirty years, qualifying it as a Newly Industrializing Country (NIC) along with Korea, Mexico, and Brazil. The United States is Taiwan's most important trade and investment partner, and opportunities abound for doing business with this island country, whose official name is the Republic of China.

The Taiwanese adhere in large part to the ethics of Confucius. Preserving face and self-respect is crucial; this value permeates all actions in the society, including business transactions. Frankly negative comments or criticisms are considered rude because they make someone else lose face.

Respect for people older than oneself or in a higher position is fundamental, and deference is due all elderly persons. A quiet, modest, calm demeanor is correct at all times. Showing any emotion, positive or negative, is seen as a loss of self-control.

Taiwan's political establishment is dominated by the 15 percent of the population which emigrated to the island in 1949 from mainland China (the People's Republic of China, or PRC). Members of this group hold most of the important political posts, and they also head the state-owned enterprises. The indigenous Taiwanese seem to feel a loss of control in their lives because of this anomalous political situation. There does not appear to be, however, any significant deterioration of overall relations with the United States since normalization of our relations with the PRC.

The government of the Republic of China consists of a national assembly and five other branches. The president, elected by the national assembly for six years, is the head of state.

In contrast to the political arena, the economic sphere is dominated by the local Taiwanese, who run most private businesses.

The economic growth of the past thirty years has been trade generated, with exports accounting for 50 percent of the GNP. Over one-third of Taiwan's exports are to the United States. As an example of the country's remarkable growth, its exports totaled $450 million in 1965. By the mid-1980s, this figure was in excess of $25 billion. The average annual growth rate between 1962 and 1973 was 10.3 percent; from 1974 to 1981, it was 8.3 percent.

Buddhism and Taoism are the predominant religions in this nation, with Confucian philosophy and ethics the basis for everyday conduct. About 5 percent of the Taiwanese are Christian, and there is a small Muslim community.

Education is a cornerstone of Confucian philosophy. Over 90 percent of Taiwan's population is literate, and primary education is mandatory and free for the first nine years.

The importance of the family is also central to Confucian teaching. Family relationships are extremely important, securing benefits for the family as a whole and for individual members. Family-owned and -operated enterprises are very common.

Women still play a traditional role in Taiwan, and rarely hold executive positions. Most Taiwanese will be surprised, but not insulted, if your negotiating team includes women. However, it may take some time for your Taiwanese counterparts to accept the women, especially at business meals.

Located about 70 miles off the coast of mainland China, the Republic of China is comprised of approximately 70 small islands. Taiwan itself, which measures 240 by 80 miles, is very mountainous, and only about one-quarter of the land is usable. Close to 20 million people live in this small area, making Taiwan one of the world's most densely populated nations. The climate ranges from subtropical to tropical, and rainfall is heavy in most areas.

Although most of the population speaks a dialect known as Taiwanese, Mandarin Chinese is the official language for business as well as for other transactions. Many Taiwanese speak English, however, and much business correspondence is in English. Catalogues, promotional literature, and other items in English are acceptable.

Business Opportunities

Taiwan imports large quantities of tools, basic metals, electrical machinery, transportation equipment, chemicals, and lumber. High-technology areas hold the best prospects for U.S. sales to Taiwan; U.S. equipment has a good reputation for quality and benefits from Taiwan's strategic industries program, which gives incentives to local manufacturers who import advanced technology. Products with the highest sales potential in Taiwanese markets include industrial process controls, scientific and engineering equipment, medical instruments, pollution control apparatus, and telecommunications equipment.

Taiwan's market for computer systems is expected to increase at a rate of 25 percent a year for the next five years. U.S. firms, with a 67 percent market share, are the leading suppliers. Minicomputers and small computer systems for the private sector have the greatest market potential.

The market for analytical and scientific instruments is growing at an annual rate of 15 percent. U.S. firms have a 50 percent market share and should keep it at that level, because of the high quality of U.S. products. The medical equipment market is dominated by imports, with 80 percent of the market. U.S. firms are the leading suppliers of cardiology and pulmonary equipment. The larger hospitals tend to purchase American medical equipment.

The three most significant purchasing groups are the state-owned enterprises, large private companies, and small local firms. They are considered to be end-users, in Taiwanese business parlance.

Initiating Contact

Approaching Taiwanese companies is best done through third-party introductions. This should help to eliminate some of the initial suspicion and uncertainty with which the Taiwanese business community often regards unfamiliar business representatives.

Most foreign trade in Taiwan is handled through agents. The Taiwanese prefer to deal with local associates because they can offer assistance quickly if there are problems. These agents also give advice pre- and post-sale, and they are responsible for service and warranty transactions. For the foreign businessperson they offer market sensitivity, and they are an excellent way of contacting the three end-user categories.

The role of private trading organizations is also expanding. These organizations can act as commission agents, or they can trade for their own accounts. Some large trading houses are associated with the large industrial groups. Establishing an association with these trading organizations can be valuable for foreign businesspeople, as the trading companies have considerable buying power, political and business connections, and financial strength.

Another effective means to locate business opportunities in Taiwan is through American banks with local offices. These banks can introduce the business executive to local clients, and also to members of the Taiwanese banking community.

For buyers, several annual trade shows in Taiwan are excellent places to make initial contact. Hundreds of manufacturers and wholesalers attend these shows and are happy to see potential American buyers. Information on the dates and types of products exhibited can be obtained from the Economic Section of the Coordination Committee for North American Affairs for the Republic of China (Taiwan) in Washington, D.C.

Arranging appointments with larger firms is best done through third-party connections, since direct sales or telex will probably be ignored. Again, U.S. banks can help in this regard. Appointments with smaller firms may be made by mail, with follow-up telephone calls. It is suggested that these appointments be made only after arrival in Taiwan, once appointments with larger firms have been made. Owners and executives of smaller firms may be more willing to meet with you and to agree to a specific time/place if you are already in the country. Your presence in Taiwan instills a proper seriousness of purpose and underlines your commitment.

For further information and assistance, write to:

Taipei World Trade Center Co., Ltd.
Sung Shan Airport Terminal

340 Tun Hwa North Road
Taipei, Taiwan
Phone: (02) 715-1551   Telex: 28094 TPEWTC

American Chamber of Commerce
Chia Hsin Building II, Room N-1012
96 Chung Shan North Road
Sec. 2, Taipei, Taiwan
Phone: (02) 551-2515

China External Trade Development Council (CETDC)
201 TunHwa North Road
Taipei 105, Taiwan
Phone: (02) 715-1515   Telex: 21671 CETRA

U.S. Commerce Department
Far East Division
Marketing Manager for Taiwan
14th Street and Constitution Avenue
Washington, D.C. 20230
Phone: (202) 377-4957

Chinese National Association of Industry & Commerce
17th floor, 30 Chungking South Road
Sec. 1, Taipei, Taiwan
Phone: (02) 314-8001

China External Trade Development Council
41 Madison Avenue
New York, N.Y. 10010
Phone: (212) 532-7055

Business Protocol and Procedures

BUSINESS ENVIRONMENT

Most Taiwanese businesses—and as many smaller ones as can afford to—are headquartered in Taipei, the political and population center of the nation. Smaller companies and operating units of larger organizations may be found in the cities of Taichung, or Kaohsiung, which is the site of Taiwan's newest superport.

It is best to bring a team of two to four people, including a senior executive with decision-making power, to Taiwan. The size of the party, to the Taiwanese, reflects the seriousness with which the foreigners regard the meeting and the respect they accord their hosts. Having a team of several people also enhances the status and image of the visiting executive.

The business day starts officially at 8:00 A.M., although most serious work does not get under way until about 9:00 A.M. Punctuality also enhances the image of the visiting businessperson; however, you may be kept waiting for half an hour. You should take a taxi to the host's office.

In a large company, the executive's secretary will escort you either to a waiting area outside the office or to the office itself. In smaller companies, or when you know the executive well, you will be personally escorted to that individual's office.

The principle of modesty guides business behavior in Taiwan. Visitors are not expected to assume rights or privileges, which implies that you are expected to wait at the door of your host's office until invited in, and to stand until invited to sit down. The host will direct the seating arrangements, placing the visiting senior executives in the opposite seat, so that they are face-to-face.

For at least the first meeting, interpreters should be used. Your hosts may have their own, but it is advisable to bring one yourself, one whom you can brief in advance about the general objective of the meeting and about any special terms to be used.

RANK AND STATUS

In this Confucian-based society, rank and status are extremely important. Status comes from age, authority comes with status, and those in authority within an organization have absolute power.

In large family-owned firms, the top executive chairs the board and is almost always the leading male in the family. The president in such firms is the link between the board and the rest of the enterprise. The president has some power, although not necessarily supreme authority.

In public enterprises, the board of directors is less a policy- and decision-making body than an advisory group, and the president will have the decision-making authority. In smaller, family-owned businesses, the head executive's title can be chairman, owner, general manager, or president. It is important, when dealing with such companies, to determine who is really the chief executive.

FORMS OF ADDRESS

In greeting you, the Taiwanese business executive will probably initiate a handshake. A very senior executive, however, may only nod, say something in greeting, and offer you a seat. When greeting a woman in the company, unless she holds a very senior position, you should only nod, unless she offers her hand.

Taiwanese names can be confusing. Usually, they start with the family name, which is never hyphenated. Thus, a colleague named Mr. Chan Tai Heng is addressed as "Mr. Chan."

BUSINESS CARDS

Exchanging cards is very important and takes place during introductions. Your card should be bilingual: English on one side, Chinese on the other. The card should be handed to the host with the right hand, Chinese side up. Titles are of paramount importance in the Oriental world, since they indicate rank and status, and your title should be clear on your card.

You will be giving out business cards constantly, so take an ample supply. If you run out, the top international hotels can usually get cards printed overnight.

BUSINESS DRESS

Conservative dress is appropriate at all times. Blue or grey suits are correct, and white or light blue shirts, to the Taiwanese, show the wearer is serious and pragmatic. Women should dress conservatively and modestly.

GIFT-GIVING

Gift-giving is common in Taiwan, and the visitor is expected to participate. For the first visit, small practical gifts are appropriate. Such items as pens, ties, or paperweights are appreciated, as are items carrying your corporate logo. If you are invited to your host's home for dinner, a bottle of imported scotch or an imported luxury food item will be very welcome.

COMMUNICATION STYLES

The Taiwanese do not expect foreigners to speak Chinese. Many executives have been educated in the United States or at least speak some English. It is best, however, to speak slowly and clearly and avoid American slang or colloquialisms.

The Taiwanese avoid physical contact with strangers. Patting on the back or touching someone's arm for emphasis is not done. The pointing of one's finger is not considered polite, and it is best to use the whole hand when pointing something out, or emphasizing a point.

In Taiwan a nod of the head means only "I understand," not "I agree." Also keep in mind that openly expressing feelings is not appropriate, and your hosts may well detect nervousness or conflict by inappropriate laughter or silence.

Overly friendly gestures make the Taiwanese uncomfortable. So does crossing the legs, which suggests undue familiarity.

When you are speaking, be alert for subtle signs that your host may not have understood you—stop and repeat points if necessary. The Taiwanese will not want to tell you they have not understood.

Negotiating in Taiwan

It is important to understand who has the decision-making power when negotiating with the Taiwanese. In family-owned firms, the senior decision maker will be the patriarch of the family. An older person's views carry much weight and can be challenged only with great care.

The oldest son is usually second in command. In many firms, two generations may be represented: the founder father and sons and nephews. These people, too, hold real power, dealing with top executives and with middle-level technical and operations people.

Lawyers are definitely *not* part of negotiations. Legal proceedings are thought to be rude and undesirable and, when conflicts arise, they are usually settled by arbitrators and preferably not in the courts.

In consummating successful business ventures with the Taiwanese, it is critically important that you establish a mutually respectful relationship with your customer. The confidence developed between you will enable successful communication, which will ultimately produce an association based on trust. Taiwanese will prefer to deal with counterparts whom they have met, wined and dined, and negotiated with personally. Additional contact via telephone and mail is vital in keeping personal links alive after you return to the United States.

The Taiwanese appreciate such sales aids as models, audio-visual materials, and samples, especially to help in technical understanding. The ability to supply your products in a timely manner is important.

In Taiwan's increasingly competitive atmosphere, the ability to provide fast, reliable, and preferably local service is crucial. U.S. exporters should consider adapting their products for the Taiwan market by stripping them down to the basic production unit, thereby avoiding the additional costs of meeting U.S. standards of sophistication.

Credit is an important issue in any business proposal, and you will need to consider short, medium, and long-range credit arrangements. In the private sector, the Taiwanese buyer is required to place a deposit with a bank to guarantee his letter of credit, a procedure that can be quite costly, given the high local interest rate structure and the shortage of capital. Your negotiations will go more smoothly if you are prepared to accept payments on a 90- to 180-day basis.

Export quotations should be on a c.i.f. (cost-insurance-freight) basis, with Kaohsiung harbor the FOB (free on board) point, to indicate that the seller pays all expenses. Kaohsiung has certain free-port privileges.

In negotiating with the Taiwanese, it is imperative that you discuss all points in detail. All possible perspectives should be covered to ensure mutual understanding. While a spirit of harmony and cooperation should characterize the negotiating atmosphere, the Taiwanese are also very competitive. Bargaining is part and parcel of doing business with them, and the individual wants to come away from the negotiations feeling that something beneficial has been accomplished for his or her firm. It is a good strategy to take this need to bargain into consideration when planning your proposal, so that you can include some things that you expect to bargain away.

The Taiwanese consider it impolite to say no directly to a verbal request. Rather than saying no directly, the executive will be silent or mention a possible difficulty. Also, nodding of the head only means understanding; it does not connote agreement.

The Chinese prefer vague and flexible contracts to U.S.-style agreements that spell out terms in great detail. You will need to make sure that all parties understand the details of any arrangement, including what is expected of each side and what timing is involved.

Business Entertaining

Entertainment is an important part of doing business in Taiwan. If you are a buyer, you will have a full schedule of activities and find little chance to initiate any entertaining. If you are selling, you may not be treated quite so lavishly, but entertainment is even more important. Choosing the right restaurant and treating your Taiwanese counterparts with friendliness and respect can greatly enhance your chances of success.

Business lunches usually start at noon. Dinners begin between 6:00 P.M. and 7:00 P.M. and are banquet style. Business is *not* discussed at meals.

At banquets, the table will be round and food placed on a lazy Susan in the center. The guest of honor starts the meal by serving himself or herself. The host sits facing away from the kitchen door, while the guest of honor faces it.

Toasting is done with wine or liquor. The host starts by raising his or her glass with two hands, one supporting the bottom of the glass. A simple statement of appreciation or of praise for the spirit of cooperation is all that is required. Even a simple *"Kan Pei"*—meaning "bottoms up"—is sufficient. The glass should be drained after the toast.

Women can be included in social evening meals, but they do not generally attend business meals. You can alleviate the potential discomfort caused by a woman's attending a business meal by letting the Taiwanese know in advance that women will be in your party.

The Taiwanese are impressed if foreigners eat with chopsticks. If you do not know how to do so, you might try learning before your trip.

If you are invited to a Taiwanese home for dinner, bring a gift, as mentioned above, and arrive about 15 minutes after the time stated. The meal is over when tea is served. Guests do not linger to talk after the meal has ended.

General Tips

• Appearing respectful and appreciative is important for getting along well with your Taiwanese hosts. Talking much about one's accomplishments is considered immodest and therefore impolite. Praising one's family or a member of it is also not done, for it is considered the same as praising oneself.

- In private, it is acceptable to ask your host's views on sensitive issues, such as the People's Republic of China or the local political situation, and your host may be glad to discuss these topics. Questions, of course, should be asked in a polite and respectful tone.
- Although the ultimate authority usually rests with the eldest man in family-owned corporations, the sons and other younger men may run entire subsidiaries. These people may have considerable power and influence.
- On the other hand, in family-run corporations, nonfamily members may hold high positions, but they will not have authority to make decisions without family backing.
- When taking a taxi, get the address written in Chinese characters. Make sure you have a card with the hotel's name and address in Chinese—for the return trip.

EXECUTIVE TRAVEL TO TAIWAN   •

DOCUMENTS

Entry regulations vary from time to time, so be sure to check with the closest Taiwan Coordination Council office. All visas require a valid passport, a completed application, two passport-type photos, and a confirmed ticket.

INOCULATIONS

Check with the Taiwan Coordination Council for the necessary entry requirements, which vary.

AIRPORT

Chiang Kai-shek International Airport is located just outside Taipei. The trip to downtown will take about 40 minutes (a distance of 25 miles).

CUSTOMS

Duty-free allowances include 200 cigarettes or 50 cigars, one bottle of wine or spirits, one movie camera, and one typewriter. Gold and silver jewelry must be declared upon arrival.

U.S. EMBASSY

The American Institute in Taiwan (AIT), an unofficial organization incorporated under the laws of the District of Columbia, represents U.S. interests in Taiwan:

> 7, Lane 134, Hsin Yi Road, Sec. 3, Taipei
> Phone: (02) 709-2000

TRANSPORTATION

Many of the large hotels provide shuttle bus service from and to the airport. It is advised that for the duration of your stay you arrange for a car and a driver/translator.

TIPPING

Tipping in hotels and restaurants is optional since a 10 percent service charge is always added to your bill. Taxi drivers do not expect to be tipped.

HOTELS

TAIPEI

> Hilton International Taipei
> 38 Chung Hsiao West Road, Sec. 1
> Phone: (2) 311-5151   Telex: 22513

> Lai Lai Sheraton
> 12 Chung Hsiao East Road, Sec. 1
> Phone: 321-5511   Telex: 23939

> Ritz Taipei Hotel
> 155 Min Chuan East Road
> Phone: (02) 597-1234   Telex: 27345

RESTAURANTS

TAIPEI

> Antoine   *French*
> Lai Lai Sheraton
> 12 Chung Hsiao East Road, Sec. 1
> Phone: 321-5511

L'Escargot   *Continental*
21 Chang an East Road, Sec. 1
Phone: 563-6515

Lucky Star   *Chinese*
160 Chung Hsiao East Road, Sec. 1
Phone: 771-1755

Trader's Grill   *Continental*
Hilton International Taipei
38 Chung Hsiao West Road, Sec. 1
Phone: 311-5151

Zum Fuss   *Swiss/German*
55 Lin Sean North Road
Phone: 531-3815

TRAVEL TIPS

• International telephone, telegraph, and telex services are available. The major hotels have bilingual staff to assist the business visitor.
• Medical and dental care is available as well as hospital emergency treatment centers.
• There are two daily newspapers printed in English, as well as the Asian edition of the *Wall Street Journal*, which can be translated for you locally, should it be required.
• As when visiting most foreign countries, drink only bottled water and avoid raw vegetables outside of hotel and better restaurant dining rooms.
• There are several excellent museums (including the National Palace) and art galleries in Taipei specializing in Chinese cultural achievements. Notable buildings include the Chiang Kai-shek Memorial Hall, Lungshan Temple, Martyr's Shrine, and the Confucian Temple.
• A business traveler staying at one of the major hotels is able to make arrangements for all sightseeing trips and recreational outings. Information on the most popular nightclubs and other nightlife will also be provided.
• Personal safety is very good in Taiwan, but being sensible about using normal precautions is always advised.
• Mandarin is the dialect spoken most often in Taiwan.

AUSTRALIA

Cultural Overview

The sixth largest nation in the world, the Commonwealth of Australia is the only country to occupy an entire continent. It is approximately the same size as the continental United States.

Australia has a democratic system of government, with four main political parties: the Australian Labor party; the Liberal party, which when in office governs in coalition with the rural-based National party of Australia; and the Australian Democrats.

This vast country has seven states, or territories: New South Wales, Australian Capital Territory, Victoria, Queensland, Tasmania, Northern Territory, Western Australia, and South Australia.

Even with a relatively small domestic market, Australia's economy is strong, due in part to a stable political situation, a plentiful supply of natural resources, steady population growth, and capital investment from other countries. Technology is advanced and there is a wide range of products available. The public service sector is the largest single industry, although both manufacturing and agriculture are important. Small businesses account for more than 40 percent of private-sector employment.

Australia is the world's largest exporter of aluminum, wool, beef and veal, mineral sands, live sheep, and refined lead. It is also among the top suppliers of wheat, sugar, coal, nickel, iron ore, and bauxite. In order to offset the decline in the importance of wool in the world textile market, Australia has increased its exports of mineral products. Also, instead of exporting primarily to European markets, Australia now sells to the developing countries, especially those in Southeast Asia. Australia's major imports are machinery, transportation equipment, petroleum, and petroleum products. Japan and the United States each account for one-fifth of the import trade.

Australia's economy is growing rapidly and this pace is expected to continue. Inflation and interest rates are down, while employment and business investment have risen. An essential factor in creating this economic stability was the accord reached on prices and wages between the government and the Australian trade union movement.

Australia is highly urbanized. More than half of its 15 million inhabitants live in the largest cities, which are all on the southwest coast. Over 20 percent of the people live in Sydney, the capital of New South Wales, and Melbourne, the capital of Victoria. (These cities are Australia's financial centers.) Brisbane, Adelaide, Perth, and Canberra are also well populated.

Most Australians are descended from European immigrants, particularly from Britain. Since World War II, however, the proportion of the population of Anglo–Celtic descent has fallen to about 60 percent. The national language is English, but many others are spoken. Most Australians are Christians.

School is compulsory from ages 6 to 16, with public education administered by the state governments and financed by federal funds. About one-fourth of the pupils attend private schools. The school year begins in February and ends in December, because the seasons are the reverse of those in the northern hemisphere.

The family plays an important role in Australian life. It is much like the United States. The average family is small, and both mother and father often work. Single-parent households are increasing. Dating begins at 16 or so; the average age for marriage is 21 for women and 25 for men. The standard of living is high, as is the life expectancy. Good medical care is provided either through private insurance or a government support program.

Australia has strong antidiscriminatory legislation, and the government actively encourages the participation of women at the higher levels of public service. Most male employers are aware of women's rights and the skills they contribute to the workforce; many have implemented affirmative action policies. In the public service, women account for approximately 34 percent of the workforce. And although still in the minority, there are 60,000 women in administrative, executive, and managerial positions, or roughly 14 percnet.

Business Opportunities

Australia is one of the world's most attractive markets for foreign investors. It can support advanced development projects, and the government is active in assisting industry. The Australian people do have some concern for foreign ownership and control; therefore, the policy of the government has been to provide opportunities for Australians to take part jointly in the industrial development of their country, in concert with foreign investors.

To enable potential investors to assess their projects, the government has established clear foreign investment guidelines covering three broad requirements: opportunities tests, economic benefits tests, and specific equity participation rules for some sectors. Foreign investment proposals are examined on a case-by-case basis to ensure that they demonstrate sufficient economic benefits to offset any losses of Australian ownership or control.

The government provides taxation investment allowances, and loans and grants for industrial development. For information, check the Australian Industrial Development Corporation, which is responsible both for promoting the development of industry and for providing finance in the form of loans and equity capital underwriting. It sometimes guarantees and participates in joint ventures, and is responsible to the Minister of the Department of Industry, Technology and Commerce. Some projects may be handled by the Bureau of Industry Economics (BIE). In addition to the government, some financial institutions will help prospective investors with up-to-date information about taxation, foreign exchange, the banking and monetary system, and entry conditions for staff.

Initiating Contact

Australia has a long-standing "old boy" network, and it helps to have an introduction from a senior executive. But the young Australian businessperson is generally capable of evaluating proposals on their own merits rather than on the basis of your connections. A banker-to-banker contact from the United States may be all that is necessary for you to establish a relationship.

Much of the international commerce in Australia is handled by agents, who are more than mere marketing representatives. They are also equipped to provide access to the financial community and to people who can manage product quality and maintenance responsibilities. Agents can also arrange visits with federal or state officials.

Frequently these agents have exclusive franchises, and you will have to agree not to create any competition in their territory. It is possible that you will need a representative for each state and territory. There are some nationwide agencies with offices in either Melbourne or Sydney. They may have warehouse and transport facilities. Agents work on a commission basis and expect travel expenses in addition.

For further information and assistance, contact:

World Trade Centre Melbourne
Corner Flinders and Spencer Streets
P.O. Box 4721
Melbourne, Victoria, Australia 3001
Phone: (03) 611-1999   Telex: AA34211

American Chamber of Commerce in Australia
50 Pitt Street
Sydney, N.S.W. 2000
Phone: (02) 241-1907

Australian Consulate General/Trade Commission
630 Fifth Avenue—Suite 426
New York, N.Y. 10020
Phone: (212) 245-4000   Telex: 12328 AUSCON
(Offices also in San Francisco, Los Angeles, Chicago, Houston,
    Honolulu, and Washington, D.C.)

Department of Trade
Stockland House
181 Castlereagh Street
Sydney, N.S.W. 2000
Phone: (02) 265-3005
(Offices also in Melbourne and all major cities in Australia.)

U.S. Commerce Department
Marketing Manager for Australia
14th Street and Constitution Avenue
Washington, D.C. 20230
Phone: (202) 377-3646

Business Protocol and Procedures

BUSINESS ENVIRONMENT

Australians usually work a 38-hour week. Businesses are generally open from 9:00 A.M. to 5:00 P.M. on weekdays. Retail establishments also often open on one or two nights during the week and on Saturday from 9:00 A.M. to noon, although in some states this extends to 4:00 P.M. Banking hours are from 9:30 A.M. to 4:00 P.M. Be punctual.

In the past, a visiting businessperson would be shown around a business office and introduced to a few of the staff. Now there is more formality. When you arrive, you will be escorted to a seat in the office or conference room (also called board room) of your host. Then, at this stage, you will be introduced. Shake hands. Since English is used in Australia, no interpreters are necessary, but colloquialisms may be confusing.

A few helpful suggestions follow:

• Confirm your appointments immediately after your arrival at your hotel.
• Recognize that a late arrival is seen as an indication of a careless business attitude. Waiting is not a part of the Australian business code.
• Anticipate that the initial introductory conversation, unrelated to the business at hand, will be quite short.

RANK AND STATUS

The corporate hierarchy is different in various industries and sectors in Australia. Although some companies are adopting U.S. titles, most still follow the British precedent. The CEO is often called the managing director. Another title may be chairperson if the individual also chairs the board. The board of directors is involved in major operating decisions, and directors frequently hold senior management positions in the organization simultaneously. The second-in-command may be called executive director, technical director, director, or even general manager. A chief manager is what we might call a group vice president.

In financial institutions, the second-in-command to a managing director is a chief general manager, who in turn is supported by a number of general managers who correspond with executive vice presidents in the United States. Reporting to these men are chief managers, who are equal to our vice presidents.

FORMS OF ADDRESS

Informal introductions are usually made around the table at the beginning of the proceedings, since members of the Australian business community often know each other. First names are adopted very quickly in Australia. It is not necessarily a sign of friendship, but is indicative of an informal atmosphere, which your hosts feel is conducive to good business.

When addressing the holder of a title, use "Sir" and the man's Christian name. "Sir John," for example. In general, the respectful form of address is "Sir."

BUSINESS CARDS

Present your business card at the opening of the meeting. This is a welcome gesture, particularly if you do not have an Anglo-Saxon name. The Australians may or may not present a card to you since they do not always use cards.

BUSINESS DRESS

The British dress tradition in Australia dictates the choice of a conservative suit in a dark, subdued tone. You will need a tie for business meetings. However, be prepared to take off your jacket when invited to do so. Men should not wear precious stones or other ornaments when doing business. Although businesswomen in Australia tend to dress conservatively, it is usually in a skirt and blouse, not in a suit.

Lightweight clothes are suitable all year round in the tropical regions, and for spring and summer in the South. During winter in the southern regions, sweaters and topcoats are needed.

GIFT-GIVING

Gift-giving in the business context is taboo. Gifts are not ordinarily presented in the Australian business world. If you wish, you may give flowers to a helpful secretary, but do not offer a valuable gift to an Australian business executive. If you visit someone's home, you can take a small gift at that time.

COMMUNICATION STYLES

The Australian style is considerate and courteous, and it is sensible to follow their example. The business community is small (for instance, there are only four or five law firms in Sydney), and Australians deal with the same people again and again. It is therefore necessary to them to keep relationships pleasant and natural. In reality, this means that Australians approach goals in a roundabout way, and are low-key and circumspect when specifying demands.

Nevertheless, Australian business executives can be straightforward when they feel that associates are applying too much pressure. The more aggressive U.S. business style is considered offensive to Australians. They like to do business with friends.

Negotiating in Australia

The major difference between doing business in Australia and in the United States is the disparity in the size and depth of each marketplace. While there have been less sophisticated lending methods and financial instruments available in Australia, this is changing. Today's Australians have become success, performance, and goal oriented, as you will learn in your negotiations with them.

During the first meeting, you should provide a complete picture of your company, including achievements and specifics that would be of interest to Australians. Also, the type of presentation common to the U.S. businessperson is now becoming the norm down under. Since Australia has censorship regulations, commercially produced films or literature may have to be referred by customs agents to relevant authorities before they are released. Films are reviewed by the Commonwealth Film Censoring Board, literature by the attorney general of the state of importation.

Australians are skillful, well informed, and pragmatic. Be forthright. Australians like to hear the good and the bad sides of a proposal, and resent it if important issues are concealed. Also, all proposals should indicate CIF terms since freight is an important cost item for Australians. FOB foreign port prices are also necessary in order that correct customs and duties can be calculated. Remember that Australia has converted entirely to the metric system.

Make your initial price a realistic one. Australians do not like to bargain. The opening price will probably be close to the final one. There may be delays as the last details are being negotiated. Your counterpart may be required to consult with technical experts or more senior policy makers. Policy and decision making is generally concentrated at the top senior management level, and approvals of agreements negotiated cannot be obtained without top management's involvement. It is also imperative not to press public employees or officials for a faster response than is usual in the normal channels.

Although both bankers and attorneys prefer to be involved in business transactions from the outset, they are usually not consulted until the later stages of negotiation in this country. Their presence is not considered as necessary as it is in the United States, where the business community relies upon such expertise to explain possible legal or financial implications throughout the discussions.

An agreement may be sealed with a handshake, but a written contract using standard clauses will be necessary to consummate a deal. The document will define all material issues and involve considerable detail. Disagreements are litigated under common law.

Additional suggestions for negotiating:

• Show interest by prolonged eye contact. Speak naturally, using gestures to emphasize and clarify what you have to say.

• Recognize that a local representative (agent) can be extremely valuable in helping the visiting businessperson to understand questions or problems that the Australian company may present.

• Be aware that there are international attorneys available in all Australian business centers.

Business Entertaining

Celebration dinners are appropriate at the termination of a successful deal but, generally speaking, Australians do not treat business associates to lavish luncheons. Work luncheons which may be served in the board room are more the norm. Also, business entertaining is customary among people on the same level. Thus, it is inappropriate to invite the executive director of the firm if your position is lower down on the management ladder; however, it is correct to invite your Australian counterpart to lunch as soon as a friendly relationship has been established between you. You can also further your social contacts by meeting for cocktails after work.

If your associate reciprocates your invitations, it may well be to a club, where the atmosphere will be relaxed and cheerful. When dealing at senior management levels, or with a serious business relationship, entertaining will likely be more formal. Both men and women are usually invited to these functions.

Table manners are European. Australians usually eat with the fork in the left hand, the knife in the right. At restaurants, a hand gesture is enough to attract the waiter's attention. Tipping is not always necessary, but is expected at better restaurants. International credit cards are widely accepted.

Australians do not usually make toasts at informal occasions; at formal or celebratory meals, the host may say a few words, customarily to express appreciation to those whose efforts contributed to the success of the deal.

Invitations to an Australian's home are not common. If you are invited, consider it to be a very special compliment. Although formal attire is not usual, do inquire beforehand as to the appropriate dress.

General Tips

• If you are teased, you are expected to reply in kind, with good humor. Such self-confidence will increase an Australian's respect for you. They do not admire a subservient attitude.
• Try not to be too idealistic in political or religious views.
• Australians are pleased when foreign visitors know something about their country, about Australian football or other sports.
• Australia is a very clean country. There is a stiff fine for littering.
• Do not show physical familiarity, touching, or hugging. Businesspeople should be reserved and conservative.
• Tea is served frequently throughout meetings.
• Personal space is important, and about the same distance as most U.S. executives need—an arm's length or so.

EXECUTIVE TRAVEL TO AUSTRALIA •

DOCUMENTS

A valid passport and visa and a return or onward ticket is required.

INOCULATIONS

None are required for U.S. citizens.

AIRPORTS

Kingsford Smith Airport (Sydney)—approximately 8 miles (40 minutes) from center of city.

Tullamarine Airport (Melbourne)—approximately 8 miles (40 minutes) from center of city.

CUSTOMS

Visitors are permitted, duty-free, 200 cigarettes or 250 grams of tobacco, and one liter of liquor; no restrictions on items for personal use.

U.S. EMBASSY

Moonah Pl., Canberra
Phone: (062) 733711   Telex: 62104

TRANSPORTATION

Taxis are abundant; however, it is recommended that you hire a car and driver for your stay.

TIPPING

Tipping is not the general custom in Australia. Hotels do not usually add service charges to bills; a 10 percent tip is therefore appropriate, if desired, to those providing special services.

HOTELS

SYDNEY

Hilton Hotel
259 Pitt Street
Phone: (02) 266-0610

Inter-Continental Hotel
177 Macquarie Street
Phone: (02) 230-0200

The Regent of Sydney
199 George Street
Phone: (02) 238-0000

Sebel Town House
23 Elizabeth Bay Road
Elizabeth Bay 2011
Phone: (02) 358-3244

Sheraton-Wentworth
61 Phillip Street
Phone: (02) 230-0700

MELBOURNE

Menzies Rialto
49 Collins Street
Phone: (03) 620-111

Regent Melbourne Hotel
25 Collins Street
Phone: (03) 630-321

Rockmans Melbourne Regency Hotel
corner Lonsdale and Exhibition Streets
Phone: (03) 662-3900

Sheraton Hotel
13 Spring Street
Phone: (03) 639-961

Windsor Hotel
103 Spring Street
Phone: (03) 630-261

RESTAURANTS

SYDNEY

Bagatelle   *French*
117 Riley Street
Phone: (02) 357-5675

Claude's   *French*
10 Oxford Street
Woollahra 2025
Phone: (02) 331-2325

Darcy's   *Italian*
92 Hargrave Street
Paddington 2021
Phone: (02) 323-706

Imperial Peking Harborside   *Chinese*
15 Circular Quay West
The Rocks
Phone: (02) 277-073

Pegrum's 36 Gurner Street Paddington 2021 Phone: (02) 357-4776	*Nouvelle cuisine*

MELBOURNE

Fanny's 243 Lonsdale Street Phone: (03) 663-3017	*French*
Fleurie 40 Ross Street Toorak 3142 Phone: (03) 241-5792	*French*
Stephanie's 405 Tooronga Road Hawthorn East 3123 Phone: (03) 208-944	*French*
Two Faces 149 Toorak Road South Yarra 3141 Phone: (03) 266-1547	*French/Swiss*
Vlado's Charcoal Grill 61 Bridge Road Richmond 3121 Phone: (03) 428-5833	*Steakhouse*

TRAVEL TIPS

• Sydney is very manageable for visitors as the main attractions are within walking distance of the city center, Martin Plaza. A harbor boatride is a must for the best view of the city and Harbor Bridge, the Sydney Opera House, and the skyline.
• Sydney is famous for its opals. You should purchase gems only from one of the city's well-established jewelers to be sure of getting what you pay for.
• Melbourne is the fashion center of Australia, with its totally stocked department stores, haute couture boutiques, and woolen goods.

• Horseracing is of national interest. Meets are held in or near all the capital cities every Saturday and frequently during midweek. Golf, yachting, fishing, and all water sports are popular.

• Australia's climate is generally warmer than the United States overall. The seasons are reversed: summer is from December to February; autumn is from March to May; winter from June to August; and spring from September to November. For most of the country the hottest month is January.

EUROPE

BRITAIN

Cultural Overview

The United Kingdom of Great Britain (England, Scotland, and Wales) and Northern Ireland (popularly abbreviated to Britain) is slightly larger (94,251 square miles) than the state of New York. Ireland, Britain, and the United States have strong common roots and a shared cultural heritage.

The government is a constitutional monarchy. The legislative authority rests in Parliament, which consists of the House of Lords (appointed by royal decree) the House of Commons, whose members are elected by popular vote. Executive power rests with the cabinet, led by the prime minister. Britain has no written constitution and no separation of powers, as in the United States. The House of Lords also functions as the supreme judicial authority. The two main political parties reflect the division between the socialism of the working class (the Labour party) and the upper and middle classes' conservatism (the Conservative party). A third party, the Social Democratic party (SDP), was formed in 1981, partly by disaffected members of the two main parties. The Liberal Party, with which the SDP has established an alliance, is the third largest in the country, having its origins (like the Conservative party) in the eighteenth century.

Britain was the home of the Industrial Revolution, and for decades it was a leading world power. After World War II, some areas of the economy were nationalized, including electricity, coal, railroads, and steel. Britain is the world's second largest producer of nuclear power, the fifth largest producer of coal and natural gas, and the sixth largest oil producer. It is the third largest trader in the world, and imports much of its food. Despite some industrial nationalization, Britain's economy is based on capitalist principles of free enterprise and market economy. In recent years the Conservative party has sought to minimize government intervention in the economy and to bring some nationalized industries (notably telecommunications) back into the private sector. Rising productivity and low inflation have been characteristics of an improving economic picture in recent years although unemployment remains a serious problem. The standard unit of currency is the pound sterling.

Britain's population is 56.3 million, with a third of the people living in Greater London and seven other major metropolitan areas; 97 percent of the population live in private households. Britain has the second lowest growth rate in the world, effectively reaching zero population growth. The population is mainly Caucasian, but there are Indians, Asians, and Africans in large numbers in Britain. There has been some racial unrest resulting from issues of housing, welfare, and competition for employment. Although English is the official language, there are local dialects and many other languages are used, especially in London.

British families are small, tight-knit nuclear groups, and they are often closed to outsiders. The average family size is 2.9 people. Most people do not support organized religion. If they do go to church it is likely to be the established Church of England, or one of many other Protestant denominations. About 9 percent of the population is Roman Catholic.

Illiteracy is almost nonexistent in Great Britain. Education is government subsidized through high school. The British private schools are referred to as "public schools." There are about forty-five universities, and a degree is required for professional positions. Higher education was once limited to the upper classes; now many working-class students receive government grants for their education.

Most women in Great Britain today work out of necessity. Because of relatively high personal tax rates, there is less spendable income. Usually, women work at traditional female occupations in the fields of education, research, and the service industries. More women are now, however, attaining executive positions in British business. The need to correct a historical disparity between the opportunities and compensation of women and men was recognized in the Equal Pay Act of 1970 and the Sex Discrimination Act of 1975. The latter made discrimination between men and women unlawful in employment.

Power and prestige among the British business executive elite are frequently related to social stature and membership in certain distinguished social clubs. British businesspeople have a well-developed sense of loyalty to their companies, but the firm is certainly not the key to their personal identity. More important are family, the community, and Britain. The British are patriotic and love their country intensely. The British possess avid respect for privacy, and may appear aloof to those unacquainted with this preference.

Business Opportunities

Britain is the third largest trading partner of the United States. The policies of the present British government are highly favorable to international businesspeople. U.S. companies offering technical expertise, high quality, and reliability enjoy excellent business opportunities in British markets. The recent strength of the U.S. dollar has imposed a serious restraint on U.S. exports to Britain, but provided an additional incentive to U.S. investment here.

There has been an emphasis on raising general productivity in Britain recently, and projects to ensure that productivity is enhanced are most welcome. Prospects are also good for exporting equipment to Britain that is designed to conserve energy, or for plant maintenance and materials handling.

Initiating Contact

The best way to initiate contact in Britain is through third-party introduction, preferably at a meal or over a drink. If this is not possible, you can contact someone via the telephone or through a letter. The customary role of an intermediary is only to make an introduction, not to be called on for help beyond the initial stage. If no references can be found, initiate the contact yourself by first sending a written inquiry, either by letter or telex, to the company with which you wish to deal. The correspondence should be addressed to the company rather than to an individual or a department. Later, when you have established a relationship, telephone calls will be more in order.

Some useful resources for obtaining references include:

• The "old boy" network (public schools, universities, clubs) of prospective clients.
• Members of the diplomatic corps and senior civil service officials.
• Banks and top-level executives in service industries.
• Senior executives in overseas subsidiaries of British companies, including those in the United States.
• Well-placed government officials, if you are interested in contacting nationalized enterprises.

For further information and assistance, contact:

World Trade Centre London
International House
Saint Katharine's Way
London, E1 9UN, United Kingdom
Phone: 01-488-2400   Telex: 884671

American Chamber of Commerce
75 Brook Street
London, W1-1 2EB, United Kingdom
Phone: 01-493-0381

Invest in Britain Bureau
British Consulate-General
845 Third Avenue
New York, N.Y. 10022
Phone: (212) 593-2258

International Trade Association (United Kingdom)
U.S. Department of Commerce
14th Street and Constitution Avenue
Washington, D.C. 20230
Phone: (202) 377-3337

British Trade Development Office
150 East 58th Street
New York, N.Y. 10022
Phone: (212) 593-2258

(Consulates general have offices in Atlanta, Chicago, and Cleveland.)

Business Protocol and Procedures

BUSINESS ENVIRONMENT

British business hours are 9:00 A.M. to 5:00 P.M. weekdays, and some businesses are also open from 9:00 A.M. to noon on Saturday. Most British managers work until 5:30 P.M., but not later. The summer months, particularly August, are not ideal for business trips because many British are on holiday. Often, a good arrangement is to make a late-morning appointment followed by an invitation to lunch. However, such business lunches are more appropriate after some rapport has been established between the executives.

Be prompt, but not more than a few minutes early. Schedules are carefully observed in Britain, and being five minutes late is frowned upon. Conversely, your host may keep you waiting for a short time. If you are dealing with a large business organization, call to reconfirm your appointment before you get to Britain.

British executives normally keep their office doors closed to maintain privacy. The executive will open and close the doors for visitors, unless this is done by a secretary. At the end of the meeting, the visiting executive should be the one to initiate a departure. Unless pressed for time, the British executive would consider it impolite to dismiss any visitor. As a matter of courtesy, you will be escorted out. It is best to go without undue leave-taking.

RANK AND STATUS

Formal rank and status matter considerably in business in Britain. The chairperson of the board is at the top of the hierarchy, and, as with boards in the United States these executives are rarely involved in the day-to-day functioning of the company. The managing director is the equivalent of the CEO in the United States. A deputy would be equal to a corporate vice president. Directors are usually divisional officers, with deputy directors under them. Managers, found in large companies, are one rank below—nonetheless, theirs is a high-level position in terms of both line and staff functions.

Senior British executives usually have large, separate offices, which are significant status symbols. A private secretary is another, as are furnishings and other appointments.

FORMS OF ADDRESS

It is customary for the secretary to introduce you to the executive. If this does not happen, introduce yourself. Shake hands firmly, but not aggressively or for a prolonged period. The proper greeting is a mutual "How do you do?"

If you are not already standing, rise when being introduced. If a woman is present, she should take the initiative to extend her hand to the men even if they outrank her in age or seniority.

When meeting a group, shake hands with the eldest person or the one with the highest rank. Then continue in order of rank. The host will probably anticipate your unfamiliarity about who is next, and will guide you through it. Notwithstanding the number of people, you must greet everyone personally. Neglecting to shake someone's hand is considered uncivilized behavior and will be noticed.

British executives are addressed by name only, not by their business titles. At first, only last names should be used. Wait for the host to initiate the informality of using first names. When addressing members of the nobility, use the title "Sir" and a man's first name (for example, "Sir John"). A woman is addressed with the title "Lady" and the family name ("Lady Smith"). Among others who should be addressed by title are military officers, university professors, and doctors of medicine, except for surgeons, who are greeted as "Mister."

BUSINESS CARDS

Business cards are not exchanged as a matter of routine in Britain. You should offer one, however, if your name is not clearly an Anglo-Saxon one.

BUSINESS DRESS

In general, dark grey or dark blue suits are favored by British executives. Black jackets and striped pants are still worn in the legal profession and in the financial center (the city) of London. Even dark brown may be considered too sporty. It is critical to conform closely to this conservative approach to dress. Also, be careful about wearing striped ties in England. Many may resemble school or military ties. It is not appropriate to wear an old school club or regimental tie unless you are entitled to do so. Your shirts should not have pockets; if they do, make sure they are not bulging with pencils, business cards, and so on. Theatre dress is formal. Loafers are too casual in most business environments; lace shoes are preferred.

Businesswomen should wear a tailored and conservative suit of a design that is tasteful and elegant. A carefully selected piece of expensive jewelry is permissible. Women frequently wear floor-length gowns to the theatre.

GIFT-GIVING

Gift-giving is not part of the British business world. There is a clear distinction between business and personal dealings. Gratitude is best expressed by an invitation to a dinner or an evening at the theatre. The exception is when you are invited to an executive's home. Then a gift for the hostess is necessary. Cut flowers are appropriate, but consult with a local florist since the type, color, and number given all have symbolic meaning. Liquors or champagne, wine or boxes of chocolate are also appropriate. This gift can be delivered by messenger on the day of your visit, or you can carry it yourself, presenting it at the door to the lady of the house. As a last resort, it can be delivered the next day with the thank-you note.

COMMUNICATION STYLES

Manners and civility are crucial to a successful business deal in Great Britain. The British respect an objective, logical, and calm approach to discussions. They do not like aggressiveness and high-pressure or hard-sell methods. British executives tend to look upon themselves as scholar-professionals. Be factual and thorough.

Physical touching to emphasize a point, or moving closer to an Englishman, is not appropriate. Avoid putting an arm around a shoulder, or tugging on sleeves. The British appreciate space around them, and do not like their privacy invaded. Also, demonstrative hand gestures should be used sparingly, even during presentations, as they are thought to be distracting and undignified.

The British have subtle ways of communicating unfriendly attitudes. An incredulous question, such as "Did you really have to . . . ?" or "Are you really saying . . . ?" may indicate that the

English disapprove of your tactics. Criticism can be inferred from statements like "I'm astonished that . . ." or "It's rather surprising . . ."

Keep facial expressions well controlled. It is polite not to display anger, frustration, incredulity, or amazement. Avoid keeping your hands in your pockets when speaking.

Negotiating in Britain

In general, British executives tend to be older than their U.S. counterparts, and this can occasionally cause uneasiness. To minimize this discomfort, it is prudent to send older executives to negotiate with British executives. The older managers favor a detached and cautious approach to negotiations. Younger officers, and those with modern management training, are apt to be impatient and conceivably less effective.

The first few minutes of a meeting are usually spent exchanging pleasantries, then substantive discussions can begin.

Be logical and make the benefits of your proposition apparent. Avoid condescension and elaboration. Respect the intelligence of your audience. Refrain from American idioms such as "bottom line," "ASAP," "no way," and the like. It is advisable to reserve one or two issues, so that pertinent discussions would warrant a subsequent meeting.

The British response to your proposal might be restrained. Do not anticipate instant feedback. Deliberations and decision making are slower in Britain, both in the private sector and in the government-owned businesses.

It is not necessary to send material ahead, but it is important to leave behind detailed documentation material describing your company and proposal. British executives ordinarily pay attention to details, and will want to analyze your information thoroughly.

When negotiating with executives and government-owned corporations, expect a more complex situation. Executives in these companies are subject to varying and conflicting political pressures and are influenced by broader national interests than the executive in the private sector. In general, be prepared for a little give-and-take in your dealings.

Decision making in British companies is the prerogative of senior management. The senior executive may appoint a committee of trusted staff advisors to help decide certain matters, but the financial decision is often based on administrative rules and procedures and will be determined by senior executives.

Inasmuch as the British are not ordinarily future oriented, a business presentation should emphasize the more immediate rather than long-term benefits. They are also less inclined to be interested in change, novelty, or innovation than in continuity and stability.

In British business, an oral ("gentlemen's") agreement is binding. The handshake of an authorized British executive at the conclusion of a deal is considered morally binding. Legally, written agreements confirm those made orally, and are usually in broad outline form. Only major agreements receive full legal attention and result in complex documents. Faith in their commercial code serves most British executives. The British value full performance of their obligations and postagreement problems are rare. If there is a dispute, it is usually settled out of court.

Ideas for negotiating that will help you:

- Instead of talking about the weather during the initial few minutes, comment on London traffic or flight conditions.
- Many British consider Americans to be condescending and smug and may react by delaying and subverting your proposal.
- British executives can be prudent, sober, analytical, and slow to make commitments.
- If mid-level managers complain about their company when senior people are absent, remain uninvolved.
- The British view buying and selling with some misgivings, but they can be hard negotiators when necessary.
- To protect yourself but without creating an atmosphere of mistrust, try to determine at what point in the negotiations it might be useful to employ the services of an attorney.

Business Entertaining

The practice of breakfast meetings has not yet been widely accepted. Many executives live in surburban areas and have long commutes.

Luncheon meetings are acceptable after you have gotten to know your British counterpart. The location is generally an informal spot, such as a pub or wine bar, which offers sandwiches and light meals. Lunch with senior British executives will only be in the company's executive dining room or a top-notch restaurant. Do not invite a British associate to dinner until you are certain that the negotiations are off to a good start. Theatregoing is also a welcome way to entertain British corporate officers. But do not invite people of different ranks to the same luncheon or evening affair. It may cause discomfort, as divergent management levels do not mingle socially.

These occasions offer a respite from business discussions and should not be used for a continuation of them. You might talk about business in general, but avoid your specific proposal. If you are having drinks with a British executive, talking about your business might be appropriate, but let your counterpart introduce the subject. Spouses should be included in any invitation to dinner.

Restaurant dinners may be quite formal in Britain. If you receive an invitation that says "formal," it could mean a variety of customs. To be sure that you rent the appropriate attire for the evening, take your invitation to a formalwear rental shop. If you are dining with someone from the upper class, expect the women to be traditional and withdraw after the dinner, leaving the men to indulge in brandy and cigars.

In most restaurants, meals are served only during scheduled hours: usually noon to 2:00 P.M. for lunch and 7:00 P.M. to 11:00 P.M. for dinner. Check with the restaurant to be sure.

The guest with the highest status should be offered the seat of honor at the head of the table. This person in turn may offer this seat to the host, who should accept it and offer the seat at the right to the same guest.

The British eat with the fork continuously in the left hand with tines down, and the knife continuously in the right hand. You will probably find more utensils on the British dinner table than you are used to in the United States. Forks are at the left of the plate, knives and spoons on the right. Start at the outside and use a utensil for each course. The knife above your plate is for butter. When not holding your utensils, empty hands should be on the table, not in your lap. Do not put your elbows on the table. When you are finished with a course, the utensils should be carefully put back on the plate. If you wish to put down a utensil for a moment, also put it on your plate.

A 10 percent tip is customary in Britain, and should be left on the plate on which the waiter brings the bill.

Toasting is common at formal dinners. Do not toast a guest older than yourself, or of higher rank, or your host and hostess, until they initiate it. A favorite toast is "The Queen," often at the end of the meal. Other toasts may then follow.

An invitation to an executive's home will be extended only after strong personal bonds have been established. If you receive an invitation, be sure to arrive punctually. Stand up when women enter the room. Also, men should open doors for women. Do not expect that your host will show you around the house.

Send a handwritten note of thanks for being entertained the next day by hand (a messenger), not by mail. It is considered uncivilized to phone to thank someone for lunch, dinner, or an evening's entertainment. The note should be brief.

The host and hostess will not ask you to leave. You must initiate that, and should do so by 11:30 P.M. or midnight.

General Tips

• Relationships between the "cousin" countries—Britain and the United States—are cordial, but colored somewhat by Britain's empire having diminished, as U.S. international power and influence have increased. This has created some uneasiness, ambivalence, and understandable resentment.

• The British do not appreciate an exaggerated or conspicious display of affluence. Showing off may very well bring a negative reaction. Comport yourself with discretion.

• Avoid discussion of religion, politics (especially Northern Ireland and socialism), personal finances, personal occupations (an invasion of privacy), money, and prices in general.

• British humor tends to be satirical and sarcastic. Avoid making jokes unless you are well versed in British ways.

• The British regard themselves as geographically and culturally separate from the Continent, although the economic advantages of European Community membership (since 1973) are well recognized by the business world. It is best however, not to refer to them as Europeans.

• Telephones are not used as extensively in Britain as they are in the United States. It is best not to place a call without an introduction, or to attempt to conduct business over the telephone, except to make arrangements for a meeting or to call at a time other than business hours.

EXECUTIVE TRAVEL TO BRITAIN   •

DOCUMENTS

No visa necessary for the U.S. traveler. Only a valid U.S. passport is required.

INOCULATIONS

None required for U.S. citizens.

AIRPORTS

Heathrow Airport—14 miles from London.
Gatwick Airport—26 miles from London.

CUSTOMS

Duty-free: one liter of liquor, 200 cigarettes, 50 cigars or 250 grams of tobacco, plus personal belongings.

U.S. EMBASSY

24/31 Grosvenor Square, London WIA 1AE
Phone: (01) 499-9000   Telex: 266777

TRANSPORTATION

Taxis are readily available, but it is suggested a car and driver be hired for the length of your business trip.

TIPPING

There is usually a 15 percent service charge added to the bill. If not, tip those at the hotel who have provided you with services (concierge, porters, maids, etc.); this also applies in restaurants where 15 percent is the standard amount. Tipping is also expected by taxi drivers, barbers, hairdressers, and so on.

HOTELS

LONDON

Browns Hotel
21 Dover Street WI
Phone: 493-6020   Telex: 28686

Claridge's
Brook Street
Phone: 629-8860   Telex: 21872

The Connaught
16 Carlos Place
Phone: 499-7070   Telex: 296376

The Dorchester
Mayfair Park Lane
Phone: 629-8888   Telex: 887704

The Ritz
Piccadilly
Phone: 493-8181   Telex: 267200

The Savoy
The Strand
Phone: 836-4343   Telex: 24234

RESTAURANTS

LONDON

Connaught   *Continental*
The Connaught Hotel
16 Carlos Place
Phone: 499-7070

Dorchester Terrace   *International*
Dorchester Hotel—Park Lane
Phone: 629-8888

The English House   *English*
3 Milner Street
Phone: 584-3002

Leonis Quo Vadis   *Italian*
26–29 Dean Street
Phone: 437-9585

Tiger Lee   *Seafood*
251 Old Brompton Road
Phone: 370-2323

Waterside Inn   *International*
Ferry Road
Phone: 881-3079

TRAVEL TIPS

• The major London department stores, except for Harrods which is in Knightsbridge, are along Oxford Street. The luxury shops are on Bond Street and Regent Street. Saville Row is where you will find the finest men's tailors.

• The best buys are in men's tailoring, ladies' wear, leather goods, silver, china, and crystal.

• Football (soccer) is one of the most popular spectator sports, with the season running from August to May. Cricket is played during the summer in London at Lord's and the Oval. Horse-racing is sponsored at four local tracks, with the Derby held the first week of June.

• Golf, tennis, and swimming facilities are plentiful.

• The South Bank complex boasts of three concert halls, the National Theatre offering plays, and the National Film Theatre. Visit the Royal Opera House for opera and ballet from September to July.

• Nightlife is to be found in theatres, nightclubs, and hotels providing top entertainment.

• You must be a member for a least forty-eight hours before you are permitted to use the gaming rooms at the Clermont, the Palm Beach, the Ritz, and other clubs.

• The Sunday *Times,* the *Observer,* and the Sunday *Telegraph* cover business news extensively.

• The most popular business newspapers read are the *Economist, New Statesman, Financial Times, Times, Guardian,* and *Telegraph.*

FRANCE

Cultural Overview

The largest country in Western Europe, France is a nation fiercely proud of its history as a political and cultural leader. Today, despite the upheavals of the twentieth century, the French people remain determined to preserve their artistic and historical heritage, maintain a place as a world economic power, and retain a high standard of living.

France is governed by a two-chambered parliament. Unlike other parliamentary systems, France's government is headed by a president with decision-making power, who is elected for seven years. The population totals well over 50 million, more than three-quarters of whom live in urban areas in the northern and eastern part of the country and in the Rhone Valley.

Fourth among the Western industrialized nations, France has the largest agricultural industry among the European Common Market nations. The nation leads the world in the construction of nuclear power plants and is among the top countries in nuclear applications, medical research, and the aircraft and electronics industries. High inflation and unemployment, growing out of the worldwide economic problems of the early 1980s, are the major challenges the French economy now faces.

A close relationship has long existed between the French government and its larger industries, with cooperation and subsidization a most common arrangement.

A top priority in France, education is entirely state controlled and supported. Social status and career are very much influenced by the school one attended and how well he or she did there. Imagination, individualism, and intellectual achievements are qualities the French value highly.

A majority of the French people are Catholic, but there are also many Protestants, a large Jewish community, and many Muslims since the influx of immigrants from North Africa.

Women in France are joining the workforce increasingly, with approximately 60 percent now employed. Many are joining businesses, especially in the service industries, and work in staff positions. They are still fighting for equality. However, French men may feel some-what uncomfortable with French women executives and treat them quite coolly.

Business Opportunities

Despite efforts to "buy French" and to encourage banks to lend only to companies that use French-made equipment, the government does view foreign investment as the key to creating more jobs, attaining new technology, and developing French exports. For the United States, France's largest foreign investor, good opportunities exist for exporting computers and peripherals, particularly microcomputers, and other electric components. Other good areas are products for the avionics industry, medical equipment, scientific instruments, and printing and graphic arts equipment. Joint ventures are encouraged.

France is second only to the United States as a franchise market. Approximately 10 percent of the franchisers are foreigners, and this sector is expected to grow and create more opportunities in the future.

Initiating Contact

Doing business in France often involves going through an intermediary contact whose credentials are impeccable. The best contacts are French people who have ties with the person you want to contact—through family status, money, or schooling. This last is perhaps the most important, for the French managerial elite are linked by having attended the prestigious *Grandes Ecoles*. You might find people to introduce you to the executive you want to meet in a number of ways. People in related industries, for example, almost always know each other well. Once you have a good relationship with someone in one firm, he or she might be able to introduce you to people in other firms within the industry.

Since it is important to deal with the most senior person possible, finding the right initial contact is crucial. You need someone high enough in the organization to have access to decision making, which is usually confined to the very top levels, but low enough to offer you an easy entree into the firm.

Members of the organization you want to contact, particularly in branches or divisions away from the one you will visit, can be very helpful. Other good contacts may be American or French acquaintances in banks or government offices, at the diplomatic level, or among customers or suppliers of the person you wish to contact. A personal introduction is ideal and may take place over lunch with you, your contact, and the person you want to meet. You may also have your contact send a letter, which should arrive well in advance of your attempt to make an appointment over the phone.

You will also need to have a representative in France who knows the local system and how to comply with EEC regulations. Any of the following alternatives will help you do business in France:

A France-based agent, who will be registered in the *registre des agents commerciaux* and will be independent of any firm. These agents work on a commission basis—a plus for the hiring business person—but their independence makes selecting them carefully a crucial matter. You should always check an agent's credit rating with the French banks. It is also prudent to check with the local Chamber of Commerce.

A limited agreement with an export house can be a good short-term solution until you gain a satisfactory knowledge of the market.

A subsidiary of your American company can be opened, which involves the filing of prior declarations with the Banque de France for real estate transactions and with the ministère de l'Economie et des Finances for all other business, or a *"succursale"* of your American firm can be opened. This is a branch of the parent company and would give you more control over your local agent than if you opened a subsidiary.

The following organizations can be particularly useful in assisting you to obtain introductions:

U.S. Chamber of Commerce
7 rue Jean Goujon, 75008 Paris
Phone: 1-359-6335

Comité Parisien de Congrès
24 Avenue de l'Opera, 75001 Paris
Phone: 296-03-61   Telex: 210 311F

World Trade Center of Paris (France)
Chamber of Commerce and Industry
2 rue de Viarmes, 75001 Paris
Phone: 508-3600

French American Chamber of Commerce in the United States
1350 Avenue of the Americas
New York, N.Y. 10019
Phone: (212) 581-4554

U.S. Commerce Department
14th Street and Constitution Avenue
Marketing Manager for France
Washington, D.C. 20230
Phone: (202) 377-4941

Business Protocol and Procedures

BUSINESS ENVIRONMENT

The business day in France usually begins at 8:00 A.M., certainly no later than 9:00 A.M. Lunch takes one and a half to two hours; then business resumes, often until 7:00 P.M. Many businesses open for a half day on Saturdays, while some close on Monday mornings. The best times to schedule an appointment are at 11:00 A.M. or 3:00 P.M. Beware the month of August if you are planning a business trip, for most French people vacation then. The two weeks before and after both Christmas and Easter are other times to avoid.

Punctuality is important in France, and visiting executives are expected to be on time—even if the French host keeps them waiting, which often happens. When you arrive for your appointment, you should give your business card to the receptionist.

The French are very polite, and any gestures of courtesy should be accepted gracefully. If the host ushers you through the door, go first. "After you" games are not expected or appreciated in France. You will be offered a seat and should take it and sit down, unless women are present. A short period of small talk may precede the meeting.

In boardroom meetings or other large gatherings, the highest ranking executive will enter the room first, followed by the others. You will probably be shown where to sit but, if not, ask before taking a seat.

RANK AND STATUS

The French are status conscious and high position is concomitant with family background, money, and education. In the business community, there is an especially strong camaraderie among graduates of the prestigious *Grandes Ecoles,* the elitist educational institutions. These people generally dominate the upper echelons of business. At a business meeting, the person with the highest status will open the discussion.

FORMS OF ADDRESS

You should not use first names unless specifically asked to do so. Titles are not used a great deal in French conversation. Instead, "monsieur," "madame," or "mademoiselle" is always correct. Furthermore, it is impolite to use "bonjour," "au revoir," or any similar greeting without appending a name, or at least "monsieur," as in "Bonjour, monsieur." Women in business are properly addressed as "madame" whatever their marital status.

Handshakes are an integral part of greetings and introductions in Europe, and they are very important to the French. You should shake the highest ranking person's hand first.

BUSINESS CARDS

In France, you should offer your business card whenever you meet a new business associate. If there are several people at the meeting, give your card to the senior person. Since the French place great value on education, business cards can include academic degrees and even the name of your university if it is particularly prestigious. You may wish to add such credentials to your card. Be sure business cards are properly translated.

BUSINESS DRESS

French attire is almost synonymous with fine styling. And French business executives appreciate fashionable clothing.

Business dress is somewhat on the conservative side, with blues or greys the preferred color for men's suits, although some French executives may wear a styled jacket with elegant trousers. Light or striped shirts are the norm. The businessperson would do well to make sure materials are of high quality, not "wash and wear."

In Paris, dress is very important, especially for businesswomen. The key is to combine a businesslike, conservative tone with some style and flair.

GIFT-GIVING

Giving gifts to your French counterpart is not usually done in France, particularly at the first meeting. You might host a dinner or other special occasion when a transaction has been successfully completed. If the circumstances do suggest that giving your French host a gift would be appropriate, books or tapes that suit his or her interests are always acceptable. The French are interested in things American, and books about the country or crafts unique to the United States would be welcome.

COMMUNICATION STYLES

The French are articulate, and they view good conversation as an art. In business, they enjoy a certain amount of general discussion. They expect clear and elegant presentations. If your French is not fluent, and your counterpart's English is lacking, it is sensible to have an interpreter at meetings. If a meeting is to be conducted in French, ask your host to arrange for an interpreter.

The French do not use hand gestures much when conducting formal discussions, although their facial expressions may be quite animated. The French also consider a discreet physical distance essential with strangers, particularly in business. Touching, except for the ever present handshake, is not appropriate.

Negotiating in France

The pace of negotiations in France is slower than that in the United States. The French like to look at all possible alternatives and consequences of what is being proposed. They do not like to be rushed, and any attempt to rush them or any show of impatience is a serious mistake.

Decision making in French organizations is centralized and concentrated with a few executives at the top. If you are not dealing with the top two or three people in a large French company, it will take time for your lower-echelon contacts to pass information on and get a decision. In smaller firms, the top manager or the owner usually makes all the decisions. Also, government enterprises or nationalized companies move slowly under bureaucratic administrations. All these factors make it most important to start negotiations at as high a level as possible, and to have the decision makers involved in discussions at the earliest possible time.

The French are fond of debate and argument. They are not likely to be convinced of anything immediately, but instead spend time debating every point. They may interrupt you during a presentation with arguments or criticisms. Understand that this kind of questioning is only part of the French executive's careful and intellectual consideration of your position. Being well versed, logical, persistent, and focused on your strong points should carry you through admirably.

The French, in general, have a low opinion of the act and profession of selling. French executives will not be impressed by extravagant or emotional presentations, but they will respond to presentations that deal with facts and that are rational, reasonable, and formal.

Price bargaining will probably not be a major issue in negotiations. In dealing with larger firms, particularly, you should emphasize superior performance and longer product life. If you can also show the French firm a clear economic advantage to itself, you will have helped your chances immensely. When dealing with smaller firms, in contrast, you can emphasize direct and tangible financial benefits. This is because many of the smaller entrepreneurial or family-owned enterprises dislike using credit and look for alternate financing methods.

In major negotiations, plan to have at least one piece of your technical literature translated into impeccable French. Perfect use of the language is important here; there are many agencies in Paris which can prepare flawless copy for you. Competent use of the French language will bring a warm attentiveness from your counterparts.

French contracts are very specific and precise, not subject to interpretation. Every detail, no matter how small, should be covered in the document, since if anything ever comes to litigation, the French courts pay attention only to what appears in writing.

Lawyers are not usually present during most of the negotiating procedure leading to a contract, although they may be with you in France to help you prepare. When the time comes to sign a contract, your firm's attorney or legal department should review the document, especially if it is a major transaction. Lawyers should pay particular attention to clarifying the issue of settlement currency, which has been known to be a problem on occasion.

Remember the following points when negotiating in France:

- If your presentation is to be in English, speak distinctly and at a reasonable pace; avoid slang and colloquialisms.
- In cities other than Paris, the atmosphere for business meetings may be more conservative. In the south, however, business-people may be more outgoing, relaxed, and informal.
- The French do not like sudden changes. Introducing changes in your proposal, no matter how good they seem to you, is not recommended.

Business Entertaining

Privacy is most important to the French, and they tend to separate their business from their social life. Most business entertaining, there-fore, is done over lunch or dinner at a restaurant. Business dinners are not usually attended by anyone but the people involved in the transaction. Your French host will let you know who is expected to attend. You should be punctual for an engagement in a restaurant.

It is perfectly correct for you to suggest lunch to your French host. You may want to ask him or her to recommend a restaurant, or you may impress him or her by doing some research and suggesting an excellent place yourself. You, of course, take the check if you do the inviting.

Even at these business meals, discussion of business is usually de-layed until coffee is served after the meal. Good conversation during a meal is highly appreciated, and favorite topics include culture, en-tertainment, books, places of interest in France, or your home.

An invitation to a French home for dinner is a rare honor. Spouses are usually included in such an invitation, since these dinners are regarded as social, not business, occasions. You should arrive about 15 minutes after the time stated in the invitation: always bring a gift to show appreciation. Flowers are an excellent choice, except for white blossoms of any sort, particularly chrysanthemums, for white flowers symbolize mourning. Fine chocolates or excellent champagne are also very good gifts. Bringing a bottle of wine is a bit risky, since your host may have very definite preferences. If you do bring wine, be sure it is very good—and expensive.

Food, of course, is a source of great pride to the French, and meals, especially in someone's home, are long, leisurely occasions. Commenting on the high quality of the food and drink is always appreciated. Toasting is not done at formal French meals but only on very informal occasions. If you are at someone's home and are offered a drink before dinner, you should stand to accept it.

Suggestions for entertaining:

• The French consider it an insult to the chef to add salt or other seasoning to your food, even after you have tasted it.
• They do not smoke between courses at the table, and visitors are expected to follow suit.
• Your hands should be kept on the table during meals.
• Bread is supposed to be torn, not cut.
• A regular knife should not be used to cut fish. If no fish knife is provided, separate the fish with the fork only.

General Tips

• The French appreciate a knowledge of or an interest in the arts and culture, particularly French art and culture. They will be pleased if you show an awareness of their country and heritage.
• Topics *not* acceptable to the French in conversation with all but intimates are religion, personal matters (including queries about someone's occupation or marital status), and politics.
• The prestigious *Grandes Ecoles* are the Ecole Nationale d'Administration, the Ecole Normale Supérieure, the Ecole Polytechnique, the Ecole Centrale de Paris, and the Ecole des Mines and des Ponts et Chaussées. The speaker is likely to be a person of high position if he or she mentions attending one of these schools.

EXECUTIVE TRAVEL TO FRANCE

DOCUMENTS

No visa is required for visits less than three months. A valid U.S. passport is the only requirement.

INOCULATIONS

None are required for U.S. citizens.

AIRPORTS

Orly Airport is 9 miles from downtown Paris (about a 50-minute ride).

Charles de Gaulle Airport is about 14 miles from downtown Paris (about a 50-minute ride).

CUSTOMS

Duty-free: 400 cigarettes, 100 cigars, 500 grams of tobacco, one bottle of liquor, and two bottles of wine. In addition, personal belongings, including cameras, tape recorder, and so on. Check with an airline or travel agent for the current list at the time you plan your trip.

U.S. EMBASSY

2 Avenue Gabriel 75382, Paris
Phone: 296-1202/261-8075   Telex: 650221

TRANSPORTATION

While taxis are plentiful, it is recomended that you hire a driver/ translator during your stay.

TIPPING

A 15 percent service charge is usually included with the restaurant bill. An additional gratuity, if you have been pleased with the service, is always appreciated. At the hotel, it is proper to tip the porter, maid, or any of the hotel staff who provide service to you.

HOTELS

PARIS

George V
31 Avenue George V
Phone: 723-5400

Hotel de Crillon
10 Place de la Concorde
Phone: 265-2424   Telex: 290241

Le Bristol
112 rue du Faubourg Saint-Honoré
Phone: 266-9145   Telex: 280961

Plaza Athénée
25 Avenue Montaigne
Phone: 723-7833

Ritz
15 Place Vendôme
Phone: 260-3830   Telex: 220262

RESTAURANTS

PARIS

Crillon   *French*
10 Place de la Concorde
Phone: 296-1081

Lasserre   *French*
17 Avenue Franklin D. Roosevelt
Phone: 359-5343

La Tour d'Argent   *French*
15 Quai Tournelle
Phone: 354-2331

Le Fouquet's   *French*
99 Avenue des Champs Elysées
Phone: 723-7060

Le Taillevent   *French*
15 rue Lamennais
Phone: 561-1290
(must book 4–6 weeks in advance)

Les Ambassadeurs   *French*
Hotel de Crillon
10 Place de la Concorde
Phone: 265-2424

Le Train Bleu   *French*
Gare de Lyon
Phone: 343-0906

Lucas-Carton   *French*
9 Place Madeleine, 8e
Phone: 265-2290

Maxim's   *French*
3 rue Royale
Phone: 265-2794

Relais Plaza   *Continental*
Hotel Plaza Athénée
Phone: 723-7833

TRAVEL TIPS

• In Paris there is an American hospital, L'hôpital Américain de Paris. Phone is 747-5300, in the event of an emergency.
• The French have a strong control over pharmaceuticals that are sold over the counter, so that it is difficult to find drugs that are not produced in France.
• France is a country where you should not be overly concerned about security problems. It is always advisable, however, to be cautious in large cities and on the French Riviera.
• France has no restriction on the amount of currency you bring into the country. However, if you have more than FF5,000 (French francs), you should get a special form from the customs to declare the amount. This assures that you will be able to take out the same amount when leaving the country.
• Telephone service in France is said to be unreliable. Public phones are within easy access: on the street and in cafés which abound. It is always preferable to use these phones instead of the hotel phones, as the hotel surcharge can be as high as 100 percent.
• All first-class hotels have telex services. In addition, there is a special office, Poste de Telex, at 7 rue Feydeau, Paris.
• If you are in Paris on a Friday night, do not miss going to the Louvre where the sculpture galleries are illuminated for special effect.
• If you have the time, take a trip on the river Seine on ships called *"bateaux mouches"* that go under the famous bridges of Paris. Some serve meals on the trip.
• July 15–August 15 is the favorite time for the French to leave

their stores and businesses and take a vacation. So plan your trip accordingly.

• Horseracing is one of the most popular spectator sports, and there are several courses on the outskirts of the city. *Longchamp* and *Auteuil*, both in the Bois de Boulogne, are two of the most famous tracks.

• One of the city's major cultural attractions, *L'Opéra*, offers performances of opera and ballet.

• Paris nightlife is extensive, including cabarets, ballrooms, discos, international clubs, and jazz clubs. Check with the concierge.

• No one goes to Paris without spending some time shopping. For expensive things, or a more original taste, try the variety of boutiques on rue de Rivoli.

ITALY

Cultural Overview

Extending far into the Mediterranean, modern Italy's natural beauty, long cultural heritage, and pleasant lifestyle have made it second only to the United States and Spain in the number of tourists visiting each year.

Since 1946, Italy has been a republic governed by a bicameral parliament, whose members are elected for five-year terms, and who represent several different parties. Parliament elects a president for a seven-year term and the president appoints the prime minister, the effective head of state.

Italy's economy is heavily export oriented, concentrating on machinery and transport equipment, textiles, foodstuffs, chemicals, footwear, and jewelry. The northern cities of Milan, Turin, and Genoa are the centers of industrial activity, although Naples, far to the south, is gaining in importance.

Although the economy is based largely on private enterprise, the state owns the electrical, transportation, telephone and telegraph systems, and the national radio and television network. The government also has joint ventures or controlling interests in a number of large commercial, financial, and industrial enterprises. Approximately one-

192   **THE GLOBAL EDGE**

third of Italy's industrial output comes from state-owned or state-controlled firms, which are predominantly operated along conventional, market-oriented business lines.

Poor in natural resources, Italy imports raw materials, consumer goods, capital equipment, and petroleum. Since the mountainous countryside is not well suited to modern agriculture, foodstuffs are also a major import. Italy's major trading partners are West Germany, France, and the United States (our third largest), accounting for approximately 9 percent of Italy's imports and 5 percent of her exports.

Most Italians are Roman Catholic, and the family remains the cornerstone of their society. Family ties are very strong and active, not only in social life, but also in business and government.

The approximately 60 million Italian people have a reputation for valuing the arts, culture, and a fairly easygoing lifestyle, although northerners are now more pressured by the demands of an industrialized society. Education is compulsory from 6 to 14 years of age. Italy has 36 universities and institutes of higher learning.

Business Opportunities

Because Italy is so dependent on foreign trade, her investment policies are liberal, with no limits on the extent of foreign ownership in business. The government encourages foreign investment as the avenue to economic growth, greater employment, and technological advancement.

There are good opportunities for U.S. companies to export sophisticated high-technological equipment, particularly to support the ten-year plan, started in 1984, designed to upgrade Italy's telecommunications network through electric circuitry. Since Italy's small- and medium-sized companies are emphasizing investment in labor and energy-saving equipment, good prospects continue for the sale of computers and peripherals. Equipment for process control, electronic production, and testing will be in demand, as the government encourages increased productivity in industry and agriculture.

Opportunities for exporting coal handling, transportation, storage equipment, and pollution control devices are growing, because of the combination of Italy's increasing reliance on coal and the European Economic Community's tightening of pollution laws. Security and technology equipment is also needed to cope with an alarming increase in political terrorism. Other major Italian imports are crude oil, machinery, transportation equipment, ferrous and nonferrous metals, wool, and cotton.

Initiating Contact

Many channels exist for marketing foreign products in Italy. For selling raw materials, semifinished products, and capital goods to the larger manufacturers, commission merchants, brokers, and independent representatives are used extensively. For reaching smaller industrial firms, and the many specialized wholesalers and retailers of consumer goods, exporters usually go through established distributors.

The numerous American, Italian, and European trade shows are excellent places to make informal personal contact with Italian firms. The most important and prestigious of these is the Milan International Trade Fair, held annually in April since 1922. A foreign organization can also make contact directly with a manufacturer or distributor by writing "cold," and including promotional and informative material in Italian. In the north, your initial written contact should be brief and to the point. In the south, there is a greater emphasis on more personal oral contacts, especially through intermediaries.

English is not spoken as widely in Italy as it is in France or Germany. Your initial correspondence with an Italian firm should be in Italian, especially if the firm is based in the southern part of the country. If the reply is in English, you can use it from then on, but your initial use of Italian is a courtesy that assures prompt and respectful attention. Catalogues and product literature should be in Italian, if possible. Never schedule an appointment early in the morning or shortly after lunch.

The following government and nongovernment agencies can assist in arranging contacts and give advice on doing business in Italy:

Italian American Chamber of Commerce
350 Fifth Avenue
New York, N.Y. 10018
Phone: (212) 279-5520

Italian Trade Commission
499 Park Avenue

New York, N.Y. 10011
Phone: (212) 980-1500

U.S. Commerce Department
Country Specialist/Italy
14th Street and Constitution Avenue
Washington, D.C. 20230
Phone: (202) 377-3462

World Trade Center Italy SRL
Palazzo WTC
Centro Direzionale Milanofiori
20090 Assago (Milan), Italy
Phone: (02) 824-4086

American Chamber of Commerce in Italy
12 Via Agnello
20121 Milan, Italy
Phone: (02) 869-0661

Business Protocol and Procedures

BUSINESS ENVIRONMENT

Business hours in Italy are usually 8:30 A.M. to 12:30 P.M. and then 2:00 or 2:30 P.M. to between 6:00 and 7:00 P.M. A two-hour lunch break is fairly common, but foreign-owned and northern firms tend to take less time. Banks are open from 8:30 A.M. to 1:30 P.M., and civil service offices are usually open from 8:00 A.M. to 2:00 P.M., with no break. August is a bad time to try to schedule business appointments, since most factories and businesses close or are operated with a very small staff.

Unless your Italian is fluent, you will probably want to use a translator. Many are available in the United States and in Italy. Business may be conducted in French or German, too, so be prepared to deal with several languages and to make sure that everyone understands all details.

When you arrive at your host's office, he or she will show you to your seat. The head of your delegation will sit at the middle of one side of a rectangular table, facing the head of the Italian group. Others in your party will also face the Italian group across the table.

The first part of the meeting will be devoted to getting acquainted. It will please your hosts if you compliment their country and city, and express your general desire to establish an ongoing business relationship. Questions about local artistic and cultural events will be welcome, and help you overcome the stereotypical view some Italians have of Americans as uncouth and uncultured, interested only in making money.

The north and south of Italy differ considerably. Dealing with the northern Italians will be much like dealing with the Swiss, French, or Germans. In the south, business may be done more as it is in Greece or in Arab countries. Long-term relationships are even more important than in the north, and trust must be built up over a long time. Business in general will be at a slower pace and conducted in a more ceremonious fashion.

As in many other countries, women are few in business. However, those who do make it in the Italian business world are likely to be sophisticated, well-to-do financially, and polished in their professional and social skills. Such women executives, however, expect to be treated like ladies.

If she is familiar with her material, an American businesswoman is likely to be treated professionally. However, if she is perceived to be "too young," her Italian counterparts might feel uncomfortable even if she is highly competent.

In this nation or elsewhere in Europe, women shake hands with each other as well as with men. The woman takes the initiative in handshakes with men, extending her hand first, even if the man outranks her in age or seniority.

If an American businesswoman is entertaining male colleagues in a restaurant, she should invite more than one Italian counterpart to prevent an unfavorable impression. There should be at least a couple of male guests.

RANK AND STATUS

Social rank and status are very important in Italy, although they are gradually becoming less so. Status, however, still derives exclusively from birth and class; it does not depend on wealth and is almost impossible to change, no matter how successful one becomes. This means that a U.S. firm should give some thought before sending Italian-American translators or even executives, no matter how prominent they might be in the United States, to negotiate in Italy.

FORMS OF ADDRESS

The head of the Italian group, whose identity will be obvious through his or her dealings with colleagues, will usually take the lead and introduce his or her associates. Introductions will be formal, including the title or position of each executive. The head of the U.S. team should introduce the American delegation in an equally formal manner and avoid saying anything like, "Just call him John." The Italians would find this disrespectful, and showing respect for colleagues is important to them.

Professional titles should always be used in addressing the Italians, unless you are given permission to do otherwise. This permission will probably only be to call someone "Signor Banzini," not to use the first name. That privilege is likely to take quite some time to earn.

On business cards and correspondence, Italians may use two last names. The second is the mother's last name; the first, the father's. In written correspondence, both names should be used. In conversation, however, only the father's name is used.

You may still encounter Italians with aristocratic titles. You should use the aristocratic title at the first introduction, but you can probably drop it after that and address the person by some less formidable but professional title. In general, however, you are safe in addressing someone as he or she was introduced and in remaining strictly formal until invited to do otherwise.

BUSINESS CARDS

In Italy, business cards are an important part of your identity. The farther south you go in Italy, the less widely English is understood and a bilingual business card would be more appropriate. If you have an M.B.A. or a Ph.D., print that on your card and it will impress businesspeople in both northern and southern Italy.

You may offer your card at your first encounter with an Italian executive, or you may wait until discussion suggests that further contact may be worthwhile.

BUSINESS DRESS

Italy is a fashion-conscious nation. Dress is very important. Polyester suits are definitely out, natural fibers in. For men, the style is still well tailored but conservative for serious business negotiations, with dark grey, blue, and black suits predominating. Three-piece suits are usually not worn unless it happens to be the current fashion. White shirts and black, laced shoes are the norm. However, loafers are acceptable in many circles, especially Guccis. Handmade shirts show that "you've made it," especially those initials on the left breast pocket—two initials only. Cotton shirts should be worn, not silk, which is considered "too pretentious."

Women executives in Europe emphasize sophistication and affluence in their dress and American women should do the same to gain the respect of male Italian executives. Classically styled dark suits are in order. Costume jewelry is out of place, but one item of good jewelry for accent is appropriate. Women should never wear "bow ties" with business suits; this will put you on a less competitive par with male counterparts. Cotton or silk dresses are more acceptable. More stylish and colorful clothes for business entertainment are acceptable for men and women.

GIFT-GIVING

Gifts of liquor are always appropriate. Beyond that, gifts should be chosen in relation to the recipient's taste and interest. If you are visiting a home, flowers for the wife (except chrysanthemums, which symbolize death and mourning) and chocolates for the family are always welcome. Only the finest of wines are acceptable; otherwise, wine should be avoided. Very good scotch is always appreciated.

Much gift-giving to people within the Italian government bureaucracy is common to make things run more smoothly. This practice, however, is illegal and the prudent visitor goes by the book, letting a well-prepared proposal and skillful, tactful negotiations stand on their own.

COMMUNICATION STYLES

Business executives in northern Italy (such as in the business centers of Milan and Turin) are quite sophisticated and part of the business elite in Europe. To be effective, you need to communicate with them as you would with business executives in northern Europe. Keep preliminary social talk to a minimum and get to the substantive part of your business proposal fairly soon. In southern Italy, on the other hand, you need to spend more time in preliminary talk to establish rapport with your counterparts.

Your presentation should be factual, detailed, logical, orderly, and concise. Avoid superlatives and exaggerations. Written communication, including charts, graphs, and other illustrations, should have all these elements, and should also be systematic and neat. A calm presentation and soft sell are likely to be more effective than an intensive, aggressive approach. Present your products/services on their own merits rather than trying to knock out the competition.

You should never talk with cigarette in mouth, hands in pockets, or conspicuous body gestures.

Nonverbal communication in Italy is in some ways different from that in the United States. An up-and-down nod of the head, with chin high and eyes closed, means "no," not "yes." People stand closer to one another when talking, and poking someone's shoulder to make a point is common. Normal conversation is often louder than it is in the United States, especially in southern Italy.

During presentations, project an air of total confidence in yourself and in your product. Do not tell jokes, for they will probably not be understood, and may be distracting.

Gestures with two hands may be inappropriate in some situations, so it is better always to use one hand. Finger gestures, it should be noted, mean in Italy what they do in the United States, so be careful!

Negotiating in Italy

Decision making in Italian organizations is usually concentrated with one executive or at most a few, and management is a top-down process. All executives are deferential to their superiors. Negotiations, ideally, should be between or among executives of equivalent rank. Middle-level people should be used for the preliminary meetings, and they should not expect to have immediate access to the top-level Italian executive. The U.S. firm should send high-level executives to stress the importance and seriousness of a negotiation.

The Italians are competent and shrewd businesspeople; therefore, vagueness in negotiations may not be because of ignorance. They will be well versed in world market conditions and in business details, and the visiting executive needs to be equally prepared. Business is not conducted on a crude bargaining level; the Italians expect set prices and good-faith negotiations over terms, rates, and discounts. It may take a longer time in Italy to conclude a business deal than it does in the United States. Patience and flexibility will help the visitor get along well.

For the negotiation, both sides will probably have an agenda which will be known and fairly flexible. Keep in mind that aesthetics are very important in Italy for presentations just as much as for dress. The style should be clear and exact, demonstrate a mastery of detail and language, and be well organized. Polish and elegance count for a great deal. Graphics should be pleasing, clear, and useful.

It is helpful to realize, when negotiating, that motivation differs somewhat between Italian and U.S. businesspeople. In the United States, money is often regarded as an end in itself. In Italy, money is often seen as merely the means by which one buys time for more meaningful pursuits: the arts, culture, leisurely and more enjoyable living. The U.S. executive who shows an appreciation for culture and the arts and is patient, elegant, and charming may somewhat disarm the Italians, who expect quite different behavior from Americans in general.

Subsequent meetings can be arranged when one series has concluded, or they can be arranged through correspondence. It is perfectly acceptable for the visiting U.S. executive to suggest a follow-up meeting. The Italians appreciate thank-you letters after meetings. These letters, and any correspondence to confirm future business arrangements, should be sent promptly.

There is little delegation of authority or effective communication between the different levels of management. As a result, business decision making is very slow. In government-owned enterprises, with bureaucratic red tape, the process is even slower and more cumbersome. Italian attitudes in small- and medium-sized companies do not rely on expert opinions, outside consultants, or in-house specialists. Instead, they rely more on their own impressionistic evaluations and judgments. Nor is there much feedback between superiors and subordinates, even on the middle and higher levels of management.

The implications of these business practices for American executives are twofold: patience is a virtue when doing business in this country and you should try to approach the key decision makers from the beginning, as even middle-echelon managers have little influence on the decisions of top managers.

The sanctity of written contracts is upheld by law in Italy. Agreements should be extremely detailed in letter and spirit, and as little as possible should be left to interpretation.

Although Italians are generally less litigious than people in the United States, having attorneys at all negotiating sessions is recommended. Italians tend to be somewhat vague in negotiations and agreements, and a lawyer can assist in defining and understanding details.

Business Entertaining

A good deal of business entertainment is done at private homes. Spouses do not attend business meals or banquets, but they are part of the social evenings in people's homes. If invited to a home, you are expected to be on time—not fashionably late, but not early either. During the evening you should compliment the food (but do not ask for the recipe). You may also offer to help serve if there are no servants, although your offer will probably be refused. You should not, however, ask to help with washing the dishes.

After the event, if you brought no gift, you may send flowers, although this is not expected. Thank-you notes are not sent, but a letter from you after you reach home would be appreciated. You are not expected to reciprocate for a meal at someone's home, except to entertain that person and his or her family if they visit the United States.

If you are largely in charge of the meeting and know it will take some time, be sure to arrange for a break with refreshments. If you break over the noon hour, remember that Italian executives are likely to live nearby and take at least two hours for lunch at home.

Italians consider it polite to keep the hands on or above the table while eating. They eat "European style"; that is, they hold the fork in the left hand, the knife or spoon in the right, and they do not switch them. When a course is finished, flatware is left on the plate.

General Tips

• Government office hours are 8:30 A.M. to 1:45 P.M. Monday through Friday. Senior staff members may return to their office in the evening by appointment.

• Most Italian firms are closed for vacation for the month of August.

- To get immediate attention to your correspondence, have it translated into Italian. You can expect large firms to respond in English.
- Religion and politics are very sensitive issues and should be approached cautiously or avoided altogether.
- Italians have a very relaxed approach to time. The Italian phrase "Dolce far niente"—"It's sweet to do nothing" personifies their attitude in social situations.
- Italians enjoy drinking wine but do not condone drunkenness. Wine is not used for escape but incorporated into their daily fare.

EXECUTIVE TRAVEL TO ITALY •

DOCUMENTS

U.S. citizens require only a valid passport and proof of citizenship for a stay up to 90 days. No visa is necessary.

INOCULATIONS

None are required of U.S. business travelers.

AIRPORTS

The distance from the Rome airport (Leonardo da Vinci) to the downtown area is 22 miles; from the Milan airport (Malpensa) to downtown —35 miles.

CUSTOMS

Personal belongings and jewelry, 400 cigarettes, and cigars and tobacco not to exceed 500 grams are allowed duty-free. Check with the airline regarding any specific items you may wish to bring.

U.S. EMBASSY

Via Veneto, 119/A, 00187 Rome
Phone: (06) 4674   Telex: 613425 or 610450

TRANSPORTATION

Although taxis are plentiful, it is recommended that you hire a car and a driver/translator for your stay, which will increase your status in the eyes of your Italian counterpart.

TIPPING

A service charge of 15 to 18 percent will be added to your hotel bill. On your restaurant bill do not be surprised to see the word *coperto* (meaning coverage charge) added to the bill. This charge will be as little as $2.00 per person. The service charge will be automatically added to the bill. However, an additional few dollars beyond this charge would be appreciated by the waiter or wine steward.

HOTELS

ROME

Hassler-Villa Medici
6 Piazza Trinita dei Monti
Phone: (06) 792651   Telex: 610208

Excelsior
125 Via Veneto
Phone: (06) 4708   Telex: 610232

Le Grand Hotel et de Roma
Via Vittorio Emanuele Orlando
Phone: (06) 4709   Telex: 610210

Lord Byron
5 Via de Notaris
Phone: (06) 3609541   Telex: 611217

MILAN

Excelsior Gallia
9 Piazza Duca d'Aosta
Phone: (02) 6277   Telex: 311160

Grand Hotel de Milan
29 Via Manzoni
Phone: (02) 870757

Palace Hotel
20 Piazza Repubblica
Phone: (02) 6336   Telex: 311026

Principe e Savoia
17 Piazza della Republica
Phone: (02) 6230   Telex: 310052

RESTAURANTS

ROME

Domus Aurea Monte Oppio Avenue Phone: 7315325	*Italian*
El Toulà 29 Via della Lupa Phone: 6786471	*Venetian,* *international*
Hostaria dell'Orso 93 Via Monte Brianzo Phone: 6564250	*Italian*
Passeto 14 Via Zanardelli Phone: 6543696	*Italian*

MILAN

Bagutta 14 Via Bagutta Phone: 702767	*Tuscan*
Brasera Meneghina 10 Via Circo Phone: 803004	*Italian*
El Toulà 6 Piazza Paolo Ferrari Phone: 870302	*Venetian,* *international*
Giannino 8 Via Amatore Sciesa Phone: 5452948	*Italian*
Gualtiero Marchesi 9 Via Bonvesin de la Riva Phone: 741246	*Haute cuisine*

Savini   *Italian*
11 Galleria Vittorio Emanuele
Phone: 8058343

TRAVEL TIPS

• Nightlife is limited in Rome, but Jackie O, Gil's, and Bella Blu
are chic, sophisticated spots to visit—other than the large rooms
in major hotels.
• The opera season runs from November until May and the Teatro dell'Opera is the main opera hall. Rome has many theatres,
and drama productions appear to be their forte. The Foro Italico
is a large sports complex where soccer is a major attraction.
• Check with your hotel concierge for the best local tourist guide
to see properly the wonders of this historic city. The Pantheon,
founded as a temple in 27 B.C., Saint Peter's in the Vatican, the
Vatican Grottoes and Treasury, the Colosseum, and the Galleria
Nazionale d'Arte are only a few of the wondrous treasures to see
during your stay.
• English-speaking doctors and pharmacists are available in most
of the larger cities.
• International telephone, telex, and cable facilities are available.
When calling the United States call collect—station to station is
less than calling direct. Most hotels will have bilingual secretarial
assistance, or can recommend secretaries.
• Sensible precautions should be observed in crowded areas to
keep your valuables protected from pickpockets.
• In Milan, the seventeenth-century Palazzo di Brera is a 38-
room gallery containing many magnificent art masterpieces.
Modern art is housed in the Galleria d'Arte Moderna.
• Milan boasts of Nepentha, the best place for nighttime entertainment.

THE NETHERLANDS

Cultural Overview

The kingdom of the Netherlands, or Holland, is approximately the size of the states of Massachusetts and Connecticut combined. It is geographically well situated in Europe, east of Germany and north of Belgium. The kingdom also includes the Netherlands Antilles, islands in the Caribbean.

The Netherlands is a constitutional monarchy with a democratic parliament. Since 1890, the Dutch sovereigns have all been queens. The constitution dates from 1814. The Dutch government is composed of three main branches: the Crown (Monarch, Council of Ministers, and Council of State); the States General (Parliament); and the courts. The monarch's functions are primarily ceremonial. The ministers, who initiate legislation and formulate and execute policy, also serve in various government departments. The Council of State is an advisory board made up of members of the royal family and court-appointed people with specific experience. The States General consists of the First Chamber, whose members are elected for six years by all 11 provinces; and the Second Chamber, whose members are elected by the direct vote of the Dutch people every four years. The judiciary has 62 regional and 19 district courts, five courts of appeal, and a supreme court. All judicial appointments are made by the monarch at the specific advice of the government.

The major political parties are: Christian Democratic Appeal (CDA), a center–right religious coalition; the right-wing Party of Freedom and Democracy (VVD); the left-wing Labor party (PvdA); and the left-wing Democrats. For years, no one party has been able to gain control of Parliament, and coalitions have been formed in order to administer the government.

The Netherlands has been referred to as the gateway to Europe. The excellent coastal location and the dearth of natural resources has obligated the nation to be trade dependent. As a result, the Dutch economy is more sensitive to changing world conditions than that of any other industrialized nation. Holland does possess abundant resources of natural gas and slate, but must import most of its raw materials and semimanufactured products. About 70 percent of what the Dutch produce is exported. Leading industries include petroleum refining, natural gas, electronics equipment, metal products, and chemical fertilizers. Holland is the world's third largest producer of natural gas.

Agriculture is most important, with 70 percent of the land under cultivation. Dutch cheeses, livestock, and flowers find markets worldwide. Services in banking and finance, insurance, tourism, trade, and transport account for 45 percent of net income.

In spite of high unemployment, the Netherlands economy is experiencing an upturn. A center–right coalition government has attempted to cut deficit spending, reduce the tremendous cost of the extensive social programs, and improve incentives for business. Industrial wage and price restraints remain a prime objective.

About 40 percent of the 14.4 million people live in the two western provinces, North and South Holland, which also contain the three largest cities: Amsterdam (the capital); Rotterdam (the port), and The Hague (the seat of government). Holland's people are referred to as Netherlanders, or the Dutch.

The nation has a high population density: 1,041 people per square mile (compared to 58 in the U.S.); 40 percent are under age 25.

Holland is situated at the mouth of three large rivers: the Meuse, the Scheldt, and the Rhine. Half of the country contains flat land below sea level; this has motivated the Dutch ingenuity to develop methods of keeping the land dry. Holland is famous for its numerous dikes, windmills, tulips, canals, patchwork farms, and polders (land reclaimed from the sea). The Netherlands has a temperate climate with year-round rainfall and gusty winds.

The population is primarily Dutch, mostly of German stock, with some Gallo–Celtic mixture. There are also Indonesians and Surinamese who have emigrated to Holland. Nederland, or Dutch, is the national language (the word *Nederlands* means lowlands), and English, German, and French are widely understood and spoken.

Family ties are strong in Holland, and children are taught to show respect for their parents. Although queens have long been the monarchs, very few women enter business in Holland.

Holland's literacy rate is high: about 98 percent. School attendance is compulsory from age 6 to 16, after which a student may attend a regular high school (HAVO); a preuniversity school, which is called a gymnasium or an atheneum; or a vocational training school. Both public and private schools receive government subsidies. Religion has long been a factor in Dutch life, starting with the Reformation-inspired revolt from Spain in the sixteenth century. Religion still has some influence in social and political life. The royal family are members of the Protestant Dutch Reformed Church, as are 40 percent of the people. The 40 percent who are Roman Catholics live primarily in the southern provinces of Noordbrabant and Limburg.

The Netherlands and the United States enjoy the oldest unbroken diplomatic relationship in the world: 200 years in 1982.

Business Opportunities

The Netherlands has many obvious advantages as an export market for U.S. business. It is strategically located, unhampered by tariff barriers, and commercially and administratively efficient. The Netherlands also has highly developed facilities for cargo handling, warehousing, and distribution by truck, rail, and barge to all of Western Europe.

The United States exports oilseeds, chemicals, animal feed grains, high-tech, medical, and transportation equipment to Holland. There is a growing market for computers, software, and peripheral equipment. High growth is also expected in the service industries and finance, commerce, and medical support systems. Other potential markets include oil and gas production equipment; laboratory, scientific, and engineering equipment; automobile parts and accessories; apparel; and medical and health care equipment.

The Dutch government has a liberal attitude toward trade. It does not discriminate between domestic and foreign companies. U.S. executives have exactly the same rights and obligations as their Dutch counterparts. Import and export licenses are rarely required; what regulations there are present few obstacles.

To encourage the development of specially designated areas, the Dutch government offers a wide range of incentives to investors, including tax-free bonuses, capital grants, interest subsidies, and credit guarantees. For details write:

Ministry of Economic Affairs
P.O. Box 20101, 2500 EC

The Hague, The Netherlands
Phone: 070-798911

Initiating Contact

To initiate contact with Dutch companies, U.S. firms should approach any large investment banking house; any international bank with representation in Holland; or a Big Eight accounting firm. Dutch merchant/investment banks can also be valuable for business introductions. One such bank is Pierson, Heldring & Pierson, with offices in the three main Dutch cities.

For small- and medium-sized businesses, the ideal starting point would be the World Trade Centers in Rotterdam, Eindhoven, and Amsterdam. Their primary aim is to promote international trade by supplying information on trade-related subjects; identifying appropriate trading partners; establishing contacts; and arranging introductions.

Trade fairs and exhibitions offer the opportunity to display products and services. Many are held in the primary exhibition centers in Amsterdam and Utrecht. Details can be obtained from the Dutch Chambers of Commerce, or from Dutch consulates.

The U.S. Foreign Commercial Service (FCS), which has representation in Holland, can also help U.S. firms to penetrate or expand their sales in Dutch markets through information gathering and reporting, promotional events, and introductions. For the FCS, or for general information concerning the Netherlands, contact one of the following:

U.S. Department of Commerce
International Trade Administration
Netherlands Country Specialist
14th Street and Constitution Avenue
Washington, D.C. 20230
Phone: (202) 377-5401

Royal Netherlands Embassy
4200 Linnean Avenue N.W.
Washington, D.C. 20008
Phone: (202) 244-5300   Telex: 89494

World Trade Center Amsterdam (R-1P)
Prinses Irenestraat, P.O. Box 7030
1007 JA Amsterdam, The Netherlands
Phone: (01) 20-5759111   Telex: 12808

Netherlands Consulate General
1 Rockefeller Plaza
New York, N.Y. 10020
Phone: (212) 246-1429

Netherlands Chamber of Commerce for America/
    Netherlands Center for Trade Promotion
Bezuidenhoutseweg 181
2594AH, The Hague, The Netherlands
Phone: (070) 478234   Telex: 32306

Netherlands Chamber of Commerce
1 Rockefeller Plaza
New York, N.Y. 10020
(212) 265-6460

General economic information, statistical data, advice on government investment policies, assistance in research, and evaluation and implementation of investment opportunities information can be obtained from:

Netherlands Industrial Commission
1 Rockefeller Plaza
New York, NY 10020
Phone: 246-1434   Telex: 125240

Business Protocol and Procedures

BUSINESS ENVIRONMENT

Commercial offices are open weekdays from 9:00 A.M. to 5:00 or 5:30 P.M., with one hour for lunch at 12:30 P.M. Banks start at the same time but close at 4:00 P.M.; in some large cities, they stay open Thursday or Friday evenings. Government offices are open from 8:30 A.M. to 5:00 P.M. weekdays. It is best to schedule morning meetings.

It is important to be punctual, and to confirm appointments before you arrive. Dutch executives travel frequently, and it is sensible to check beforehand to be sure that they will be there when you arrive.

There is no set procedure for seating arrangements during business meetings, but usually each negotiating team sits on the opposite sides of a rectangular table. If at later stages a senior executive joins the working sessions, this executive sits at the head of the table.

Interpreters are not necessary, the Dutch speak English fluently.

RANK AND STATUS

The corporate hierarchy in the Netherlands differs from that of a U.S. firm. Usually, there is an identifiable CEO or chairperson who is head of the firm. But the daily business of a Dutch corporation is often conducted by one or more managing directors, equal in authority but with different responsibilities. They may even rotate jobs on occasion.

Managing directors are appointed by the general assembly of shareholders during their annual meeting. Dutch companies do not have a board of directors but a board of supervisory directors, which supervises the company's management board. The management board is composed of two or more managing directors. The supervisory board, mandatory by law for large corporations and optional for smaller companies, is composed of at least three members. It has the authority to dismiss managers and to approve major management decisions.

The management board formulates corporate policy, and is responsible for preparing the annual financial statements. Its decisions may be challenged by the shareholders or by a trade union in court. The Dutch Court of Appeals in Amsterdam can also change management decisions, and may dismiss and replace managing directors. In most large companies, the management board is also accountable to the shareholders.

What level of management you will deal with depends on the importance of the proposed business venture. Any joint venture will eventually be directed to the top levels of management for negotiation.

FORMS OF ADDRESS

For correspondence in English, it is acceptable to use "Mr.," "Mrs.," or "Miss" as forms of address. If the business correspondence is in Dutch, correct use of business titles is required. Titles are considered important and family titles, educational degrees, and business titles should always be used in correspondence.

A handshake is appropriate when greeting people of all ages. Usually your host will introduce you but, if not, it is proper to introduce yourself as you shake hands. When leaving, shake hands again. It is best to use last names until a closer relationship is established, at which time you are invited to use first names.

BUSINESS CARDS

Present your business cards to all the executives you meet. It is not necessary to print the cards in Dutch. However, the longevity of a business is impressive to the Dutch. If you represent an old established firm, have the founding date printed on the card.

BUSINESS DRESS

Most Dutch executives dress conservatively. Follow their example. Men should wear dark suits to meetings. Women should wear suits or dresses.

GIFT-GIVING

Business gift-giving is not customary. Giving something ostentatious or extravagant would be viewed as unfriendly. It may be acceptable to give company logos or U.S. memorabilia.

COMMUNICATION STYLES

The Dutch are conservative in behavior, and courteous and earnest in their business dealings. Many are well organized and dislike doing things spontaneously. On the whole, they view people from the United States with a mixture of admiration, delight, and paternalistic reproach. They welcome the friendly, outgoing nature of the U.S. executive as a change from the more reserved European. But they are also wary of an instant, too-friendly rapport, and of high-pressured salesmanship. What the Dutch do respect is the expertise in business development and administration and the technological know-how possessed by Americans.

Continued eye contact is important, conveying interest and respect, as are facial expressions. Avoid informal physical gestures such as slapping on the back. The only acceptable contact is when shaking hands or touching a good friend's shoulder.

Negotiating in The Netherlands

Competition in Holland's marketplace is tough, and both the Dutch executive and the consumer are very demanding. They are quality and price conscious, expect delivery dates to be honored, and demand courteous, competent service. They also respond with unshakable loyalty if you perform as expected. Dutch businesspeople are among the most sophisticated in Europe and prefer to deal with associates in long-term relationships.

There is little preliminary conversation in meetings before you settle down to business. You can expect to come to the point right away. When making your presentation, keep in mind the value of comprehensive and succinct information, and the competitiveness of the Dutch market. If it is possible, prepare documents that outline your proposal and have them ready for the meeting to facilitate free-flowing discussion of the proposal. Visual aids that clarify the major objectives are valuable tools. Stress economies of scale and formal quantity discounts; the Dutch may perceive lower price as lower value. Package your discounts with valid reasons.

The Dutch are methodical and conscientious when they make business decisions. After presenting your proposal, expect executives to request time to consider it at length. Rushing them to respond or pressuring them will be counterproductive. Depending on the size of the firm, any agreement reached with a managing director or equivalent in rank will be subject to ratification by the supervisory board.

It is not necessary to have an attorney present at the first meeting, which is to present a proposal, but it is advisable to prepare a letter of intent or a memorandum of understanding at the meeting's conclusion, summing up the terms and conditions discussed. You should have an attorney at subsequent meetings. It is proper to ask your Dutch colleague at what stage this would be appropriate. Also, it is best to have legal contracts drawn up for agreements with agents. In the Netherlands, oral agreements and statements of intent are binding.

The Dutch government purchasing policy is to issue tender summaries (formal offers) in Dutch and English. All other tender documents are in Dutch. Bids made in English may be refused; it is better to make the bid in Dutch. For highly technical projects in fields such as aircraft and electronics, bids can be made in English, provided the specifications are drawn up in English. The minimum deadline time for bidding on tenders is 30 days; 40 days is average. Tender summaries need only be a few pages in length.

The Netherlands Government Purchasing Office generally uses the open tendering system. Selective tendering is usually done by entities that deal with construction contracts. Although U.S. firms do not require a local agent to bid on government tenders, it may well have a positive influence on a bid. If interested in participating in future Dutch tendering, you should confirm that interest in writing with the Netherlands Government Purchasing Office. U.S. firms are advised to be exact on pricing, using CIF quotations not FOB; also, metric standards, and electric current in 220 volts, 50 cycles measurement. U.S. firms should also be aware of the need to meet Dutch and EEC specifications.

Suggestions to help you negotiate successfully:

• Avoid the hard sell, but point out the high quality, good construction, and practicality of your U.S.-made product.
• It is important to establish trust and credibility, since the Dutch cherish long-term business and personal relationships.
• The Dutch are polite. If a conversation initially centers on non-business-related subjects, do not rush them.
• The Dutch admire the British people. To enhance the appeal of your proposal, find English parallels and comparisons.
• Prompt replies to price quotes, orders, and correspondence are critical. Maintain close contact with your Dutch colleagues.
• U.S. exporters should plan on stockpiling in Europe to service and supply customers speedily.
• Since oral agreements are often binding, be careful before promising terms, dates, and deliveries.
• Insisting on an interpreter may offend the Dutch by making them feel their English is not adequate.
• It is best to support your distributor's sales efforts by sharing advertising costs.
• Be aware of, and do quote, competitive credit terms. Letters of credit are generally disliked by Dutch executives. In most cases, sight or time drafts are used as the means of payment.
• For a list of attorneys practicing in Holland, contact the Office of European Community International Trade Administration, U.S. Department of Commerce, Washington, D.C. 20230.
• There is less friction between management and labor in Holland and fewer labor strikes than in other countries.

Business Entertaining

The Dutch executive likes both to entertain and to be entertained. Business lunches and dinners are common, and many deals have been struck over coffee or cognac. Usually, spouses are not invited along if business is going to be discussed. But when a deal is closed, spouses should be invited to the celebratory dinner or evening activity. Your colleague's spouse will be seated next to you.

The Dutch refer to 6:30 as "half-seven." Be sure to clarify times to avoid misunderstandings.

If you are invited to a dinner party at your colleague's home, the lady of the house may serve herself first, a tradition from medieval times when it was necessary to prove the food had not been poisoned. Unless otherwise announced, men wait until all the women are seated before taking their own seats.

It is proper to bring flowers (an uneven number) and present them unwrapped to your hostess. Should your host pick you up at the hotel, it is appropriate to ask to stop at a florist on the way. Do not bring wine, unless your colleague is also a close friend. The Dutch have fine wine cellars, and the executive could be insulted by such a gesture. You should leave about an hour or an hour and a half after dinner is finished.

All types of food are eaten with fork and knife, including sandwiches, fruit, and sometimes pieces of bread. The Dutch hold the fork in the left hand, the knife in the right. Strive to eat everything on your plate; asking for seconds is very complimentary to your hostess.

Do not get up during a meal, as this is considered rude. You may smoke between courses, but ask first. If the hostess leaves the table for the kitchen, the men should rise as she returns.

General Tips

- The Dutch are politically oriented. So do some homework on current events before arriving, but avoid being contentious.
- Acknowledge the Dutch Royal Family. The Dutch are fond of them and many have pictures of the Queen in their home.
- Men should stand when a woman enters the room.

• The Dutch take great pride in their homes. Compliment them on the paintings, carpeting, and furnishings.
• Personal compliments should only be given when people know each other well, and only if they are sincere.
• The Dutch do value their privacy. You may ask personal questions to show interest, but do not pry.
• Good topics of conversation are travel, vacations, soccer, cycling, and ice skating.
• Avoid discussion of money or prices.
• Women executives will have little difficulty taking a Dutch male executive to dinner, especially if they use a credit card.
• Refrain from impromptu suggestions.
• When using the telephone, one should say "Good morning; this is Mr. Smith speaking," instead of just "Hello." The other person will state his or her business when replying.
• Businesswomen should not be offended by queries regarding their marital status, or why they chose to pursue a career rather than raise a family. Use patience and humor and the Dutch will take the hint.
• Stick to business for the most part and avoid personal questions.

EXECUTIVE TRAVEL TO THE NETHERLANDS •

DOCUMENTS
A valid passport is the only requirement for a U.S. citizen.

INOCULATIONS
None are required for U.S. citizens.

AIRPORT
Schiphol Airport is located 12 miles from Amsterdam, and the trip to the downtown area is about 25 minutes. There are excellent rail connections to all major cities from the airport.

CUSTOMS

There are no currency restrictions and customs procedures are fairly simple; you can import a reasonable amount of any item for your own personal use. Visitors from outside Europe should not bring more than 400 cigarettes, 100 cigars, and one liter of liquor or two liters of wine. Gifts up to $90 in value are duty-free.

U.S. EMBASSY

Lange Voorhout 102
APO NY 09159, The Hague
Phone: (070) 624911   Telex: (044) 31016

TRANSPORTATION

Major cities are connected by rail, and the highway system is modern. For your stay it is recommended that a car and driver be retained.

TIPPING

All hotels include a 15 percent service charge and VAT (value-added tax) on the bill and it is printed on their rate cards and menus. Extra gratuities are welcome for special service. Taxi drivers include tips in their fees.

HOTELS

AMSTERDAM

Amstel Hotel
1 Professor Tulipplein
Phone: 020-226-060   Telex: 11004

Amsterdam Hilton
138 Apollolaan
Phone: 020-780-780   Telex: 11025

Amsterdam Marriott
19–21 Stadhouderdkada
Phone: 020-835-151   Telex: 15087

Apollo
2 Apollolaan
Phone: 020-735-922   Telex: 14084

Hotel de l'Europe
2–4 Nieuwe Doelenstraat
Phone: 020-234-836   Telex: 12081

Hotel Okura Amsterdam
175 Ferdinand Bolstraat
Phone: 020-787-111   Telex: 16182

Sonesta Amsterdam
1 Kattengat
Phone: 020-212-223   Telex: 17149

THE HAGUE

Hotel Des Indes
54–56 Lange Voorhout
Phone: (070) 469553   Telex: 31196

Kurhaus House
30 Gevers Deynootplein
Phone: (070) 520-052   Telex: 33295

Promenade
1 van Stolkweg
Phone: (070) 574121   Telex: 31162

ROTTERDAM

Hilton International
10 Weena
Phone: (010) 144044   Telex: 22666

The Park Hotel
70-72 Westersingel
Phone: (010) 363611   Telex 22020

RESTAURANTS

AMSTERDAM

De Boerderij   *International*
69 Korte Leidsedwarsstraat
Phone: 236929

La Rive   *Continental*
Amstel Hotel
1 Professor Tulipplein
Phone: 226060

Swarte Schaep   *Dutch*
24 Korte Leidsedwarsstraat
Phone: 223021

Vijff Vlieghen   *Dutch*
294–302 Spuitstraat
Phone: 236404

THE HAGUE

Saur   *Seafood*
51 Lange Voorhout
Phone: 463344

ROTTERDAM

Cote de Boeuf   *Continental*
Hilton International
10 Weena
Phone: 144044

Coq d'Or   *French*
25 Van Vollenhovenstraat
Phone: 366405

TRAVEL TIPS

• The telephone system is excellent and direct dial service is available to the United States and most parts of Europe. Cable, telegram, and telex facilities are efficient and readily available.
• Good medical and dental attention are readily available.
• Museums of the Dutch masters and art galleries of present-day artists, the Royal Palace, canal boat rides, the flower markets, are all not to be missed.
• Gambling casinos similar to Las Vegas or Monte Carlo, with blackjack and roulette, are located in the towns at Zandvoort on the North Sea, Scheveningen a little further down the coast, and in Valkenburg, Limburg.
• Using either "Holland" or "The Netherlands" in conversation is correct, and will not offend the Dutch.

• The Netherlands has at least twelve symphony orchestras and a great number of music ensembles.

• All flower bulbs to be sent or taken out of the country must be inspected by the Plant Disease Service.

• Be aware that a shop clerk waits on only one person at a time and may even escort the customer to the door. Never interrupt, no matter how much of a hurry you are in.

SWITZERLAND

Cultural Overview

Tucked into an Alpine pocket, Switzerland (officially called the Confederation of Helvetian States) is roughly the size of Connecticut, Rhode Island, and Massachusetts combined; its population size is approximately that of New York City. This small country, however, has an important reputation as a center for banking, precision industries, and tourism, and many countries vie to do business there. German, French, or Italian customs and attitudes shape the culture in different regions. Appropriate business or social conduct in an area depends a great deal on what is acceptable in the neighboring country. As a result, there are German, French, and Italian zones of influence within Switzerland, with each zone using the language of its predominant culture.

With its natural resources largely limited to hydropower, timber, and salt, the nation has developed as an importer of raw materials and energy-related items and an exporter of high-value, high-quality finished products. Its industry and economy in general have been challenged in recent years by technological advances and other changes in the world's economy, but the Swiss response has been to increase productivity, update and automate its industry, and maintain the high quality of its manufactured goods. Switzerland possesses a highly skilled labor force.

Because the country is so dependent on foreign commerce, its trade policies are liberal. The constitution guarantees free enterprise and a free market economy, and relatively few laws affect the investment climate. The purchase of real estate by foreigners, the licensing of foreign banks, and permits issued to foreign workers, however, do come under government regulation.

Switzerland is a federation of 22 cantons, or states (19 full and six half-cantons), divided into about three thousand municipalities (called communes). It stretches over an area of 15,941 square miles. The Swiss form of confederation (first established in 1291) is looser than the federal form of government in the United States, with power significantly decentralized and each canton maintaining its own autonomy. The federal government does have exclusive power over foreign affairs, national defense, customs, post and telecommunications, railways, legislation on civil, criminal, and industrial problems, and some aspects of social security and taxes. The significance of this system to foreign businesspeople is that they will need to pay attention not only to trade laws and regulations of the Swiss federal government but also to those of the individual cantons, as they have more powers than state governments in the United States.

Ninety-nine percent of the Swiss people are literate. The nation is divided about equally between Protestants and Catholics. Its climate is moderate, with warm summers and cold winters. In the Alpine mountains, of course, the winters are severe and long.

Business Opportunities

Switzerland is a most attractive market, and competition for Swiss business is formidable. U.S. firms do well by stressing their products' superior quality, cost effectiveness, and technological sophistication. Strict adherence to such contractual details as delivery dates and terms of payment, and careful attention to quality and service guarantees, are essential to maintain a place in the Swiss market.

Since Switzerland is Europe's most highly computerized country, computers and peripheral equipment are much in demand. U.S. firms can gain and maintain an edge in this field through aggressive marketing strategies that offer complete systems and strong support services.

U.S. firms have been major suppliers of process control instruments and systems and microprocessors. To maintain their share of this market, however, more careful attention will have to be paid to exacting Swiss standards.

There are other opportunities for U.S. firms in supplying industrial and commercial security systems, apparel, sporting goods, and biomedical equipment. In marketing biomedical equipment, U.S. firms need to stress increased cost effectiveness and technological advances, and should pursue vigorous marketing strategies. This particular market has become increasingly competitive.

Local industry in Switzerland also welcomes cooperation with U.S. firms in the form of licensing and joint ventures.

Initiating Contact

Trade fairs are excellent places to make business contacts and generate sales in Switzerland. In the past, price and quality were the main features the Swiss sought in U.S. products exhibited at these fairs, but novelty and styling are becoming more important. The principal trade fairs include the International Motor Show in Geneva, in March; the Swiss Industries Fair *(Mustermesse)*, and the European Watch, Clock, and Jewelry Fair, in Basel each spring; the Swiss National Fair *(Comptoir Suisse)* for the national agricultural and industrial products, in Lausanne in September; and OLMA, an agricultural fair, in St. Gall in October.

Major Swiss banks in the United States serve as intermediaries between American businesses and potential Swiss customers (as well as Swiss customers and prospective American buyers). The heads of the international divisions can provide useful initial contacts and introductions. The major Swiss banks operating in the United States, by order of size and importance, are: Union Bank of Switzerland; Swiss Banking Corporation; and Credit Suisse. All have U.S. headquarters offices in New York and some have branches also in other major cities.

Initial contacts can also be obtained through the several U.S. and Swiss governmental and nongovernmental trade offices listed below.

To arrange an appointment by mail with a Swiss organization, write at least two to three weeks in advance. An appointment can be made by telephone or telex as little as three or four days in advance.

The embassies can provide information on doing business in Switzerland, as well as initial contacts and introductions.

For information on business opportunities and making contact with Swiss business organizations, the following agencies can be very useful:

Swiss Office for the Development of Trade
Avant-Poste Ch-1001

Lausanne, Switzerland
Phone: 021-20-3231

Swiss Consulate Trade Department
444 Madison Avenue
New York, NY 10022
Phone: (212) 757-5944
(Offices also in Chicago, New Orleans, Los Angeles, and San Francisco.)

World Trade Center
P.O. Box 306
CH 1215, Geneva—Airport 15, Switzerland
Phone: 022-989-989   Telex: 289950

Swiss–American Chamber of Commerce
Talackerstrasse 41, CH-8001, Zurich, Switzerland
Phone: 01-211-2454

Swiss Desk
International Trade Administration
U.S. Department of Commerce
14th Street and Constitution Avenue
Washington, D.C. 20230
Phone: (202) 377-2897

In addition, the Swiss-American Chamber of Commerce publishes a yearbook that lists all Swiss companies represented in the United States. The cost is $100. The yearbook is also available for referral in Swiss consulate offices in the major U.S. cities.

Business Protocol and Procedures

BUSINESS ENVIRONMENT

While most businesses are open the usual 9:00 A.M. to 5:00 P.M. with an hour for lunch, many businesses have extended hours during the summer, starting at 8:00 A.M., with a two-hour lunch break from noon to two o'clock. Some Swiss executives work much longer hours, starting as early as 7:30 A.M. The visiting executive, however, should not try to schedule appointments for the beginning or end of the day, as these times are usually set aside for in-office activities.

Punctuality is important all over Switzerland, and the Swiss expect replies to their business letters to be very prompt. Other subtleties of business conduct, such as the importance of preliminary small-talk meetings, vary from region to region. In northern areas near Germany the German language prevails, and so do German ideas of etiquette and proper conduct. In southern Switzerland, the Italian language and business style are dominant, while the French influence permeates those areas in between. In general, in the German areas, business will be conducted in a more formal atmosphere and at a quicker pace. In the French and Italian areas, people will be more casual and business will be conducted at a more relaxed pace.

You will not need an interpreter to do business in Switzerland, even for written communications, as English is widely spoken in all parts of the nation.

RANK AND STATUS

The Swiss expect the negotiator to be technically competent and to have a position of sufficient authority to conclude an agreement. The nature of the transaction determines the appropriate level of management to approach when doing business with a Swiss company. To establish formal ties with a company, a senior officer of the firm should contact his equivalent in rank. In dealing with an international company, you would first contact the head of the international division in the United States. To establish a joint venture between two companies, contact the top man in the firm. Long-term agreements or contracts would be in the domain of the president of the company.

The Swiss equivalent of the title of president might be president, chairman, director, general director, or general manager. The equivalent of a vice president would use that title or *Prokurist*, which means an officer with authority to sign for the company. The head of a very large firm would be the *Geschaeftsfuehrer*, the equal of an executive vice president.

FORMS OF ADDRESS

As a rule, refer to everyone by their title and family name. Never go to a first-name basis unless the Swiss take the initiative. Men and women are greeted with a handshake and a greeting including the person's title. For example, you would greet a doctor as "Herr Doktor" and his wife as "Frau Doktor."

BUSINESS CARDS

Upon arrival for a first meeting, present the receptionist with your business card. Be certain your contacts in the company each receive one. It is not necessary to have the cards translated, as almost all Swiss businesspeople speak English. If you represent an established older firm, have the founding year printed on the card. Include any titles and degrees you may hold as well as your corporate title.

BUSINESS DRESS

There is a large emphasis placed on appearances, so care is required in choice of dress as well as posture. For business meetings, conservative, well-tailored suits and ties are appropriate. For women, tailored dresses or suits are the norm.

GIFT-GIVING

A good bottle of liquor, such as cognac, is proper as a business gift. Avoid large or expensive gifts, which are considered vulgar and ostentatious. If invited to a meal in a Swiss home, nonpersonal gifts are considered in good taste. Flowers are customary, and are presented unwrapped. Choose colors other than red (symbolizing passion) and never give chrysanthemums or white asters, as these are considered funeral flowers. Unless there are more than nine flowers in the bouquet, arrange to give an uneven number of flowers. Other acceptable gifts are fine candy and chocolate. Send flowers to your hostess beforehand, if invited to a large social occasion, and afterward if invited to a home on the spur of the moment.

COMMUNICATION STYLES

Eye contact conveys interest and respect. Conversation space is similar to American practices. One should avoid informal physical gestures, such as a slap on the back. As the Swiss are reserved by nature, they are suspicious of overenthusiasm and hard sell. It is best to be somewhat reserved and correct. They prefer reticence and have a sharp, dry wit. Coarse language and humor are to be scrupulously avoided.

Negotiating in Switzerland

Swiss executives are well known for their financial acumen and their personal and professional integrity. To deal with them effectively, it is essential to be very knowledgeable about your business and theirs and to be prepared to negotiate on their terms.

Decision making is relatively slow and deliberate in Switzerland, and patience is a virtue in negotiations. Establishing a long-term relationship is most important. To cultivate this, ongoing personal contact through visits and communication is essential.

Most Americans operating in Switzerland conduct their business deals in Zurich or Bern. Since these cities are in the German-speaking part of the country, Swiss business practices also reflect those of Germany. Consequently, negotiations there should take place as they would in Frankfurt or Hamburg. Be formal, factual, thorough, and logical in your approach.

The soft sell is likely to be more effective than an aggressive approach, as executives in that part of the country believe that a good product should speak for itself. Draw attention to quality features of your product and let your counterparts recognize them by samples and technical documentation. Do not play up superiority of your goods and services; emphasize instead mutuality of interests and tangible immediate benefits even more than future values.

In dealing with the federal government, technical superiority is again more important than price. The federal government exercises a great deal of caution in inviting bids. The authorities are not required to inform the bidders of the tender that has been accepted, or of the reason for the choice. Foreign firms are sometimes required to have a Swiss bank guarantee.

Many public projects are carried out by the local authorities, cantonal or communal. They usually prefer to deal with suppliers in their own region. The cantonal and communal authorities, unlike the federal, are required to inform bidders of the tender accepted, and the reasons for the selection.

If you plan to maintain a permanent representative or an office in Switzerland, you should know that the organization of Swiss corporations is much like that of U.S. firms. The shareholders approve laws and amendments, appoint the board of directors, and have other responsibilities similar to those of U.S. stockholders. Officers are appointed by the board of directors, a majority of whom must be residents and citizens of Switzerland. The chairperson must be a resident, but not necessarily a citizen, of the country. Most American businesses that have an ongoing physical presence in Switzerland are organized as Swiss corporations, or as branches of a corporation.

Lawyers will not play a major role in the course of business negotiations in any part of Switzerland. Your Swiss counterparts are likely to make use of a variety of preprinted legal forms. If additional clauses or modifications are needed, they are likely to add or modify them without the help of a lawyer. In major transactions, however, professional legal staff will be involved (but in the documentation rather than in the negotiation side of the transaction). In either case the legal documentation will be detailed, comprehensive, and precise, leaving little room for subsequent misinterpretation.

Business Entertaining

Business dinners are more common than business lunches in Switzerland. A business lunch is more likely to be in the company cafeteria than in a restaurant, and any business entertaining is more likely to be in a restaurant than at home.

Consider it an honor to be invited to a Swiss home as the Swiss are very private people. If you are the guest of honor, expect to be seated in the middle of one side of the table (not at the head). The Swiss, like most Europeans, hold the fork in the left hand, the knife in the right, and do not switch implements while eating. It is important to keep your hands and wrists on the table at all times. It is considered very impolite to put your hands in your lap after you are finished eating.

Never begin to drink your wine until the host has made an official toast. It is polite, when a toast has been made, to look your host in the eye and say, "To your health." The toast should be made in the language of the region your host is from. It is also expected that you clink glasses with everyone at the table. You will probably find cocktail and dinner parties to be very intimate and the host very selective as to the guest list. Before entering, you should go through a brief ritual of wiping your shoes on the mat, even if they are dry and clean.

In a home, it is polite to offer to help, even though your offer will probably be declined. Dinner parties end around midnight. If there are Swiss guests, take your cue about leaving from them and, when leaving, shake hands all around.

General Tips

• In all parts of Switzerland, the word used for thanking someone is always the French "merci." The Swiss use it often and are impressed when visitors do the same.

• In a restaurant, it is acceptable to ask a waiter for a description of a dish before ordering it.

• The Swiss consider it impolite to keep your hands in your pockets during conversation. Crossing your legs is acceptable, but stretching them out is not.

• In choosing wines, select local Swiss labels, even if they may not seem as desirable as some others.

• As a general rule, when you do business in a given part of Switzerland, take your cues from the neighboring country that each region emulates. For additional specific details, see corresponding sections in the chapters on Germany, France, and Italy.

EXECUTIVE TRAVEL TO SWITZERLAND   •

DOCUMENTS

U.S. citizens need only a valid passport for business travel to Switzerland, visits not to exceed 60 days.

INOCULATIONS

None are required for U.S. citizens.

AIRPORTS

Cointrin International Airport (Geneva)—20 minutes from city.
Kloten Airport (Zurich)—30 minutes from city.

CUSTOMS

Visitors may bring in duty-free 200 cigarettes, 50 cigars, two liters of wine, and one liter of spirits. There are no restrictions on the import or export of currency.

U.S. EMBASSY

Jubilaemstrasse 93, 3005 Bern
Phone: (031) 437011   Telex: 32128

TRANSPORTATION

The country has very good public transportation. It is recommended that business executives hire a car and a driver/translator during their stay.

TIPPING

Service charges are usually included in the bill. If not, a 15 percent tip should be handed to the waiter (not left on the table). Taxi drivers expect 10 percent.

HOTELS

ZURICH

Baur au Lac Hotel
Talstrasse 1, CH-8022
Phone: (1) 2211650   Telex: 813567

Dolder Grand Hotel
Kurhausstrasse 65, CH-8032
Phone: (1) 2516231   Telex: 53449

Eden au Lac Hotel
Utoquai 45, CH-8023
Phone: (1) 479404   Telex: 52440

GENEVA

Le Beau-Rivage Hôtel
13 Quai du Mont-Blanc, CH-1201
Phone: (022) 310221   Telex: 23362

Le Richemond
Jardin Brunswick, CH-1201
Phone: (022) 311400   Telex: 22598

Noga-Hilton
19 Quai du Mont-Blanc, CH-1211
Phone: (022) 319811   Telex: 23362

RESTAURANTS

ZURICH

Agnes Amberg   *French*
5 Höttingerstrasse
Phone: 2512626

Chez Max   *Haute cuisine*
53 Seestrasse
Phone: 3918877

Eichmuehle   *French*
933 Neugutstrasse, Waedensvil
Phone 7803444

Zur Rebe   *French*
5 Schuetzengasse
Phone: 2211065

GENEVA

Auberge du Vieux Moulin   *French/seafood*
89 Royte d'Annecy, Troinex
Phone: 422956

Le Chat-Botté   *French*
Hotel Beau Rivage
13 Quai du Mont-Blanc
Phone: 310221

Le Gentilhomme   *French*
Hôtel Richemond
Jardin Brunswick
Phone: 311400

Parc des Eaux-Vives   *French*
82 Quai Gustave-Ador
Phone: 354140

TRAVEL TIPS

• Zurich is emerging as one of the major art centers of the world, and the many galleries offer a wide range of fine art.
• Music boxes, hand-woven Swiss lace, delicious chocolates, precision watches, and wood carvings are some of the wonderful examples of Swiss artistry available in the shops.
• Excellent symphony orchestras, theatre, opera, and ballet abound. This cultural crossroad pays homage to the music and arts of the world, and you are sure to find a program or performance of the highest caliber in the major cities.
• The postal system is excellent, as is the federally operated telephone system. Most long-distance calls can be dialed directly. Public telex facilities are available at most port offices and hotels.

• Good medical treatment in modern facilities is easily obtained, as are quality pharmaceuticals. Health and sanitation conditions meet the highest standard in all Swiss cities.
• Soccer is a major sport, with skiing and bicycling also very popular. The visitor has all the popular participant sport facilities available (golf, tennis, swimming, etc.), either at the major hotels or in the immediate vicinity.

WEST GERMANY

Cultural Overview

Officially called the Federal Republic of Germany (FRG), West Germany is a country of more than 95,930 square miles, about the size of Wyoming. It is comprised of ten states (plus the city-state of West Berlin) and five distinct geographic areas. These areas are: the north German lowlands; the hills of Mittelgebirge; the west and south German plateaus and mountains; the south German Alpine foothills and lake area; and the Bavarian Alps. The latter includes Germany's highest mountain, the Zugspitze (altitude 9,721 ft.).

West Germany is in the temperate zone; the climate is generally comparable to that of northern New England. It has frequent weather changes, even in the course of the same day. Rain falls all year round.

Established in 1949, West Germany is governed by a bicameral parliament. The Bundesrat is the upper chamber, with delegates appointed by the state governments. The Bundestag, the lower house, elects the chancellor, who heads the government and can be removed from office at any time by a constructive vote of confidence by the Bundestag electing a new chancellor. West Germany is the leading economic power in Europe today and a dominant force worldwide. Its currency is among the strongest and most stable of any nation, and it is the world's foremost exporter of manufactured goods.

It is considered a model of Western capitalism, a position supported by a large and prosperous middle class. Labor–management relations are generally more harmonious in Germany than in the United States; in part, because by law German workers participate in the decision-making process of business.

Most of the approximately 60 million people are of German stock. Less than 10 million immigrant workers, largely from Turkey, Greece, and Yugoslavia, perform unskilled labor. Germany's population is about one-fourth that of the United States.

High German is the official language, but many younger Germans speak or understand English. The population is split about equally between the Catholic and Protestant faiths, along with a small minority of other denominations. Church attendance is not high.

German families are nuclear and small, and the birth rate is the world's lowest. Within the household, the father is dominant and the values of order, discipline, responsibility, and achievement are instilled in the children from an early age.

Education plays a major role in West Germany, and public education is compulsory for the 6- to 18-year age groups. The literacy rate is extremely high and adult education is encouraged by evening courses at "people's universities" (*Volkshochschulen*). West Germany has 52 universities, many technical and research institutes, and numerous seminaries and teacher-training schools. Tuition is free. University standards are very high, in some cases, even higher than those of American graduate colleges.

Although women constitute well over one-third of West Germany's workforce, they are mostly in traditional female jobs (secretaries, teachers, nurses, etc.). Women must by law receive equal pay for equal work, but male German executives tend to treat them casually and with some distance. Discrimination against women in employment is not uncommon, as their primary role is still perceived to be that of a homemaker.

Less than 20 percent of German business executives are women, mostly in lower management positions. A German female business executive doing business in Germany is likely to treated in the same professional manner as her male counterpart.

Business Opportunities

Since West German goods are of excellent quality and price, they have a solid position in the domestic market. More competition for U.S. exporters comes from Japan and the European Economic Community; the current strength of the dollar also puts U.S. business at a decided disadvantage.

Despite these drawbacks, there are attractive prospects for exporters in certain areas, including advanced medical equipment and products that support the health care industry, such as computer software, microfilm services, and consulting.

Good markets may also exist for telecommunications equipment, microcomputers, electronic components, and electric power equipment. In addition, since West Germany is the site of several NATO bases, there are business opportunities in a variety of NATO infrastructure projects.

The Battelle Institut in Frankfurt, with a staff of over seven hundred, can provide customized research regarding almost any aspect of doing business in German markets. For further information, contact: Battelle Institut, AM Roemerhof 35, 6000 Frankfurt 90, Federal Republic of Germany. Phone: (69) 79080.

West Berlin has a population of about 2 million, a high standard of living, and a thriving economy. It is the largest city in West Germany and a major industrial center. Due to its geographical location deep inside East Germany, West Berlin cannot serve as a regional distribution center.

Nevertheless, West Berlin does have extensive manufacturing plants, together with numerous research and engineering facilities. Raw materials, fuels, and capital goods are imported; the latter represents potential prospects for U.S. businesses. Foreign workers from southern Europe are abundantly available.

Initiating Contact

Two excellent avenues to finding new business contacts in West Germany are trade fairs, or *Messe,* and the German Chambers of Commerce. West Germany has a complete range of fairs and exhibits in all industries. These prestigious events, occasions for industry leaders to meet and talk informally, offer marvelous opportunities for U.S. executives to make contacts.

Other useful sources of business contacts include bankers who do business with a firm; German peers in the same industry; family members and friends; well-placed public officials; and industrial, trade, and employers' associations.

When dealing with the government, it is important to have an intermediary, since the bureaucracy is cumbersome and best dealt with by Germans. Such go-betweens can be those who provide the initial introductions, and their help can be enlisted in the places listed above.

Initial contact with a West German firm should be by letter or telex. A telephone call is appropriate only after the first contact has been made.

The first letter should be addressed to the firm as a whole, not to an individual executive or a particular department. "Gentlemen" or "Dear Sirs" are appropriate salutations. If you do know the specific person to contact, you may use that executive's name but the firm's name should still come first, the individual's next, after "To the attention of . . ."

Always try to contact an executive at the highest possible level. In small- to medium-sized companies, which comprise about 75 percent of all West German businesses, contact the head of the firm, the *Geschaeftsfuehrer*. Typically, this executive will be the firm's owner, or a member of a family that has a controlling interest. In larger companies, try to get an appointment with the chief executive, although your request will probably be passed down to a lower level.

For further information and assistance, contact:

German–American Chamber of Commerce
666 Fifth Avenue
New York, N.Y. 10019
Phone: (212) 582-7788   Telex: 0023-234209 GACC

American Chamber of Commerce in Germany
Rossmarkt 12
6000 Frankfurt 1, West Germany
Phone: 283401/2

U.S. Commerce Department
Marketing Manager for the Federal Republic of Germany
14th Street and Constitution Avenue
Washington, D.C. 20230
Phone: (202) 377-2841

German Foreign Trade Information Office
P.O.B. 108007, Blaubach 13
D-5000 Cologne 1, West Germany
Phone: (221)-20571

Business Protocol and Procedures

BUSINESS ENVIRONMENT

Germans respect order and discipline, and they observe formality and solemnity in business meetings. Breezy and informal attitudes are not appreciated, and visitors are expected to keep ties and jackets on and refrain from such relaxed behavior as putting feet up on desks, leaning back in a chair with hands behind the head, or fidgeting with objects. Erect posture and a neat appearance are essential for making a good first impression. The atmosphere tends to be less formal in the northern and western parts of the country, but the best rule is strict formality until you know your hosts well.

In general, the best months for meeting businesspersons in Germany are in January, from April to June and from September to November. The best time to establish new business contacts is during the prestigious trade fairs and exhibits when all principal executives mingle and meet informally with others.

The best hours for business appointments are between 11:00 A.M. and 1:00 P.M. and between 3:00 and 5:00 P.M.

The least favorable times for business contacts are between June 1 and August 30 (especially the month of August, when most Europeans are on vacation); between Christmas and New Year's Day; before and after Easter; during February and March, when German managers take short skiing trips or their winter vacations; during the three-day *Fasching* or *Karnival* (that ends before Ash Wednesday) when normal business almost stops during the celebration in the mainly Catholic regions of the Rhineland and in Bavaria; when some entire firms temporarily shut down in observance of the *Betriebsferien* (summer recess); and on Friday afternoons, in general, as government offices and many private businesses close at 2:00 P.M. or 3:30 P.M.

When foreign executives are dealing with German businesswomen, they should avoid much casual conversation unless the two are well acquainted. Women, however, expect to be treated with courtesy. They should be the first to extend their hand for a handshake.

Business hours are from 8:00 A.M. to 5:00 P.M., but executives arrive earlier and work later. Many will schedule appointments early or late, or even on Saturdays. If you are meeting with top-level executives, the meeting is likely to take place in their offices. With middle managers, the meeting will probably be in a conference room. Germans are very punctual and expect others to be so. If you are unavoidably delayed for a meeting, telephone to tell your hosts as soon as possible.

Security is tight in West German firms. When you arrive at your host's building or floor, you will probably encounter a guard or a checkpoint. Once your appointment has been confirmed, you will either be escorted to the site of your meeting or asked to proceed along. If you are not escorted, ask for detailed instructions, as in most industrial complexes the executive offices are quite far from the checkpoint.

In Germany, executive status is indicated by the number of doors one must pass through before reaching the executive's office.

It would serve you well to pay special attention to the secretary of the businessperson you will be meeting with, as in Germany, the secretary has a special relationship with her employer—more of an office wife, where her opinion bears weight and often is considered in evaluating an individual as well as his or her business presentation. It is advisable to present your business card to the secretary, and always address her with utmost courtesy and respect.

At the beginning of the meeting, you will be introduced and you are expected to shake hands with each person present. Senior executives will extend hands first. Handshakes should be firm, but a lady's hand should not be squeezed. You should remain standing until the senior host not only offers you a seat but also invites you to sit down.

Business meetings usually start only after the office door has been shut. (Privacy is highly repected in Germany.) A short period of small talk will precede the business discussion and you may be offered tea, coffee, or an alchoholic beverage. Appropriate topics for the preliminary small talk include your flight, the city you are visiting, your home city-state, nonpolitical current events, sports, cars, and the like. The initial meeting is likely to be short, and it is up to you, the visitor, to sense the appropriate time to initiate departure. An effective way to communicate readiness to end the meeting, without an explicit statement to this effect, is to collect papers from the table, put them in your briefcase, move your chair slightly away from the table, summarize your favorable impressions, and approach a formal thank you and handshakes.

If your West German host does not understand English, it is up to you to provide an interpreter. Since good translations depend on understanding, you may want to brief the interpreter before the meeting, especially if it concerns technical subjects.

RANK AND STATUS

Rank, status, titles, and formal hierarchy are far more important in German business organizations than in the United States, and job descriptions and lines of authority are more sharply defined and followed. The style of management tends to be centralized and authoritarian; bypassing the proper channels is not acceptable. The status gap between upper and middle management is far greater than that in U.S. corporations. The workplace in Germany plays a key role in self-perception and social status.

Prestige and status among West Germans comes from individual achievement, indicated by education or job title, rather than from wealth, family history, or land ownership. Titles are used constantly, even between the Germans themselves. Business titles, in descending order of rank, are as follows:

Geschaeftsfuehrer	top executive
Generaldirektor	general manager
Direktor	top-level manager
Generalbevollmäechtiger	executive with general authority to commit the firm
Prokurist	executive with specific authority to commit the firm
Abteilungsleiter	department head

The right side is the "place of power" in Germany. Expect to see women and persons of higher status on the right side, in the office, at dinner tables, in the streets, and elsewhere. A woman walking with two men should walk between them, as should a man walking with two women.

In business meetings, expect the most senior executive to project authority and self-confidence by voice modulation, facial demeanor, and a structured presentation. Try to adopt the same approach, without blind imitation, in order to command respect and inspire confidence.

Power and status are also appreciated by Germans. Some visitors are said to place phone calls to their home offices or tell others what to do in order to impress their West German hosts. In general, however, this might be looked on unfavorably and considered pretentious.

Some local German hotels (not part of the international chains) have high prestige and are viewed by Germans with pride and even some awe. Having a room in one of these establishments will often elevate you in the eyes of your German counterparts.

FORMS OF ADDRESS

In West Germany a younger person, or one of lower status, is introduced to the higher ranking or older person, not vice versa. Men are introduced before women.

At the beginning of a meeting, last names only will be used, preceded by titles. You are expected to use last names until requested to do otherwise. The most common titles are "Herr" (Mr.) and "Frau" (Mrs.). The title "Fraulein" (Miss) is considered obsolete and "Frau" is substituted wherever it is appropriate unless addressing a very young woman. These are followed by another title, a family name, or both. For example, someone might properly be addressed as "Herr Doktor Schmidt."

If you do not know someone's name but do know his or her occupation, you may address him or her by "Herr" or "Frau," followed by the business title. It is polite to use "Frau" if you do not know a woman's marital status. In West Germany women use their own first names with their husband's last name. They do not have to address men by their titles unless there is a great disparity in age or status.

Titles carry great weight in Germany, as they signify the social status of individuals. The Germans are very careful about titles and you should be, too.

BUSINESS CARDS

Business cards can be exchanged briefly during a first meeting with the visitor taking the initiative, or clipped to the written material you leave behind with your host.

If your firm has been in business for a long time, print the founding date on your card. Add also any academic degrees you may have. Germans appreciate business longevity and formal higher education.

BUSINESS DRESS

Proper business attire in West Germany is formal and conservative, with dark colors the norm. Women are expected to wear suits at all times, although short-sleeved dresses may be appropriate in the summer. Sleeveless outfits are never acceptable in business.

GIFT-GIVING

Gifts are not appropriate at the first meeting, and even modest souvenirs may make your German counterparts uncomfortable.

If you receive a rare invitation to a business associate's home, you should arrive on time and bring a gift. Flowers—an uneven number, and never red roses—souvenirs, and good chocolates are appropriate. Unwrap the flowers and present them to the hostess. Wine is not recommended as a gift, since that might be interpreted as an insult to the host's wine cellar. If the party is in your honor, you should send flowers in advance.

COMMUNICATION STYLES

Communication is formal and businesslike in meetings. Germans appreciate a direct, to-the-point approach that is factual, concrete, and precise. They are not impressed by flowery or imaginative presentations, but a tone of self-confidence that demands respect is most effective.

To communicate integrity and overcome initial skepticism on the part of your German host, maintain direct eye contact at all times. As part of their respect for privacy in business matters, Germans do not sit close to one another at meetings or stand close when talking. Physical gestures, like backslapping, are not appropriate. When you are talking, avoid using hand gestures as much as possible. Good posture and neatness, not only in appearance but in all correspondence and presentations, are highly regarded in Germany.

When communicating through an interpreter, look at the party who is addressed, not at the interpreter. The same applies when listening to an interpreter.

Formality and good manners count most in German business transactions. *Do not* take off your jacket, loosen your tie, put your feet on desks or chairs, lean back with hands behind your head, put your hands in your pockets, or fidget with objects. Be orderly and formal not only in appearance and manners, but also in your oral and written presentations.

Over 40 percent of German managers have an engineering-oriented education, and 20 percent a theoretical economics background; most have training in industrial management which approaches business management scientifically. Be thorough, systematic, and careful with numbers and technical details in your written communications.

Negotiating in West Germany

Power in German business organizations is quite centralized and concentrated at the top. In small- or medium-sized organizations, one person will make virtually all the important decisions. Consequently, decision making in German business organizations tends to be slow. In large corporations, operational decisions are made by the Vorstand, an executive committee of six to ten members. Most international transactions are decided upon within this body, and based in part on the submitted recommendations of middle management. Decisions are generally arrived at by consensus. If you are not meeting with the top people, you can do little after making your presentation and submitting your proposal. Your counterpart will move the matter on to higher levels for a final determination.

In negotiations, you should be direct, factual, and concrete. Such factors please German businesspeople and are likely to increase the effectiveness of your negotiation. Pointing out the mutuality of interests between your firm and the German organization is a good strategy, as is emphasizing features of your product or service that appeal to Germans in general, such as efficiency, performance, and quality. However, be careful not to overemphasize the superiority of your product or service, since the Germans are proud of their own achievements. Keeping discussions and presentations low key and avoiding a hard-sell approach is most effective, especially in early stages.

Price will be an important factor in your proposal, and it will have to be highly competitive. German executives concentrate on the present and do not plan too far in advance. Thus, you need to stress the immediate benefits of your proposal. On the other hand, your German counterparts will prefer long-term relationships to one-shot deals, so you will be laying the foundation for future business even as you discuss only the most immediate issues. Presentations should not take a gimmicky approach. Germans do not appreciate "tricks" of advertising or marketing.

Before you leave, be sure you have contacted the appropriate management level to arrange a follow-up discussion. Leave your German counterparts written material—catalogues, reports, brochures, and so on—all in German, to substantiate your proposal. Technical data should conform to German standards by using the metric system and referring to the deutschemark.

Be thorough in your written reports and proposals and be meticulously careful about details, because your German counterpart will take a long and hard look at your material and scrutinize it carefully. Furthermore, the material should not only be thorough and accurate, but also well organized. Germans appreciate neatness and order, and a touch of professionalism will make a strong impression on them.

Only a written contract will constitute evidence of an agreement; an oral agreement may be binding morally but not legally.

Lawyers are not generally present for negotiations, nor do they play a major role in the final contract except for very large international transactions. German firms rely instead on preprinted, standardized contract forms. If, however, you are going to maintain a physical presence and ongoing operations in West Germany, you will need to work with German attorneys.

As in the United States, German counterparts will want to be sure every detail is covered in the final agreement. The contract will include no leeway, no ambiguity, and no chance for misinterpretation.

Binding documents in German firms usually have two signatures. On the right side, the signature will probably be that of the chief negotiator, the officer whose area is most immediately affected by the agreement, or a company specialist in the relevant area. The more important signature is on the left, where the officer with binding authority signs the agreement. Any signature that is binding will be preceded by the letters *ppa* for *"per prokura"*; or *i.V.*, for *"in Vollmacht,"* which means in full power, or *"in Vertretung"* (on behalf of). Executives who precede their signatures with *i.V.* have authority only to commit the firm in specific areas. The chairman of the executive committee (*Vorsitzender*) and the managing director (*Geschaeftsfuehrer*) are empowered to commit their firms to contracts. Internal company bylaws may require that even these top-level executives obtain higher approval from the board of directors.

Additional tips for negotiating in West Germany:

• German executives have a strong sense of order and a definite preference for predictability. Never do anything that might be perceived as inordinate, and never pull any surprises.

• Considerable privacy and secrecy is prevalent within German corporations. For an outsider, it is even more difficult to procure information about a company.

• Under German law, if you induce a party to believe an agreement will be concluded, you may be liable for damages if this does not happen. Be careful in choosing your words, especially if you are speaking in German.

• Sending youthful executives to negotiations in West Germany can be a mistake. Most Germans in key posts are in their mid-fifties, and they may not take younger counterparts very seriously.

Business Entertaining

Business lunches and dinners are common in West Germany, but an invitation to a business associates's home is rare. Breakfast meetings are unheard of.

Business lunches are usually set for 1:00 P.M., lasting about an hour to an hour and a half. Dinner invitations are customarily for 8:00 P.M., and generally include spouses.

When you are a guest in a restaurant, do not try to pick up the bill. On the other hand, if you do the inviting, you will be expected to pay. German executives enjoy being taken to lunch, even if their corporations have excellent in-house dining facilities.

Lunch is the main meal of the day, and any business discussion should be of a general nature. Supper is a lighter meal enjoyed about 6:30 P.M. It is inappropriate to discuss business at dinner.

A male guest of honor will sit to the left of the hostess, a female guest of honor to the right of the host. Husbands and wives are separated at a formal dinner. Whenever a woman leaves the table, all the men are expected to rise. Guests are expected to make the first move to leave a dinner party, which should not extend past 11:00 P.M.

In Germany, people eat "European style." The fork stays in the left hand, the knife in the right. No switching of these implements takes place, as it does in the United States. When you are finished eating, put the knife and fork diagonally, side by side, on your plate with the handles at five o'clock pointing to the eleven o'clock position. If you wish to be served more food, silverware should be placed on the left-hand side of the plate slightly angled to the right.

Toasts are common at dinner parties. Do not take a drink until the host has toasted the group and taken a drink. The host will raise his glass to the lady on his right, then toast the rest of the party. You should follow suit when you host a party. Acknowledge a toast with a nod and a smile. After the first toast, guests may offer toasts. The guest of the highest rank toasts first, and others follow later throughout the evening. Men toast women, but women never toast men.

In home entertainment, the men will rise, but not the ladies, when the host enters the room, and remain standing until offered a seat again. It is also polite for men to stand when a woman enters the room.

Thank-you notes after dinner parties are expected.

General Tips

- The German sense of humor may be unlike yours, so it is a good idea to avoid jokes.
- Men precede women when entering a restaurant or other public places. Otherwise, men hold doors open and let women or seniors precede them.
- Appropriate topics for dinner conversation or any "small talk" are the German countryside, travel abroad, hobbies, and sports. Taboo subjects in most situations are World War II; personal questions, especially about marital status, spouse, and children; and personal finances. Even jokes are not advisable.
- If you say "Let's get together sometime" to a West German colleague, he or she may take you up on it, so be sure to set a definite date.
- In restaurants, summon the waiter or waitress by raising a hand. Address a waiter as "Herr Ober," a waitress as "Fräulein."
- Germans rise from their chairs whenever people older or of higher rank enter and/or leave the room.
- Like most Europeans, Germans shake hands frequently, both upon meeting and departing, with strangers and among friends.
- West German business correspondence is often signed by two people, without their full names and titles printed under the signature. If this happens, note the reference numbers or initials under the letterhead and politely ask in another letter that the names and titles of the signatures of that letter be sent to you.

• In Germany, it is polite to wait until one of your German colleagues has taken the lead before smoking, or to ask permission before lighting up.

• If you are male, do not be surprised if a German woman links arms with you when walking down the street (especially before or after business entertainment in a theatre, etc.). If you are a woman, do not be surprised if a German kisses your hand in some parts of the country.

• Germans are embarrassed by direct compliments, and they dislike it if people are too ebullient, too friendly, too nonchalant, or too pushy.

• The proper form of writing a postal address is to put a zip code before the name of the town (on the same line) followed by a street names and building number. The sender's address (or return address) appears in the same format, at the lower (not upper) left corner of the envelope preceded by the word *Absender,* meaning sender.

EXECUTIVE TRAVEL TO WEST GERMANY •

DOCUMENTS

The only requirement is a valid passport for U.S. citizens.

INOCULATIONS

None required for travelers coming from the United States.

AIRPORTS

The distances from the airport to the downtown areas are: Frankfurt —6 miles; West Berlin—4 miles; Munich—6 miles; Düsseldorf—5 miles; Hamburg—8 miles. There are no direct flights to West Berlin from New York, but a connecting flight from Frankfurt takes about one hour.

CUSTOMS

You may bring with you duty-free 400 cigarettes, 100 cigars, or one pound of tobacco; one quart of liquor; perfumes and cologne for personal use as well as a small amount of gifts (check with the airline when planning your trip, as requirements change).

U.S. EMBASSY

Delchmannsaue 5300, Bonn 2
Phone: (0228) 3393390   Telex: 885452

TRANSPORTATION

The rail system is Germany's pride and should be considered if traveling throughout the country. It is recommended that you hire a car and a driver/translator for your stay in each city in which you have business.

TIPPING

In restaurants, a 10 to 15 percent gratuity is usually added to the bill in hotels and restaurants. It is usual to add another 5 to 10 percent to restaurant bills. Small tips to bellhops and hotel maids are appreciated. Tip taxi drivers about 5 percent.

HOTELS

WEST BERLIN

Bristol Hotel Kempinski Berlin
27 Kurfuerstendamm
Phone: (30) 881091   Telex 183553

Inter-Continental Hotel Berlin
2 Budapester Strasse
Phone: (30) 26020   Telex: 184380

Steigenberger Hotel
32 Rankestrasse
Phone: (30) 21080

BONN

Hotel Bristol
Poppelsdorfer Allee
Phone: (228) 20111   Telex: 8869661

Steigenberger Hotel
Am Bundeskanzler Platz
Phone: (228) 20191   Telex: 886363

FRANKFURT

CP Frankfurt Plaza Hotel
2-10 Hamburger Allee
Phone: (69) 770721   Telex: 412573

Hotel Frankfurt Inter-Continental
43 Wilhelm-Leuschner Strasse
Phone: (69) 230561   Telex: 413639

Steigenberger Frankfurter Hof
17 Am Kaiserplatz
Phone: 20191

STUTTGART

Steigenberger Hotel Graf Zeppelin
7 Arnulf Klett Platz
Phone: (711)-299881   Telex: 722418

Stuttgart International Hotel
100 Plieninger Strasse
Phone: (711)-62021   Telex: 7255763

RESTAURANTS

WEST BERLIN

Anselmo   *Italian*
17 Damaschkestrasse
Phone: 323-9094

Exil   *Viennese*
44a Paul Lincke Ufer
Phone: 612-7037

Heinz Holl   *German/international*
26 Damaschkestrasse
Phone: 323-1404

La Puce   *Viennese*
20 Schillerstrasse
Phone: 312-5831

Maitre   *Haute cuisine*
31 Podbielskiallee, Dahlem
Phone: 832-6004

Rockendorf's   *French*
1 Duesterhauptstrasse
Phone: 402-3099

BONN

Ambassador Club   *International*
Steigenberger Hotel
Am Bundeskanzler Platz
Phone: 20191

Am Tulpenfeld   *French*
an der Heuss Allee
Phone: 219081

Beethovenhalle   *German*
3 Theaterstrasse
Phone: 633348

In Stiefel   *German*
30 Bonngasse
Phone: 634806

TRAVEL TIPS

• In almost every case, German banks and currency exchange offices will pay a higher rate for traveler's checks than for cash. Do not pay hotel and restaurant bills directly with traveler's checks as it will be more expensive.

• While Germany has no currency restrictions, the United States does. You must file a report with U.S. Customs if you deposit or return with more than $5,000 in cash, foreign currency, traveler's checks, money orders, or any negotiable instruments.

• Emergency medical service is available by telephone twenty-four hours a day, outside of hospital service. Ask the operator for *"Arztlicher Notdienst."* The major cities have pharmacies open twenty-four hours a day.

• To safeguard your passport, leave it in the safe deposit box of your hotel during your stay.

• Restaurant bills are usually paid at the table, but tips are given directly to the waiter/waitress.

• The arts play a more significant role in the German lifestyle than in almost any other country. A full calendar of music festivals, symphony concerts, opera and ballet performances, and theatre productions are daily fare in most cities. Check with your hotel for current attractions.

• Do not be offended if you find strangers staring at you. It is common among the Germans themselves, and extends to visitors as well. This behavior is merely a sign of interest and curiosity.

MIDDLE EAST AND AFRICA

SAUDI ARABIA

Cultural Overview

Approximately one-third the size of the United States, the kingdom of Saudi Arabia is the twelfth largest country in the world. Until petroleum prices rose sharply in the early 1970s, the kingdom was growing at a relatively slow pace living on modest oil revenues. Then, with the world's largest petroleum reserves, Saudi Arabia leaped onto the world stage and took its place among the wealthiest of nations and became an important factor in regional and world affairs.

Saudi Arabia is a monarchy based on Islamic law and Bedouin tribal tradition. The royal family, its relatives, religious leaders, and the sheiks (tribal leaders by birth or through recognition of their power) constitute the power structure.

Its relations with the United States are very strong, despite periodic disagreements over regional foreign policy decisions. The kingdom has no diplomatic relations with any communist country and opposes the expansion of communism.

Consumer and government spending have increased greatly since the 1970s and international trade and investment have boomed. In the seventies, development of the kingdom centered on infrastructure projects such as: air, land, and sea transportation; schools and universities; highways; telecommunications; medical centers, hospitals, and clinics; petrochemical projects; military facilities; and industrial cities. In the early 1980s, emphasis began shifting to expanding the country's industrial base and reducing its dependency on petroleum exports. Future development plans are aimed at building up the role of the private sector.

Life in Saudi Arabia revolves around the laws and rituals of Islam.

Visitors must respect these laws and American authorities have no power in the legal system. Infractions, even by foreigners, are severely punished. The penalty is severe for alcohol use or possession—even of one of the little bottles one might pick up on a plane—and frequently leads to jail and deportation.

Men completely dominate the society. While legally men may take up to four wives, most have one wife. Family life is very important, and it is common for several generations to be living in one home. Men and women lead very separate lives. When Saudi women appear in public, they must wear long black coverings over their clothes (*abaya*) and usually veil their faces. They cannot drive cars or ride bicycles and few work. Single foreign women have difficulty getting a visa into Saudi Arabia, although this is being relaxed for businesswomen who belong to recognizable organizations.

Saudi women are being educated along with the men, however, for the government mandates and finances education for all Saudis from kindergarten through the university level. More women than ever before are getting university degrees and entering the workforce, though they are still restricted to "women's" jobs in such areas as education, social work, and the health field. Many Saudis are sent abroad for higher education and specialization, often to the United States.

As part of the code of Islam, Saudis value hospitality, generosity, honesty, friendship, loyalty, and modesty. They greatly respect poetry and oratory in Arabic, the official language. English, the language of business, is widely spoken, especially by young Saudis, and it is taught as the second language.

The country is a peninsula composed mostly of a desert plain, with very little rain. Summer temperatures often exceed 120 degrees Fahrenheit. Saudi Arabia has a small population of 8 million people, 2 million of whom are expatriates who migrated to the kingdom as laborers to participate in the many development projects.

Business Opportunites

Uniformly liberal trade policies, low customs duties on imports, and an absence of controls on the transfer of capital are advantages of trading with Saudi Arabia, one of the United States' largest markets. As the kingdom's number one supplier, the United States exports over $20 billion worth of products and services a year, which represents approximately 20 percent of the total imports.

Major opportunities for U.S. business participation lie in financial services; technology, particularly computers; telecommunications equipment and other electronic products; service industries; and real estate. Saudi Arabia's emphasis on developing agriculture makes land-use technology and products attractive exports. Demand for more and better consumer goods has risen recently and other major imports include metals and metal products, foodstuffs, transportation equipment, clothing, medical equipment, chemical products, ceramics and glass, nonferrous minerals, and wood products. In addition, wealthy Saudis invest some of their capital abroad, creating more opportunities for U.S. businesses.

Initiating Contact

As a rule, foreign firms must, by Saudi law, work through Saudi agents or partners. The main reason for this is to provide "accountability" for the activities of the foreigner. That is, it is the Saudi who becomes ultimately responsible toward the government. A more practical reason is bringing in Saudis as participants in the business development and growth of the kingdom and, most important, sharing the profits to be made.

Such agents or partners serve valuable functions and can be vital to the success or failure of your enterprise. Hence, your choice is very important and should not be made lightly. Frequently, a preliminary trip to Saudi Arabia to study the market and to locate an agent/partner is recommended in order to avoid future difficulties.

The functions of these agents/partners are to keep your lines of communication open to those buyers and users of your goods and services. They should provide the "lubrication" in your relationship in the market, especially with the government officials and departments.

These representatives should be chosen carefully to be sure their reputations are beyond reproach. Do not limit reference inquiries to Saudis alone, for they rarely criticize one another. Talk with other clients, local bankers, or diplomats during your search. The following agencies can help find an agent, check credentials, or offer additional assistance:

Saudi Arabian Consulate General
866 United Nations Plaza

New York, N.Y. 10017
Phone: (212) 752-2740

U.S.–Arab Chamber of Commerce
1 World Trade Center
New York, N.Y. 10048
Phone: (212) 432-0655

Royal Embassy of Saudi Arabia
Ministry of Commerce
1155 15th Street N.W.
Washington, D.C. 20005
Phone: (202) 342-3800

U.S. Department of Commerce
Office of the Near East
14th Street and Constitution Avenue
Washington, D.C. 20230
Phone: (202) 377-5341

Jeddah World Trade Center (R-1P)
Saudi Economic & Development Co. Ltd. (SEDCO)
P.O. Box 4384
Jeddah, Saudi Arabia
Phone: (02) 644-0920-1   Telex: 400197 SEDCO SJ

Riyadh Chamber of Commerce & Industry
P.O. Box 596
Riyadh, Saudi Arabia
Phone: 22600, 22700

Once your agent has made initial contact, write to the Saudi organization to request an appointment, offering two or three possible dates, at least six weeks before your trip. It is not appropriate to telephone for appointments until you have established a solid relationship with a Saudi executive or official, and even then telephone calls may be ignored.

Your letter should clearly identify the purpose of your visit in a way that engages your potential host's interest. The Saudis are deluged with proposals and will only consider dealing with well-connected foreigners with intriguing ideas. Persons sent to do business in the kingdom should rank high in the organization, so that a similarly powerful Saudi will meet them. Any foreign representative should have power of attorney to act on behalf of his or her organization.

You should receive written confirmation of your appointment at least a week before you leave. If you do not, have your agent work locally to set things up. If you still have no confirmation, you can make your trip anyway, taking a copy of your letter with you to use for access. It is not appropriate, however, to "drop in" unexpectedly, without having tried to arrange a visit in advance by mail.

Pay attention to religious holidays when planning your trip. During the month of Ramadan, for example, Muslims cannot eat, drink, or smoke from dawn to dusk. This fasting is not conducive to business discussions or decision making. However, it is not uncommon for many businesses in Jeddah, Dhahran, and Alkohbar to open *after* sundown and work through the night! In addition to religious holidays, Jumad I and Jumad II are not propitious months to schedule appointments with government departments, because most officials are preoccupied with budgets. Check these dates ahead as they change yearly because of the lunar holiday.

Business Protocol and Procedures

BUSINESS ENVIRONMENT

The pace of business in Saudi Arabia is much slower than that in the United States; the establishment of trust and personal relationships, much more important. The Saudis have tended to regard Americans as morally degenerate, albeit technologically admirable. This attitude, however, has begun to change. Knowing and respecting Saudi protocols and expectations will help you overcome unpleasant stereotypes.

In government offices, business hours are generally from 9:00 A.M. to 2:00 P.M.; in businesses, from 8:00 A.M. to 1:00 P.M. and 4:00 P.M. to 8:30 P.M. Friday is the Muslim day of rest. Business closes Thursday afternoon, but government offices close both Thursdays and Fridays. Early-morning appointments, if made, may run into delays since high-ranking officials and executives tend to arrive about an hour late. The business day will be interrupted by prayer calls, mandated by law.

The visiting executive is expected to arrive on time for appointments, but the Saudi may be quite late, and may even not see the visitor for hours or even days. This does not convey disrespect. Your ultimate success may depend, in part, on your patience and persistence in returning again and again to see the Saudi.

Since being punctual is important, when going to your appointment your should arrange transportation in advance with the hotel or your agent, and allow for delays from various causes.

Some Saudis have modern, Western-style offices. Here you will receive focused attention, although the Saudi may be interrupted occasionally by family members or co-workers. Other Saudis, however, conduct business in a *majlis* or a *diwan*. A *majlis* is an audience-type setting while the *diwan* is like the *majlis* except that it is in the Saudi's home. People wait together to see the executive or official in a large room where visitors are received.

You will be invited to speak at the Saudi's discretion. While you are waiting, your host may place or take phone calls, attend to paperwork, or talk at length with other visitors. Your turn may be long in coming or not materialize at all the first day, when you may get only an invitation to return. This first meeting, and perhaps several subsequent ones, may have nothing to do with business. These are crucial, however, for you will be making the all-important personal impression upon which much of the success of your business depends.

At any meeting, you will be served small cups of coffee or tea continually. It is polite to drink at least three cups. After that, you may refuse by tilting your empty cup a few times from side to side and saying *"bes"* (pronounced "bess"), meaning "enough."

When a meeting is over, the leave-taking may be prolonged with much conversation, or it may be abrupt. Many meetings conclude with more coffee or tea, which you should accept. Stay until you have finished it, for this is a sign that you desire further meetings. If your local agent is with you, leave details of future meetings in his hands. If not, you may suggest meeting again the following day.

RANK AND STATUS

Rank and status are important in Saudi Arabia. High-ranking Saudis want to deal only with people of similar rank. Sending a middle-level executive to deal with a high-ranking Saudi is interpreted as an insult, meaning that you consider either the Saudi or the business itself to be of little importance.

The person of highest rank enters a room first, followed by the next ranking person, and so forth down the line. As a guest, you will be shown into and out of rooms first. You should make a polite protest about this and then accept it graciously. People are expected to rise to show respect for persons of higher rank or greater age. At a business meeting or meal, the position of honor is to the right of the host.

To show respect, you should address Saudi colleagues as their names appear on their cards, or else as introduced. Use first names only if you are invited to do so. Titles used most frequently in Saudi Arabia are "Mr.," "Sheik," and "Your Excellency." Men who have achieved status in society are called "Sheik." "Your Excellency" is reserved for members of the royal family. If you meet the king, speak to him only through the interpreter and address him as "Your Royal Majesty."

FORMS OF ADDRESS

A limp, prolonged handshake is the proper, standard greeting. Saudi Arabian men often greet friends by extending the left hand to the other's right shoulder and kissing both cheeks. Such a greeting is not appropriate between casual business acquaintances, however, and is not expected from foreigners. If you meet a Saudi accompanied by a veiled woman, he may not introduce her. In that case, you should not acknowledge her presence.

If your meeting is at a *majlis* or a *diwan*, you are expected to shake hands with the others waiting to see the Saudi host. As a foreigner, however, you are not expected to bow or to kiss the host's hand, even though others do.

BUSINESS CARDS

Cards are not necessarily exchanged at the beginning of a meeting. Wait until your hosts offer theirs. Yours should be printed in English on one side and Arabic on the other. Offer your card, Arabic side up, to your host.

BUSINESS DRESS

For meetings, conservative dress—suits, dress shirts, and conservative ties—is appropriate. Women should wear modest suits, dresses, or pantsuits and a minimum amount of jewelry and makeup. Their arms and legs should be covered; knees should not show.

GIFT-GIVING

Saudis appreciate gifts, and U.S. souvenirs (such as an electronic gadget or a small item bearing your company logo) will be very welcome. The end of the first or second meeting with your host is a good time to give such a gift. Avoid giving leather items that might be made from pigskin.

Saudis are very generous and they also believe in strict reciprocity. If you express strong admiration for something in a Saudi's office or home, he or she will feel obliged to give it to you. Then he or she will ask for something of yours, and you will be expected to give it or something of equivalent value.

Some suggestions on giving gifts:

• If you are dining at a Saudi's house, do not bring gifts of food, which would imply that you did not expect to dine well. Flowers or books are quite appropriate.
• You should not bring a gift for a Saudi wife or any woman in a household. However, gifts for children are quite acceptable.

COMMUNICATION STYLES

Usually, one of your host's party will speak English and the Saudis do not expect you to know Arabic. If you are holding talks through an interpreter, however, express regret at not knowing the language. If you are dealing with several Saudis at once, they may talk among themselves for some time in Arabic.

Maintaining a respectful attitude and avoiding any suggestion of condescension toward the Saudis are essential. If you are speaking English, speak slowly. Avoid the tendency to raise your voice if you are not understood. Do not use slang (such as "ball park figure"), acronyms, or coarse language. Even strong slang (such as "you sly dog") is out of place. Joking banter may be interpreted by Saudis as insulting. Anything that makes a Saudi seem to lose face in public is to be avoided, so care must be taken to avoid criticism or putdowns regarding your hosts.

Politics is the number one topic of conversation in the kingdom, and Saudis tend to be well informed about U.S. affairs. They do not generally understand U.S. foreign policy attitudes, especially toward Israel and the Arab nations. Do not hesitate to express your opinions tactfully, for your hosts will expect you to. However, it is wise to be familiar with both sides of the Arab–Israeli conflict, as well as with the overall world picture.

Sports makes an excellent topic in initial conversations. The Saudis are especially fond of soccer, tennis, and the Olympics. You should not ask about the women in your host's family, but you may ask about the family's health in a general way. Any more discussion of anyone's family, however, is not appropriate, nor are references to alcohol or pork or casual references to religion. If you have entertained your Saudi host in the United States or in another Western country, and he has indulged in alcohol or other things not accepted in the kingdom, do not remind him of these instances.

Periods of silence are normal in Saudi conversations and respecting them can help you to establish rapport. Do not jump in to fill them or feel uncomfortable when they occur. On the other hand, a very long silence coupled with your host's staring into space indicate that a conversation is over.

Nonverbal communication is especially important in a country as different from the United States as Saudi Arabia. Saudis stand close during conversations, perhaps as little as eight to ten inches away. Avoid backing up, which can be interpreted as a rebuff. Furthermore, being close is often quite necessary to hear and to be heard.

Talking with the hands is considered impolite in Saudi Arabia, as are such vigorous gestures as backslapping or arm-punching. On the other hand, gently tapping a person or resting a hand on someone's arm or shoulder is acceptable to emphasize a point.

A lowered tone of voice shows deference and respect. In contrast, crossing one's legs so a Saudi can see the sole of the shoe conveys great disrespect. Placing hands on hips is a sign of a challenging attitude. Sneezing, nose-blowing, sniffing, coughing, or hiccuping are not considered polite and should be muffled. Using the left hand for eating, holding, or handling anything is *not* done, for it is associated with poor hygiene.

Negotiating In Saudi Arabia

Negotiations proceed at a slower pace in Saudi Arabia than they do in the United States and may last for weeks. The more patience, respect, and perseverance you display, the more you will be overcoming your host's natural wariness with strangers. Such an environment is clearly no place for an aggressive or hard-sell approach.

The decision-making process in this nation also adds time to negotiations. Decisions are made by top government and business leaders. Many people may need to be consulted. It is best to submit proposals, which should be in Arabic, well in advance of meetings.

Do not underestimate the Saudis; they are shrewd businesspeople. They will know about your competition even if they are dealing only with you. They may suddenly take an arbitrary stance for a while, which may only be a means of testing your patience and desire for the business.

Price discussion usually comes near the end of negotiations. The Saudis do not object to people making a profit but, being well informed about the competition and the market, they will not tolerate an outrageous price. Avoid any reference to compromising or "splitting the difference." Saudis interpret compromise as giving up something that belongs to them.

Once an agreement has been reached, you should get it in writing. Lengthy contracts irritate the Saudis, but everything should be explicitly stated. If litigation ever arises, nothing is inferred or interpreted, and every word is used in its literal sense. Lawyers from both sides should be used in drawing up this agreement. Your lawyer should work with an Arab lawyer who will assist in the wording since the ruling language of the contract is in Arabic.

When negotiating, remember that the Saudis do not like to discuss the future because they believe everything is in the hands of God. The Saudis prefer to wait for transactions to be consummated before announcing anything about plans. Let your Saudi counterparts choose the time to make public announcements about the results of your negotiations.

Early in the negotiations, your host's natural graciousness may express itself in positive comments about some possible transaction. This is only a courtesy, representing no commitment.

You may have to ask your agent to make frequent inquiries and apply mild pressure to see that the agreement is carried forward or that steps are taken as they should be. The Saudis have been known to forget promises or to get distracted by other activities.

Saudis like to feel they are getting special consideration and hospitality. Another extra you might offer could be training for your counterpart or a family member or manager in the United States, on special or new technology.

Sometimes a contract will be awarded to a firm from another country because it is "their turn" to get it. The Saudis have also been known to refuse contracts because of the foreign policy of the firm's home country. You may not be aware of these factors operating during negotiations.

Business Entertaining

Entertaining is an important part of doing business in Saudi Arabia. Your host should be the one to initiate such social interactions, which are usually lunches or dinners in a restaurant. An invitation to a home is an honor. You are expected to reciprocate before leaving the kingdom. Western women are rarely invited to business meals.

Dinner in a restaurant will start between 8:00 P.M. and 10:00 P.M., and even later in a home. No matter where you are eating, it is polite to take an interest in the food, which is an important part of the culture. Many courses will be served, and it is polite to try a small portion of everything offered. You may decline more food, however, with a slight nod of the head and the word "*bes*."

Eating is generally communal, with the main dishes placed in the center of the table. Some Saudis eat with their hands and visitors may do the same, although most homes and restaurants provide utensils. If a Western woman is invited to a home, she will join the Saudi women unless the dinner or reception has mixed nationalities.

At the end of the meal, after being served fruit or pastry and coffee, the guest should make the first move to leave. Lingering longer than 15 or 20 minutes is not recommended. If the meal is dinner, the hour will be quite late; if the meal is lunch, you should leave to allow the Saudis time for their afternoon rest.

The laws against alcohol are strictly enforced. However, you may be offered liquor in your host's home if he knows you well or feels comfortable with you.

In a restaurant, whoever issued the invitation picks up the check. It is polite, however, to offer to pay, even if your host invited you, and to repeat the offer. When it is your turn to entertain, choose a large hotel with private dining room facilities and a homey atmosphere. Follow your host's lead in deciding whether to hold a lunch or a dinner. The bill will be presented to your table and paid to the waiter or cashier. The tip is usually added to the bill, but generally an extra amount of cash is given to those who served you.

After you are entertained, write a thank-you note; it will be appreciated, as will a telephone call before you leave the country.

General Tips

• Always refer to the Islamic religion as Islam; its followers as Muslims or Moslems. The terms Muhammadism and Muhammadan are inaccurate and impolite.
• When meeting the king, men are expected to bow and women to curtsy.
• It is considered impolite to ask about the Saudis' clothing or to ask them to remove their headgear.
• Taking pictures of Saudi women should be avoided.
• When you encounter Saudis praying, it is not polite to stare, walk in front of them, or step on the prayer mat. Maintain a respectful silence and distance until the person is finished.
• Food is a good "ice-breaker" in conversation, but do not discuss dishes that include pork or that are cooked in wine or alcohol.
• Smoking is common in Saudi Arabia and, where it is not permitted, there will be signs. However, you should not smoke in public from dawn to dusk during Ramadan, or anytime in front of the Royal Family. Women are not supposed to smoke.
• It is not acceptable in Saudi Arabia for men to go without shirts or to wear shorts in public.
• Saudis respond well to offers of extra benefits, such as trips to the United States, a weekend at your home, or a trip you might arrange to a special spot in the United States.
• Save every business card you receive. Many Saudis have unlisted telephones and addresses.
• For advertising in Saudi Arabia, remember that they do not represent the human body in any kind of art. In ads they favor pastoral scenes and the colors blue, green, and white. Black is reserved for funerals. Religious symbols or sayings from the Koran are not appropriate.

EXECUTIVE TRAVEL TO SAUDI ARABIA   •

DOCUMENTS

You cannot enter the country without a valid visa. Visa requirements and regulations vary, depending on the purpose of the trip, and it is best to check with the U.S. Department of Commerce for the most current information. Allow adequate time prior to your departure for visa formalities.

INOCULATIONS

Cholera and smallpox shots are not required but are recommended. It is suggested that you check with your physician, should you have any question.

AIRPORTS

Jeddah International airport—approximately ½ hour from the city.
Riyadh airport—approximately 5 miles from the city.

CUSTOMS

Regulations are extremely strict and you should obtain a copy of *Special Travel Instructions to Saudi Arabia* from the consulate to avoid complications.

U.S. EMBASSY

> P. O. Box 149, Palestine Road, Ruwais, Jeddah
> Phone: 667-0080   Telex: 405175

TRANSPORTATION

Taxis are the chief mode of transportation. Business travelers should arrange to have a car and a driver/translator for the length of their stay.

TIPPING

A 15 percent service charge is usually included on your hotel and restaurant bill. Any additional tipping is optional.

HOTELS

DHAHRAN, DAMMAM, AL KOHBAR

Dhahran Palace
P.O. Box 381 Dhahran
Phone: 45444   Telex: 601227

Gulf Meridien Hotel (Al Khobar)
Cornich Boulevard
Phone: 864-6000   Telex: 670505

JEDDAH

Al Badr Jeddah Hotel
Airport Road
Phone: 6310000   Telex: 40512

Al Salam Meridien Hotel
King Khaled Street & Mecca Road
Phone: 6314000   Telex: 401276

Hyatt Regency Jeddah
Medina Road
Phone: (02) 6519800   Telex: 402688

RIYADH

Hyatt Regency Riyadh
Redec Plaza
Phone: (01) 4771111   Telex: 202963

Marriott Riyadh Hotel
Maather Road
Phone: 4779300   Telex: 928-200-983

Riyadh Inter-Continental Hotel
Maazar Street
Phone: 465-5000   Telex: 201076

Riyadh Palace Hotel
Prince Fahd bin Abdulaziz Street
Phone: 4012644   Telex: 200312

RESTAURANTS

The best restaurants are located in the first-class hotels. It is suggested that you inquire of the concierge or your Saudi host as to the quality of the local restaurants.

TRAVEL TIPS

• If bringing in prescription drugs for personal use, be sure they are clearly labeled with your name, doctor's name, pharmacy, and contents.

• Observe standards of dress and personal conduct as referred to in the Saudi Arabia country outline, and seriously heed the absolute ban on alcohol.

• International telephone, telegraph, and telex services are available.

• Dental and medical care are available, with the majority of the doctors and dentists Western trained. Both Jeddah and Riyadh have twenty-four-hour emergency service at their local hospitals.

• Water supplies are generally safe in the better hotels, but visitors are advised to drink bottled water or carbonated beverages. Caution should be exercised consuming fresh fruit and vegetables.

• Saudi radio broadcasts are in both Arabic and English, and two daily newspapers are printed in English. TV programs are limited, some with English dialogue.

• The larger cities have modern shopping centers thriving alongside the traditional *souq*, or market, filled with old and new treasures. Gold, fine jewelry, and hand-woven goods are some of the favorite choices.

• The hotels provide tennis courts, exercise rooms, and swimming pools, which are restricted for male use only.

• There is little nightlife. Dinner out or an invitation to a resident's home are the main choices.

IVORY COAST

Cultural Overview

The Republic of the Ivory Coast occupies an area (about the size of New Mexico) in western Africa on the Gulf of Guinea between Ghana and Liberia.

Since 1960, the Ivory Coast has been independent of France. The constitution of the Ivory Coast empowers the president to name his own successor. The president also appoints his Council of Ministers, 29 in number, who are responsible to him only. The National Assembly is a 147-member legislative body. There is a single political party, the Ivory Coast Democratic party.

Full economic development for the Ivory Coast has been the goal of the independent government, and its relative stability has made this nation a leader in economic development. Its agriculture based economy enjoyed rapid growth during the 1960s and 1970s. During the early 1980s the falling prices for cocoa and coffee, slowing oil production, and rising interest rates made it impossible for the Ivory Coast to pay its international debts. Austerity measures were imposed, the debts were rescheduled, and the country is again moving toward recovery and renewed economic growth.

Recent revisions in the investment codes reinforced the government's liberal approach to private enterprise and foreign investment, including special incentives for labor-intensive, small-scale industrial schemes that provide employment in rural areas.

The Ivory Coast has a population of 8 or 9 million of varying ethnic groups, including the Malinke, Don, Bete, Wobe, Akan, Senoufo, and Kron peoples. An expatriate population of fifty thousand is primarily composed of French technical, government, management advisors, and businesspeople, and there are many Lebanese. The workforce is augmented by 2 million migrant laborers from neighboring Mali.

The government pays for public school education, and builds a school for students through sixth grade in every settlement with 500 families. Close to 80 percent of the children receive a primary education, although fewer girls than boys attend classes. A public university with many disciplines has campuses throughout the country. About a fourth of the people are Muslims. Many others follow traditional beliefs such as ancestor worship, animism (harmony with nature), and spirit religions.

The Ivory Coast has three rivers flowing north and south, which dominate the central plains. Forests in the western region are the basis of the large number of wood products industries, including mahogany. The climate varies from hot and dry in the north to hot and humid in the coastal south. The economic capital is Abidjan which is on a series of islands on the coast, and which has been called the "Riviera of Africa." The administrative capital is Yamoussoukro, a "new city" being developed in the interior of the Ivory Coast, and government departments and operations will move there when the Abidjan–Yamoussoukro road is completed.

Although many women are found in business in the Ivory Coast, they generally work in the marketplace. It is not usual to find women in executive positions in international business. The Ivory Coast has several traditional languages, but French is used in the business world.

Business Opportunities

The Ivory Coast has many opportunities for business: natural resources, manufacturing, agriculture, construction, and the business of national development. But the key is researching the possibilities from both traditional and profitable points of view. Serious considerations are the ready availability of workers, or the ability to train them; or prohibitive tariffs that protect French interests. Currently, France supports 35 percent of the import needs of the Ivory Coast.

The Ivory Coast has good railroads, airports, waterways, and roads, which makes it possible to have access to development areas and to get goods to market.

Initiating Contact

Business in the Ivory Coast is almost always initiated in Abidjan, the country's economic capital and largest port city. Contacts are easily made. The following organizations will help put you in touch with a trading partner in the Ivory Coast:

Ivory Coast Embassy
Bureau of Investment
177 East 55th Street
New York, N.Y. 10017
Phone: (212) 355-6975

Department of Foreign Trades
Abidjan, Ivory Coast
Phone: 322627

Consul Economique et Social
Abidjan, Ivory Coast

General Surveillance Co. (Export-Import)
Abidjan, Ivory Coast
Phone: 321290

Since Ivorian businessmen travel frequently to New York in search of opportunities for business, you may be able to arrange a meeting in the United States. It is helpful to start exploring business opportunities with an Ivorian who has had some experience with the United States and its customs.

For additional information, contact:

World Trade Center Abidjan
(Centre de Commerce International Abidjan)
P.O. Box V.68
Abidjan, Ivory Coast
Phone: 32-38-69   Telex: 23460

Ivorian Center of Foreign Trade
P.O. Box V.142
Abidjan, Ivory Coast
Phone: 322635

International Economic Policy (Ivory Coast)
International Trade Administration
14th Street and Constitution Avenue
U.S. Department of Commerce
Washington, D.C. 20230
Phone: (202) 377-4388

Business Protocol and Procedures

BUSINESS ENVIRONMENT

Be sure to confirm your appointment by letter or telex. Once there, it is best to reconfirm by phone with the secretary of the person you are meeting.

Business hours are from 8:00 A.M. to 12:00 noon, and from 3:00 P.M. to 6:00 P.M. This is based on the old tradition of taking advantage of the light, and being practical about avoiding the midday heat. It is not uncommon for African businessmen to have sunrise meetings. The long lunch hour is to enjoy a leisurely lunch, freshen up, and get ready for the balance of the day.

You may have been met at the airport, either by your host or a member of the staff, and driven to your hotel. If necessary, you will be picked up at your hotel and delivered to the meeting. It is best to be punctual. Once you are comfortable, drinks will be served (either cold soft drinks, coffee, tea, or cocoa). Some time will be spent in discussing non-business-related subjects as a way of getting acquainted.

If you do not speak French, you will need an interpreter. Although some Ivorian businessmen do speak English, it is usually with difficulty. You may want to audiotape the sessions, and translate them later. Your host may supply an interpreter as part of the business transaction. But any documents or written material will also probably be in French.

RANK AND STATUS

The structure of Ivorian companies is European in style, with a general manager as the top executive, who is equal to the president or CEO here. Second-in-command is the director or vice president, followed by managing directors who have specific functions, such as Managing Director of Corporate Development.

FORMS OF ADDRESS

If you have been met at the airport, you will go through the formalities of greeting there. If not, at the first meeting, give a firm handshake when being introduced. When the relationship matures, you can expect to be greeted with a hug and what seems like a kiss but is actually more a touch on each cheek. First the left, then the right, then the left again, three times. Try not to bump noses. The gesture is easier with practice.

BUSINESS CARDS

Cards are important. In addition to your name and title, they should have the name, address, and telex and telephone numbers of your company. You can present them when you are being introduced.

BUSINESS DRESS

By French standards, better clothes make a good impression. Africans are not quite so concerned. With the tropical climate, it is advisable to wear suitable lightweight, practical clothing. In the rainy seasons an umbrella and a raincoat are necessary.

GIFT-GIVING

Gifts are common in the Ivory Coast. Electronic gadgets are good: singing calculators, exotic phones, radios. Be sure anything electric is 200 volt/AC 50 cycles. Small battery operated goods are fine but do not forget to supply the batteries!

Gifts are usually presented to the family. Never present a gift to the wife only. Women love perfume or makeup. Bring the children some chocolate.

COMMUNICATION STYLES

Discussions are conducted in a friendly manner and in quiet voices. Even an absolute no is expected to be nice, diplomatic, and civilized.

The chief negotiator's aides will sit in such a way that they can make eye contact with him. Signals are highly structured means of answering questions. Whatever the question, if Ivorians say, "Let's wait and see," they almost always mean no.

Negotiating in the Ivory Coast

Many Ivorian businessmen have a background of government service. As in many developing countries, the government has the first choice from among the trained and educated people. The result is that when they do become businessmen, they are well connected in government circles, and are able to cut through red tape and handle bureaucratic tangles. This is very important when working with the new trade codes of the Ivory Coast. Entrepreneurs are encouraged, but the government remains involved in many industries.

Remember that personal relationships will be the foundation of any business deal. Africans rarely do business with a person who is not within the extended family, or at least a friend. Much time will be spent developing the rapport and trust necessary to carry you through the enterprise. The one-on-one relationship is very important.

If your negotiating team includes women, it may be difficult for both sides. Ivorian men are still used to dealing with women as people who serve them, not as equals. The problem is less if the Ivorian host has been educated in the West, but the situation requires delicate handling.

It is best to be well prepared, to do thorough research, and to understand and present the project thoroughly. If you can get French documents for the proposal, it will simplify the start of the negotiations. The major negotiators should meet to set up the framework for the working relationship. The managing director is usually part of the transaction and, if you lose his confidence by not being well prepared, you may not be able to regain it.

The terms of the agreement will be discussed point by point. All parties must understand each point and agree on them individually and in sequence. Teams of negotiators can work on difficult points, and bring their agreement to the principal negotiators.

Lawyers are important. Choose one experienced in international transactions, and one with impeccable language skills. Ivorian contracts are drawn up under the jurisdiction of Ivory Coast law, which is patterned after the French system. So much will be unfamiliar to you that you must rely on your lawyer's expertise and advice.

These observations will help you negotiate successfully in the Ivory Coast:

• Gratuities are given for formalities and introductions in the Ivory Coast. They are not condoned by the authorities, but it is true that they make the wheels turn faster. If you think you need this help, discuss this carefully and frankly with your host, and find out how they should be handled.
• Coax instead of push. Outline your points one by one in a clear manner.

• Be patient. Business in Africa is much slower than in the United States.

• Sending a woman as the sole negotiator could prejudice the business proposal.

• With difficult technical discussions, it may be best to have a professional interpreter, one who has experience in the field you are discussing.

Business Entertaining

Business entertaining is a way of promoting the friendship that is so necessary for a good business relationship. Most Western food is imported and therefore expensive. But invitations are expected and a good impression is important. Choose a good restaurant, preferably French. For your first invitation, it will be up to you to choose and make the arrangements. Later, one can discuss the plans with your Ivorian counterpart and try local menus and the hot, spicy African dishes.

Dinner usually begins at 8:00 P.M. and goes on until 10:00 or 10:30 P.M. It is proper to invite your host's spouse, especially if your spouse is with you.

If you are invited to someone's home, bring a gift of flowers with you. These are greatly appreciated. Imported whiskey also makes a nice gift for your host.

The classic toast, *"Santé,"* "Good luck," "To our friendship," is accompanied by a clinking of glasses. In salute to the ancestors, a small amount of the liquid to be consumed is poured on the ground.

General Tips

• The initial get-acquainted period is a way of getting to know each other's tempo and demeanor. It is seen as a means of welcoming you and making you feel at home.

• Ivorians are not flamboyant, but they do have the French flair for enjoying the finer things, and appreciating the quality, of life. Usually, they do not drink wine without food or eat a meal without wine.

• The personal relationship will develop through a series of invitations to eat together or to visit your host's home, or perhaps through a trip to the African country.

• Be prepared to try *fou-fou,* a starchy cassava paste eaten with the fingers and used to sop up the spicy soups and stews.

• In restaurants and cafés, a service charge is added to the bill. If not, 10 percent is the usual amount to tip.

• Africans are passionate about politics. If you talk about politics, you may choose the wrong position. Be careful.

• Ivorians are polite about bad French, but find it amusing when one cannot deal in their language.

• One who always talks business is suspect. Making friends means you have to consider the human aspect.

• It is best not to keep score or expect returns on favors. Whatever you do is an investment in friendship, and one friend may give more than another to a relationship.

EXECUTIVE TRAVEL TO THE IVORY COAST •

DOCUMENTS

A valid passport and a visa are required. Business travelers should support their application with a letter from their firm giving full details of the business to be undertaken and accepting financial responsibility for the applicant.

INOCULATIONS

A valid international certificate against smallpox is required from all persons visiting the Ivory Coast. It is advisable to be vaccinated against yellow fever and cholera. Malaria prophylaxis is strongly recommended.

AIRPORT

Abidjan airport (Port Bouet) is approximately 10 miles from the center of town.

CUSTOMS

Personal effects, along with 200 cigarettes or 400 grams of tobacco, are allowed duty-free, as well as a camera, portable typewriter, and so on. Check with the airline or your travel agent for specific items you may wish to bring.

U.S EMBASSY

> 5 rue Jesse Owens
> Abidjan, Ivory Coast
> Phone: 324630 or 322581

TRANSPORTATION

Taxis are available, but it is recommended that you hire a car and a driver/translator for your stay.

TIPPING

A service charge of 10 to 15 percent is usually added to the bill. If not, tip in that range. It is customary to tip those at the hotel that provide services (porters, maids, etc.).

HOTELS

Abidjan

> Du Parc
> Avenue Chardy
> Phone: 222386

> Forum Golf
> Boulevard Lagunaire
> Phone: 431043

> Ivoire Inter-continental
> Boulevard de la Corniche
> Phone: 441045

> Palm Beach
> on the beach at Vridi
> Phone: 368116

> Relais Aeriens
> at Cocoday
> Phone: 349661

RESTAURANTS

The larger hotels have restaurants of international standards and are preferred to local ones unless you are specifically recommended to one by a resident whose opinion you value.

TRAVEL TIPS

- Best buys: woven and printed cloth, sculpture, bead necklaces, ivory carvings, and leatherwork.
- Abidjan has several air-conditioned cinemas and a theatre in the university complex at Cocody. The French Cultural Center presents films and plays.
- A wide choice of water sports is available with many hotels offering sail and motor boating, water skiing, and so on. Deep-sea fishing is very popular.
- The African character of the city can best be felt in Treichville, which is surrounded by many restaurants and nightclubs. You will, no doubt, be taken there by your host as it is not advisable for tourists to go there alone.
- The heat can be oppressive so be sure to pack for the weather.

NIGERIA

Cultural Overview

Nigeria, on Africa's west coast, is about the size of Texas and Wyoming combined. It is the most populous country in Africa, with 94 million people or one-fifth of the total on the continent.

After over ninety years as a British protectorate, Nigeria became independent in 1960. Although it experimented with democracy and the elective process, it is again under military rule. The military suspended the constitution and imposed austerity measures, along with prohibitive economic decrees about foreign exchange. The military government has maintained good relationships with the West. Government-owned and -run enterprises are being opened up to the private sector.

Nigeria's petroleum (called "sweet oil" in the marketplace) is in heavy demand. Since it's discovery in 1958, the development of petroleum resources has helped Nigeria's economy to become one of the most vigorous and powerful in Africa. With this prosperity, Nigeria has constructed the country's much-needed infrastructure.

Nigeria has swamps, rain forests, savanna, and woodland, and a long coastline with sandy bays. It borders on the Sahara in the north and is well watered by two major rivers: the Niger and the Benue.

The climate is tropical, with two well-defined seasons. The rainy season lasts from April to October and sometimes has very high humidity. The dry season lasts from November through March.

Nigeria has 19 states. The principal cities are Lagos, Kano, and Port Harcourt. Ibadan, Kaduna, Ogbomosho, Enugu, and Benin are also important. Abudja, a "new city" being built in the interior, has been designated as the nation's new capital.

Many languages are spoken, primarily Hausa, Yoruba, and Ibo. However, English (the language of administration and education) is used almost exclusively for business matters. It is also spoken in shops and hotels everywhere. Freedom of worship is guaranteed and the predominant religions are Islam, which is found chiefly in northern Nigeria, and Christianity, which is prevalent in the south. Traditional African religions such as ancestor worship are found throughout the country.

Nigerians have a high regard for education, and in 1975 the government launched a universal primary education policy aimed at providing free education for all. Nigeria does have universities, and the government supports students who study in other countries in fields that will be useful for building the nation. Nigeria has a 37 percent adult literacy rate.

Nigerians marry young, sometimes with arranged partners. Under customary law a man may have many wives, but practically the economics of polygamy are harsh. The practice is disappearing in urban areas. The concept of extended family is important in Nigerian life.

In Africa, the woman's role has been traditional, limited to the family, taking care of her husband and children. Indeed, in Nigeria, women are not considered complete unless they marry and have children. Without these traditional relationships, women are not taken seriously, even though many have had an education and some have achieved high positions in government and in careers.

Business Opportunities

Nigeria has been an important trading partner for the United States, and a major supplier of petroleum of both the United States and Europe. The nation has a huge market for foreign investment, technology transfer, capital equipment, and consumer products. Opportunities range from steel and manufacturing projects and the multibillion-dollar seaport to simple export-import transactions.

A Western businessperson should design a business plan that coincides with the nation's priorities, which are stated in the government's Development Plan. You can get a copy of the plan from the Nigerian Consulate.

Finding a Nigerian partner is most important. A prospective investor should investigate these with care and choose the one who blends with desired objectives.

Lagos is the commercial center of the nation.

Initiating Contact

In order to do business in Nigeria, your company must incorporate locally, unless it has been invited or approved by the government. Business in Nigeria must conform to the Nigerian Enterprise Decree of 1977, which encourages foreign investment but also ensures local participation. Copies of the decree are available from the Nigerian Investment & Promotion Center, 575 Madison Avenue, New York, N.Y. 10022.

Getting a business permit may take up to six months. Correct completion of the ten-part form is essential because if the form is incorrect, it may be rejected, and submitting a new application could take another considerable amount of time. Paperwork is a constant problem when doing business in Nigeria.

The following organizations may be of help in establishing business in Nigeria:

• Both the United Bank of Africa and the National Bank of Nigeria, with branches in New York, have staff who can help you get started with the formalities in the banking areas.
• The commercial consuls of the Nigerian consulates can make sure that your company registration and licenses are in order.
• The Commercial Section at the consulate can help reduce your risks by checking on your partners to verify their financial status and reliability. The consuls can also clarify the rules regarding foreign exchange restrictions and bank procedures.

In addition, contact the following for assistance:

World Trade Center of Nigeria, Ltd.
Western House, 8th floor

8/10 Broad Street, P.O. Box 4466
Lagos, Nigeria
Phone: 631499/632151

Nigerian-American Chamber of Commerce, Inc.
P.O. Box 5298, FDR Station
New York, N.Y. 10150
Phone: (212) 421-3580

Nigerian Association of Chambers of Commerce, Industry, Mines
  and Agriculture
Union Bank Building
131 Broad Street, 3rd floor
P.O. Box 109
Lagos, Nigeria
Phone: 664202

International Trade Administration
U.S. Department of Commerce
14th Street and Constitution Avenue
Washington, D.C. 20230
Phone: (202) 377-4388

Consulate General of Nigeria
575 Lexington Avenue
New York, N.Y. 10022
Phone: (212) 936-6100

Business Protocol and Procedures

BUSINESS ENVIRONMENT

Official business hours are from 8:00 A.M. to 12:00 noon and from 2:00 P.M. to 5:00 P.M. weekdays, and on Saturdays from 8:00 A.M. to noon. Government hours are from 7:30 A.M. to 3:30 P.M. Mondays through Fridays.

It is best not to schedule more than two appointments a day and allow plenty of time in between. Nigerians do not have a rigid sense of time. Your host may show up later than the scheduled hour.

In addition, a meeting is often interrupted by staff, visitors, or business matters. It will serve you well to be patient in Nigeria. Senior executives often have many responsibilities that require, and divide, their attention. Likewise, you can make an unscheduled call in Nigeria. Businesspeople obviously tolerate them, and often you will be graciously received.

Make arrangements while you are in your Nigerian host's office to use the telex for a report to your office. Telexes are not widely available in the country.

RANK AND STATUS

Both rank and status are enhanced by education. Technocrats are highly regarded, and a man or a woman with a Ph.D. is given respect and called "Doctor." Two other titles, *"Al Hajji"* and "Chief," are respected. *"Al Hajji"* indicates a Muslim who has made the pilgrimage to Mecca; thus, this title indicates both maturity and responsibility toward his religion.

FORMS OF ADDRESS

If the Nigerian has a title, it should always be used in direct address. If not, use "Mr.," "Mrs.," or "Miss" and the last name. It is proper to shake hands when being introduced or when greeting someone. In Nigeria, the gesture is more a lingering grasp of hands without pressure or a pumping motion. Take extra time to inquire about a person's health, spouse, children, friends, and relatives.

BUSINESS CARDS

Business cards are sometimes called "compliment cards." They often say "With the compliments of" and are considered meaningful, more than just a handy reference for names and addresses. You are expected to have a card. When you offer your card to a Nigerian, you can ask for one in return.

BUSINESS DRESS

The U.S. businessman should be dressed in a conservative, tropical suit, light shirt, and tie. Short sleeves are acceptable. Businesswomen should be dressed stylishly. The Nigerian may be dressed in a Western suit or in colorful national dress.

GIFT-GIVING

In view of the government's attitude and its War Against Indiscipline, to discourage corruption it is best not to give monetary or other gifts; only small items, such as a calculator or a pen with your company logo, are appropriate.

It is acceptable, however, to bring some small gift when invited to someone's home.

COMMUNICATION STYLES

Nigerians are a happy, friendly people. Their business style is spirited but, because it is influenced by British etiquette, it is also quite formal. In general, Nigerians are confident and secure in the future and greatness of their country, and will negotiate from this viewpoint.

Negotiating in Nigeria

Since Nigeria is only a recent trading partner in the world marketplace, the customs of doing business are not set, and will be determined by many factors: the background and training of your trading partner; the size of your project; and whether it is part of the public sector or the private sector.

In general, the Nigerian way of business is a mix of various styles. Having learned the British system of administration and American technical know-how, they also employ unique Nigerian attitudes about winning, honed since the thirteenth century, when the country was an important route for caravans moving across Africa. Nigerians have been trading since then, and do not operate within the win-win system common to Western negotiations. Nigerians play only to win, and expect you to win on your own, not by any concessions that they offer. In essence, Nigerian businesspeople play hardball. The stakes are usually big.

It is important to start your negotiating with the person who has ultimate authority in the company. Also, do not take anything for granted. Every detail is important because it could cause huge losses in time and money. Have patience. If you walk out of a meeting, it is considered a sign of disrespect. You will never be able to recover your position.

A common practice in Nigeria is the "dash," or a tip. In order to get a job done, it is necessary to dash. The practice is very common and expected everywhere, although the new military government has created a campaign against it called War Against Indiscipline. WAI has helped modify the behavior of Nigerians a little but dash still continues.

In dealing with the government, you will have to work with an extensive civil service system. Another legacy of British rule is the complicated system of barristers and solicitors. It is best to find a lawyer who knows the intricacies of the administrative and legal systems.

Some ideas to help you:

• Doing business in Nigeria requires patience and wit.
• Resign yourself to dealing with forms and more forms, signed and countersigned and carried through ministries, clearinghouses, and registries for signatures and stamps.
• Ask your Nigerian host or contact how best to deal with the practice of dash. It may be necessary to get a job done.
• Expect business negotiations to be long term.

Business Entertaining

It is probable that you will continue business negotiations over lunch at a restaurant near your host's office. You may offer to pay the bill. Since Nigerians are cordial and generous, it is likely they will want to take their guests instead of vice versa.

Breakfast meetings are popular as Nigerians start their day early, and discussing business over breakfast is often productive. Nigerians appreciate this opportunity to extend their business day.

Usually, social evenings are reserved until you are near the end of business negotiations. By this time you have established friendly relations and you will probably be invited to the home of the Nigerian executive. You should return the invitation by being host at a dinner or lunch at your hotel.

General Tips

• Lagos is the second most costly city in the world. Be prepared to spend about $250 a day to get your business done.
• Try not to be upset if your host shows up late for an appointment.
• Lagos has a serious traffic problem during the rush hour. Therefore, consider this when scheduling appointments and allow sufficient time for commuting.

- In Nigeria what status you have will not impress people. Only what you do will be counted. Do not brag.
- Do not use black market currency.
- It is best not to discuss politics.
- Nigerians are very proud of their country, and your praise of its prosperity and growth will be well received.

EXECUTIVE TRAVEL TO NIGERIA   •

DOCUMENTS

Valid passport, visa, and international health certificate are necessary. When applying for a visa, enclose a letter in duplicate from your firm giving full details of the business to be conducted, including the names of your business contacts, and confirming financial responsibility for the applicant. In addition, a letter of invitation from a Nigerian firm or government representative relevant to the visit is required.

INOCULATIONS

Antimalarial medication is advised.

AIRPORTS

The principal airports are Ikeja (Murtala Muhammad) International Airport, which is 16 miles from Lagos; Kano airport, which services the north; and Port Harcourt, which serves the oil areas.

CUSTOMS

Exempt from import duty are one one-quart bottle of liquor, one one-quart bottle of wine, 200 cigarettes or 50 cigars, or ½ pound total tobacco.

U.S. EMBASSY

2 Eleke Crescent, Lagos
Phone: 610097   Telex: 21670

TRANSPORTATION

Taxis are available, but it is advisable that you hire a car and driver for your stay.

TIPPING

Tip 10 percent, if not included in the bill. Tipping is also proper for taxi drivers, porters, and other services. Some hotels and restaurants add a 10 to 20 percent service charge to the bill. If they do not, add this yourself.

HOTELS

LAGOS

Holiday Inn
Victoria Island, PMB 12724
Phone: 615000   Telex: 22650

Federal Palace Hotel
Victoria Island
Phone: 610030/31   Telex: 21432

Ikoyi Hotel
Kingsway Road
Phone: 603200-8   Telex: 22632

KANO

Daula Hotel
150 Murtala Muhammad Way, PM Bag 3228
Phone: (064) 5311-3   Telex: 77241

PORT HARCOURT

Presidential Hotel
Aba Road, PMB 5141
Phone: 335655 or 229647   Telex: 61182

RESTAURANTS

The larger hotels have restaurants with international standards; they are preferred to local ones.

TRAVEL TIPS

• Water sports are the most popular and facilities for riding, golf, tennis, football (soccer), and cricket are available—mostly through clubs or your hotel.

- English language movies are shown in many cities and live theatre and art exhibits are well supported.
- Medical and emergency care can be received at both government and private hospitals.
- Radio, television, and 17 daily newspapers are in English.
- Carry your passport and travel documents with you at all times to certify that you are a traveler in transit.
- Nigerian currency may not be changed back into foreign exchange at hotels and banks. You may be able to arrange for this at the airport bank before your departure, if the foreign currency you want is available. Avoid transactions with money changers (touts) at the airport.
- International telephone, telegram, and telex facilities are available. Your hotel will instruct you as to closest locations.

NORTH AMERICA

CANADA

Cultural Overview

Canada is the second largest country in the world, but only a third of the land is developed. Most Canadians live within two hundred miles of the United States, with which Canada shares the world's largest unguarded international border.

Canada is an independent federal democracy of ten provinces and two northern territories. The 1867 British North America Act of the British Parliament created Canada's two-level structure of government, and Canada's new constitution, the Canada Bill (1982), outlines areas of responsibility. The territories are under federal jurisdiction, which includes banking, transportation, trade and commerce, criminal law, defense, and external affairs. The provinces (like U.S. states) have partial self-government, with jurisdiction over education, property law, municipal affairs, natural resources, labor law, and direct taxation for provincial purposes.

Canada has three primary political parties: the Progressive Conservatives, Liberals, and New Democrats. The party in power is elected for five years. But the government in power can call an election at any time if it is to their advantage to do so, and by doing so can be elected for another five-year term. The prime minister is the leader of the majority party in the House of Commons (whose members are elected by the people for not more than five years) and the effective head of government.

The governor general is the nominal head, a ceremonial position, and is chosen by the Canadian government and confirmed as the British sovereign's representative by the Crown. Although the governor general appoints members of the other legislative branch, the Senate, for life, these appointments are on the recommendation of the prime minister and the cabinet. The prime minister chooses the cabinet from members of the same party holding seats in Parliament. Each minister heads a department in the government.

All provincial legislatures consist of unicameral elected assemblies similar to the House of Commons. Each province has its own lieutenant governor, the sovereign's representative.

The Canadian government has been heavily involved in the economy through Crown, or state-owned, corporations such as Air Canada. However, as a result of a change in parties in power at the federal level, the Canadian government is actively looking for buyers of state enterprises.

Foreign companies control a significant portion of Canadian industry, particularly in manufacturing and resource development. U.S. companies account for three-fourths of foreign ownership. In recent years, Canada has had some problems from the increase in foreign ownership, rapid urbanization and industrialization, the exploitation of natural resources, the resurgence of French-Canadian nationalism, and both inflation and recession.

Canada has one of the fastest rates of population growth for an industrialized nation. But, because it is so large, it also has a low population density. It has a tenth the people of the United States, or 25 million. Three of four Canadians live in urban areas; 60 percent live on 2 percent of the land, in a six-hundred-mile strip from Quebec City to Windsor, Ontario. Much of Canada's land is mountainous and rocky; fully 89 percent has no permanent settlement. The nation has four seasons, and the weather can change frequently.

There are five distinct regions in Canada: the resource-rich Atlantic provinces; the Prairies; British Columbia; and the two industrialized areas of Ontario and Quebec. Provincial rivalry and separatism are strong, stemming from the fact that more than 40 percent of Canadians are of British origin, while 30 percent are French.

By federal law, Canada has two official languages: English (spoken by 61 percent) and French (26 percent). French is the only official language of Quebec. The province of New Brunswick is officially bilingual but English is dominant elsewhere.

Education in Canada is government financed, and school is compulsory to age 15. About 20 percent of the population goes on to university or technical training. The French Canadians are primarily Roman Catholic, while the rest follow a variety of Protestant faiths, principally that of the United Church of Canada.

The family unit is important in Canada, but there is a trend toward smaller families and an increase in the number of single-parent families. The women's movement is as successful as it has been in the United States, and women do fill executive positions.

The closeness of the United States and Canada and the similarity of values makes it difficult to detect differences. But it would be a mistake for U.S. businesspeople to assume that Canadian hosts share their attitudes. One basic difference for Canadians is the existence of two distinct cultures in their country, and the continued threat of separatism. While 80 percent of the business world in Canada has a British heritage and speaks English, the official policy of bilingualism affects all dealings. Thousands of miles away from French-speaking Quebec, Saskatchewanians who apply for a civil service job must speak both languages.

Business Opportunities

Many industries in Canada's free enterprise economy are controlled by federal and provincial legislation but none are closed to private enterprise. The same holds true for foreign companies, with some exceptions in areas of energy, telecommunications, and transportation.

Foreign investment in Canada has played a significant role in the growth of the economy. Although it has been declining, foreign ownership still accounts for about 33 percent of the total economy, and the new government is more disposed to welcome U.S. companies than the former government was. In previous years, a screening framework, called the Foreign Investment Review Agency (FIRA) was set up to pass on investments that could prove to be of demonstrable benefit to Canada. In reality, it was a blocking agency that held up business investors through a complex and time-consuming process. It would often take as long as a year to get a ruling. Now the new regime is dismantling that organization and changing it to Investment Canada, which is set up to help people invest.

Canada and the United States are each other's largest trade partners and Canada depends on U.S. management skills, markets, capital, and technology. There is a saying among Canadian businesspeople that "When the U.S. economy gets a cold, we get pneumonia." Although the United States may be more powerful, both countries need each other to realize the best potential for North America.

Established industries in this country that have good potential for growth include petrochemicals, plastics, machinery, railroad rolling stock, grain exports, high-tech industries such as semiconductors, satellite communications, computers, new plastics that conduct electricity, drugs, and medical products. The service sector's share of total Canadian output is increasing.

As a result of the great distance between the east and west coasts, transportation costs are of paramount importance. Also, the ethnicity of the Canadian market is significant. There are differing tastes in chicken and chocolate marketed in the French and English areas. Quebec province is not expected to experience much growth, primarily because of lagging capital investment. In the nineteen years of a proseparatist provincial government, a number of major English-speaking investors have left Quebec.

Initiating Contact

Finding a business partner in Canada can be as simple as finding one in Georgia if you are based in Chicago. Although the countries are separate and distinct, the volume of trade and the similarity of cultures have made doing business in Canada seem more like a regional matter than a national one.

You can call an executive directly, or send a telex, to say that you will be in Toronto, or Montreal, and would like a meeting. The best approach is to send a letter first, outlining your proposal and the special merits of your company.

Other methods of finding an association, beginning a business, or finding out about markets include the following:

• The Canadian Department of Industry and Commerce has trade offices in major U.S. cities. These councils sponsor trade shows and exhibits and can even arrange introductions for U.S. businesspeople going to Canada, and vice versa.
• The Ontario provincial government puts out informational circulars on a monthly basis for Ontario businesspeople. It lists U.S. companies looking for Canadian products. Check the other provinces for similar circulars.
• Contact the local Chambers of Commerce or local Boards of Trade in a specific Canadian city.

For additional assistance, contact:

World Trade Centre Montreal
Montreal Chamber of Commerce
772 Sherbrooke Street West
Montreal, Quebec, Canada H3A 1G1
Phone: (514) 288-9090

World Trade Centre Toronto
Toronto Harbour Commissioners
60 Harbour Street
Toronto, Ontario, Canada M5J 1B7
Phone: (416) 863-2154   Telex: 219666

Canadian Consulate General
1251 Avenue of the Americas—16th floor
New York, N.Y. 10020
Phone: (212) 586-2400
(Also offices in Atlanta, Boston, Buffalo, Chicago, Dallas, Detroit,
   Los Angeles, Minneapolis, San Francisco, and Seattle.)

U.S. Commerce Department
Country Specialist/Canada
Washington, D.C. 20230
Phone: (202) 377-5327

Department of Industry Trade & Commerce
235 Queen Street

Ottawa, Ontario, Canada K1A 0H5
Phone: (613) 995-5771

Business Protocol and Procedures

BUSINESS ENVIRONMENT

Business hours for commercial firms are from 9:00 A.M. to 5:00 P.M.; government offices are open from 8:30 A.M. to 4:30 P.M.; banking hours are from 10:00 A.M. to 3:00 P.M.

Meetings may be held in your Canadian host's office, in boardrooms or conference rooms, or even during lunch.

Except in Quebec, where French is the primary language, you will not need an interpreter. You will find interpreting and translation services in Montreal. The Canadian firm may provide an interpreter, but it is better to employ your own.

When setting up appointments and planning your schedule, it helps to understand that the differences between Canada and the United States are similar to the differences between California and New York. In essence, they are regional, except for Quebec. Use the same sort of discretion. Also, the area in Canada corresponds to the same geographic area in the United States. Winnipeg is like our west, Vancouver like California.

RANK AND STATUS

Business titles are much the same as in the United States including president or CEO and vice president. There may also be senior vice presidents and executive vice presidents. All indicate senior positions and decision-making responsibility. The next level will be managers, and they will be responsible for a specific department, such as a marketing or product manager. They may also be called directors or supervisors, such as director of personnel. This will vary from industry to industry.

FORMS OF ADDRESS

The Canadians are slightly more formal than people from the United States, and less reserved than the British. Informality in the use of first names is common. When meeting someone for the first time, either during a business meeting or socially, shake hands and say your first and last name, as "Dan Winkler," or "I am Dan Winkler." If you are introduced by a colleague, follow the example set by that introduction. You may be introduced to a top executive, such as the president of the firm, as "Mr. Jones," for instance. If this tone is set, do not use first names until Mr. Jones suggests you do. With peers, first names are used as informally in Canada as they are in the United States.

If you are dealing with the president or CEO, it is a matter of discretion how informal you can be. Some may want to use first names right away. Older executives may prefer being addressed as "Mr. Smith."

When dealing with female executives, the use of "Ms." is commonly accepted, particularly in written communications.

BUSINESS CARDS

Business cards are used as extensively as in the United States. You may exchange them whenever and wherever business is discussed, at a formal business meeting or a cocktail party. You should carry them at all times. If you are going to an appointment with individuals you have not met, it is useful to leave cards with both the executives whom you meet and their secretaries.

BUSINESS DRESS

You should dress conservatively, in a subdued business suit, although the dress code varies from region to region. In Toronto wear blue, grey, brown, or pinstriped suits, traditionally cut. With the French influence in Montreal and other parts of Quebec, dress is more relaxed. Sports jackets and slacks are seen. This is also true in western Canada, where businesspeople may wear Western boots and hat and a string tie. Businesswomen should dress conservatively in suits, dresses, or blouses and skirts.

GIFT-GIVING

It is best not to present gifts to your business host in Canada. Business ethics regarding gifts (or bribery) are the same as in the United States. It is not done. If you have developed a sincere friendship, it might be appropriate for you to bring a souvenir type of gift, a memento from the United States or a particular region, such as a Western-style belt.

COMMUNICATION STYLES

The Canadian businessperson is apt to be less aggressive than a U.S. counterpart. He or she will use hard-sell and high-pressure techniques if necessary, however.

U.S. businesspeople have noted a subtle resentment from the Canadians in the past. It is important to remember that being neighbors is not always easy, and that U.S.–Canadian relations are constantly in a state of flux. In recent years, when the Foreign Investment Review Agency was operating, tensions were high. Since foreign companies are now more welcome, attitudes have also changed.

One factor that adds to the Canadians' sense of resentment is the image of their country that is portrayed in the U.S. media. Canada is not a French outpost and it does not have only arctic weather. Moreover, not all Canadians are lumberjacks or Mounties. These misconceptions persist despite efforts to eradicate them.

Negotiating in Canada

Canadian businesspeople face a different set of problems than do their U.S. counterparts, primarily because of the size of the market (one-tenth of the U.S.), the legal requirement for bilingual packaging, and their own desire for quality. Without totally bilingual packaging, the Canadian businessperson cannot market a product in Quebec, and this province represents 20 percent of the Canadian market. Every piece of literature, every catalogue, and every advertising campaign has to be, in effect, implemented twice, and the additional expense justified in the face of a smaller market. U.S. manufacturers must realize these requirements when dealing with Canadians.

If you are doing business in Quebec, it is best to know in advance if the key negotiators speak English, because if you have to rely on an interpreter your task will be much more difficult. The value system is different and the language can be a barrier. You will have to prepare differently. And it is essential that all written information be translated into French.

The business decision-making and negotiating style in Canada may be less dynamic than in the United States, but the Canadian will be familiar with the American style and may play a similar game if necessary to settle a fair and equitable deal. The Francophone executive will be slower to get down to business, preferring to enter into social banter first.

Professional presentations with slides, display, or a presentation book will be appreciated. Brochures or samples, especially those you can leave behind, will also be very helpful. Annual reports and leaflets describing your company and its place in your industry are also good. If you are not well prepared, especially if you are the seller, there is more of a chance of creating resentment than if you are someone from another culture with whom the Canadians have less in common.

Contract law in Canada is based predominantly on the British system and is identical to the U.S. legal practice. You will need a lawyer present as you begin final negotiations.

Business Entertaining

Canada does quite a bit of business entertaining, either in hotel restaurants or private clubs, for lunch or for dinner or for cocktails. You can reciprocate as you would if you were doing business in U.S. cities other than your hometown. It is not customary or necessary to invite your host's spouse. You can do so to be polite, but it also depends to some extent on the strength of your relationship.

Any internationally known hotel will have a world-class restaurant. This would be suitable, as would any of the well-known restaurants in the city. Ask your host. A few in various price ranges will probably be suggested, and you may be able to get an idea of where he or she would like to go. Many restaurants may not serve after 11:00 P.M. Call to be sure.

As your relationship develops you may get an invitation to the Canadian's home for dinner, to a country club for golf, or to a cottage in the northern lake area for a hunting or fishing trip. Business discussions will continue on these occasions.

General Tips

• Canada is changing from the Imperial system of weights and measures to the Standard International (metric) system.
• The Francophone Canadian people take their culture and lifestyle seriously. They like to share its richness with their guests. Be attentive.

• It is good to attempt to use basic French courtesy phrases when conducting business in Quebec.

• Slow down. Things are done with more circumspection and deliberation in Canada, and it is necessary to exercise patience in negotiations and discussions.

• It is important to remember you are in a foreign country. Do not talk to Canadians as if they were your compatriots, with the same attitudes as yours.

• Avoid talking down to Canadians just because the country is economically smaller. Canada's market is as large as California's. They are colleagues, and equals.

• Be sensitive to issues of contention between Canada and the United States, including acid rain and economic domination.

• It may help to deal with Canadians if you understand that they have long been under the economic domination of either Britain or the United States.

• The average Canadian assumes he or she knows more about the United States than the U.S. businessperson knows about Canada. This is often true. It helps to do some research and to be knowledgeable about the country.

EXECUTIVE TRAVEL TO CANADA   •

DOCUMENTS

There is no visa requirement for U.S. citizens, but it is advisable to carry proof of citizenship, that is, driver's license or social security card.

INOCULATIONS

None are required for U.S. citizens.

AIRPORTS

Montreal: Dorval Airport—14 miles to the city.
Toronto International Airport—18 miles to the city.
Quebec city—7 miles to downtown area of the city.

CUSTOMS

Regulations are not rigid and you are permitted to bring in reasonable amounts of personal effects as well as one 40-ounce bottle of liquor and 200 cigarettes, or 50 cigars and two pounds of tobacco.

U.S. EMBASSY

> 100 Wellington Street, Ottawa K1P, 5T1
> Phone: (613) 238-5335   Telex: 0533582

TRANSPORTATION

All major cities have good local transportation as well as taxis. You may wish to hire a car and driver for your stay.

TIPPING

Gratuities are included in hotel room prices, but an additional tip for extra service is appreciated. At restaurants 15 percent is proper, with the same for taxi drivers.

HOTELS

MONTREAL

> Bonaventure Hilton International
> 1 Place Bonaventure (P.O. Box 779, PQ H5A 1E4)
> Phone: (514) 878-2332   Telex: 24480

> Le Chateau Champlain
> 1 Place du Canada, PQ H3B 4C9
> Phone: (514) 878-1688   Telex: 60048

> Le Quatre Saisons
> 1050 Sherbrooke Quest, PQ H3A 2R6
> Phone: (514) 284-1110   Telex: 25142

> Ritz-Carlton Hotel
> 1228 Sherbrooke West, H3G 1H6
> Phone: (514) 842-4212 or (800) 327-0200   Telex: 24322

TORONTO

> The Four Seasons Hotel
> 21 Avenue Road
> Phone: 964-0411

King Edward Hotel
37 King Street East
Phone: 863-9700

Royal York Hotel
100 Front Street West
Phone: 368-2511

Toronto Hilton Harbor Castle
1 Harbor Square
Phone: 869-1600

The Windsor Arms
22 Saint Thomas Street
Phone: 979-2341

CALGARY

Palliser Hotel
133 Ninth Avenue S.W.
Phone: 266-8621

VANCOUVER

The Four Seasons
791 West Georgia Street
Phone: 689-9333

RESTAURANTS

MONTREAL

Chez la Mère Michel 1209 Guy Phone: 934-0473	*French*
Les Chenets 2075 Bishop Street Phone: 844-1842	*French*
Les Halles 1450 Crescent Street Phone: 844-2328	*French*
René Varaud Les Terrasses 705 Saint Catherine Ouest Phone: 843-8592	*French*

TORONTO

Courtyard Café Windsor Arms Hotel 22 Saint Thomas Street Phone: 979-2212	*Nouvelle cuisine*
Fenton's 12 Gloucester Street Phone: 961-2440	*Nouvelle cuisine*
Hy's Restaurant 73 Richmond Street West Phone: 364-3326	*Steakhouse*
Panarello's 123 Front Street West Phone: 366-8199	*Italian*
Truffles Four Seasons Hotel 21 Avenue Road Phone: 964-0411	*Continental*
Winston's 104 Adelaide Street West Phone: 363-1627	*Continental*

CALGARY

Owl's Nest 320 Fourth Avenue S.W. Phone: 266-1611	*French/continental*

VANCOUVER

Umberto's 1376–1383 Hornby Street Phone: 687-6316	*Italian*

TRAVEL TIPS

• Toronto has one of the highest pollen counts in North America; hay-fever sufferers should bring their regular medication along during season.

• Personal safety is not a major factor, but at night stay in well-traveled areas, and avoid isolated streets.

• Hockey, baseball, football, tennis tournaments, and thorough-bred racing are popular spectator sports. A full range of partici-pant sports—ice skating, tennis, golf, swimming, and skiing in season—are all readily available in the major cities.

• Canada observes the same four standard time zones as does the United States. Check with your airline or travel agent for the city you will be visiting.

• Summers are warm: average 71°F; winters are long and cold with average around 23°F, and plenty of snow. If traveling be-tween December and April, bring hats, boots, gloves, and heavy outer clothing.

• Canada recognizes the driver's licenses of most other countries. Road signs and traffic symbols are graphic in design and easily understood.

• Foreign currency should be exchanged at federally chartered banks to receive the best rates. The Canadian dollar is based on 100 cents.

• The summer holiday period extends from July through August, with some offices and factories shutting down for a two- to three-week duration during this period.

MEXICO

Cultural Overview

Los Estados Unidos Mexicanos, or Mexico, has grown dynamically in the last twenty years. It is one of the prominent NICs (Newly Industrializing Countries). The dramatic industrialization which is taking place is expected to continue as the population grows rapidly.

In recent years, the influence of U.S. culture has spread in Mexico. Yet more traditional values—family loyalty, personal relationships, and a conservative outlook—rule Mexican society.

Mexico is a federal democratic republic consisting of 31 states and the federal district of Mexico City. The government is headed by the president, who serves six years and cannot be reelected. Mexico is essentially a one-party state with the official government party, the Institutional Revolutionary party (PRI), winning most elections. Presidents are hand-picked by their predecessors and have often been important in the previous administration. There is a bicameral legislature as well as a judicial branch.

Recently, opposition parties have demonstrated for greater representation and have defeated some PRI candidates in northern states. However, the PRI is likely to continue to be dominant. It has tremendous popular appeal and is the party of Mexico's political and economic elite. Although basically conservative, its foreign policy rhetoric can sound moderately leftist.

Mexico's well-publicized problems with a huge foreign debt can be traced to the focus on development of its oil industry during an earlier administration. Dependence on oil revenues left the country ill equipped to deal with the depressed oil markets of the early 1980s. Also, Mexico's ability to feed its people declined as oil production increased. The present government understands the need to be financially prudent while generating economic development and jobs.

Mexico is the second largest economy in Latin America, and the government shares equally with the private sector in contributing to the GNP. Government agencies or government-owned or -controlled companies dominate in the areas of public utilities, petroleum, banking, and basic manufacturing, mining, commerce, entertainment, and service industries.

The United States is Mexico's major trade partner, while Mexico ranks third among U.S. trading partners. Mexico exports crude oil and agricultural products to the United States. Many U.S. firms take advantage of lower wage rates in Mexico to decrease the manufacturing costs of their products. Among markets that seem most promising to foreign producers are all types of consumer products. The two largest unsatisfied local markets are agricultural equipment and housing, especially low-cost units.

The leading imports from the United States are agricultural products such as corn and soybeans, motor vehicle parts, automatic data processing equipment parts, and paper.

Rules for foreign investment are not as constraining as for other Latin American countries, but they need reform. An important example is the limitations imposed on majority equity investments by foreign investors. The huge state-owned industrial complex is another weighty problem because of its inefficiencies and mismanagement.

Until the revolution of 1911, Roman Catholicism was the state religion; Catholicism still predominates among Mexicans today.

The federal government provides free education for all children through six years of primary school and three years of secondary school. It also funds the three largest universities in Mexico City. Some state governments help support education at all levels.

Marriage and family are very important to Mexicans. It is usual to have large families, and divorce is rare. Since traditional attitudes regarding the roles of men and women prevail, Mexican society is male dominated.

Mexico is one-fourth the size of the United States, but there is a wide variation in altitude. Most of the country is a highland plateau bordered on the east, west, and south by mountains. The northern part includes Mexico City, located at an altitude of 7,500 feet above sea level (by comparison, Denver is 5,280 feet).

Half the country is arid or semiarid, including the northern part that borders on Texas. Mexico City and the central part of the country have a temperate or semitropical climate with moderate temperatures ranging in the low seventies. Most of the coastal regions, including the Yucatán peninsula, have a humid, tropical climate, with temperatures averaging in the eighties. The rainy season runs from May to October, although the coast near the Gulf of Mexico has rain all year.

Mexico's population, now about 77 million, has one of the world's highest growth rates. It is primarily an urban nation, with three-fifths of its people living in large towns or cities. Over one-fifth live in Mexico City, the political and economic capital of the country.

Mexicans speak Spanish, although English is understood and spoken by many members of the business and political community. As Mexico has a major tourist industry, many service industry employees speak a number of languages. Indian dialects still survive in certain areas.

Business Opportunities

One important aspect of setting up business in Mexico is understanding the size and scope of the government's participation. Certain industries such as banking, petroleum and basic petrochemicals, railroads, and telecommunications are reserved for the state. And the government owns and operates a broad spectrum of companies in aviation, food distribution and processing, fertilizers, iron and steel, mining, forestry, sugar, and textiles.

Initiating Contact

When initiating contact, letters should include information on your firm's objectives, products, services, and management. Associated materials should be written in Spanish.

Third-party introductions are preferred, however, since they eliminate a degree of uncertainty for both parties. Otherwise, the following suggestions may be helpful:

• Make contacts through Mexican representatives in the United States, particularly the foreign trade offices. The Mexican Institute for Foreign Commerce has offices in New York, Chicago, Los Angeles, and Houston. It can help in providing contacts in Mexico City and other cities. Write the Institute at 950 Third Avenue, New York, N.Y. 10022.
• Or contact Mexican banks, with branches in large U.S. cities. Write Bancomer, 299 Park Avenue, New York, N.Y. 10017; Banco Nacional de Mexico, 375 Park Avenue, New York, N.Y. 10022; and Banco Serfin, 88 Pine Street, New York, N.Y. 10005.
• To do business with the government, a foreign businessperson must register with the Secretariat of Programming and Budget. Some government concerns require registration with their own purchasing departments. Since registration is a long, complex process, it should be handled by your firm's Mexico City representatives. If you do not have representation, the National Association of Importers and Exporters of the Republic of Mexico will assist you.
• Handle dealings with private business through an agent. The agent should have good market contacts and experience, the necessary technical skill and service capability, and sufficient financial resources.

For further information, contact:

American Chamber of Commerce of Mexico
Lucerna 78, A.P.O. 83
BIX, Mexico D.F.
Phone: (905) 566-0866

National Chamber of Commerce of Mexico
Paseo de la Reforma 42
Mexico, D.F.
Phone: (905) 535-0289

Mexican Chamber of Commerce in the U.S.
233 Broadway
New York, N.Y. 10007
Phone: (212) 227-9171

United States–Mexico Chamber of Commerce
1000 Potomac Street, Suite 102
Washington, D.C. 20007
Phone: (202) 296-5198   Telex: 892683

World Trade Center de Mexico
Central de Comercio Mundial S.A.
Mariano Escobedo 491-494
Delegación Miguel Hidalgo
C.P. 11570 Mexico City, Mexico
Phone: 254-1659

Business Protocol and Procedures

BUSINESS ENVIRONMENT

The foreign business executive should understand that Mexico has a relaxed business environment, with less pressure than in the United States. A Mexican's view of business is long range. He is interested in developing trust and a personal relationship with a high degree of reliability. For most Mexicans, personal relationships are essential before serious discussions can take place.

Business hours in Mexico are between 9:00 A.M. and 6:00 P.M. Lunch (sometimes called dinner in Mexico) is the main meal of the day and is later than in the United States at 2:00 P.M. or 2:30 P.M. Business is often discussed during lunch, to clarify or amplify points made during morning meetings.

However, the main purpose of a business lunch is enjoyment. Spend time expressing your favorable interest in the country. Lunch may conclude the business day for many executives.

The U.S. negotiating team should consist of at least one senior decision-making executive. This executive should be accompanied by one or more middle-level managers. A lawyer should not be present on the first trip.

Women still occupy traditional positions in Mexican life. While some of the younger upper-class women become professionals such as teachers, doctors, dentists, or lawyers, very few enter the business or political worlds. Certainly, women will not be found in higher level management positions. The foreign female executive may find business situations awkward and strained at first. It would not be prudent to send a woman as the main representative of a company.

Since Mexican executives travel a great deal and schedules often have to change, your secretary should reconfirm the scheduled appointment one or two weeks before the meeting.

You should arrive in Mexico a day in advance in order to reconfirm appointments. It is best to make morning appointments so that lunch will not interfere.

Be punctual when arriving at your host's office. However, do not become impatient if you are kept waiting a while.

Unless there is a formal presentation before several executives, most meetings will take place in the senior executive's office. Wait until your host directs you to a seat, which will usually be the one opposite.

The first 10 to 15 minutes are spent in conversation unrelated to business and geared to establishing a personal connection between the two executives. Talk about your trip, your impressions of Mexico, or news of the day. The visiting executive should slowly move the discussion toward matters of business.

After the first meeting, the Mexican executive may send the visitor to the middle-level executives and technical people. This should not be taken as an affront, but as an encouraging sign that your proposals will be carefully evaluated by trusted technical and operating specialists.

RANK AND STATUS

Mexican rank and status are related to personal accomplishments, whether in business or government or other fields. People in the arts and literature are highly regarded in Mexico, and its most accomplished practitioners enjoy a respected status.

One aspect of success in Mexico is a decided lack of flashiness. Mexicans do not show off their high position, but exhibit it in a low-key style.

Business titles are different in Mexico. The top executive is a *director general* or *presidente*. This is the same as a chairperson, or chief executive officer. Below him are *directores*. These men operate with power and authority, as division heads. They are comparable to senior or executive vice presidents. Further down are *gerentes* or managers of smaller departments, who are equivalent to vice presidents or functional managers.

A government department is headed by a *secretario*. He is generally a political appointee whose top staff wields great power. Powerful technocrats in the public sector include *subsecretarios*, *directores*, and *subdirectores*. All individuals who have earned a doctorate degree are addressed as *"Doctor."* The same holds true for engineers (*ingenieros*) and lawyers (*licenciados*). Often, the title *licenciado* is also bestowed on holders of other advanced degrees.

FORMS OF ADDRESS

When addressing a male Mexican executive, call him *"Señor."* Women are addressed as *"Señora."* Top executives or those with titles are addressed by their title and name.

BUSINESS CARDS

While no great ceremony is involved, business cards should be exchanged at the start of a meeting immediately after introductions have been made.

BUSINESS DRESS

Conservative suits for both men and women are recommended, with dark grey and navy the most favorably accepted. Shirts and ties are worn at all occasions, except perhaps at informal meals on weekends, and at other casual activities.

GIFT-GIVING

Gift-giving is not common or necessary, but small gifts are appreciated. On the first visit, bring corporate logo gifts or other nonpersonal items. After a relationship has formed, more personal gifts may be given, such as books, cassette tapes, or artwork. Scotch whiskey or French wine is also appropriate. If you are invited to a Mexican home for dinner (which will not occur until a solid relationship has been established), flowers for the hostess should either be sent ahead or brought with you. Caution should be used, however—since white flowers are considered to be uplifting, yellow flowers connote death, and red flowers are thought to cast spells.

COMMUNICATION STYLES

Public behavior in Mexico is dominated by European norms of courtesy, dignity, diplomacy, and tact. This means that business communication is more subdued than in the United States. The tone is often indirect, cautious, and exploratory, especially with new people. Foreign executives should avoid direct questions. Also, since disagreement is to be avoided, many Mexican businesspeople say what their visitors want to hear, which often leads to misunderstanding.

Since the Mexican executive's goal is to develop trust and a sense of *"simpático,"* your company's affiliation is less important than how you are perceived. A good indication of progress is increased physical contact. Your Mexican host may touch your shoulder while making a point, or hold your arm.

Regional differences do influence the communications process, particularly in the Monterrey area, where a business elite dominates, and management practices and social interactions are influenced by the United States. Most senior executives here have a no-nonsense, bottom-line approach to business.

Negotiating in Mexico

The process of negotiation in Mexico proceeds according to Mexican attitudes about time. Mexicans are usually indifferent to deadlines, and a foreign executive's desire to get matters clarified right away is apt to go unfulfilled. A personal relationship cannot be developed during one morning's discussion. The negotiations will proceed slowly.

Lawyers will not be used as extensively as they are in the United States. Only if there are difficulties will a Mexican lawyer be brought into discussions and negotiations.

Spanish is the preferred language. However, interpreters should be used, at least at the first meeting, to avoid misunderstandings.

The issue of financing purchases of foreign goods and services is central to the negotiating process because of Mexico's fragile financial situation. Deals have been made and subsequently lost on the basis of cost and availability of financing for foreign goods. Foreign executives may have to offer creative financing, incorporating the latest techniques of countertrade and offset.

Decision making in Mexican companies is concentrated at the senior levels. However, most senior decision makers depend on lower level managers to negotiate, analyze, and make recommendations. These lower level officials have a direct link to the senior decision maker.

Here are some suggestions on negotiating successfully in Mexico:

• Understand that Mexico is and will remain an important future market for U.S. products. If you present an image of long-term commitment and interest, this will enhance both individual and corporate perceptions.

• In selecting a representative in Mexico, assess the person's qualifications. While local contacts and influence may be enough in some cases, it is not enough in others. Check the ability of the firm to market, distribute, and service your products effectively. Also, be sure of the financial stability of the Mexican firm, as it may have to carry receivables for months. Make sure that all contingencies are covered, or can be covered, in a short period of time.

• Realize that, although, after many hours of meetings, little of substance may have been discussed, this fits in with the desire of the Mexicans to develop personal relationships. Avoid pressure tactics or trying to control conversation.

• Take time to listen carefully, responding in a way that increases your counterpart's willingness to do business with you as an individual. The ability to be flexible will be helpful.

• Realize that senior Mexican executives and government officials are highly educated, many with technical backgrounds. Many have been educated in Europe and the United States.

• Be sure to secure a written contract defining the terms when agreement has been reached. Lawyers are usually involved in this phase of the negotiating process.

Business Entertaining

Entertaining is very important in Mexico. After-hours cocktails or dinner will accelerate the development of close personal relationships. If lunch has not been long, before-dinner cocktails at around 7:00

P.M. provide a relaxed opportunity to go over the day's discussions and clarify details. This cocktail hour is especially popular among younger executives.

The foreign businessperson should select a good restaurant (French or Italian, preferably) and plan on a long, relaxed dinner to relieve the pressures of the day.

While wives are not normally included in such arrangements they are welcome to join in. If wives are present, business will not be discussed. During evening entertaining, discussions of family, friends, hometowns, and politics will bring the foreigner and the Mexican closer together.

Make sure there is generous rest and conversation at the meal's end. Then signal the waiter quietly. The bill will include a 15 percent service charge. Arrangement for payment of the bill should be made in advance to avoid any contest as to who will be paying.

Seating arrangements at a formal dinner, whether hosted by the visitors or by the Mexicans, will put senior executives facing each other if seated at a rectangular table, or next to each other at a round table.

General Tips

• If this is your first visit to Mexico, schedule some time to walk around the city before your first meeting. Your impressions will be valuable for initial conversation.

• Mexican businesspeople do not want to hear about how things are done in the United States. They are the experts on the local situation, and it is fairly certain that their information and instincts about the local establishment are reliable.

• The relationship between the United States and Mexico is still a sensitive one, and U.S. methods and values should not be compared with those in Mexico. Historically, Mexico and America have had an inferior–superior relationship. Present problems include drugs, illegal immigration, and financial difficulties.

• Mexicans are especially respectful of their *patrón* (someone of power or wealth) or employer. It is similar to a father–son relationship, and implies more than just friendship.

EXECUTIVE TRAVEL TO MEXICO •

DOCUMENTS

U.S. citizens need only a valid passport and visitor's card, available at the Mexican Consulate or through the airlines when purchasing your ticket.

INOCULATIONS

None required for U.S. citizens.

AIRPORT

Central International Airport is 8 miles from Mexico City (about a 20-minute drive).

CUSTOMS

U.S. residents are exempted from paying duty on items with a total retail value of up to $400. You are allowed to bring in 200 cigarettes and 100 cigars and one liter of alcohol.

U.S. EMBASSY

Reforma 305, Mexico City
Phone: (905) 553-3333

TRANSPORTATION

It is recommended that you arrange for a car and a driver/translator for use during your stay, both for your comfort and to enhance your image.

TIPPING

Tipping is appreciated by all Mexican service workers. The average tip is 10 to 15 percent to waiters, 10 percent to barbers and hairdressers; a standard tip for porters and bellboys is the peso equivalent of 50 cents per bag.

HOTELS

Mexico City

Camino Real
Mariano Escobedo 700
Phone: (905) 545-6960   Telex: 01773001

El Presidente Chapultepec
Campos Eliseos 218
Phone: (905) 250-7700   Telex: 01776392

Galería Plaza
Hamburgo 195
Phone: (905) 286-5444   Telex: 01771808

Hotel Maria Isabel Sheraton
Reforma 325
Phone: (905) 211-0001   Telex: 01773936

RESTAURANTS

Mexico City

Ambassadeur   *French*
Paseo de la Reforma 12
Phone: 535-6435

Churchill's   *English*
Boulevard Avila Camacho 67
Phone: 520-0585

Del Lago   *Continental*
Nuevo Parque de Chapultepec
Phone: 515-9585

El Paseo   *French*
Paseo de la Reforma 146
Phone: 546-5124

La Cava   *Mexican*
Insurgentes sur 2465
Phone: 548-5887

Maxims   *French*
Presidente Chapultepec Hotel
Campos Eliseos 218
Phone: 250-0025

Prendes	*Seafood*
Avenida 16 de Septiembre 10	
Phone: 585-4199	
San Angel Inn	*Mexican*
Palmas 50 at Altavista, San Angel	
Phone: 548-6746	

TRAVEL TIPS

• Money and traveler's checks can be exchanged at most large hotels and banks located in the main business districts of each city. Banks are open from 9:00 A.M. to 1:30 P.M. daily.

• Domestic and international communications facilities are excellent. International telex and telegram services are reliable. English language newspapers and magazines are available, and U.S. news can be heard from 7:00 P.M. to midnight by tuning into Radio VIP, 1560 on the AM dial.

• Most medical problems suffered by visitors are the result of overindulgence. Eat in moderation, especially highly spiced foods, and drink only bottled water. Most large hotels have in-house doctors available for more serious illnesses.

• Mexico is a shopper's paradise. Mexico City's "Pink Zone" is filled with boutiques, galleries, and shops of every kind. Museum shops specialize in paintings, ceramics, and art objects.

• The archaeological wonders of Mexico are among the country's greatest national treasures. The accomplishments of the ancient Aztec and Mayan civilizations are visible in the great pyramids of Teotihuacán outside Mexico City, and at Uxmal, Chichen Itzá, and Tulum in the Yucatán peninsula.

• The great spectator sport of Mexico is the bullfight. Mexico City's bullring, Plaza Mexico, is the world's largest and seats fifty thousand. Other spectator sports include baseball, basketball, soccer, boxing, and jai alai; golf, tennis, and horseback riding facilities are readily available in the cities and the coastal resorts.

• The Ballet Folklórico is a unique presentation of Mexican folk music and dance and is performed regularly in Mexico City at the Palacio de Bellas Artes or opera house. The Plaza Garibaldi is the famous mariachi square where bands assemble at 8:00 P.M. and play until early morning.

• The high altitude in Mexico City and several other cities over seven thousand feet above sea level may affect people with heart problems, and joggers should consider this as well.

• Be sensible about personal safety by avoiding strange neighborhoods at night and not targeting yourself for pickpockets and petty thieves through flashy dress and carelessness with valuables.

SOUTH AMERICA

ARGENTINA

Cultural Overview

The third largest country in Latin America, the Argentine Republic is distinguished by its abundance of natural resources. Since the early seventies, the country has seen economic problems, war with Great Britain over the Malvinas, and major political changes. Argentines, however, appear to be meeting these challenges with optimism, and to have embarked on a more coherent political and economic course than they formerly followed.

Most Argentines are descended from Italian or Spanish immigrants, and Western European values are evident in their conservative attitude toward manners, appearance, style, family, and religion. Titled academic achievement and artistic accomplishments are held in high esteem. The upper classes are extremely fashion conscious and have a penchant for international travel.

Argentina is well endowed, and has been rich for many decades. By the 1800s, profits from its abundant harvests and meat industry had created an affluent society, which in building Buenos Aires significantly chose as its model the then most prestigious capital of the world: Paris.

In the past, Argentines have had a reputation for being somewhat arrogant, an attitude emanating at least in part from the country's wealth, and particularly from its European heritage. The difficult political and economic situations of the past several years, however, appear to have altered this attitude. Argentina now seems to be seeking friends among other nations.

In late 1983 Argentina ended ten years of military rule, electing a civilian president, Raul Alfonsin, in a campaign characterized by free access to the media and open political debate—a sharp contrast to the way government was conducted under the military regime. The federal government consists of an executive branch, headed by the president, a bicameral legislature, and a judicial branch, headed by the Supreme Court of Justice.

The 1983 election brought with it the return of many former political exiles as well as the first defeat of the Perónist party since 1939. The rise of a viable two-party system, with the Perónists as a minority, may offer significant value in getting Argentina back on a sound political and economic course.

Restoring the economy, however, will be a major challenge. Despite its natural wealth, Argentina has experienced severe economic difficulties in recent years. Inflation is a major problem. Between 1974 and 1984, for example, the annual inflation rate dropped below 100 percent only once—in 1980. In 1984, it reached 400 percent. In addition, the early 1980s saw an economic decline in all industries except agriculture, and increases in both unemployment and foreign debt. The national debt jumped from $2 billion in 1979 to $44 billion in 1985, and bankruptcies in manufacturing, construction, and services were not uncommon.

Although based on free enterprise, the Argentine economy has the largest public sector participation of any South American country. The state controls 118 enterprises, which employ about 25 percent of the people and spend 40 percent of the GDP. The state participates in virtually every sector of the economy, including energy, telecommunications, pulp and paper, foodstuffs, food processing and packaging, electronics, railways, and airlines. It also controls the Fabricaciones Militares, a multibillion-dollar military-industrial complex with interests in weapons and other areas such as timber, petrochemicals, and construction.

Agriculture, the basis for the wealthy society that arose in the nineteenth century, is still Argentina's principal industry. The country is one of the world's largest grain exporters and a major competitor of the United States in the international grain markets. Other important agricultural products are oilseeds, cattle and sheep, sugar, fruit, wine, and tea.

The major industries involve the production of oil and gas, steel, machinery, and vehicles. Manufacturing, overall, represents 36 percent of the GDP. Imports have declined dramatically in recent years due to the severe financial situation. The U.S. share of Argentina's imports, however, has remained around 22 percent for the past several years.

The country's religion is predominantly Roman Catholic. Other Christian faiths are also practiced, however, and Argentina has one of the world's largest Jewish communities outside of Israel.

Literacy in Argentina is high: about 95 percent. Primary education is free and compulsory, and the state also finances secondary education and university degree programs. The labor force is comparable in skills and aptitudes to that in most developed countries.

Family life is very important, with its generally conservative, European influenced attitudes. Women, in general, play a secondary and traditional family role. Middle- and upper-class women are usually responsible for raising the family and rarely work outside the home.

Argentina is situated in the southern part of South America and has an area of about 1.1 million square miles—a little less than one-third the size of the United States. On the west, the Andes separate Argentina from Chile. The country also shares borders with Bolivia, Uruguay, Brazil, and Paraguay.

The climate varies widely, from subtropical to subantarctic. Much of the country, however, enjoys a temperate climate and adequate rainfall, along with fertile soil—ideal conditions for agriculture. Maximum summer temperatures, even in Buenos Aires, are usually between 80° and 89° Fahrenheit, and winters are relatively mild. In most places it freezes only occasionally, and snowfall is usually limited to the mountains and the southern regions.

Argentina has close to 30 million people; a third live in the Buenos Aires metropolitan area. Unlike the situation in most South American countries, there is little trace in Argentina of the original Indian inhabitants. Problems of race, religion, or color seem quite unknown.

Spanish is the official language, although English is the usual second language for businesspeople, academics, and political officials. Reflecting the pervasive European influence, many Argentines also speak French, Italian, or German.

Business Opportunities

State-owned companies are extremely attractive markets for U.S. products and services. Among the largest state enterprises that purchase products and services abroad are:

- Administracion General de Puertos (Port Authority)
- Yacimientos Petroliferos Fiscales, or YPF (oil/gas company)
- Servicios Electricos del Gran Buenos Aires (SEGBA) (power authority)
- Empresa Ferrocarriles Argentinos (railroad)
- Agua y Energia Electrica (water and electrical power)
- Empresa Nacional de Telecommunicaciones (ENTEL) (local and international telecommunications)

Foreign investment will necessarily play an important part in Argentina's economic recovery. The areas with the greatest potential for investment include oil and gas development, mining, and fishing. These industries formerly have had a low priority, because agriculture has been so successful.

Initiating Contact

For sales to state companies, the national press usually carries invitations for bids, which are submitted to the appropriate state entity. Some state-owned enterprises, however, purchase from restricted public vendors. Invitations for bids in such cases are sent only to firms on the list of approved suppliers. Therefore, any company wishing to bid on such contracts must be represented by an agent, importer, or distributor, or enter into a joint venture with a local firm.

This kind of representation is suggested for sales to any organization. Finding agents is becoming more difficult, however, since a large number of such connections have already been established, and existing agents are committed. The economic problems of the early eighties have also made the search for good representation even harder, and consequently third-party contacts are becoming increasingly valuable. American banks can be useful in arranging introductions since they have been in the country for a long period and have heavy commitments there.

For additional information, contact:

Argentine–American Chamber of Commerce
50 West 34th Street
New York, N.Y. 10001
Phone: (212) 564-3855

American Chamber of Commerce in Argentina
Avenida R. Sáenz Peña 567
1352 Buenos Aires, Argentina
Phone: 33-5591

Argentine Trade Office
555 Madison Avenue
New York, N.Y. 10022
Phone: (212) 759-6477

Argentine Embassy
1600 New Hampshire Avenue N.W.
Washington, D.C. 20009
Phone: (202) 387-0705
(Also offices in Chicago, Los Angeles, Houston, New York, and
   Puerto Rico.)

U.S. Department of Commerce
Marketing Manager Argentine Desk
14th Street and Constitution Avenue
Washington, D.C. 20230
Phone: (202) 377-5427

Business Protocol and Procedures

BUSINESS ENVIRONMENT

Argentine business style is much like that in other South American countries. The pace is slower than in the United States and building personal relationships is important. High-pressure techniques are not likely to be effective. Correct and polite behavior is expected and appreciated.

Business hours are traditionally from 9:00 A.M. to early evening. Meetings should be arranged through an initial letter, telex, or telephone call, and they should be confirmed a week in advance. Since you will have had a long journey, plan to arrive the day before your first meeting, which is best held in the morning. Lunch, an important part of the Argentine business day, will probably follow. Business discussions can be continued over the meal, which usually does not start before 1:30 P.M. and lasts about 2 hours. Argentine executives return to the office late in the afternoon and stay until about 7:00 P.M.

Meetings will be held at your Argentine host's offices. Guests will be escorted to their chairs, and the senior visiting executive will be seated opposite the senior officer of the Argentine firm. In the first meeting, business discussions will be put off for about half an hour while the parties become acquainted. Small talk about your trip or discussions of general business topics are appropriate, as are specific introductions. Plan to arrange for an interpreter for at least the first meeting, since quite possibly your counterparts will speak only Spanish, and Italian or French, not English, may be their second language. Meetings should be conducted in a relaxed manner, maintaining eye contact and avoiding the use of excessive gestures.

Traditional Argentine executives will want several meetings and extensive detailed discussions, in order to obtain as much information as possible and become secure about the deal. The thrust in this case is risk-aversion. The Argentine executive who has had prior dealings with Americans or other foreign executives will be more knowledgeable of other business customs and feel comfortable dealing with them. In this instance, business may proceed with fewer delays.

RANK AND STATUS

In Argentina, social and business prominence depend a great deal on education, professional accomplishment, and wealth. The professions of medicine and law are highly respected, as are the arts. Family loyalties and commitments, friendships, and business associations are all important in determining one's social status and prestige. These connections foster an Argentine's ability to gain support for ideas or deals, and to get things done.

Politicians have not been generally held in the highest esteem in Argentina; the military was cheered when it first took power. The relatively new democratic government's handling of Argentina's problems will have an unprecedented impact on the image of future civilian politicians.

Despite the male domination in Argentine society, women do sometimes occupy top positions in business. Nevertheless, the Argentine executive may prefer dealing with the men on the foreign business team. An honest approach, emphasizing the women's professional status and responsibility, should alleviate most problem situations. Defensive behavior on the part of businesswomen, on the other hand, will damage credibility and diminish their ability to deal effectively on an equal basis.

FORMS OF ADDRESS

It is correct form to address an Argentine male as "señor," and last names are used until your host proposes a less formal style. Women should be addressed as "señora" unless they are quite young; in such cases, "señorita" is appropriate.

Older Argentine business associates will probably not call you by your first name, but will address you as "Señor X," "Mister X," or "Señora X." Younger businesspeople will be less formal and may use your first name after customary opening formalities. Your best posture, however, is to wait for your Argentine host to make the first move in this rather delicate area.

BUSINESS CARDS

It is good form to leave your business card with your host's secretary before entering his or her office. Immediately after introductions are completed in a meeting, business cards are presented to everyone in the room. Bilingual cards are not necessary, although some Argentine executives do appreciate them, as they indicate courtesy and respect.

BUSINESS DRESS

Argentine executives dress conservatively, with a fondness for British style. Light colors, plaids, polyesters, or excessively designer-style fashions are not appropriate. Conservatively styled navy blue or dark gray suits, with light dress shirt and tie, are correct for any business or evening occasion. For casual weekends, blue blazer, grey slacks, shirt, and tie are always in good taste.

Women doing business in Argentina can dress fashionably and not too conservatively. Argentines expect women to have a touch of flair, and this does not detract from a woman's professional credibility or image.

GIFT-GIVING

Gift-giving is not necessarily reciprocal in Argentina, and you are not expected to present a gift until a fairly close relationship has developed. Expensive gifts may carry the stigma of a possible bribe attempt. Appropriate business gifts include a bottle of imported whiskey, a French or Italian silk tie, or books or music in accordance with your host's tastes. Flowers or silk scarves are appropriate for wives. A small gift of a silk scarf or other item to your counterpart's secretary will help ensure fast communication with her boss. Argentina is a wine-producing country, and consequently they do not appreciate gifts of foreign wines.

If you are presented with a gift, you are expected to open it at once and express your pleasure and gratitude.

COMMUNICATION STYLES

Argentines can be animated in discussions, using gestures and touch for emphasis. During meetings, your Argentine associates will look for uncomfortable fidgeting, wandering eyes, and yawns in order to judge your feelings and interest. Direct eye contact is important, especially during greetings, leave-takings, and presentations. When you are not using your hands to stress a point, they should be kept in your lap or on your desk.

Negotiating in Argentina

Coloring virtually all negotiations with the Argentines is the issue of rampant inflation. Priorities and decision making in a nation where inflation can reach 90 percent are totally different from one where 4 percent is the norm. Successful negotiations will depend on your having a clear understanding of the cost structure and of such issues as levels of investment required, repatriation of capital and profits, and extended financing. Up-to-date knowledge of these subjects is essential to conduct business successfully.

Developing positive and friendly relationships with your counterparts will be important to consummating successful transactions. Personalizing negotiations, moreover, will shorten the time needed to reach compromises and decisions.

Keeping a longer term view than is common in the United States will help prevent unrealistic immediate expectations from damaging your entire venture. Remember that Argentina's long-range future is quite bright, with its abundant resources and relatively small population.

Decision making in Argentine companies tends to be concentrated in the most senior positions, usually held by the business and social elite. The *presidente*, corresponding to the president or chief executive officer here, and *vice presidente*, equivalent to a senior vice president, are the main formulators of corporate policy. Ultimate authority rests with them.

In state entities, retired senior military officers usually hold the top posts, which are generally regarded as sinecures that are rewards for long service. Career technocrats and middle-level managers may have operational authority, but the chairpersons and directors of these enterprises have the final authority on business matters. How much of this management system will survive is uncertain, given the change in government and in the current attitude toward the military.

Some suggestions for negotiating:

• Learn, if possible, about the amount of experience with international business, especially with the United States, that the company or executive you are negotiating with has had. The more traditional executive with little international experience will require more meetings and more detailed discussions than will the more experienced businessperson before feeling secure about a venture.

• Take a relaxed approach to negotiations. Argentines appreciate this and dislike the hard sell. If an Argentine wants more information, he will ask for it.

Business Entertainment

Your host will probably have a restaurant or club in mind to which he will invite you. It is perfectly acceptable, however, for you to initiate the hospitality and organize a pleasant business lunch. At lunch, the main meal of the day, it is likely that business discussions will continue.

Dinner never starts before 9:00 P.M., and evenings will be long, since the business day may last until quite late. Dinner is primarily a time for socializing and developing personal relationships, but a limited discussion of an important business issue is not inappropriate. Spouses often join executives for dinner. Seating is informal except that the senior executives appropriately sit opposite each other (or side by side at a round table).

When entertaining at a restaurant, it is in order for you to try to pick up the check. You can arrange this in advance with the maître d' to avoid discussion. If that is not possible, you can insist on paying, and do insist more than once.

If you are invited to your host's home for dinner, send flowers beforehand or bring chocolates or scotch with you. Check with your host to see if you are expected to arrive punctually, or 30 to 45 minutes later, as is more typical of the Latin American style.

General Tips

• Remember in all conversations that the islands over which Argentina and Great Britain fought are the *Malvinas*. This conflict is a very sensitive subject and should be broached only with great care once a relationship has been established. Argentines are also sensitive about discussions of family life and religion, and frequently prefer to avoid political issues.

• Argentina used to have very close ties with Great Britain. Since the conflict over the Malvinas, naturally, this relationship no longer exists.

• America has a very positive image with the Argentines, who see similarities between our two countries' immigration patterns and frontier experiences.

• The Argentine people are very sensitive to criticism and comparison with other South American nations, especially Brazil.

• Extremely fashion conscious, Argentines will notice such accessories as cufflinks and watches. They generally appreciate a neat and well-kept appearance, and will predicate their opinion of you on how you project yourself personally.

• Telephone systems are not dependable and frequently out of order. Confirm all appointments by telex before your arrival date.

EXECUTIVE TRAVEL TO ARGENTINA   •

DOCUMENTS

U.S. citizens require a valid passport and visa, which can be picked up at the nearest Argentine consulate or through the Embassy in Washington, D.C. A prerequisite is possession of a round-trip or onward ticket.

INOCULATIONS

No special inoculations are required.

AIRPORTS

Ezeiza Airport, located about 30 miles from the center of Buenos Aires, is the main international terminal. Jorge Newbery Airport is located within the city limits and handles mostly domestic flights.

CUSTOMS

Two liters of liquor, 400 cigarettes, and 50 cigars are allowed duty-free entry. Airport taxes vary because of the fluctuating currency.

U.S. EMBASSY

> Avenida Colombia 4300
> 1425 Buenos Aires
> Phone: 7748811

TRANSPORTATION

Although Buenos Aires has an excellent transportation infrastructure, it is recommended that the executive make arrangements for a private car with a translator/driver for the duration of his or her visit.

TIPPING

Gratuities have theoretically been outlawed in Argentina, but your hotel or restaurant adds 24 percent service and tax to your bill. Add 5 to 10 percent if you expect to return to the establishment or for special services. There is no need to tip cab drivers.

HOTELS

BUENOS AIRES

Buenos Aires Sheraton
Calle San Martín 1225
Phone: 3116311   Telex: 9222

The Elevage Hotel
Calle Maipu 960–962
Phone: 3932082   Telex: 7374

Hotel Libertador
Avenida Córdoba 698
Phone: 3922595   Telex: 24264

Plaza Hotel
Calle Florida 1005
Phone: 315011   Telex: 122488

RESTAURANTS

BUENOS AIRES

Claridge Hotel Grill   *International*
Avenida Tucuman 535
Phone: 324-001

La Cabaña   *Steakhouse*
Calle Entre Rios 436
Phone: 382-373

La Raya   *Argentine*
(popular for business lunches)
Avenida Pavón 3062
Phone: 941-5782

The London Grill   *English/Argentine*
455 Calle Reconquista
Phone: 312-233

Tomo Uno   *French*
1598 Calle Monroe
Las Heras 3766
Phone: 801-6253

TRAVEL TIPS

• Money changers *(cambios)* are located along Corrientes and Calle San Martín.
• International direct dial telephone service, as well as telex and cable services, are available in the larger international hotels.
• Personal safety is not much of a problem, and the streets of the major cities are fairly safe at all hours.
• Health facilities are among the best on the continent. Drugstores *(farmacias)* are plentiful, and many are open all night.
• Fine clothing, leatherware, shoes, and traditional gaucho products are indigenous to the country. Among the top stores are H. Stern, the Brazilian jeweler; James Stuart for ready-made and custom men's suits; Botticelli for Italian and Argentine shoes; Pullman & Lopez for luggage and leather goods.
• Buenos Aires is a beautiful city made for walking tours. It is laid out in an easy-to-follow grid pattern.
• For your cultural pleasure, Buenos Aires has the National Art Museum, the Museum of Spanish-American Art, and the Teatro Colón, one of the finest opera houses in the world. The National Ballet Theatre and National Symphony Orchestra also perform there. The San Martín Performing Arts Complex occupies a whole city block and includes movie theatres, an art gallery, and a main theatre facility. In addition, some 42 theatres are constantly presenting a wide variety of plays.
• Tennis, golf, boating, shooting, and skiing in the Andes Mountains are popular participant sports. *Futbol* (soccer) matches are a year-round sport. Polo, auto racing, and boxing are popular spectator sports.

BRAZIL

Cultural Overview

Brazil (officially the Federative Republic of Brazil) is the largest nation in South America, and the most dominant in the area's economy. Although there is some difficulty doing business because of financial constraints, Brazil will continue to have a strong role in the international markets because its economy is solidly based. Brazil has been called the "colossus of South America."

Well aware of its size and power, Brazilians see their land as unique among South American countries. They speak a different language— Portuguese, not Spanish—and do not want to be confused with their Spanish-speaking neighbors.

Brazil is a country of five distinct regions. In each, the economic development has varied; consequently, the special culture of each region lends diversity to the country as a whole. Regional ties are as important as family ties, and most Brazilians are proud of being from a particular state or region.

Brasília is one of the most modern and beautiful federal capital cities in the world. It has been built in central Brazil over the past four decades, but the location was conceived over one hundred years ago. It was situated there to encourage the dispersal of the population concentrations along the coast, and to develop the rich interior of this vast nation.

In March of 1984, after twenty-one years of military rule, Brazil elected its first civilian president. This election was the climax of a decade-long preparatory state called *abertura* (opening up), which the last two military administrative presidents encouraged and developed. The president-elect died before he could take office; the primary question for Brazilian democracy was how the various parties and the armed forces would respond. The succession issue and the fate of *abertura* is unfolding, and the current political situation appears to be relatively stable.

The federal constitution provides for three branches of government —the executive, legislative, and judicial. There is also an important state hierarchy, with governors of the richest states wielding substantial authority in national affairs.

Brazil has the eighth largest economy in the free world, and has enjoyed a high growth rate in the last twenty years. However, massive infrastructure investments, oil shocks, and high interest rates during the early 1980s produced an economic crisis brought on by the foreign debt problem.

Brazil remains the world's largest coffee producer, a major source and exporter of raw materials, and a world-scale producer of gold, iron ore, bauxite, copper, and manganese. In recent years, it has started producing automobiles, finished aluminum, steel, ships, chemicals, textiles, shoes, aircraft, arms, and weapons. In addition, it exports many foodstuffs: sugar, orange juice, soybeans, corn, and beef cattle.

The political situation must remain normal for a time before the government can negotiate with its creditor banks and the International Monetary Fund. Despite qualms about instability, Brazil's abundant natural resources, technical resources, and large consumer market continue to make it attractive for foreign investment.

Family relationships are extremely important in Brazil. Several business empires are family owned, and depend on their members to run the company's various operations. Roman Catholicism is the dominant religion but many Protestant faiths are practiced. Also of particular importance are the rituals and ceremonies brought from Africa by the slaves. Significant Jewish and Lebanese communities are found in the major cities.

For the most part, Brazilian society is male dominated. A woman's place is still at home, caring for children and running the day-to-day operations of the household. Brazilian women tend to defer to their male partners, and very few women in business or government have positions of authority. Most traditional males would rather negotiate with men, although this depends to some extent on where you do business. For example, São Paulo is more progressive, in the commercial sense, than Rio de Janeiro and both are more so than the rest of the country.

Brazilians tend to look to the future and do not dwell on the past. Their optimism is symbolized by the term *jeito* (jay-toh), which suggests that there is always a way of solving a problem. Brazilians admire the culture and economic success of the United States, but have great national pride, believing their country is the best place in the world to live.

In addition to being the fifth largest country in the world, Brazil has the sixth largest population, with more than three-quarters of its 120 million people under age 40, and nearly half under the age of 20. Brazilians are a mix of many races and cultures, including Iberian (Portuguese), Italian, German, African, Indian, and Japanese. Brazil, interestingly, has the largest Japanese community outside of Japan.

Many Brazilians live in cities—more than 12 million in São Paulo, and 9 million in Rio de Janeiro. The country has forty-six hundred miles of coastline on the southern Atlantic and borders every nation in South America except Chile and Ecuador. Mainly flat, Brazil is dominated by the huge Amazon River Basin and its forest. The Amazon River is the largest in the world, with ocean-going ships able to navigate two thousand miles inland.

As a result of its vast dimensions, this nation has a wide range of climatic conditions, ranging from the equatorial in the north to the tropical and temperate in the central and south.

Business Opportunities

Most of Brazilian business is conducted in its two main cities. São Paulo is the commercial, industrial, and financial center. Although Rio de Janeiro is known for its beaches, it is also a center for trading companies of all sizes and many multinationals worldwide. It enjoys a major port location, and is the home of the country's most important airport, Galeão.

Exporting to Brazil is difficult now because of the reduced imports. The need to conserve foreign exchange and increase exports puts pressure on Brazil's trading companies. In dealing with countries in Africa and Europe, many Brazilian companies use nontraditional finance methods such as barter, countertrade, and offset. Often, foreign sellers bid against each other solely on the basis of financing arrangements. The prospective exporter should understand that cash payments are often difficult to arrange.

Nevertheless, international trade, specifically with the United States, is given high priority by the government. And now is the best time to begin working, in order to reap the anticipated rewards to be experienced over the next five to ten years.

Initiating Contact

Third-party contacts and introductions are the preferred way to enter the Brazilian business world, but also contact the Brazilian Government Trade Bureau at 551 Fifth Avenue, New York, N.Y. 10036. Computerized lists are available with names of Brazilian agents, distributors, import houses, trading companies, and manufacturers, as well as information and tips on what products are needed in or available from Brazil. Prospective associates and customers can be checked through bank references.

Most Brazilian companies will respond to a letter that discusses your firm's products and services. The letter should be from a senior executive, and it should be professionally translated into Portuguese.

Financial considerations can make the difference between success and failure in dealing with Brazil now, and there is concern over the state of its financial situation in both public and private sectors.

It is important that you select Brazilian partners with special care, because there has been a tremendous growth in the number of companies and individuals involved in international trade in recent years and, of course, not all are reliable. Check all potential associates with the Brazilian government, banks, and key people in industry. The Association of Brazilian Chambers of Commerce can be helpful in checking references. When researching a firm, ask about its financial condition, resources, technical and service capabilities, and marketing experience in your product line, as well as its capabilities in Brazil's various regions. Remember that, once signed, a Brazilian agent is protected by law from unilateral termination of his contract by a foreign principal without "just cause," and it is *Brazilian* authorities who determine what is meant by this phrase.

In order to bid to supply goods or services to the government, foreign firms are required to have local (legal) representation in Brazil. You may also need a prominent presence in the country, since many bid periods are as short as a month. Your chances of success are improved if you have an association with a Brazilian company in the same business, or if the bid includes a subcontract with a Brazilian firm.

For further information, contact:

World Trade Center do Rio de Janeiro
Rua Mexico, 111/Gr. 1504–andar
Rio de Janeiro, Brazil 20031
Phone: (021) 2243065/ 2529524   Telex: 22239 or 31299

World Trade Center de São Paulo
Servlease S.A.
Rua Estados Unido, 1093
01427 São Paulo—SP—Brazil
Phone: (011) 2804811   Telex: 22917

U.S. Trade Center
Edificio Eloy Chaves

Avenida Paulista 2439
São Paulo, APO Miami 34030
Phone: (011) 8532011/2455/2778

American Chamber of Commerce for Brazil
Caixa Postal 916-2000
Rio de Janeiro, Brazil
Phone: (021) 2221983

U.S. Department of Commerce
Marketing Manager/Brazil Desk
14th Street and Constitution Avenue
Washington, D.C. 20230
Phone: (202) 377-5427

Business Protocol and Procedures

BUSINESS ENVIRONMENT

Business meetings are held at the offices of your Brazilian hosts. Office hours are generally from 9:00 A.M. to noon, and from 2:00 P.M. to 6:00 P.M. on weekdays. Factories operate on Saturday morning shifts, and it is not uncommon to arrange Saturday meetings with manufacturers. However, most other businesses will be closed on weekends.

Seating arrangements are not formalized, but your host will probably lead you to a chair opposite his. In any meeting, the visitor will be served a small cup of strong Brazilian black coffee, a *cafezinho*, several times. You should accept and drink the coffee. After the second cup, you can refuse politely without being considered rude.

Be as technically prepared when calling on a business executive in São Paulo as you would be in the United States. Include technical drawings, models, visual aids, and computer printouts in the presentation, if they are relevant. In the past twenty years, Brazilians have become very knowledgeable in both modern business practices and industrial technology.

Unless you speak fluent Portuguese, it is recommended that you have an interpreter at the meetings. Some business and government officials speak English but would prefer to negotiate in their native tongue. Younger Brazilians who have been educated abroad may speak French or other European languages. The "Paulistas" (as the natives of São Paulo are called) are similar to U.S. executives: hard-driving and ambitious. There, an executive's schedule is tight, being on time is important, and careful business analysis is evident. To "Cariocas" (citizens of Rio de Janeiro,) the quality of life is more important, and while the business environment is more aggressive than in most other South American countries, patience is still needed. The pace of most initial discussions is slow. Only in São Paulo will you find a more rapid pace, sometimes as hectic as that in New York.

Trust is important in business dealings, even when sophisticated analytic techniques are used to evaluate a business proposal. Intuition, or a feel for the correctness of a business deal, plays an important role in decision making. Most Brazilian businesspeople prefer to build long-term relationships with the individuals they negotiate with as well as with the firms they represent.

RANK AND STATUS

Rank and status in Brazil are related to this nation's rapid economic growth. Since Brazilians have an entrepreneurial impulse much like that in the United States, business success is rewarded with respect. The greatest Brazilian business heroes are the major exporters of Brazilian goods. Also, the older men who run the family-controlled businesses in Brazil are accorded considerable esteem.

Many Brazilian companies are privately owned and operated. The founder chairman usually has the title of *presidente* and exercises almost total executive control. The founder's children may also hold executive positions and have considerable authority, although the final decision rests with the father.

FORMS OF ADDRESS

A firm handshake and "How do you do?" or "Pleased to meet you," are the appropriate forms of greeting. If you can, try to learn a greeting in Portuguese; it will be greatly appreciated.

The correct address for "Mr." is "Senhor," for "Mrs." it is "Madáme" or "Senhóra." "Senhorita" is used for "Miss," and "Dóm" is used as a familiar form of address.

BUSINESS CARDS

Business cards should be printed in both English and Portuguese, and should be presented immediately after the introduction at the start of any meeting, without formality.

BUSINESS DRESS

In keeping with the European influence in their fashions, conservative business suits should be worn at all times. In São Paulo, a dark blue or grey suit should be worn with a white or light blue long-sleeved shirt, with French cuffs, preferably, and a subdued tie. In Rio de Janeiro, lighter color suits may be worn, especially during the summer. Most bankers and executives in large companies will wear darker suits year round.

GIFT-GIVING

While gift-giving is not customary in Brazil, it is appreciated. It is appropriate to bring flowers to the wife of your host if you are invited to their home for dinner. A bottle of scotch whiskey is a gift well-received.

COMMUNICATION STYLES

Brazilians tend to be emotional, yet often hide their annoyance. When speaking with someone, they like to stand close. When making a point, they frequently touch the other person. Eye contact, sitting up straight, and listening carefully are very important to Brazilians.

Good personal relationships leading to good business relationships are valued by the Brazilians. As friendships develop, the customary hug, called an *abraco*, is used between counterparts, signifying growing friendship or a successful meeting.

It is not unusual to see men exchange kisses on the cheek, during an *abraco;* it is common between good friends and associates.

Negotiating in Brazil

A team approach is not necessary in Brazil. Sending one or two executives is enough to indicate the seriousness of your proposal. You will probably meet with a senior Brazilian executive and several close aides. Once the meeting is set, you should confirm it with a letter, and then follow up with a telephone call before you leave.

Business decisions tend to be made more spontaneously in Brazil because inflation, currency movements, and government regulations change so rapidly, necessitating expediency. The process of making decisions based on long-range projections of business and economic conditions, common in the United States, is rare in Brazil.

Most contracts with a Brazilian firm will be under Brazilian law. Credit is vitally important, and financing questions and issues should be clearly understood before contracts are signed.

Here are some suggestions for negotiating in Brazil:

• Brazilians have a strong entrepreneurial attitude, giving the lone businessperson considerable respect. Recognize this.
• While the younger Brazilian executives may speak several languages, because of international educational experiences, many older businesspeople have limited proficiency beyond Portuguese.
• Five to ten-year projections cannot be used in Brazil because the rate change is so fast; forecasts can become obsolete by the time you present them.
• Do not patronize a Brazilian. They realize they have made strong progress in business. Too much praise can have a negative effect.

Business Entertaining

Entertaining is an important part of doing business in Brazil. Lunches may help to continue the morning discussions in more informal settings. Dinners are more social, and nonbusiness topics are discussed. Your host would be happy to tell you about Brazil from his perspective.

Interesting subjects for discussion could be politics, sports (soccer is a national passion), popular music, the beaches, the Amazon, and Brazil's economic potential.

A prospective purchaser of Brazilian goods can expect to be treated to a variety of entertainments, but the prospective seller should plan his or her entertainment strategy as carefully as a negotiating strategy. The selection of the right restaurant is as important as is the choice of alcoholic beverages.

Dinner usually starts between 8:00 and 9:00 P.M. You should plan dinner at a restaurant other than the one at your hotel. Drinks before the meal are common. You will make a proper impression serving imported whiskey and vodka, as imported brands are very expensive in Brazil. The price for imported scotch may be two to three times the price in the United States. If wine is served, choose a Chilean or

Argentine wine. Ordering of French wines may offend or seem too pretentious.

Your dinner invitations should make it clear whether wives are invited or not. Brazilians love to go out at night, so you might investigate with your hotel management the newest and most "in" clubs in the city.

Scheduling a Saturday business lunch is a very effective tactic among manufacturers.

While toasting is not important or even common, raising your glass and giving an enthusiastic *"Saude"* (pronounced Sa-ooge) or "Cheers" will contribute to a pleasant atmosphere.

It is considered unlucky when dining to pass the salt shaker directly to another person. It must be set down on the table and then picked up by the next person. When the salt shaker is handed around, it signifies bad luck between the two parties so this should be scrupulously avoided.

General Tips

• The traditional *abraco* (embrace) is an obvious sign of warm feelings, and should be regarded as a positive gesture during negotiations.

• The familiar "thumbs up" sign is used to show approval. However, the traditional American okay sign, with thumb and index finger forming a circle, is considered an obscene gesture.

• When meeting someone for the first time, at a dinner table or cocktail party, talk about the weather, the city, or world politics. Two subjects, soccer and Brazilian economic development, are favorite topics. Family matters are very private in Brazil, and asking total strangers about their private family life is considered rude.

• Do not compare your experiences in this country with your normal lifestyle, or complain about petty issues.

• Praise the Brazilians for their accomplishments, but not too lavishly. Too much praise tends to be patronizing, and, although progress has been made, there is much to do in the future.

• Most Brazilians do not like being called Latin Americans. Remember the great pride they have in their cultural diversity, economic development, language, and history.

• Brazilians appreciate any effort on the part of a foreign visitor to speak Portuguese. The ability to address your business associate in Portuguese (no matter how labored) will enhance your relationship.

EXECUTIVE TRAVEL TO BRAZIL •

DOCUMENTS

Visas are required for business travel. Free to U.S. citizens, they are valid up to 90 days and may be extended for an additional 90 days. Visa applications may be made by mail at all Brazilian consular offices except in New York City where you must apply in person. To get a business visa, the following must be presented:

• Valid passport
• Application form in triplicate.
• Three passport-size photographs (2x3).
• Letter from your company outlining the purpose of your trip and assuming moral and financial responsibility for you.

INOCULATIONS

There are no specific requirements for U.S. citizens.

AIRPORTS

Rio de Janeiro has Brazil's largest international airport and is the commercial gateway to Brazil. Visitors to São Paulo must first fly to Rio de Janeiro and then transfer to a domestic flight to São Paulo. The flight time for this shuttle service is 55 minutes. Galeao Airport in Rio de Janerio is about 25 miles from the various hotel sites, and this trip will take about 45 minutes. There is connecting air taxi service to Brasília from main centers.

There is an airport departure tax that must be paid in cruzeiros. This tax differs from city to city, although the range on international flights is between five and ten dollars.

CUSTOMS

Customs law provides for visitors to bring up to 400 cigarettes and two bottles of liquor.

U.S. EMBASSY

Avenida das Nocoes, Lote 3, Brasília
APO Miami 34030
Phone: (061) 2230120   Telex: 0611091

TRANSPORTATION

There are licensed taxis and air-conditioned airport buses between the airport and the hotel. Do not accept offers of rides in private cars. It is advisable to rent a car and get a driver/translator for your stay; prices are reasonable and the convenience will save you time. The Brazilian lifestyle includes such amenities, and you should take advantage of them.

TIPPING

Although taxi drivers do not normally receive tips, 10 percent of the fare would be gratefully accepted. In restaurants, if a 10 to 15 percent service charge has not been added to your bill, that amount should be left as a tip.

HOTELS

RIO DE JANEIRO

Caesar Park
460 Avenida Vieira Souto, Ipanema
Phone: 287-2121/or 2133   Telex: (21) 21204

Copacabana Palace
1702 Avenida Atlantica, Copacabana
Phone: 257-1818   Telex: (21) 22248

Meridien Hotel
1020 Avenida Atlantica, Copacabana
Phone: 275-9922   Telex: (21) 23047

Ouro Verde
1456 Avenida Atlantica, Copacabana
Phone: 257-1880   Telex: (21) 23848

Rio Othon Palace
3264 Avenida Atlantica, Copacabana
Phone: 255-8812   Telex: (21) 22655

Rio Palace
4240 Avenida Atlantica, Copacabana
Phone: 521-3232   Telex: (21) 21803

São Paulo

Caesar Park
1508 Rua Augusta
Phone: 285-6622

Maksoud Palace
150 Alameda Campinas, Bela Vista
Phone: 251-2233   Telex: 1130030

São Paulo Hilton
165 Avenida Ipiranga
Phone: 256-0033   Telex: (011)21981

Brasília

Nacional
Setor Hoteleiro Sul, lote 1
Churrascaria do Lago
Phone: 226-8180   Telex: 1062-380

RESTAURANTS

Rio de Janeiro

Enotria   *Italian*
115 Rua Constante Ramos, Copacabana
Phone: 237-6705

Le Bec Fin   *French*
178 Av. N.S. de Copacabana
Phone: 255-3384

Le Pre Catelan   *Nouvelle cuisine*
Rio Palace Hotel
Phone: 287-9992

Michael's   *French/seafood*
25 Rua F. Mendes, Copacabana
Phone: 235-2127

SÃO PAULO

Ca d'Oro   *Italian*
129 Rua Augusta Centro
Phone: 256-8011

La Cocagne   *French*
129 Rua Campos Bicudo
Phone: 282-4275

Marcel's   *French*
98 Rua Epitacio Pessoa
Phone: 257-6968

The Rodeio   *Barbecue*
1498 Rua Haddock Lobo
Phone: 852-4613

BRASÍLIA

Tarantella   *Brazilian*
Comercio Local Sul
202, Bloco A
Phone: 224-9408

TRAVEL TIPS

• Banks, most hotels, and stores (when making purchases) give the official rate of exchange, some *cambios* (currency changing offices) and travel agencies may give more.
• Always carry your passport for identification.
• The official unit of currency is the cruzeiro (Cr$).
• Medical care is excellent in the large cities, and many renowned surgeons are Brazilian. If you have an emergency, call the American Consulate in Rio. The international operator will speak English and may be able to help. The telephone number is 001081.
• Sensible precautions should be taken when walking in unfamiliar neighborhoods at night.
• Brazil is famous for its precious and semiprecious stones, which can be purchased as jewelry or separately. Two of the largest dealers are H. Stern and Roditi. Brazil has quality leathergoods and shoes, and boutiques offer a wide array of Brazilian designed and produced clothing.

• You will find in some stores that paying with dollars can result in a substantial discount, although this practice is frowned upon by the government.

• Brazil offers the visitor a vast choice of natural wonders, including the beaches of Rio de Janeiro and the Iguacú Falls to the south. Both São Paulo and Rio de Janeiro provide a large number of discos, nightclubs, and theatrical revues for your evening entertainment. The shows at Scala and Plataforma in Rio de Janeiro are outstanding.

• The Brazilian national sport is *futebol* (soccer), and the Maracana Stadium in Rio seats one hundred eighty thousand fans.

• The federal government operates a sophisticated international telecommunications network offering telephone, telex, and cable via satellite. Most large cities have direct-dial capability.

• If possible, avoid travel to Brazil around the time of the Carnaval holiday, which begins immediately prior to the commencement of Lent and runs officially for four days and three nights. The country literally closes down for this biggest holiday of the year and no business is conducted.

CHILE

Cultural Overview

Chile's attitude toward U.S. trade and investment is one of the most favorable among South American nations. Between one-quarter and one-third of the country's imports are from the United States, representing several billion dollars annually. New markets are opening up, and the climate for foreign investment is very attractive.

Chilean values and culture, like those of Argentina, reflect the citizens' European roots. Chile's middle class is one of the larger ones in South America and conservative values prevail in politics, economics, and social attitudes.

A military junta, presided over by an elected president, has run Chile since 1973, following the overthrow of socialist President Salvador Allende.

Copper is the foundation of Chile's economy. There are some 6 million tons of proven copper reserves, and the national company,

CODELCO, is the world's largest copper producer. Foreign-owned mines were expropriated by President Allende, and the government, after compensating the owners, still owns and operates the mines.

Other major products include nitrates, gold, silver, coal, iron, manganese, sulphur, fruit, and fish. Wine production is also an important industry with France as its most important customer.

During the worldwide recession of 1982 and 1983, copper prices declined and Chile's economy suffered. Recovery began in 1984, but the foreign debt, while stable, remains one of the world's largest on a per capita basis. Future economic growth depends on diversification: increasing noncopper exports and internal savings; lowering inflation; strengthening the private sector; maintaining an attractive foreign investment climate; and working closely with the International Monetary Fund and creditor banks.

Roman Catholicism is Chile's major religion, but Protestant faiths form a substantial minority.

With free and compulsory elementary education, 90 percent of Chileans over 15 are literate.

Family respect and loyalty are primary concerns in Chile, for the family is the individual's main support system. Family obligations take precedence over business responsibilities.

Men dominate the business world, but women do occupy some middle and even senior management positions. The Chilean executive will treat a visiting businesswoman with great courtesy, expecting this to be taken as a compliment and a sign of respect for her position.

Geographically, Chile is long (2,625 miles) and narrow (312 miles at the widest). The country encompasses every kind of land, from the soaring Andes to the barren desert in the north. The climate is equally varied, although Santiago enjoys weather similar to that of southern California, but with more rain.

Roughly one-third of Chile's 11.5 million people live in Santiago. Most Chileans are descended from Spanish immigrants, but English, Scottish, and Italian heritages are also represented. Unlike many South American countries, Chile has only a small native Indian population, and intermarriage is rare.

Spanish is Chile's official language. Well-educated businesspeople, particularly in more senior positions, may speak English, but most feel more comfortable speaking their native tongue.

Business Opportunities

Because Chile needs to earn or conserve foreign exchange, markets for imported consumer goods will not be expanding. The situation, however, should lead to opportunities for sales of primary and intermediate materials and capital goods to Chile's export-oriented and import substitution industries. Markets for mining, agriculture, food processing, and forestry equipment should be opening up. Proposals that will help Chile increase exports or decrease imports have the best chance for success, and nontraditional products for export such as timber should receive some attention.

U.S. suppliers of goods and services will find several projects now under way that offer excellent prospects. These include:

- Expansion of CODELCO's mining operations, plus new private mining projects.
- Expansion and modernization of the telephone and telecommunications systems.
- Construction of methanol and ammonia/urea plants.
- Construction of hydroelectric and thermoelectric plants.

Chile's rules for foreign investment are liberal, and investors receive nondiscriminatory treatment. Loans to Chile have been quite scarce in recent years, and foreign investment is regarded as a good way to attract technology and capital.

Initiating Contact

Chilean commerce is centered in and around the capital, Santiago. Third-party contacts, especially banks, consulting firms, and U.S. companies already operating in Chile, are important for making initial introductions.

Chile has more than two thousand import houses, most of which are small to medium in size. Some of these handle a few specific lines, although many also represent a variety of products. The majority of firms have their central offices in Santiago and are controlled by Chilean nationals. These firms either import for their own accounts or act as representatives for overseas interests.

Firms that act solely as commission agents are also common. Questions about their technical, servicing, and financial resources, however, make dealing with them more risky than dealing with the import firms.

If you are selling to government entities, it is advisable to obtain legal representation by registering with the Bureau of Government Supplies. Government entities generally do their own buying. Chilean law calls for public bidding, although in some cases negotiation is permitted. Bidders must put up a guarantee bond of 10 percent of the total bid.

National entities active in foreign procurement include:

- Servicio Nacional de Salud
  (National Health Service)
- Direccion de Aprovisionamiento del Estado
  (Bureau of Government Supplies)
- Ministerio de Obras Publicas
  (Ministry of Public Works)
- Empresa de Transportes Colectivos del Estado
  (Public Transport Enterprises)
- Ferrocarriles del Estado
  (Chilean State Railways)
- Empresa de Comercio Agricola
  (Agricultural Commerce Enterprise)

PROCHILE, the government trade promotion bureau (see below), can help identify possible market opportunities and arrange first meetings with Chilean agents, import houses, and distributors. The other listed organizations can also assist in initiating contact and providing information:

PROCHILE
866 UN Plaza
New York, N.Y. 10017
Phone: (212) 980-3255

U.S. Commerce Department
Marketing Manager for Chile
14th Street and Constitution Avenue
Washington, D.C.
Phone: (202) 377- 4303

Chamber of Commerce of the U.S.A. in Chile
Huerfanos 669, Officina 608
P.O. Box 4131
Santiago, Chile
Phone: 393163

Asociación Nacional de Importadores
(National Association of Importers)
Santa Lucia 302, P.O. Box 1015
Santiago, Chile
Phone: 397859

North American–Chilean Chamber of Commerce, Inc.
220 East 81st Street
New York, N.Y. 10028
Phone: (212) 288-5691

Business Protocol and Procedures

BUSINESS ENVIRONMENT

The Chilean business atmosphere combines South American and U.S. styles. Chile and the United States have done business together for a long time, and many Chilean executives have been educated in the States. The U.S. way of doing business is understood and its business styles are admired and emulated. Chileans are extremely bottom line oriented.

The Chilean business style tends to be more formal than in the United States or many other South American countries. Correct dress and behavior are expected, and the more senior executives, especially, may find the easy familiarity common among U.S. executives to be offensive. Chileans put great emphasis on the importance of strong personal relationships in business.

Meetings will be held at your host's offices. Traditional business hours are from 9:00 A.M. to 5:00 P.M. and many executives stay at the office until 7:00 P.M. Business discussions often continue over lunch, an important part of the Chilean business day that starts around 2:00 P.M. and lasts for two hours. It is best to set up the first meeting for the morning, with lunch to follow. This meeting should be confirmed a week in advance by telephone or telex.

Doing business in Chile requires at least one visit by a senior executive, who should be accompanied by one or two junior colleagues. Follow-up meetings are most often conducted with middle-management staff.

During the initial meeting, the first 20 to 30 minutes will be devoted to getting acquainted. Discussions on impersonal topics are appropriate. After about 20 minutes, the visiting executive should try to steer the conversation slowly toward business issues. The main purpose of this initial meeting, however, will be to discuss general issues about potential opportunities and to start developing personal relationships. Arranging for an interpreter, at least for the first meeting, can ensure that the relationship gets off to a good start, with no misunderstandings.

RANK AND STATUS

Family, education, and professional accomplishments are the main factors determining rank and status in Chile. The arts are also important in Chilean society, particularly literature and fine art.

In the business world, Chilean titles may not mean quite what similar titles would in the United States. The *presidente* or *gerente general* is usually the equivalent of chairman of the board or chief operating officer. *Vice presidente* means senior vice president, and ranks second in a company. The Chilean equivalent of the U.S. vice president is a *gerente*.

FORMS OF ADDRESS

Chilean men should be addressed as "señor," and women are always addressed as "señora," (very young ladies as "señoritas"). Younger executives may be less formal than their older colleagues; however, even with them it is best to be conservative and respectful, unless and until your host invites a less formal form of address.

When entering a room, you should acknowledge each person individually. The proper greeting is a firm handshake, direct eye contact, and a slight smile.

BUSINESS CARDS

Cards should be presented, with the right hand, to everyone in the office except the secretaries. Your title should be clearly visible on the card. Bilingual cards are not necessary.

BUSINESS DRESS

Business dress is more conservative in Chile than in the United States, with dark blue or grey suits, light shirts, and subdued ties acceptable. Bright or light colors, plaids, and very up-to-the-minute fashions are not appropriate.

GIFT-GIVING

Gift-giving need not be reciprocal, and you are not expected to give one until a fairly close relationship has been established. Appropriate gifts for your counterparts include imported whiskey and such personal items as silk ties or books. A small present for your counterpart's secretary can help smooth the way in future dealings with the executive.

Some suggestions on gift-giving:

- Any gift you receive should be opened at once, and you should express gratitude.
- It is considered impolite in Chile, as in many places, to offer a gift to your host in the presence of his or her associates if you do not have something for each person.
- If you go to your Chilean colleague's home for dinner, send flowers to his wife *before* your arrival. If you cannot arrange for flowers, bring a box of chocolates, perfume, or a bottle of scotch.

COMMUNICATION STYLES

Chileans are very physical and frequently emphasize points with hand gestures. Flinching or retreating from such gestures is interpreted as a lack of sensitivity to your host and disinterest in what he or she is saying. Direct eye contact is thought to show sincerity and openness.

Negotiating in Chile

Decision making in Chilean businesses is quite centralized. Senior officers—the *presidente*, the *vice presidente*, or the *gerente general*—have the greatest authority to initiate, conduct, and conclude negotiations. *Gerentes*, the equivalent of vice presidents in the United States, may have decision-making authority, but not in all cases. Middle- and lower-level staff usually provide technical and operational support for the decision makers.

Negotiations are taken seriously. Using an interpreter is advised, to be sure that all contractual obligations and expectations are clear. If your products require service on a regular basis, it is an excellent strategy to have a Chilean representative and to make this clear during negotiations. Chileans will appreciate your willingness to serve the customer, even at a distance of ten thousand miles, and your commitment to such service will help business relationships. Any marketing strategy must include a strong financial package, incorporating extended financing terms, and perhaps nontraditional arrangements such as barter or offset.

Business Entertaining

Entertaining plays a major role in developing the personal relationships so crucial to doing business in Chile. Dinner is usually the main event, either at a restaurant or at your host's home. In a restaurant, it is appropriate—and appreciated—for you to pick up the check. You can make arrangements with the maître d' in advance, to avoid any discussion about who pays.

Chileans are very conscious of table manners. In addition to standards that hold in any society, it is impolite in Chile to keep your hands under the table during meals.

After dinner at a Chilean's home, it is not necessary to send flowers or a thank-you note.

General Tips

- Appropriate subjects for small talk include Chilean cuisine and wines, the beauty of the country, and other neutral topics. Domestic politics, religion, marital status, and other more personal topics are not considered polite subjects for small talk among new acquaintances.
- Chileans often criticize their country, but they do not like foreigners to agree.
- A serious, businesslike image is important and demonstrates your intention to develop a mutually beneficial relationship. Chi-

leans have a sense of humor, but they do not appreciate excessive joking or crude behavior.

EXECUTIVE TRAVEL TO CHILE   •

DOCUMENTS

A valid passport and round-trip ticket are required to enter the country. A tourist card, which is issued at no charge by the airline upon arrival, is valid for 90 days.

INOCULATIONS

There are no special requirements for business travelers from the United States.

AIRPORT

The International Airport (Comodoro Arturo Merino) is located about 15 miles from downtown Santiago and should take about 30 minutes by taxi.

CUSTOMS

Tourists may bring in personal belongings, 500 cigarettes, 100 cigars, two liters of alcoholic beverages, and gifts. There is a small departure tax.

U.S. EMBASSY

1343 Agustinas, Codina Building, Santiago
Phone: 71-01-33

TRANSPORTATION

While public transportation is excellent in Santiago, it is recommended that a car and a driver/translator be hired for the length of your stay. These arrangements can be made with your hotel concierge.

TIPPING

Restaurants and bars add 10 percent to the bill, but waiters will expect a 10 percent cash tip in addition. Taxi drivers do not expect a tip unless cabs are hired for long hauls or extended periods of time.

HOTELS

SANTIAGO

Hotel Carrera
Avenida Teatinos 180
Phone: 6982011   Telex: 645265

Holiday Inn Cordillera
Avenida O'Higgins 136
Phone: 465158   Telex: 441306

Sheraton San Cristóbal
Avenida Santa María 1742
Phone: 745000   Telex: 440004

RESTAURANTS

SANTIAGO

Aquí Está Coco La Concepción 236 Phone: 465985	*Seafood*
El Alero de los de Ramón Avenida Las Condes 9889 Phone: 472192	*Chilean*
Enoteca Cerro San Cristóbal Phone: 2321758	*Chilean*
La Cascade Avenida Francisco Bilbao Phone: 2237286	*French*
Los Adobes de Argomedo Argomedo 411 Phone: 2229794	*Steakhouse*

Renato   *Italian*
Mardoque Fernández 183
Phone: 2322739

San Cristóbal   *International*
Sheraton Hotel
Phone: 745000

TRAVEL TIPS

• International communication links are excellent. Direct-dial telephone service is available at most large hotels, as is telex and cable service. Mail service is generally good, although incoming deliveries are often slow.

• Personal safety is good in Santiago and the crime rate in all Chilean cities is low.

• There are almost no import restrictions in Chile, and therefore stores and shops are stocked with both Chilean and imported goods. Among the best buys are the various textile products, including colorful hand-woven ponchos and vicuña rugs. Leather goods are of excellent quality and the prices are low. Semiprecious and precious stones are also widely available, as are copper products.

• The best view of the city is afforded from San Cristóbal Hill, twelve hundred feet high and adorned with a statue of the Virgin Mary, France's gift to Chile. There is a sixty-six-hundred-foot cable car ride to the top where there are gardens, a café, and walkways.

• Santiago's museums include the Colonia Art Museum, the Popular Arts Museum, and the Fine Arts Museum. There is also a Historical Museum in the downtown area.

• Chile has one of the world's top ski resorts at Portillo, located five hours by train from Santiago. In the city proper, several country clubs offer golf and tennis. The city is also an angler's paradise, with both freshwater and ocean fishing available. Spectator sports include soccer, tennis, volleyball, and horseracing.

COLOMBIA

Cultural Overview

The Republic of Colombia, a mountainous country the size of Texas and California combined, is the only nation in South America with both Atlantic and Pacific coasts. The geography of the country divides it naturally into five distinct regions: a coastal area, the highlands and valleys, vast plains, a jungle, and a tropical rain forest. Much of this country is as yet unexplored and uninhabited.

Colombia is a democratic republic with a constitution that was adopted in 1886, and which remains much the same. The government has three branches: the legislative, a bicameral congress that has a senate and a house of representatives; the executive, with a president and 13 cabinet members appointed by the president; and a judicial, which is a system of courts, with a 20-member supreme court. Direct popular vote elects the legislators and the president every four years. The president cannot succeed himself. While in office, he has broad executive power and authority. There is a two-party system, with the Liberals having a majority over the Conservatives. The military has historically had very little power.

Colombia has a proud heritage based on a native pre-Columbian civilization, combined with influences from the Spanish colonization of the country. Also, each region of the nation has a character of its own, with distinctive beliefs and qualities. Regional politics feed into the national scene as loyal bases of support. Government ministers have been known to resign their national posts to run for political office in their home *departamento* (state).

Colombia has a coffee-based economy, even though coffee has been decreasing in total output and exports. Agriculture and manufacturing are also important. The Colombian economy has recently slowed because of falling coffee prices, difficulties in the textile industry, and regional economic problems. However, mining has expanded, and it is expected that it will continue to grow with Colombia's world-scale coal and nickel projects. Mineral exports are expected to overtake coffee exports sometime in the future.

With 28 million people, Colombia is the fourth most populous country in South America. Three ethnic groups largely embody the

Colombian people: Spanish, Indian, and Black. Mestizos, who are part Spanish and part Indian, make up 60 percent of the people. Only 20 percent of the population is considered to be Caucasian. Even though there is a very poor distribution of wealth, and the country is controlled by an oligarchy, there appears to be little social conflict. Roman Catholicism is the predominant religion.

Half of all Colombians are under the age of 21. Colombia is primarily an urban nation, with 75 percent of the people living in its cities. The largest cities are Bogotá, the capital, with 5 million people, Medellín with 1.7 million, and Cali with 1.5 million. Nine other cities have populations of more than two hundred fifty thousand people.

Colombia's society is male dominated, although women participate somewhat in both business and politics. Several have served as government ministers, and some women have run small business enterprises. On the whole, however, most senior (and second-in-command) posts are held by men, with the exception of a few family businesses that have women members in high executive positions.

Business Opportunities

Colombia's development has been restrained and cautious, and consequently, the country has enjoyed a positive reputation in the international financial community for being fiscally conservative and prudent. Indeed, Colombia has not experienced the economic trauma endured by other South American countries in recent times. As a result of this restraint, considerable resources that could have been exploited or developed have not been, and they remain available to contribute to the substantial economic growth predicted for Colombia's future.

Because of its coffee industry, this nation has had substantial exposure to the international business world. Half of its export business is still in coffee. But there are many opportunities for new business ventures to be pursued, especially in the fields of agribusiness, coal, and petroleum. As one conspicuous example of this, Colombia is now the leading exporter of fresh-cut flowers to the United States.

Current trade regulations forbid imports without a provision to permit the export of a like value of Colombian products. However, coffee is obviously excluded from this arrangement. Colombia's future is heavily tied to coal exports and the production of nickel. Other products being offered for export are leather goods, timber, meats, and seafood. Substantial investment is required for rehabilitation of the infrastructure of the nation's transportation systems, which are in need of modernization, and especially to assist in the most advantageous utilization of Columbia's rivers. It is now also possible to enter into joint venture agreements concurrently with both private enterprises and the government, a consolidation which increases the chance of success for specific development projects.

Initiating Contact

The preferred method of introduction in Colombia is through a third-party contact. The nation's society is dominated by a political and economic elite, and family and regional connections can pierce through bureaucratic delays. Banking contacts are very helpful. Check those U.S. banks with offices in Bogotá.

If you are selling in Colombia, the most effective channels include the following:

- Import houses that import under their own name.
- Commission agents.
- Subsidiaries of foreign manufacturers, particularly in the areas of oil and gas production and the mining of coal and nickel ore.
- Local users, including the government and its agencies, which purchase foreign goods through public bids for specific projects. Those businesses that are substantial purchasers in their own right are: CARBOBOL (coal company), ECOPETROL (oil company), and TELECOM (communications company).

To check the technical, financial, and marketing resources of import houses and commission agents, you may contact the U.S. offices of the Colombian Trade Promotion Agency, PROEXPO, or the Camara de Comercio de Bogotá (Chamber of Commerce)—see below. For further information, contact:

Colombian–American Chamber of Commerce
Calle 35, No. 6–16
Apartado Aereo 8008

Bogotá, Colombia
Phone: 329701/791

Colombian Government Trade Bureau
140 East 57th Street
New York, N.Y. 10022
Phone: (212) 758-4772

International Economic Policy (Colombia)
International Trade Administration
U.S. Department of Commerce
14th Street and Constitution Avenue
Room 3027
Washington, D.C. 20230
Phone: (202) 377-4302

Colombian Government Trade Bureau
Calle 28, No. 13A–15
Apartado Aereo 17966
Bogotá, Colombia
Phone: 269-0777

Ministry of Economic Development
Carrera 13, No. 27-00
Apartado Aereo 3412
Bogotá, Colombia
Phone: 234-0540

World Trade Center Bogotá (Grupo 100 Ltda.)
P.O. Box 6005
Bogotá, Colombia
Phone: 2184411   Telex: 45666 CEMCO

Camara de Comercio de Bogotá (Chamber of Commerce)
Carrera 9, No. 16–21
Apartado Aereo 29824
Bogotá, Colombia
Phone: 2819900

Business Protocol and Procedures

BUSINESS ENTERTAINMENT

Business meetings will be held at the offices of your Colombian host,
usually between 10:00 A.M. and noon or after 3:00 P.M.

Most offices open at 9:00 A.M. and close at 5:00 P.M., with an hour or two for lunch, about 12:30 or 1:00 P.M. Senior executives may extend their workday to 6:00 P.M.

At least one senior executive from the U.S. firm should be at the first meeting, accompanied by one or two associate managers. On subsequent visits, the senior executive may come alone. Middle-level executives can be sent if the subsequent meeting will not be decisive.

You should be on time for each meeting, although it is likely you will be kept waiting. This is a symbolic tactic; the wait should only be between 15 and 45 minutes. Colombian executives at all levels do this as a matter of practice.

You and your colleagues will meet with the senior Colombian executive and one or two senior associates, usually in the executive's office, or in a large meeting room if there are many participants. The senior executives will be seated directly opposite each other. Strong Colombian coffee will be served throughout the meeting. You should accept and drink the first cup, but it is not impolite to refuse successive offers. Many offices can also serve you a soft drink or ice water if you prefer.

A first meeting can be useful in introducing you to business opportunities in Colombia, and to potential partners. You may have a specific proposal or project in mind. If not, it is appropriate to initiate a general exploratory discussion about your firm's business, and about the possibilities in Colombia. If the fit is good between your firm's products and services and the Colombian concern, substantive discussions can ultimately take place. Do take such an initial discussion seriously; the Colombians will certainly do so.

RANK AND STATUS

Colombia has a clear social stratification based on education, occupation, and race, among other factors. It is fairly rigid, with mobility between the lower and upper levels quite difficult. Putting it another way, the division is between those who do manual labor and those with jobs that require mental effort. However, one may certainly move from the working class to a higher position through education.

The upper class comprises two separate groups: the lawyers, doctors, and small business owners said to be the middle class, and the members of the oligarchy, who are linked by political power, education abroad, and high levels of income. There have been several isolated instances of technically trained members of the middle class becoming nationally prominent through a leadership position in a public agency.

FORMS OF ADDRESS

Greet your Colombian host with a firm handshake, a smile, and direct eye contact. Colombians are addressed as "señor," using the first (father's) name of the double last name. Senior executives and professionals are commonly addressed as "doctor," even though they have not earned a Ph.D. degree. Married women should be addressed as "señora."

BUSINESS CARDS

Present your business cards immediately after the introduction. Bilingual cards are not necessary. Titles are important, and should be clearly visible on the cards.

BUSINESS DRESS

Colombian men and women are fashion conscious. Men's suits should be dark-toned, conservatively cut, and worn with a white or light blue dress shirt and subdued ties. Accessories such as cufflinks and watches are noticed for their quality. In coastal cities such as Cartagena and Barranquilla, suits of a lighter weight and color are appropriate. In Bogotá and Medellín, a lined raincoat is advised year round because of the cool temperatures and the likelihood of rain.

GIFT-GIVING

The business executive is a person first and a business executive second. You will often be shown an individual's other interests and abilities. To promote *"simpatía,"* you should in turn share your own enthusiasms, whether they are collecting art, fishing, or visiting the host country. The corporation is an abstraction to your associate executives; it is the individual who matters. In gift-giving, try to select an item that coincides with your hosts' hobbies and interests. Your thoughtfulness will be very much appreciated.

COMMUNICATION STYLES

Colombians are often direct and straightforward. They are highly literate and sophisticated, many having been educated in Europe and the United States. Colombians from the higher elevations (and this includes Bogotá) are known as the "Swiss of South America" because of their relative isolation and conservatism. At first, they may seem distant and restrained in conversation, but this will change as trust is established.

Physical contact is customary. During a discussion, a Colombian may touch your arm to accentuate a point. Use of the hands to emphasize, or attract attention, is common. Eye contact is important to Colombians, and you are measured by your response.

Your eye contact suggests to Colombians that you are sure of yourself and comfortable with them.

Negotiating in Colombia

Negotiating with Colombians is not very different than doing business in the United States. As the coffee trade has been so significant in the world markets, many Colombian businesspeople have become extremely sophisticated in the ways of international business. Government agencies are also seasoned in global trade, and possess a matured experience in negotiating complex joint venture agreements with the largest industrial complexes in the world.

Regional ties and personal networks are very important in Colombia. Most Colombians will identify themselves with their provincial state or department, rather than with the country. Government ministers are interested ultimately in the greater welfare and development of their home region. The states provide the base for national political power and influence.

The *presidente* of a Colombian company holds most of the decision-making power. *Vice presidentes* at the senior level can also have substantial authority. If you are dealing with individuals in either of these two senior executive positions, it is evidence of their interest in your proposal. The views of lower-level executives are rarely considered, except where technical issues are raised in which they are proficient.

Business contracts are essential in Colombia, even for the smallest of details. You can expect to sign several agreements during the course of your negotiations. Be sure everything is clear to all concerned.

Business Entertaining

Entertaining at dinner is popular, and it is a good way to extend business discussions in more comfortable surroundings. It also gives you and your Colombian host the opportunity to get to know each other better without the pressure of a business setting. This is important in Colombia. Dinners usually begin at 7:30 P.M. and end at 11:00 P.M.; often, they represent a continuation of the business day, and you may not have the opportunity to return to your hotel to freshen up.

Cocktail parties, held to celebrate any occasion, are most enjoyable. They offer an exceptional opportunity to meet informally with the Colombian hosts, their associates, family, and friends. In Colombia the family extends to first and second cousins, uncles and aunts, grandparents, and so on.

If your stay in this country is for three or four days, hosting a dinner and a cocktail party on separate nights will make a very favorable impression. If you receive an invitation and of necessity must refuse, take pains to make sure that your host understands that your inability to accept was for a very legitimate reason. Remember that social occasions are important for going beyond business to develop an enduring rapport with your Colombian business associates.

Formal toasting is not usually a part of the meal, and would be considered unusual. A simple *"salud"* (cheers) is sufficient.

Colombians are sensitive to three issues: the illegal drug trade, personal security (especially the issue of kidnapping), and the Marxist guerrilla movement. They will discuss them, but these are topics that they would prefer to avoid.

Grilled meat is a specialty in Colombia, and seafood is often a specialty on the coast. Wine is served with the meal and beer and whiskey may be served toward the end of a successful meeting, as rewards for the hard work.

Table manners are important. There is a European tradition governing cleanliness and polite deportment while dining.

General Tips

- A sense of humor is as valuable in Bogotá as in New York.
- Gaining support and securing the right partners will be easier if you understand the value of the extensive personal networks existing in business and in government. Colombia's major institutions are managed by members of the political, economic, and social elite.
- Take time to hear all expressions, opinions, and perspectives,

and to develop an understanding of the subtleties of the Colombian political and business environment. This will eventually foster the mutual trust necessary to bring on effective cooperation.
• Be prepared for various types of countertrade offers that may be introduced, since the overall South American economic crisis has to some extent affected Colombia's trade balance negatively. Trade regulations forbid imports without a provision to export a like value of Colombian products, exclusive of coffee.
• U.S. firms willing to market Colombian coal abroad are looked on favorably and gain considerable business leverage in this country.
• Visiting businesswomen can overcome the traditional bias against professional women by showing competence, knowledge, skill, and discretion.
• Loyalty to superiors, teachers, and friends is important to Colombians. Frequently, a manager will perform something for his superior out of personal loyalty rather than out of his commitment to the good of the company.
• Remain calm and patient if you are kept waiting by a Colombian executive, especially a high-ranking one. If this continues to happen, and a junior official keeps you waiting, it is appropriate to express your dissatisfaction. But do realize that Colombians do not consider their waiting tactic rude.
• Your personal appearance will influence the Colombian's evaluation of you. A certain flair is appreciated, but do not detract from your credibility by being ostentatious.

EXECUTIVE TRAVEL TO COLOMBIA •

DOCUMENTS

A valid passport and tourist card, which can be picked up at the Colombian Embassy in Washington, D.C., or in New York, are required.

INOCULATIONS

While not required for travel through most of the country, typhoid, tetanus, polio, yellow fever, and hepatitis inoculations are advisable when traveling to the Amazon region of Colombia.

AIRPORT

The El Dorado International Airport is about 7½ miles from the center of Bogotá. There is a moderate airport departure tax for international flights.

CUSTOMS

Duty-free entry is allowed for 400 cigarettes, 50 cigars, or up to one pound of tobacco, and two bottles of liquor are also allowed duty-free. You can expect a thorough customs search before departure because of the country's efforts to inhibit drug traffic.

U.S. EMBASSY

Calle 38, No. 8–61, Bogotá
Phone: 285-1300

TRANSPORTATION

Taxis are plentiful, but it is advisable when traveling on business to arrange to hire a driver/translator for your stay.

TIPPING

Taxi drivers will expect a small tip. In restaurants 10 percent is average, with 15 percent for special service.

HOTELS

BOGOTÁ

Tequendama Inter-Continental Hotel
Carrera 10A, 26–21
Phone: 286-1111   Telex: 45418

Bogotá Hilton
Carrera 7, 32–16
Phone: 287-0788   Telex: 44467

RESTAURANTS

BOGOTÁ

Casa Vieja   *Colombian*
Carrera 10, 26–50
Phone: 284-7359

Eduardo   *International*
Carrera 11, 89–43
Phone: 236-1251

La Fragata   *Seafood*
Carrera 13, 27–98
Phone: 255-9504

La Reserve   *French*
Carrera 15, 37–15
Phone: 255-9504

La Table du Roi   *International*
Carrera 8-A, 15–31
Phone: 234-9508

TRAVEL TIPS

• The major hotels have bilingual staffs and direct international telephone service as well as efficient telex and cable service. Colombia boasts of an efficient postal service and sophisticated radio and television capabilities. A wide variety of international publications are available as well as four local daily newspapers.
• There are excellent hospitals in the major cities, and the Red Cross, which functions throughout the country, responds to all emergencies. The Barraquer (eye) and Shaio (heart) clinics treat patients from all the Americas.
• The unit of currency is the Colombian peso, abbreviated Col. $.
• A wide range of reasonably priced, high-quality leather goods and woolen products are available. Colombian emeralds are the highest quality in the world. There is a large selection of pre-Colombian gold and ceramic artifacts. (It is illegal to transport authentic pre-Colombian pieces out of the country.)
• Remnants of the rich pre-Columbian past can be seen in visits to archeological sites throughout the country, most particularly the San Augustín stone monuments in the southwestern part of the country, which date back to 400 B.C. Bogotá's Gold Museum contains the most spectacular collection of pre-Columbian gold, over fifteen thousand gold objects.

• A word of caution to the jogger: Bogotá's high, thin air can make your usual run a dangerous experience. With clothing, too, be aware of the altitude of the city you are visiting.

• Petty thievery is a serious problem and you are cautioned not to target yourself by wearing expensive, flashy jewelry and making your valuables easily accessible. Have your hotel doorman flag a taxi for you; don't hail one yourself if you can avoid this.

VENEZUELA

Cultural Overview

There are two Venezuelas. The best known is the 1,750 miles along the Caribbean coast, which has 80 percent of its 14 million people in the capital city of Caracas. But Venezuelans say the *llanos* (vast, empty plains) in the west and south are the "real" Venezuela. From this region come national legends and heroes, particularly the *llaneros* or plainsdwellers who raise cattle and live quietly on the frontier. The region is a symbol of self-sufficiency, courage, and romance for Venezuelans. The *llanero* can be compared to our Western cowboy.

Venezuela is a federal republic consisting of 20 states; the federal district of Caracas, two federal territories, and 72 islands known as federal dependencies. The states are autonomous but must comply with federal laws and the 1961 constitution, which guarantees freedom of speech, religion, and assembly.

The president (elected for five years) has wide-ranging power. A bicameral legislature, the national congress, includes a 49-member senate and a 203-member chamber of deputies. All are elected for a five-year term. Congress elects the 15-member supreme court justices for nine-year terms. State governors are appointed by the president. Venezuela has a true two-party system with one of the longest sustained democratic traditions in South America. Both parties are sophisticated, sometimes using political consultants from the United States.

For forty years, Venezuela's economy was dominated by its oil industry. As it developed, the agriculture and manufacturing industries suffered. Oil production (including refining and petrochemicals) continues to be the largest industry in Venezuela. The other main industries are iron ore, steel production, and aluminum. In recent decades, the government has sought diversification by encouraging the local manufacture of imported goods. Other areas of potential diversification include bauxite mining and agricultural products such as corn, rice, sugar cane, tobacco, cotton, and livestock. Venezuela's long and beautiful coastline can be developed for fishing, marine transport, and tourism.

The family is the cornerstone of a Venezuelan's life, and responsibility to it is paramount. The family unit provides the social connections that a person needs to be considered strong and complete. One's name, reputation, and family relationships define a person in Venezuelan society. And, in turn, success or failure reflects on the individual's family.

Men run the federal government, state companies, and private enterprises, and even dominate the professions. This has become even more pronounced in recent years, since only men receive education leading to technical careers. Tradition still rules the Venezuelan woman's outlook, attitude, and behavior. Wives take care of the children and the details of family life. Visiting businesswomen will not find many Venezuelan women in business. The constitution provides religious freedom; most Venezuelans are Roman Catholics.

The Ministry of Education controls education at all levels: six years of elementary school is mandatory; five years of secondary and three to six years of university or technical school are also offered; and all are free. Spanish is the official language, but many Venezuelans speak English because of the U.S. influence. Caracas is cosmopolitan, and you will hear many languages there.

Venezuela has two seasons: a rainy season from June to November, and a dry season from December to May. The climate is temperate to hot, but cooler in the mountains. Temperature in the major business city, Caracas, is moderately warm, ranging from 67 to 80 degrees Fahrenheit.

Business Opportunities

Venezuela is the richest nation in South America on a per capita basis because of its oil production. In terms of foreign exchange, it exports oil. The United States has found strong markets in Venezuela for chemicals, automobiles, food, and industrial machinery. However, the recent decline in the price of oil has meant that Venezuela must diversify its economy and exports. Also, the country is experiencing problems of high inflation and inefficiency, which are further compounded by the needs of government, industrial, and consumer subsidies. The recent devaluation of the bolivar (the currency) may spur an increase in nontraditional exports such as textiles, foodstuffs, and aluminum products.

Venezuelan planners seek to reschedule Venezuela's huge foreign debt, simplify the multiple exchange rate system, and improve the efficiency of the public sector by returning certain state enterprises to private hands; there is also a need to revitalize agricultural development and to relax restrictions on foreign investments. Success in these measures should precipitate a more stable economic adjustment.

Opportunities for U.S. firms to trade and invest should expand, although the stability of the Venezuelan economy must be strengthened before there can be any large increases in imports. One example of a possible market is in producing and processing food. Venezuela now imports 50 to 60 percent of its food supply.

Initiating Contact

The preferred way to make contact with Venezuelan business executives is through a third-party introduction, conceivably through another businessperson or perhaps a banker with Venezuelan contacts. Other contacts might be initiated in one of the following ways:

- A senior executive of your firm should write a letter describing your company, its products or services, and management, and what it hopes to accomplish in Venezuela. It should be addressed to a senior executive of the Venezuelan firm and sent via air carrier or registered letter. Promotional literature such as brochures should be in Spanish, and the letter should be professionally translated. If the reply is in English, you can use it in further communications. Follow up the letter with a personal phone call made during Venezuelan morning office hours, to explore the possibilities of a senior member of your firm visiting Venezuela.
- Venezuela does not have a major trade office in the United States. To research trade and investment opportunities with either private industry or the government, write the Venezuelan–

American Chamber of Commerce and Industry in Caracas (see below).

• Your letter should introduce your company, its products and services, and the reasons for your interest in Venezuela, and it should be signed by a senior executive. Follow up with a phone call.

• Or write the Banco de Venezuela, 450 Park Avenue, New York, N.Y. 10022, for suggestions in trade and investment opportunities and identifying specific Venezuelan companies and businesspeople that would be compatible with your company.

Four types of import channels are available in Venezuela:

• Import houses are well-financed concerns that usually import only for their own account but might agree to represent a foreign exporter on a commission basis.
• Commission agents usually sell to wholesalers and, depending on the product, collect 2.5 to 15 percent commission.
• Direct importers—these include retail stores, manufacturers, and agencies of the government.
• Branch offices or subsidiaries of a non-Venezuelan company.

Choose an import house or a commission agent with care. Some have the reputation, facilities, and technical qualifications to provide good representation. Others are small, inexperienced, or stretched too thin. Check any type of importer through banks and Chambers of Commerce. Visit Venezuela to discuss the proposal in detail.

If your firm wants to establish a marketing subsidiary, it must limit its equity to 20 percent or less to comply with the country's foreign investment code. The choice of partner, then, is crucial to the success of the venture. It may be best to consider this route after some experience in the Venezuelan market.

For further information, contact:

U.S. Department of Commerce
Marketing Manager of Venezuela
14th Street and Constitution Avenue
Washington, D.C. 20230
Phone: (202) 377-4302

Venezuelan–American Chamber of Commerce & Industry
Apartado 5181
Caracas 1010, Venezuela
Phone: (582) 283-8355

Caracas Chamber of Commerce
Los Caobos, Avenida Este 2/5
Caracas 1010, Venezuela
Phone: (582) 234-8598

Business Protocol and Procedures

BUSINESS ENVIRONMENT

Plan to arrive in Caracas the day before your first meeting, and reconfirm the appointment. Meetings will be held at the office of your Venezuelan host. Punctuality is appreciated in Venezuela. It is best to schedule meetings for the morning hours to avoid interfering with lunch appointments.

Commercial offices open at 8:00 A.M. for an eight-hour day. Lunch begins around 1:00 P.M. and lasts for several hours.

You will be escorted to an office or to a conference room if a number of individuals are to participate in the meeting. The senior Venezuelan executive will probably direct the senior executive of the U.S. firm to a specific seat.

Coffee will be served, which is a sign of friendliness and respect. The first 15 to 20 minutes are spent getting acquainted, a practice favored by most South Americans. However, if your host has worked in the United States or been influenced by the U.S. business world, this initial phase may be interrupted after only a few minutes by asking you about your business. This is a clear signal to begin business discussions.

Interpreters should be used. Arrange this when you arrive in Caracas unless your host has said they would be provided. In the meeting, interpreters are seated next to both executives.

RANK AND STATUS

The senior executive has great power and position within the business organization. Executive titles may be misleading, since they do not correspond with those in the United States. At the top, the *presidente* is equal in power and authority to a president or chief executive officer in the United States. The *vice presidente* is similar to an executive or senior vice president. Middle-level managers, called *gerentes*, usually head a department. With little responsibility for corporate policy, they are not usually included in top-level discussions unless the business relates to their own specific area.

FORMS OF ADDRESS

When meeting, shake hands firmly and announce your name, such as "John Anderson." The Venezuelan will reply, say, "Pedro Atencio." This is the custom in Venezuela, to introduce yourself. Until you develop a close relationship, address any businessman as "señor," and any businesswoman as "señora," using the first (father's) of the double last names. In letters, full names should be used, including both last names.

BUSINESS CARDS

Exchange business cards right after the introductions. Your title and company should be clearly visible. This will convey to the Venezuelan your rank and status.

BUSINESS DRESS

Conservative suits in blue or grey tropical weight wool are best for Venezuela's year-round warm climate. Dress shirts in white or light blue, and a conservative tie, are appropriate. A high-ranking Venezuelan executive is likely to be impressed by details of an individual's personal appearance. Quality in jewelry, wristwatches, and leather goods is noticed. Venezuelan women, whether spouses of executives or in government or business themselves, are as fashion conscious as French women. A U.S. woman executive should wear her best business clothes.

GIFT-GIVING

Good-quality corporation mementos make appropriate first-visit gifts; on subsequent visits, more personal gifts will be appreciated. Imported scotch and thoughtfully selected books are also well received. Gifts for wives might be imported perfume, silk scarves, or leather goods.

COMMUNICATION STYLES

The accepted greeting is a firm handshake.

Venezuelans will get quite close when speaking to you, and may touch your jacket or chest or squeeze your arm when making a point. You may be uncomfortable with touching, but it is a sign of insincerity or rejection to flinch, stiffen, or pull away from such contact.

The arm squeeze, or *abrazo* (brief embrace), may accompany salutory greetings. Venezuelans are friendly people.

Negotiating in Venezuela

There are two types of Venezuelan executives. The older generation is more traditional, entrepreneurial, and conservative. The younger is less traditional, and better educated, but just as conservative. Many of the older men founded the large industrial and commercial businesses. The younger generation is technocratic; they usually have experience touching on Venezuela's oil economy. Many were educated in the United States and worked in U.S. oil firms before the nationalization of non-Venezuelan oil firms.

It is important to show your respect for the accomplishments, age, and position of an older Venezuelan executive, and to adopt a serious, businesslike manner. The older person is apt to react to you, rather than to the company you represent, and to make intuitive judgments. Although the younger executive will be less subjective in both analysis and decision making, much will depend on the perceptions and feelings about whether you can be considered competent and experienced.

Dealing with either, the pace of business negotiations is slower than it is in the United States. The focus is on the future, as in most South American countries. Developing a firm relationship will eventually be far more important than a six-month increase in profits.

Sending one executive to the initial meeting is acceptable, as Venezuelans are used to negotiating with an individual instead of a team. However, subsequent visits should include other executives to enhance the channels of communication between the companies.

Only senior executives in Venezuela have the authority to make decisions, especially in family-owned enterprises, where power rests with one or two members who run the company. Without the interest and support of the top managers in any concern, little will be accomplished. Likewise, the senior manager in a government organization has tremendous influence and power. In enterprises (public or private) where technical skills are important, this power can be obscured somewhat by the technocrat. But such discussions with junior or middle-level management, no matter how technical, are only preliminary. The senior officers will always prevail.

Compromise in Venezuelan business is not common. In their oil-rich past, there were always other suppliers and other buyers, and the Venezuelans were afforded the luxury of taking the position they wanted. In the South American context, compromise means relinquishing or surrendering, and appearing less in control of things—a negative image that is very difficult for a Venezuelan to accept. These attitudes are changing, however, particularly in view of today's pressing economic situation. There has been a need to compromise with the International Monetary Fund and its creditor banks on repayment terms, and flexibility in dealing has become somewhat more customary.

Lawyers are seen as facilitators to business, not leading participants in the negotiating process. They can be included in a supportive role. Since negotiations may not be concluded on the first trip, it is best to wait to bring a lawyer until the legalities are negotiated, and this can take place after the first meeting.

Most state enterprises, and those headed by executives with U.S. experience, rely on detailed contracts. Firms with less international experience may avoid contracts, and use documents that outline general principles of the proposal.

Some suggestions for successful negotiating:

• Third-party introductions can clear the air of any initial mistrust or uncertainty.
• Business courtesies are important. There is much traffic and congestion in the city during morning rush hour. Allow adequate time. It is far better to be a few minutes early than to be late.
• Use the first part of the meeting to relax and get to know your host, as is being done with you. It is important not to appear restless during this get-acquainted period. Review your presentation and opening statement.

• Tactics to avoid in negotiating are too much pressure, dominating the conversation, and instant camaraderie.
• Be calm and unhurried, and prepared to go through your material slowly. Take pains to listen to your host's questions and observations.
• If your company's products and services tie in with the economic diversification of Venezuela, stress this point but make no outlandish claims.
• Business analysis may influence a decision, but it rests primarily on the visiting executive's style and method of dealing with the owner of the firm or the top executive. Find out first what is really wanted or needed.
• Visiting businesswomen must be professional in behavior at all times. With the older Venezuelan business community, a businesswoman who has established her competence and seriousness may become very effective by using charm in a subtle manner.
• A gracious way to close the negotiating process is with a personal letter from the senior executive of the U.S. firm to the senior Venezuelan, expressing satisfaction and appreciation of their cooperation.

Business Entertaining

Entertaining is important to develop the more personal side of the relationship. Lunch is a good time to continue discussions begun during morning meetings. Make reservations at a good restaurant and arrange to have the bill given to you directly.

Dinner is a more social event, beginning late, at 8:30 P.M., and lasting until midnight. Invite the spouses of the Venezuelan executives. In mixed company business discussions are avoided, although some small points can be made. A visiting businesswoman should not dine alone with a Venezuelan businessman, only with a group of businessmen and their wives.

Seating should be arranged so that the two senior executives sit facing each other. Other people are seated according to the personal relationships established, or representing their rank or business responsibility.

If it is an elaborate occasion, with several guests from each country, the senior visiting businessperson may give a small toast. You don't have to stand, but convey good wishes for the negotiating process or congratulations on its success.

If toasting, memorize a Spanish phrase that expresses your pleasure at being associated with the Venezuelans.

General Tips

• Topics that are sensitive to discuss are family, personal relationships, the government, and the influence of the United States on South America.

• The family is a person's base, a place of retreat, a world closed to outsiders. Asking a direct question about a spouse or about children is considered rude unless you have a very solid relationship. Respect their privacy.

• Venezuelans are rightfully proud of their long history of democratic government. Criticism, veiled or direct, is not appreciated. Avoid critical comments.

• Marriage, long friendships, and business relationships all provide a close-knit network that is difficult for visiting executives to penetrate. The key is to place personal relationships above the needs of abstract entities such as companies.

TRAVEL TO VENEZUELA •

DOCUMENTS

A valid passport and transit visa good for 45 days is required of visitors entering Venezuela for business reasons. If the trip is only for initial meetings, no samples or machinery are brought in, and no final business will be consummated, a tourist card issued by the airlines may be sufficient. Check with the Venezuelan Consulate for your specific requirements.

INOCULATIONS

None are required for U.S. citizens.

AIRPORT

Maiquetia Airport is located about 13 miles from Caracas, and the trip to the downtown area takes about 30 minutes.

CUSTOMS

Duty-free entry is allowed for personal belongings, 400 cigarettes, 50 cigars, and two quarts of liquor.

U.S. EMBASSY

Avenida Francisco de Miranda, La Floresta
Phone: 284-6111

TRANSPORTATION

While taxis are readily available, it is recommended that you hire a car and a driver/translator for the length of your stay.

TIPPING

Ten percent is usually added to the check in the majority of restaurants. It is customary, however, to leave an additional 10 percent on the table if you were satisfied with the service and food. Bellboys and chambermaids should be tipped a moderate sum.

HOTELS

CARACAS

Avila Hotel
Avenida Washington
Phone: 515 155   Telex: 21637

Caracas Hilton
Avenida El Conde
Phone: 571 2322   Telex: 21171

Tamanaco Inter-Continental
Avenida Urbanizacion Las Mercedes
Phone: 914 556   Telex: 23260

RESTAURANTS

CARACAS

Da Emore   *Italian*
Centro Comercial Concresa
Phone: 978 0079

El Gazevo Avenida Rio de Janeiro, Las Mercedes Phone: 975 568	*French*
El Porton Avenida Tamasaco, El Rosal Phone: 716 071	*Creole*
El Tejar Avenida Pichincha, El Rosal Phone: 710 095	*Venezuelan*
La Belle Epoque Avenida Leonardo da Vinci Phone: 761 342	*French*
Bistro Altamira Torre Centrale Phone: 283 8008	*French*
La Estancia Avenida Principal de la Castellana Phone: 337 937	*Steakhouse*
Los Pilones Avenida Pichincha, El Rosal Phone: 718 376	*Venezuelan*

TRAVEL TIPS

• Telephone service is somewhat mediocre in Venezuela, and international long distance is unreliable. Many businesses use messengers in an effort to overcome the poor communications situation. Your hotel will assist you in placing international calls.
• Medical assistance is available through the International Association for Medical Assistance to Travellers in Caracas, called "Clínica Caurinare," phone 763-033. The doctors are well qualified and speak English.
• In the heart of Caracas is Plaza Bolívar, a tree-lined square flanked by the Cathedral of Caracas and the gold-domed Congress Building. Nearby are the twin 32-story towers of the government's office complex that dominates the skyline.
• Caracas' Nacional and Municipal Theatres house a continous stream of concerts, ballets, plays, operas, and other attractions.

The Atene de Caracas in the cultural center on Plaza Morelos presents plays, classic films, and concerts.

• Caracas boasts the largest and most modern racetrack in South America, La Rinconada. Participant sports are readily available with excellent golf, swimming, and tennis facilities at the better hotels.

• Caracas' new shopping centers, called *"centros comerciales,"* have a wide range of shops. Fine gems and jewelry, pearls, native rugs and tapestries, handmade shoes, handbags, and leather merchandise of fine quality are the good buys.

UNION OF SOVIET SOCIALIST REPUBLICS

Cultural Overview

The Union of Soviet Socialist Republics (U.S.S.R.) is two and one half times the size of the United States. The population of 270 million is diverse; it is concentrated in a triangle between Leningrad, Odessa in the west, and Sverdlovsk in the eastern Ural Mountains. Almost all international business negotiations, however, take place in Moscow, the center of government and trade.

The prospect of significant improvement in the levels of U.S.– Soviet trade is, however, dim. The United States does not extend Most Favored Nation (MFN) tariff treatment to products from the U.S.S.R. in compliance with the Jackson–Vanik amendment; and U.S. Export-Import Bank (EXIM) facilities for U.S. exports to the U.S.S.R. are prohibited under the Stevenson amendment. Furthermore, Soviet business managers now look upon U.S. firms as "suppliers of last resort" because of past cancellations of signed contracts by the U.S. government, in retaliation for Soviet activity in Afghanistan and Poland and the KAL 007 shoot-down. Until an acceptable "contract sancitity" clause is written into the U.S. export control legislation, Soviet trade officials will be extremely wary of undertaking significant long-term contracts with U.S. suppliers for major projects.

The U.S.S.R. encompasses some 70 different nationalities, and nearly 200 languages and dialects. Russian is the language of education, trade, government, and national discourse, and almost all citizens speak it, at least as a second language. Many people speak English, the most commonly studied second language in the schools. Literacy is about 95 percent.

As a communist state, the U.S.S.R. recognizes no official religion, although religion's existence is acknowledged by the maintenance of a Ministry of Ecclesiastical Affairs, which to a degree defuses some popular dissent. Approximately 18 percent of the people are Russian Orthodox, 9 percent are Muslim and 3 percent are Jews. There are small numbers of Roman Catholics and Protestants. Marriage is a civil ceremony recognized by the state, and the family remains a strong force in Soviet society.

Politically, the U.S.S.R. is a federal union of 15 republics. Controlled by the Communist party of the Soviet Union (CPSU), the government has three branches: executive, judicial, and a bicameral legislature, the Supreme Soviet, which is elected every five years.

In general, the Communist party makes policy, and the government implements it. Comprised of delegates elected by local party cells, the Communist party congress elects the 320 members of the Central Committee. This body, in turn, chooses the Politburo, which determines general policies and direction, and the Secretariat, responsible for the day-to-day operation of the country. Secretariat members are the ministers heading various government departments.

The Soviet Union economy is socialist. The state controls every aspect and sector of the economy except for some small agricultural plots which are privately held. While area for private production is restricted, it accounts for about 25 percent of the total output. There is also an extensive "second" or underground economy.

Five-year plans set economic objectives, in response to which resources are deployed, instead of the demands of the marketplace. The market overtime, however, does influence production resources allocation. Economic relations between the United States and the Soviet Union depend largely on political relations between the two countries, and to do business with the U.S.S.R. one must remain current regarding the state of U.S. export control regulations and relevant aspects of the international situation.

The United States has never had a negative trade balance with the Soviet Union and, even when relations between the two powers have been tense and chilly, the United States has remained one of the Soviet Union's significant trading partners. Because of the negative Soviet trade balance with the United States and a worsening hard currency deficit in trade with the industrialized West, growth of U.S. exports to the U.S.S.R. will depend more and more on how much the Soviet Union can expand its sales to the U.S. market.

Although about 85 percent of Soviet women work, sometimes even in construction and other heavy manual activity, they still occupy something of a traditional position in society. Many women are in the professions, sciences, education, and business, but few occupy upper-management positions in business or other high-level bureaucratic posts. Soviet businessmen are not entirely comfortable dealing with foreign women executives, and, at least in initial meetings, it is best not to have women play key roles on the team. They may be brought into the process later, when the Soviet officials have gotten to know the U.S. team. Nonetheless, a number of successful small American trading firms are headed by female CEOs and some major firms dealing with the U.S.S.R. have key female executives on their Soviet staff.

Business Opportunities

The Soviets are more concerned with importing capital equipment processes or with obtaining licenses than with importing manufactured products other than food and feed grains. Long-term business relationships with the U.S.S.R. are more likely to develop with U.S. firms that can entertain alternatives to traditional financing or that can purchase Soviet manufactured goods. Entering into partnership with various industries for such projects as leasing and licensing agreements or science and technology agreements can also be successful.

Determining the need for a specific product or service is the first step in doing business with the Soviet Union. Keeping abreast of the five-year plan goals is essential, since they indicate requirements for products and industrial services. The following organizations can give information on goals, commercial agreements, and export controls regulating specific products and services:

• The U.S. Department of Commerce International Trade Administration (ITA) Office of Export Control, Washington, D.C. 20230 (The Explorer's Service Division, phone [202] 377-4811,

is prepared to give guidance concerning export licensing requirements).
• The Department of Commerce, Bureau of East–West Trade,
U.S.S.R. Affairs Division, phone (202) 377-4655, and the Trade
and Development Assistance Division, Washington, D.C. 20230.
• The Trade Representation of the U.S.S.R. in the U.S.A., 2001
Connecticut Avenue N.W., Washington, D.C. 20008, phone
(202) 232-0975. The staff of this Soviet Embassy organization
includes representatives of the individual Foreign Trade Organi-
zations (FTOs).
• Amtorg Trading Corporation, 750 Third Avenue, New York,
N.Y. 10017, phone (212) 972-1230 (a Soviet-owned company
established in New York in 1924).
• The Consulate General of the U.S.S.R., 2790 Green Street,
San Francisco, CA 94123, Commercial Section.
• The U.S.–U.S.S.R. Trade and Economic Council, Inc., 805
Third Avenue, New York, N.Y. 10022, phone (212) 644-4550, a
joint private U.S. business and Soviet trade organization, trade
and business facilitation and procuring organization, with an of-
fice in Moscow staffed by U.S. and Soviet personnel (publishes
Who's Who in Soviet Foreign Trade).
• A visiting Soviet trade mission, usually arranged to examine a
specific product.

Another excellent source of information is a handbook published
by the Soviet Ministry of Trade, *The Unified List for Foreign Trade*.
This publication lists products that have been identified through the
planning process and must come from foreign sources. The handbook
sets forth specifications, and showing that your product conforms to
these can simplify the process of making contact with the appropriate
Soviet agency.
The Business Man's Moscow, in English and Russian, published
by FTO Vneshtorgreklama (31 Kakhova Ul, Moscow 113461,
U.S.S.R.), contains detailed descriptions of all FTOs and their subsidiaries with a description of their activities. It contains the names of
key officials, addresses, telex numbers, and phone numbers.

Initiating Contacts

For business purposes, Soviet sponsorship is required for entry, so making successful initial contacts is very important. Among the various Soviet government agencies you will be dealing with, the Foreign Trade Organizations (FTOs) of the ministry of Foreign Trade are perhaps the most important. Sixty-six of these umbrella-type companies represent specific industries. Composed of highly trained, professional businesspeople, the FTOs negotiate technical and financial details and are the only groups that can sign contracts. Unsolicited offers, properly researched, can be submitted to a specific FTO. Each FTO is headed by a director general, with several deputy director generals beneath him. FTOs issue all import orders, and sales may be concluded without reference to other organizations. To initiate contact, write with a specific proposal to the appropriate Soviet Foreign Trade Organization, which can be identified through the Amtorg U.S.–U.S.S.R. Trade and Economic Council, U.S.S.R. Trade Representation, or the U.S. Department of Commerce International Trade Association. Any proposal should be clear, concise, and as brief as possible, and it should include the following:

- Details of the product's technical capabilities and its advantages.
- Details of the output of the process or equipment.
- Total price, including transport, taxes, and so on.
- Details about any discounts that might be available.
- Information about your company, its history, technical capabilities, financial position, reputation, and key executives.

Although once impossible, it is now an accepted and a usually advisable practice to contact other Soviet entities in addition to the FTO, as part of the marketing effort. While difficult, principal contacts should be with the end-user, normally the relevant sponsoring ministry but also the individual firms when possible. Such contacts may be necessary for technological products and processes with exacting specifications. You can contact an industrial ministry by addressing inquiries to its Foreign Relations Department.

In addition, it is also important to develop contacts with individuals in the Ministry of Foreign Trade and the State Committee for Science and Technology. This committee is responsible for improving the technological base of the U.S.S.R.; a U.S. firm can submit unsolicited proposals to it. However, current U.S. export controls regarding technology transfers in a large number of sectors are very restrictive.

Trade fairs and exhibitions in the U.S.S.R. or elsewhere are among the best opportunities for business contacts. Lists of such fairs and exhibits are available from the organizations noted above.

For further information, contact:

World Trade Center Moscow
v/ov/o SOVINCENTR
12 Krasnopresnenskaya nab.
123610 Moscow, U.S.S.R.
Phone: 2566303   Telex: 411486 SOVIN SU

Trade Representation of the U.S.S.R. in the USA
2001 Connecticut Avenue N.W.
Washington, D.C. 20008
Phone: (202) 232-5988

U.S.–U.S.S.R. Trade and Economic Council
3 Shevchenko Embankmant
121248 Moscow, U.S.S.R.
Phone: 2435228

U.S.S.R. Chamber of Commerce & Industry
6 Ulitsa Kuibysheva
121248 Moscow, U.S.S.R.
Phone: 2210811/2234323

International Economic Policy (U.S.S.R.)
International Trade Administration
U.S. Department of Commerce
14th Street and Constitution Avenue
Washington, D.C. 20230
Phone: (202) 377-4656

Business Protocol and Procedures

Once initial contact has been made, a meeting in the United States can be requested, through Amtorg, the U.S.–U.S.S.R. Trade and Economic Council, or a trade commission with the relevant FTO. If these discussions go well, the Soviets will seek more details on the proposal and will issue an invitation to meet in the U.S.S.R. or, in some cases, in a European location. The meetings will be arranged only after important issues for discussion have evolved. The FTO will provide "visa support" to the embassy and Intourist in New York to make necessary arrangements, while the U.S. delegation applies for visas and makes travel plans through their travel agents.

BUSINESS ENVIRONMENT

Government offices are open Monday to Friday, 9:00 A.M. to 6:00 P.M. Banking hours are 9:30 A.M. to 1:00 P.M. Business offices are open Mondays 9:00 A.M. to 6:00 P.M. and Tuesday to Saturday from 9:00 A.M. to 9:00 P.M. Businesses close two hours for lunch.

An initial meeting begins with formal introductions, using titles. The U.S. delegation leader should introduce in rank order all members of the team. Preliminaries are usually brief in early meetings. After several meetings, the atmosphere relaxes a bit, and casual conversation precedes business.

The meeting agenda should be preset, and communicated to all participants in advance. Since meetings are expensive in terms of both time and money, the agenda should be adhered to as much as possible.

Unless the U.S. team is bilingual, interpreters are necessary; and the U.S. team should, if at all possible, have its own, provided that the granting of a visa proves that he or she is acceptable to Soviet authorities.

Visiting businessmen should treat any woman in the Soviet delegation as an equal. Flirting is out of order, but such courtesies as opening a door for a woman or lighting her cigarette are appropriate and appreciated. A Soviet woman offers her hand for a handshake.

A non-Soviet interpreter can provide more reliable translations than one attached to the Soviet team or provided by Intourist, and can also be a resource in all phases of the trip.

In order to ensure a successful presentation, the U.S. team should be informative and very specific in terms of the technical and financial points. The team should expect that the Soviet delegation will be very well trained in its field.

When a meeting has finished, arrangements for the next round of talks will be made or the next steps both sides are to take will be discussed. It is essential to send thank-you and follow-up letters to all agreements made, and they should focus on positive aspects of the meeting and on the desire to keep building a good relationship.

RANK AND STATUS

To show respect for the Soviet team, titles should be used when possible. The U.S.S.R.'s society is supposedly classless, and rank and status derive only from official titles.

It is advisable to consult the interpreter before a meeting to be sure about using the correct titles and forms of address. "Comrade" would be an inappropriate title for a noncommunist visitor to use.

FORMS OF ADDRESS

The most appropriate way to address Soviet citizens, once contact has been well established, is by their first names and patronyms, derived from the father's name. For example, a woman named Elena Niko-laevna Petroy would be addressed as "Elena Nikolaevna," with no title. However, those Soviets who regularly deal with Americans are used to the American style of "Mr.," "Mrs.," or "Miss" and respond appropriately.

It is correct form to refer to the citizens of the U.S.S.R. as "Soviets" since the nation is composed of so many nationalities. The term "Russian" refers only to the citizens of the Russian republic who are designated as Russians on the nationality section of the passport.

BUSINESS CARDS

Business cards in English and Russian are an essential part of developing relations and should be used widely.

BUSINESS DRESS

Conservative dress is the watchword for businesspeople visiting the Soviet Union. Dark colors, suits, sports coats, and ties are recommended. Flashy or very stylish clothes and jewelry might accent differences in the availability of consumer goods in the United States and U.S.S.R. and are not appropriate.

GIFT-GIVING

Small gifts are appropriate, but the visitor must be careful since bribery is a serious crime. For your Soviet counterparts, French cognac,

American whiskey, or a carton or two of cigarettes are acceptable. Fountain pens, lighters, and other items with your company logo are also appreciated, and FTO's often reciprocate with this type of P.R. However, beware of giving too generous a gift, one that your colleague could never match in value.

COMMUNICATION STYLES

Until your relationships are well established, quiet conduct, the use of silence, and formality characterize correct behavior in meetings with the Soviets. Inside jokes and anything that might suggest ideas of U.S. superiority are inappropriate, as is seeming to be in a rush or seeming to know all the answers. Speaking slowly and avoiding colloquial expressions are also important. An easier relationship will evolve over time and you will find the Soviets are interested in displaying their English language ability, including colloquial expressions.

In terms of nonverbal communication, handshaking is a constant activity, but other forms of physical camaraderie are not, until a sense of familiarity has been established over time. In general, Soviets are quite direct and, if something is disturbing them, they will let you know.

Negotiating in the U.S.S.R.

In negotiating with the Soviets, the U.S. firm should basically be prepared with as much information as possible, be ready to spend an enormous amount of time forging an agreement, be determined to make a profitable transaction, and be prepared to walk out if a deal is not forthcoming. Concentrating on building long-lasting relationships will lay the foundation of good business in the long run, for the Soviets have proven themselves loyal to suppliers who have worked with them over time.

Technical negotiations are handled by teams of qualified experts, and the visiting executives must be very knowledgeable. Sending sales representatives as the only delegates is not recommended, because of the need for detailed knowledge of technicalities.

The ostensible leader of the Soviet negotiating team should be easy to spot, by virtue of title and command of the proceedings. Decisions, however, are not made publicly, and decision making is slow, with all foreign trade decisions coming out of the Ministry of Foreign Trade, via FTO. It is politic for the visiting executive, however, to treat any Soviet team leader as the ultimate decision maker.

Negotiations usually have two distinct segments, technical and commercial. This is because the end-user must satisfy their technical requirements, and then the centralized foreign trade apparatus must negotiate to get the best commercial terms possible.

In terms of pricing, the Soviets may ask for detailed information in initial proposals, but ball-park figures will be acceptable. If your counterparts are interested, price negotiations will follow. The Soviets have excellent market knowledge, so it is a mistake to include too high a price in initial discussions. A discount anticipated as part of the initial price quotation will be expected, however, and should be forthcoming. Remember that the official from the FTO wants to look good to the organization by negotiating a good price, and it is to your advantage to help this person look successful.

The Soviets may employ many strategies to gain lower prices. One is to compare unequal proposals or promise large future orders for better initial terms. Sometimes, after large-order discounts have been agreed to, the Soviets will cut the order and still demand the discounts, or they will ask for more spare parts than agreed to, or they will demand more training and support services than the agreement included.

Another strategy, called "whipsawing," involves a large buyer (in this case, the FTO) playing off potential sellers against one other to gain price concessions. Whipsawing may include such tactics as winning concessions from the weakest competitor and telling other competitors that they must meet these terms; or putting competitors in the same hotel so that they encounter each other. To defend against this, the U.S. executive needs to know as much as possible about the potential customer, the competition, and the present political/economic atmosphere in the Soviet Union. In addition, any businessperson seeking to do business in the U.S.S.R. should take full advantage of the experience of banks, trading companies, and other organizations, and of the resources of the U.S. and other governments. And the executive should be prepared to leave empty-handed if a satisfactory agreement cannot be reached.

Many U.S. firms, large and small, make excellent use of representatives who have a very deep familiarity with doing business in the

U.S.S.R., and consideration should be given to establishing a contractual agreement with such firms or individuals. The U.S.–U.S.S.R. Trade and Economic Council, Amtorg, and the U.S. Department of Commerce can help in this.

The visiting team should include attorneys for key negotiating sessions, though not initially, for the Soviets are a law-conscious people. The FTOs seek to use a standard two-page contract that is rarely modified, except during very complex negotiations. Trying to modify a contract form may bring added delays, since a higher level authority may have to approve any changes; still, this is often done.

Contracts are governed by Soviet law. They must be in writing, and any oral agreement entered into by your Soviet counterparts should be viewed with suspicion until it is in writing. Any contract must be signed by two Soviet officials, the president of the FTO and another person authorized to sign a foreign trade contract. The charter of each FTO may include specific provisions that must be met, and it is important to try to ascertain these before negotiations. Sometimes your representative, if you have one, may know the provisions.

Contracts should be spelled out in exquisite detail. The foreign executive should be very clear about who can sign the contract and what country has jurisdiction, should a dispute arise.

Although the Soviets drive a very hard bargain in contract negotiations, they will abide faithfully by its provisions, and expect the other party to do the same. They have an excellent record on honoring their financial commitments.

Suggestions that will help your negotiating:

• When you are submitting proposals or other written documentation, it is important to provide one copy in Russian and one in English. Remember that most translators will not be familiar with the specific technical terms of your industry. Translator services are available in many major U.S. cities.
• In follow-up or thank-you letters to your Soviet counterparts, the effectiveness of the group should be stressed, rather than any one individual. If individuals are to be noted, the group leader should be named, not any officials under them. In the Soviet classless society, it is not appropriate to single out individuals for commendation.

• The Soviets have good market information. By providing them with public information about your firm, you show respect for them and facilitate negotiations.

• On the other hand, if the Soviets ask for information that is not supposed to be made public, you will have to make a judgment call. The same holds true if they request a piece of equipment or a product sample for a field testing. In such cases, you will need to check proprietary or technical information that might be subject to export control regulations.

• Note that the names of all people authorized to sign foreign trade contracts are published in the *Official Gazette of the Ministry of Foreign Trade*, available at Amtorg and the Embassy Trade Representation.

• It is not common for the Soviets to type the name of the signatory under the signature. Since signatures are often illegible, a polite request should be made to have the name typed in.

• The Soviets will usually provide English copies of documents and contracts. You should be extremely cautious about interpretations and nuances and go over the entire document with your attorney and your interpreter. The use of a third language in clarifying points with the Soviets is often helpful.

Business Entertaining

Business lunches and receptions at public places or at the U.S.– U.S.S.R. Trade and Economic Council office in Moscow are standard forms of entertainment.

Dinner parties are not a common entertainment in the Soviet Union. In very rare instances, you may be invited to your counterpart's home, and you should arrive at the time stated. A small gift of flowers or imported liquor is appropriate and welcome. Dinners and lunches are leisurely affairs, with much drinking, for which many Soviets have an infinite capacity, toasting to friendship and cooperation; there is conversation at the table.

The visitor should not say he or she does not drink; you should take part in all activities to avoid offending your hosts. Oftentimes, as many as seven different wine glasses will be placed in front of you. You will be required to "drink up" when a vodka toast is made at the beginning of the meal. Vodka with the first course may be followed by white wine, red wine, sherry, port, brandy, and so on. Toasting is a very important part of the occasion, and you will be expected to toast the person seated next to you on the right.

It has been customary in the past for spouses not to be included in any business entertainment. However, under Secretary General Gorbachev's leadership, this custom might become more relaxed.

General Tips

• The Soviets are very sensitive about their place in the world, the state of their economy, and their leadership role in world affairs. Conversation should not include criticism or pointed questions about such things as human rights or other sensitive issues.

• Tips to maids, taxi drivers, waiters, and such can be small gifts. A pack of cigarettes or some "Western" candy will be appreciated.

• Avoid totally dealing with the underground economy; exchange your dollars or traveler's checks only at official establishments and keep meticulous records and receipts.

• Declare on entry all jewelry, watches, gold pens, and so on and be prepared to demonstrate that all such items are still in your possession on departure.

• Caviar is hard to get in the Soviet Union, and is not ordinarily served in people's homes. However, it is much appreciated, and if you are entertaining, serving Russian caviar is considered a very gracious gesture. Caviar and other Soviet delicacies are available at certain shops which deal only in foreign exchange. They are usually associated with major hotels.

• Register with the U.S. Embassy upon arrival so that should any difficulty arise the Embassy will be aware of your presence. However, in any conflict with Soviet authorities, it should be remembered that the U.S. Embassy's powers are limited to official protests.

• The theatre, ballet, and cinema are very popular for business entertainment. The number of seats available for visitors is limited and they may take as long as five months to obtain. Apply to the Service Bureau at your hotel as soon as possible, or make advance reservations with your travel agent for key events.

• It is important to remember that what might be the simplest offense in another European country could develop into a major political incident in the U.S.S.R.

• Because the Soviets do not have much chance to speak English, they may appear to understand much less than they actually do. They may, for example, understand remarks made as asides to colleagues or under your breath.

EXECUTIVE TRAVEL TO THE U.S.S.R. •

DOCUMENTS

U.S. citizens require only a valid passport and visa.

INOCULATIONS

None are required for U.S. citizens.

AIRPORT

Sheremetyevo Airport is about 17½ miles from the center of Moscow.

CUSTOMS

There are no restrictions on alcohol, tobacco, and personal articles that are for personal use.

U.S. EMBASSY

19/21/23 Ulitsa Chaykovskogo, Moscow
Phone: (096) 2522451-59   Telex: 413160

TRANSPORTATION

Taxis may be difficult to get. It is recommended that you hire a car and a driver/translator for your stay.

TIPPING

In general, in the Soviet Union you don't tip in money, but it will not insult anyone. Items such as cigarettes, felt tip or ballpoint pens, chewing gum, and books (nonpolitical) are sometimes more appreciated. A 10 percent tip for taxis and restaurants is appropriate.

HOTELS

Moscow

Berlin
3 Zhdanov
Phone: 221-04-77

Intourist
3–5 Gorky Street
Phone: 203-40-08

Kosmos
150 Prospekt
Phone: 217-07-86

Mezhdunarodnaya International
Mantulinskaya Ul. 5
Phone: 256-83-96

National
14/1 Prospekt
Phone: 203-65-39

Rossiya
6 Razin Street
Phone: 298-55-00

RESTAURANTS

Moscow

Arbat   *Georgian*
29 Kalimin Prospekt
Phone: 291-14-03

Belgrade   *Russian/Yugoslav*
Belgrade Hotel
5 Smolenskaya Square
Phone: 248-66-61

Berlin   *Russian/German*
Berlin Hotel
Phone: 223-35-81

Intourist   *Russian*
Intourist Hotel
Phone: 203-40-08

National   *Russian*
National Hotel
Phone: 203-55-95

TRAVEL TIPS

• Bring all the film you want, however, do not take photographs of airports, rail stations, or military installations, and do not photograph anything which might be considered as "sensitive." Make sure you bring your film home to be developed.
• Do not offer a dollar bill or a pound note as a tip. All of these are covered by some law or other.
• Carry your passport with you at all times. Keep it in a *safe* place on your person—not in a hip pocket. It is customary during check-in at the hotel that your passport be retained for registration. The registration process usually requires twenty-four hours; after this, your passport can be picked up at the front desk.
• There is not much nightlife (nightclubs or bars) in the Soviet Union. Some bars in hotels and restaurants are open until 2:00 A.M. There are discos in a lot of hotels but they close early (11:00 or 12:00 P.M.) by Western standards.
• Coffee is in very short supply in the Soviet Union. If you are a big coffee drinker, it is recommended that you bring in a container of instant coffee.
• *Beriozkas,* or foreign currency shops, are located in many of the hotels, where you can spend only foreign currency. One advantage to these shops is that prices are lower. Another advantage is that everything purchased in a *beriozka* is wrapped in a special paper, and you will have no trouble getting it past customs and out of the country.
• If you have a medical problem, make sure you bring more than enough medicine for the whole time you are there.
• It would be a very nice gesture, if you are going to have an interpreter travel with you, to bring him or her a nice gift: for example, an inexpensive calculator, a really fine pen, or American literature, hardcover or even paperback—again, you have to

be careful that it's not anti-Soviet. Classics such as Dickens, or modern fiction are very much appreciated.

• Be discreet in your actions and statements so as not to arouse unnecessary attention or cause concern during your visit.

PART III

DOING BUSINESS IN THE UNITED STATES: A GUIDE FOR FOREIGN BUSINESS EXECUTIVES

Cultural Overview

The United States of America is the world's leading industrial nation. Vast natural resources, manpower, highly developed transportation and communication facilities, and enormous agricultural and manufacturing production constitute the strength of the country.

The capital is Washington, D.C., and the government is that of a federal republic set up by the Constitution of the United States. There is a division of power between the federal government and that of the 50 states. The federal government's division of power is threefold: executive (president, vice president, cabinet); legislative (Congress—Senate and House of Representatives; and judicial (Supreme Court, lesser courts).

The United States is an extremely diverse nation, geographically, historically, ethnically, racially, and politically. Its population is a unique blending of many nationalities, not duplicated anywhere in the world; it is a dynamic welding.

Located in the temperate zone, the country has a seasonal climate. In the northern part of the nation the winter weather can be extremely cold, while the southern areas can border on the tropical.

The population is 99 percent literate, with an ever increasing number of college educated people. The majority of the population are members of one of the many denominations of Protestantism; Roman Catholicism constitutes about 20%, and Judiasm represents about 5%. English is the language of the country; the monetary unit is the dollar.

The United States has the reputation for being informal. This does not mean, however, that a familiarity with or understanding of protocols and customs is unnecessary for the visiting executive.

Business Opportunities

With an ethnically mixed population of some 235 million and a high standard of living, the United States constitutes a lucrative market with extensive business opportunities, some with the world's largest corporations. The many major cities are centers of different industries. For example:

New York City: The cultural and financial capital of the nation, New York City is also the center of the communications industry, including book publishing, advertising, and radio and television broadcasting; the legal profession in the United States; the apparel industry; and the precious gems and metals industry. The city is also headquarters for a wide range of other service companies and the marketing center for much of the world's goods.

Los Angeles: This sprawling city is the gateway to the United States for Eastern countries. The film industry is centered in Los Angeles, and both Los Angeles and San Francisco are financial centers for the western part of the country. In the valleys between the two cities are a major agricultural industry, and the headquarters of many high-tech companies.

Chicago: A regional banking and financial center, this midwest city is a distribution hub for the entire country and the center of the Midwest's giant agribusiness.

Detroit: This northern midwest city is the center of the automobile industry.

Boston: Another important city of the industrial Northeast, Boston is a center for the east coast high-tech industries and for many other manufacturing and service concerns.

Washington, D.C.: The nation's capital, Washington has government relations offices of all major industries that want to influence legislation. The city is also headquarters for all major government agencies.

In addition to the opportunities in these cities, each of the 50 state capitals is an excellent place to investigate for business.

Initiating Contact

The first step in arranging your U.S. business trip is to write for appointments with those you wish to see. Do this at least one month in advance of your departure. When you are contacting a firm for the first time, address your letter to the president of the company. The letter will be forwarded to the appropriate contact.

If you want to see a specific individual, make this clear in your request. If this person has moved on (job mobility is high in the U.S.)

or is not the appropriate person for you to see, another name will be suggested.

Your letter should state clearly and concisely your purpose in dealing with the organization. You should also specify your arrival date, if possible, and suggest a date on which you will telephone to make or confirm an appointment.

Using the name of a mutual acquaintance or business associate can encourage a favorable reply. Such references, however, are generally less significant in the United States than they are in many other countries, and they are not necessary for successful ventures.

Before your meeting, try to supply the U.S. executive with basic information about your firm: its financial status, products, and reputation. An annual report and a list of corporations you deal with worldwide are excellent items to send.

For additional assistance, contact:

United States Chamber of Commerce
1615 "H" Street N.W.
Washington, D.C. 20062
Phone: (202) 659-6000

BOSTON

International Business Center of New England, Inc.
22 Batterymarch Street
Boston, Mass. 02109
Phone: (617) 542-0426

Boston Chamber of Commerce
125 High Street
Boston, Mass. 02110
Phone: (617) 426-1250

CHICAGO

Chicago Chamber of Commerce
135 Michigan Avenue
Chicago, Ill. 60603
Phone: (312) 786-0111

Club International
Drake Hotel
140 East Walton Place

Chicago, Ill. 60611
Phone: (312) 787-2200

HOUSTON

World Trade Center Houston
1520 Texas Avenue—Suite 1D and 1E
Houston, Tex. 77002
Phone: (713) 225-0968

Houston Chamber of Commerce
1100 Milam Street
Houston, Tex. 77002
Phone: (713) 651-1313

LOS ANGELES

Los Angeles Chamber of Commerce
404 South Bixel Street
Los Angeles, Calif. 90017
Phone: (213) 629-0711

The Port of Long Beach
925 Harbor Plaza
P.O. Box 570
Long Beach, Calif. 90801
Phone: (213) 437-0041   Telex: 65-6452

MIAMI

Execucentre International
444 Brickell Avenue—Suite 650
Miami, Fla. 33131
Phone: (305) 374-8300   Telex: 519636

Miami Chamber of Commerce
1601 Biscayne Boulevard
Miami, Fla. 33132
Phone: (305) 350-7700

NEW YORK CITY

New York Chamber of Commerce
200 Madison Avenue
New York, N.Y. 10016
Phone: (212) 608-1925

World Trade Center of New York
Port Authority of New York & New Jersey
1 World Trade Center—Suite 63 West
New York, N.Y. 10048
Phone: (212) 466-8380   Telex: 285472

SAN FRANCISCO

San Francisco Chamber of Commerce
465 California Street
San Francisco, Calif. 94104
Phone: (415) 392-4511

World Trade Center of San Francisco, Inc.
1170 Sacramento Street, Penthouse B
San Francisco, Calif. 94108
Phone: (415) 928-3438

WASHINGTON, D.C.

World Trade Center Washington
1000 Connecticut Avenue N.W.—Suite 707
Washington, D.C. 20036
Phone: (202) 955-6164   Telex: 311762

Business Protocol and Procedures

BUSINESS ENVIRONMENT

Meeting visiting businesspeople at airports is not standard procedure in the United States. You should have enough currency with you for transportation to the hotel and initial expenses; since currency exchanges in airports usually operate only during regular business hours —generally 9:00 A.M. to 5:00 P.M. Monday through Friday.

A taxi is probably the easiest way to get to your destination. Many airports also have bus transportation to a central downtown terminal, often with stops at major hotels. At the larger airports, surrounding hotels and motels offer free van service to their doors. Of course, you may also rent a car or, in many cities, take public transportation— subways (underground trains) or buses. These last three seem best avoided, however, unless you are familiar with the language and the area.

When you get to your hotel, confirm all business appointments. Be sure to leave your phone number in case there has been a change in plans. Do not be offended if a secretary or assistant confirms the appointment, for this is standard procedure in many organizations.

As background for your meetings, you may want to look at the many "trade" publications geared to specific industries, which can be found on newsstands. Many businesspeople across the country read the *Wall Street Journal* for business news.

Most U.S. banks are open from 9:00 A.M. to 3:00 P.M. Other businesses usually operate from 9:00 A.M. to 5:00 P.M. Several factors, however, make these times only rough guidelines. Many U.S. executives arrive early and work late, particularly the younger professionals. On the other hand, many people commute long distances to the office and are subject to the vagaries of public transportation or the tyranny of limited schedules. With such people, it is best to schedule appointments no earlier than 9:30 A.M. and no later than 4:00 P.M.

Business hours also vary from region to region and from company to company. In New York City and other east coast centers, business tends to start earlier and close later than in the Midwest or West.

The fiscal year should be taken into account when you plan your trip. It may be very difficult to make any transaction near the end of the fiscal year, for executives are awaiting results of the current period and developing budget guidelines for the future. Try to schedule appointments early in the fiscal year, when much of the budget is not yet expended. In most U.S. firms, the fiscal and calendar years coincide, but many companies operate on different schedules.

LEGAL HOLIDAYS

Most businesses and banks close for the following holidays:

- New Year's Day (January 1)
- Good Friday (variable—early spring)
- Memorial Day (the Monday before May 31)
- Independence Day (July 4)
- Labor Day (first Monday in September)
- Columbus Day (October 12, often the closest Monday)
- Thanksgiving Day (the fourth Thursday in November)
- Christmas Day (December 25)

The following holidays are observed by some businesses and most government offices:

- Lincoln's Birthday (February 12)
- Washington's Birthday (February 22—often, these two holidays are celebrated together as Presidents' Day, on a Monday between the two)
- Election Day (first Tuesday in November—but not every year)
- The Friday after Thanksgiving
- Veterans Day (November 11)
- The Friday after Christmas Day when it falls on a Thursday
- The Friday after New Year's Day when it falls on a Thursday

Many businesses close on the day before or after a holiday that falls on a Tuesday or a Thursday. In addition, people in the United States tend to vacation in the summer, particularly in August. And the period between Thanksgiving and New Year's Day is a time when many people travel; and a holiday mood may interfere with doing business.

RANK AND STATUS

High-ranking executives' offices are usually larger and more elegantly appointed than those of lower-echelon staff. In many cities, the large corporations have offices in giant high-rise buildings. The higher the floor an executive's office is on, and the better the view, the greater his or her rank will usually be.

Rank and status in the United States is not expressed by using people's business titles, such as "Mr. Chairman." Titles are used in this way only in meetings being conducted under strict parliamentary procedures; they virtually never occur in business negotiations. Younger executives tend not to defer to those of higher rank or status and may even disagree with them in public. Such behavior is often encouraged by senior executives who are eager to encourage a free flow of ideas.

Differences in title and structure exist from firm to firm but the following organization is found in most corporations:

- Board of directors (the highest ranking officers, responsible for the company's overall welfare)
- Chairman of the board
- President
- Executive vice president
- Senior vice president

- Vice president
- Assistant vice president
- Managers
- Directors
- Staff

Other titles to recognize include:

- CEO (chief executive officer): often also the president or chairman of the board, responsible for everyday business.
- COO (chief operating officer): a senior position, deputy to the CEO.
- CFO (chief financial officer): the senior executive in charge of finance.

In U.S. firms, and especially in banks, there may be many vice presidents and assistant vice presidents, with very little power or authority.

WOMEN IN BUSINESS

Many women hold middle-management positions in U.S. firms, and a steadily growing number are in top executive posts. Women with the same title and responsibilities as male colleagues have equal status, and it would be a serious mistake to assume that an executive lacks authority because she is female.

The same respect and courtesy is due women as men in business. Special or traditional courtesies, however, such as opening doors, lighting cigarettes, or giving preferential seating are not appreciated by many female executives; to them, such courtesies indicate condescension. It is best for the foreigner to be basically polite and observe how the U.S. men act toward the women in the party.

The new designation "Ms." ("mizz") perplexes many men, American and foreign. It is used to avoid designation of a woman's marital status by either "Miss" or "Mrs." Although most women are not adamant about this point, it may be wise, especially in New York city, to use "Ms." until told to do otherwise.

DECISION MAKERS

Identifying and reaching the real decision maker is a challenge for U.S. and foreign businesspeople alike. Decision making is decentralized and dispersed among many individuals and groups within larger organizations. Decisions may be made at lower levels, or, if they are major, may have to be passed on, with approval and recommendations, to a higher authority. Inquiries when you are setting up appointments, or even when you are in meetings, to discover who has the final say on your project are entirely appropriate.

FORMS OF ADDRESS

A firm, brief handshake, with no bowing, is the usual greeting when people are introduced, or when they meet. If several people are attending a meeting, the highest ranking person will probably be introduced first.

Contrary to popular myth, Americans do not use first names immediately and not without asking permission. It is true that many Americans will probably tell you to use their first names as soon as they are introduced—and expect to do the same with you. But it is no more appropriate in most of the United States to use a first name, before you are requested to, than it is in any other part of the world.

BUSINESS CARDS

After introductions, business cards are usually exchanged. Keep those of your U.S. colleagues in front of you so you can refer to names and titles. Your card should be in English. Carry a good supply, even to social events. In New York City and many other places, any event is an opportunity to advance business, and it is customary to exchange business cards when meeting at social occasions.

BUSINESS DRESS

Conservative attire is almost always appropriate for doing business in the United States, despite its reputation for informality. Suits are the rule for both men and women although, in the entertainment and communications industries, a more informal atmosphere may make a dark blazer and slacks or a skirt acceptable. Again, regional variations affect dress codes, and things do get more relaxed the farther west you go.

GIFT-GIVING

It is critically important that the foreign business executive be sensitive to the issue of gift-giving in the United States. The practice is discouraged or prohibited in 80 percent of U.S. firms. Gift-giving presents an ethical dilemma for the U.S. executive. Either avoid giving gifts or present nothing more than tokens of little expense, such as logo items or a souvenir of one's home country.

COMMUNICATION STYLES

Meetings will almost always be in English. If you have difficulty with the language, it is perfectly appropriate to bring along a translator or a bilingual colleague.

The first rule for U.S. meetings is, *Be punctual!* Most executives operate on a tight schedule. If you arrive late, you may not have as much time as you would like.

It is not unusual for the U.S. executive to invite another colleague to the meeting without telling you in advance. Most meetings are held in individual offices or in a conference room, where there is no set protocol for seating except that the senior executive usually sits at the head of the table. In banks, some officers have their offices in an open area, and meetings in conference rooms are the rule, or they may be held in the private office of a senior executive who is away.

Before or during a meeting, you may be offered coffee or another hot beverage (never an alcoholic one), which you are free to accept or refuse as you wish. Initial small talk is very brief in most U.S. meetings, and business starts almost at once. As the initiator of the meeting, you will be expected to outline your objectives for the session and to make a brief, precise presentation. Submitting a brief of your business and supporting materials in English, in advance of the meeting, can be useful.

After some rapport has been established, your American counterpart may relax visibly, stretching out arms or leaning back in chair, hands behind his or her head. Far from indicating disrespect for you and your proposal, such actions are positive, indicating that the American feels comfortable with you. On the other hand, Americans, reputation to the contrary, do not generally welcome backslapping or other familiar physical contact except from good friends.

Negotiating Procedures

U.S. businesspeople expect detailed, well-documented oral and written presentations. Be prepared with appropriate materials, samples, and documentation, including slides, graphs, charts, and computer printouts.

In general, a down-to-earth, straightforward approach will be most effective. Maintain direct eye contact with your colleagues. In planning your presentation, remember that profit, the "bottom" line, is the paramount consideration in most companies. Showing how your proposal will enchance your customer's position and ultimately improve profits will serve you well.

In most corporations, forecasting and long-range strategic planning are crucial. Relating your proposal to specific long-term goals will be a point in your favor. On the other hand, immediate benefits are very important to U.S. executives. If you can show that your proposal will help improve the next quarterly report, it will also help your cause.

U.S. executives, particularly the younger ones, are attuned to quantitative analysis as a basis for business decisions. The more you can quantify your proposal with sophisticated analysis, the better off you will be. Innovation and creativity are also appreciated in most U.S. concerns. Executives may be willing to give an unusual proposal a try if it sounds likely to succeed.

Personal achievement is another important factor in U.S. business. If you can show your counterpart that your proposal will help him or her look good and move up, that will help your chances of success.

It may take a long time for a decision to be made on your proposal. Again, contrary to popular belief, speed does not always characterize the U.S. decision-making process, especially in large organizations and for major expenditures or ventures. When you are awaiting a decision, discreet inquiries to an executive you know are perfectly acceptable, as is a polite question to learn if you can do anything to speed up the process.

Bear in mind when negotiating that price is not a matter of bargaining and bartering in the United States. Before really "hard" discussions of price and terms, there may be some negotiation or trade-offs or quid pro quos ("If you can do this, we can do that") but, once prices and terms have been stated firmly, they are considered settled.

A formal written contract signed by both parties is the only really binding agreement. Once matters evolve to contract, attorneys will be present. (They may have been in on the negotiations from the start.) Contracts in the United States are very detailed and lengthy, with much small print, which you should read carefully.

After meetings, you should always send your U.S. counterpart a letter of appreciation for his or her hospitality and attention to your business. This letter offers a good opportunity to reiterate important points that came up in the meeting and to confirm any further steps that you feel should be taken.

For successful negotiating in the United States here are a few suggestions:

- Do not be disturbed if one or more U.S. executives leave before the meeting is over. This is not considered disrespectful; nor is it a sign of lack of interest in your proposal.
- During negotiations, especially those lasting for a long time with many meetings, your U.S. counterpart may from time to time request drafts in writing. Do not regard this as threatening or as something to which you will be held. Many drafts or agreements or parts of agreements are common, and serve to help executives review progress and clarify points.
- If the meeting concludes without a decision, it is not impolite to refer to your limited time in the country or city, and suggest a time when you might meet or call again.
- Schedules and deadlines are very important in the United States. When you agree to them, you will be expected to meet them. Failure to do so can have immediate and adverse consequences.
- Expect U.S. firms, like companies around the world, to use their buying power leverage to obtain concessions.

We asked Mr. Nelson Lees of W. R. Grace & Co., an international marketing executive with vast experience, to give us an overview for those interested in doing business in the United States, and we have incorporated many of his thoughts into the following general recommendations:

- Establish the credentials of your company up front before you meet with your U.S. prospects. Provide the equivalent of a Dun & Bradstreet, an annual report, or other information in advance, describing your financial condition, reputation, and services.
- Carefully assess what your marketing requirements will be; check what methods are currently being used to market products similar to yours.

• Determine how your products and services might have to be adapted or modified in order to sell them in the United States. Packaging, labeling, brand name, trademarks, patents, and warranties should be examined.

• If your product becomes a component of a finished good for export, it is possible that the import restrictions or limitations on your product could be modified to give it preferential treatment.

• Evaluate your competition through careful analysis of the market, price competitiveness, product quality, and service.

• Make clear the features, benefits, proof of benefits, and functions of your products and services to give more impact to your sales presentation, and make them compatible with U.S. practice. Many U.S. companies sell their products on the basis of a competitive price/performance ratio, translating product features into benefits.

• Know what the prospective customer believes the product will do for him or her, not what it is, to be successful in marketing benefits. Know the needs of your customer's customer.

• Check good sources of information about U.S. economic activity, such as the Standard Industrial Classification System (SIC) and the Standard International Trade Classification System (SITC). These are classifications of U.S. firms, products, and services.

BUSINESS ENTERTAINING

It is quite common in the United States to discuss business over lunch or dinner, or even over breakfast or cocktails. Many business transactions, in fact, are actually sealed over meals, or perhaps on the golf course, and just polished and finalized in later meetings.

Business breakfasts have become popular in New York City and other eastern locations, although they are not yet common in the West. Breakfasts are usually held in hotel dining rooms and last for an hour or more, starting around 8:00 A.M. It is probably not appropriate to schedule a first meeting with someone for breakfast. A more formal first encounter, followed perhaps by lunch, would be more fitting.

Particularly in New York or other large cities, lunch may be ordered and eaten in the office while the meeting continues. Some large corporations have club-like private dining rooms reserved for senior executives and their guests. An invitation for lunch in one of these is an honor, a sign your U.S. host holds you in high esteem.

Luncheon meetings, starting between noon and 1:00 P.M., are very common. Cocktails and dinner are less so until a good rapport has developed between visitor and host. Dinners often include spouses and are more relaxed occasions, but business discussions are still acceptable and common. It is appropriate for you as a visitor to reciprocate by inviting your hosts to dine. If you host a luncheon, make sure it is at a restaurant near the offices, quiet enough for conversation and private enough for business discussions not to be overheard. In the United States, gratuities are not included in most restaurant bills. A tip of about 15 percent is customary, although in New York City more may be in order, depending on the restaurant and the quality of the service.

Note that it is entirely acceptable and even expected for female executives to invite male colleagues out for business lunches or dinners. In such a case the woman pays, although it would not be impolite for a man to offer to take the check. Insisting, however, would be most inappropriate.

Conversations at business meals can alternate between business and personal issues. In the United States it is not considered impolite to ask about someone's family, home, children, spouse, or interests. You may find yourself asked questions you would find objectionable at home. No disrespect is intended.

If you are invited to an American home a small gift—wine, flowers, candy, something from your country—is in order. Ask about proper clothing, for in many areas home entertaining can be informal and outdoors, perhaps around a swimming pool. Mealtimes may vary. In the Midwest, dinner is likely to be at 6:00 P.M. In New York and on the West Coast, 8:00 P.M. or later is standard.

General Tips

• Place, or choose, a knowledgeable representative in the marketplace as an effective way to establish an initial business relationship in the United States.
• Try to establish personal relationships with your counterparts once they have been identified. Include your wife; wives are welcome in the United States business/social scene.

• Be sensitive to the implications of gift-giving. Gift-giving can pose an ethical dilemma for the U.S. executive, and is discouraged or prohibited in most companies.
• Conduct meetings and negotiations in English if at all possible. While the United States is a nation of immigrants, it is nevertheless a monolingual society.
• Remember that U.S. companies pride themselves on being efficient, purposeful, direct, single-minded, and materialistic. The bottom line is all-important.
• Be aware that the decision maker in an American firm may be closer to the market than his or her counterpart would be in a comparable firm in another country.
• Understand that decision making in the United States usually takes place much faster than it would if you were negotiating with the Europeans or the Japanese. Be prepared for this.
• Remember that U.S. executives tend to be uncomfortable with extended silence, and are accustomed to being frank and open during negotiating discussions. They can appear impatient if progress seems impeded.

EXECUTIVE TRAVEL TO THE UNITED STATES •

DOCUMENTS/INOCULATIONS/CUSTOMS

Check with your airline, travel agent, or consulate for travel requirements which are based on your country of origin/departure.

AIRPORTS

Chicago—O'Hare International Airport
18 miles N.W. (45–70 minutes) to downtown.

Houston—Houston International Airport
22 miles N. (45–60 minutes) to downtown.

Los Angeles—Los Angeles International Airport
15 miles S.W. (35–55 minutes) to downtown.

Miami—Miami International Airport
7 miles N.W. (30 minutes) to downtown.

New York—La Guardia Airport
8 miles (25–35 minutes) to downtown.

John F. Kennedy Airport
15 miles S.E. (30–60 minutes) to downtown.
Newark Airport
16 miles S.E. (30–40) minutes to New York.

San Francisco—San Francisco International Airport
14 miles S. (30–35 minutes) to downtown.

Washington D.C.—Dulles International Airport
26 miles W. (45–60 minutes) to downtown.

TRANSPORTATION

It is recommended that you have a car and driver in each city in which
you plan a business stay.

TIPPING

The appropriate amount to tip at better restaurants is between 15
percent and 20 percent. Taxi drivers expect the same, with smaller
amounts to the hotel staff who provide services to you.

BOSTON
(telephone area code is 617)

HOTELS

Copley Plaza
Copley Square
Phone: 267-5300 or (800) 225-7654
Telex: 951858

Parker House
Tremont and School Streets
Phone: 227-8600   Telex: 3216707

Ritz-Carlton
15 Arlington Street
Phone: 536-5700   Telex: 940591

RESTAURANTS

Café Plaza
Hotel Copley Plaza
Copley Square
Phone: 267-5300

Durgin Park
340 North Market Street, Faneuil Hall Marketplace
Phone: 227-2038

Maison Robert
43 School Street
Phone: 227-3370

The Voyagers
45½ Mount Auburn Street, Cambridge
Phone: 354-1718

CHICAGO
(telephone area code is 312)

HOTELS

Ambassador East
130 North State Parkway
Phone: 787-7200   Telex: 910-221-2120

Ritz-Carlton
160 East Pearson Street
Phone: 266-1000   Telex: 910-221-1000

Tremont
100 East Chestnut Street
Phone: 751-1900

RESTAURANTS

Cape Cod Room   *Seafood*
Hotel Drake
North Michigan Avenue at Walton Place
Phone: 787-2200

Chez Paul   *French*
660 North Rush Street
Phone: 944-6680

Crickets   *French*
Hotel Tremont
100 East Chestnut Street
Phone: 751-2400

Eli's, The Place for Steaks   *Steakhouse*
215 East Chicago
Phone: 642-1393

Pump Room   *International*
Hotel Ambassador East
1301 North State Parkway
Phone: 266-0360

HOUSTON
(telephone area code is 713)

HOTELS

Hyatt Regency
1200 Louisiana Street
Phone: 654-1234   Telex: 775791

Inn On The Park
4 River Way
Phone: 871-8181   Telex: 794510

Warwick
5701 Main Street
Phone: 526-1991   Telex: 762590

Westin Gallerie
5060 West Alabama Street
Phone: 960-8100   Telex: 4990983

RESTAURANTS

Brownstone Restaurant   *International*
2736 Virginia Avenue
Phone: 528-2844

Tony's   *International*
1801 South Post Oak Road
Phone: 622-6778

The Palm   *American*
6100 Westheimer Street
Phone: 977-2544

Uncle Tai's Hunan Yuan   *Chinese*
1713 South Post Oak Road
Phone: 960-8000

LOS ANGELES
(telephone area code is 213)

HOTELS

Bel Air
701 Stone Canyon Road, Bel Air
Phone: 472-1211   Telex: 674151

Beverly Hills Hotel
9641 West Sunset Boulevard
Phone: 276-2251   Telex: 691459

Beverly Wilshire
9500 Wilshire Boulevard, Beverly Hills
Phone: 275-4282   Telex: 698220

L'Ermitage
9291 Burton Way, Beverly Hills
Phone: 278-3344   Telex: 698441

RESTAURANTS

Chasen's   *Continental*
9030 Beverly Boulevard
West Hollywood
Phone: 271-2168

L'Ermitage   *French*
730 North La Cienega Boulevard
Phone: 652-5840

Ma Maison   *French*
8368 Melrose Avenue
Phone: 655-1991

Perino's   *Italian*
4101 Wilshire Boulevard
Phone: 612-1300

MIAMI
(telephone area code is 305)

HOTELS

Grand Bay
3250 South Bayshore Drive
Coconut Grove
Phone: 858-9600   Telex: 441370

Hyatt Regency
400 S.E. Second Avenue
Phone: 358-1234   Telex: 810514316

Omni International
1601 Biscayne Boulevard
Phone: 374-0000   Telex: 515005

Pavillon
100 Chopin Plaza
Phone: 577-1000   Telex: 525102

RESTAURANTS

Café Chauveron   *French*
9561 East Bay Harbor Drive
Phone: 866-8779

Dominique's   *French*
Alexander Hotel
5225 Collins Avenue
Phone: 861-5252

Pavillon Grill   *French*
100 Chopin Plaza
Phone: 577- 1000

NEW YORK CITY
(telephone area code is 212)

HOTELS

Carlyle
35 East 76th Street
Phone: 744-1600   Telex: 620692

Helmsley Palace
455 Madison Avenue
Phone: 888-7000   Telex: 640543

Mayfair Regent
610 Park Avenue/65th Street
Phone: 288-0800   Telex: 236257

Regency
540 Park Avenue/61st Street
Phone: 759-4100   Telex: 147180

Waldorf-Astoria Towers
301 Park Avenue
Phone: 355-3000   Telex: 666747

RESTAURANTS

Christ Cella   *American*
160 East 46th Street
Phone: 697-2479

Four Seasons   *Continental*
99 East 52nd Street
Phone: 754-9494

La Cote Basque   *French*
5 East 55th Street
Phone: 688-6526

La Grenouille   *French*
3 East 52nd Street
Phone: 752-1495

Le Cirque   *French*
58 East 65th Street
Phone: 794-9292

Lutece   *French*
249 East 50th Street
Phone: 752-2225

Maxim's   *French*
680 Madison Avenue
Phone: 751-5111

Nanni Al Valletto   *Italian*
133 East 61st Street
Phone: 838-3939

Tse Yang   *Chinese*
34 East 51st Street
Phone: 688-5447

"21" Club   *American*
21 West 52nd Street
Phone: 582-7200

SAN FRANCISCO
(telephone area code is 415)

HOTELS

The Fairmont
Powell/Geary Streets
Phone: 772-5000   Telex: 3726002

Huntington
1075 California Street, Nob Hill
Phone: 474-5400   Telex: 57363

Mark Hopkins
1 Nob Hill
Phone: 392- 3434   Telex: 340809

Stanford Court
Nob Hill
Phone: 989- 3500   Telex: 340899

RESTAURANTS

Empress of China   *Chinese*
8383 Grant Avenue
Phone: 434-1345

Le Club   *French*
1250 Jones Street
Phone: 771-5400

L'Etoile   *French*
Hotel Huntington
Phone: 474-5400

Le Trianon   *French*
242 O'Farrell Street
Phone: 982-9353

Modesto Lanzone's   *Italian*
900 North Point, Ghiradelli Square
Phone: 771-2880

Ernie's Restaurant   *Italian*
847 Montgomery Street
Phone: 397-5969

WASHINGTON, D.C.
(telephone area code is 202)

HOTELS

Four Seasons
2800 Pennsylvania Avenue, N.W.
Phone: 342-0444

Hay-Adams
16th Street/H Street N.W.
Phone: 638-6600

Ritz-Carlton
2100 Massachusetts Avenue N.W.
Phone: 293-2100

Sheraton-Carlton
923 16th Street N.W.
Phone: 638-2626

RESTAURANTS

Jean-Pierre   *French*
1835 K Street N.W.
Phone: 466-2022

Jockey Club   *American*
2100 Massachusetts Avenue N.W.
Phone: 659-8000

Maison Blanche   *French*
1725 F Street N.W.
Phone: 842-0070

Prime Rib   *Steakhouse*
2020 K Street N.W.
Phone: 466-8811

TRAVEL TIPS

• Open a small bank account to accommodate special cash needs in the event you arrive in the United States at a time when the currency exchanges are not open. Automatic banking provides twenty-four-hour service, seven days a week.

• In most major cities, translators are available. However, it is recommended that you make reservations for this service well in advance of your planned visit to assure that your requirements will be met. When you make your hotel reservation, the hotel will be able to assist you in locating a translator.

• Secretarial/typing services are available in all cities, and most of the better hotels have these facilities on the premises.

• The climate may vary greatly from one U.S. city to another during the same time period. Check with your travel agent so that you may pack the proper attire, should you be visiting more than one city.

• In California, where Los Angeles and San Francisco are only four hundred miles apart, there are vast cultural differences which, no doubt, will be immediately obvious to the visitor. Because of the consistently warm weather, the Los Angeles residents tend to take life at a slower pace and dress in lighter, less formal, more colorful clothing than the San Franciscans. The weather in northern California is always cooler, with many fewer sunny days, because of the almost constant foggy conditions around the San Francisco Bay area. You will note that this difference extends to the business climate as well.

• The New York attitude has been stereotyped in the print and film media as fast moving, fast talking, and hard driving. You will also find that New Yorkers are, as a rule, courteous, prompt for appointments, friendly to visitors, and eager for them to enjoy their stay and think well of New York. In addition to your business wardrobe, comfortable shoes are a "must" because walking around New York City is sometimes the best and/or only way to get to your next appointment. During peak hours, taxis are scarce and traffic can be a nightmare, and walking can be the quickest way to get there. In addition, visiting the well-known museums and historical landmarks—that is, Statue of Liberty/Ellis Island, Metropolitan Museum of Art, Empire State Building, New York Public Library, and so on—also requires a lot of walking. The world's greatest shopping and internationally famed restaurants are at hand—much more than one can take in on a limited business stay.

• Houston has experienced an oil boom in the last decade and has been paying the price of sudden progress with its growth, by leaps and bounds, seemingly unrestricted. The people are very friendly and uninhibited in their boisterous greetings, physical backslapping, and bone-crushing handshakes. It is hard to resist such well-intentioned, gregarious people who are determined that you have a good time when you are in their city, and no doubt you will!

• Washington, D.C., is built on a grid pattern, making it relatively easy to learn how to get around. You will probably have much more difficulty getting around the government agencies, departments, embassies, consulates, and myriad office complexes, so be sure to get explicit instructions to assure that you reach your appointments on time. Washington is the nation's showplace of culture and history with the Smithsonian Institute its shining jewel. The Lincoln and Washington Memorials, Space Museum, National Museum of Natural History, National Portrait Gallery, and National Museum of American Art are only a few of the galleries and museums open to the public.

• A business trip to Chicago will be more pleasurable if you can avoid a winter cold spell. Built along the eastern shores of Lake Michigan, the city has brisk winter winds that make crossing State Street, the main artery, quite an experience. The people, however, are warm and friendly and they are proud of the progress that is currently being made in rebuilding "The Loop" (downtown area). The Near North Side offers excellent restaurants, hotels, and boutiques with a number of informal cafés for your evening's entertainment. Concert music, theatres, and major art galleries are all available.

• Greater Miami has become an international business hub, with more foreign banks than any other city except New York. It is the regional headquarters for more than one hundred large multinational corporations, and more than four thousand manufacturing firms are located here. On the other hand, Miami is one of the cleanest, most beautiful cities in the world and a business traveler would do well to stay a few extra days to take advantage of the resorts, excellent deep-sea fishing, jai alai matches, dog-races, and average 75° weather, which can be enjoyed even in the winter months of December through February.

• Select a U.S. hotel that caters to the foreign business traveler, one that provides check-in and check-out times and services convenient to your international flight schedules.

AFTERWORD
WHERE DO WE GO FROM HERE?

We start off by becoming involved in improving our global business communication skills in concert with others who believe that these techniques will assist us in gaining and maintaining a competitive edge in world commerce. The competition in today's global marketplace is growing increasingly fierce, and it is imperative that the skills required to compete effectively be developed and employed.

Protocol is no longer the art form in the purview of the international diplomatic community alone; a knowledge of business protocol procedure is mandatory for anyone engaged in global business and exchange. Today's foreign business interaction demands that all of us be envoys for our country, equipped with a knowledge and understanding of the business and social customs of the diverse cultures with which we are negotiating. It is this know-how that will bring success, and Snowdon International can deliver it to you. We believe the exercise of diplomacy in our international business affairs to be equally important to our world relationships as that employed by our governmental ambassadors.

Snowdon International, my firm, is a management consulting company with a network of specialists available to provide expert advice on international business and social protocol as well as negotiating techniques and strategies.

Consultation service, seminars, and business briefs for more than thirty countries are obtainable through our office. We also advise on proper entertaining procedures in global business, gift-giving propriety, communication styles, and executive travel arrangements.

You will find the material that we have provided in this text to be most useful to you in your international negotiating involvements, particularly if you follow our business protocol principles, and utilize the insights on the countries we have selected.

The commitment of corporations must be to recognize and support the global executive. The most effective way to provide this support is through the establishment of an in-house protocol department, which we can help you set up; such a department can furnish the information necessary for the corporation's management to function at their best in the international marketplace, and thereby achieve The Global Edge.

The organization most prominent in the protocol field globally is the *International Protocol Officers Association*, which I recently founded. Our intent is to bring together former ambassadors, government officials, protocol chiefs, business professionals, and others to develop a resource of protocol intelligence and international networking for you in your everyday encounters in the world trade area.

The Chartered Purpose of the International Protocol Officers Association is as follows:

- Maximize the business opportunities for governments, corporations and individuals engaged in world commerce.
- Encourage a spirit of universal understanding in international trade.
- Bring both government and business professionals together for the purpose of creating a global network to exchange ideas, expertise, advice and contacts for those engaged in international trade.
- Provide assistance, direction and guidance to those responsible for briefing and de-briefing global executives.
- Develop, expand and cultivate fellowship among members of the world business community.
- Address the importance of the office of business protocol to corporations, governments, municipalities, hotels and travel services, and all others engaged in foreign commerce.
- Help build bridges for peace.

As a member of the IPOA you will receive:

- Six in-depth country studies annually, to be included in our Business Protocol Advisory Newsletter
- Your IPOA Associate Certificate
- International Protocol Officers Association identification card
- Business protocol workshops and seminars
- Annual convention planned to be held in a different country each year to study the protocols of that country with the assistance of its government
- Protocol advisory services.

APPENDIX
KEY PHRASES AND GREETINGS

PRONUNCIATION KEY

ah	as in *car*
eh	as in *set*
ee	as in *sheep/sit*
oh	as in *not/raw*
oo	as in *Sue*
ü	French u / German ü (combination ee + oo)
uh	as in *but*
y	as in *yes*
ai	as in *I*
ay	as in *say*
oy	as in *boy*
kh	as in *loch*
gh	voiced kh combined with r
r	generally rolled (main exception: French)
sh	as in *share*
shj	as in *huge* (occurs in German)
zh	as in French *Jacques*
dzh	as in *Jack*
an	as in *ban*
on	as in *on/awning*
oon	as in *moon*
an	French nasal vowels.
on	Do not pronounce final *n*.
in	Instead, nasalize the vowel.

The syllables represented in UPPER CASE bear a tonic stress and must be pronounced with greater intensity than the syllables in lower case.
Example: How do you do? = HAO do yoo DOO?

Please note that any phonetic transcription can only approximate the actual utterance. Your best source for pronunciation is a speaker of the native language. Ask him or her to say the phrases and help you with the pronunciation. Use the transcription as a learning help and reminder.

ARABIC

Good morning	Sabah al-khayr	sah-bahh al-KHEHR
(Reply to good morning)	Sabah al-noor	sah-bahh an-NOOR
Good afternoon/good evening	Masaa al-khayr	mah-sah ahl-KHEHR
(Reply to good evening)	Masaa al-noor	mah-sah an-NOOR
My name is	Ana Asmy/or	anah AHSS-mee
	Asmy whoowa	AHSS-mee HOO-wah

413

What is your name?	Ma huwa ismuka? (to a man)	ma hoo-wah eess-MOO-kah?
	Ma huwa ismuki? (to a woman)	ma hoo-wah eess-MOO-kee?
I am glad to meet you	Tasharrafna bi-maarafat-a-kum	ta-shah-RRAHF-nah bee mah-arFAHT ah-KOOM
May I Introduce you to	Ismahali an al-rifukan ala	iss-MAHH-lee ahn ahl-REE-fookah ala
How are you?	Kayf Halak? (to a man)	kehf hah-LAHK
	Kayf Halik? (to a woman)	kehf HAH-leek?
Fine, thank you.	Bi khayr, el-hamdu li'illah.	bee-KHEHR ehl-HAM-doo leel-LAHH
How are you?	Wa anta? (to a man)	wah ahn-TAH?
	Wa inti? (to a woman)	wah een-TEE?
You are welcome	Ah'lan wa Marhaaba'	AHH-lahn wah mar-HHA-bah
Excuse me	Afwan	AH-fwahn
Please	Min Fadhlak (to a man)	meen FAHD-lahk
	Min Fahdlik (to a woman)	meen FAHD-leek
Thank you	Shukran	SHOO-krahn
Yes	Na-am	NAH-AHM
No	La'a	LAAH
Mr./Mrs./Miss	Sayiid/Sayiida/A'nissa	SAH-YEED/sah-YEE-DAH/AH-nee-sah
Goodbye (as said by host); go with safety, go in peace	Ma'al-Salaamah	MAHA-ssah-LAH-mah
Said by guest: Peace be on you	Allah yesallamak (to a man)	AHL-lahh yeh-SAHL-lah-MAHK
	Allah yesallamake (to a woman)	AHL-lahh yeh-SAHL-lah-MEEK
Peace be on you	Al-Salaam Alaykom	ahs-sah-LAHM ah-LAY-koom
(The answer to this)	Wa-Alaykom Al-Salaam	wah ah-LAY-koom ahs-sah-LAHM

This traditional greeting is used at every meeting.

CANTONESE

Good morning	Jousahn	dzho-SAHN
Good afternoon	Man	mm-AHN
Good evening	Man an (good night)	mahn-AHN
My name is	Ngo ge meng hoih	gwoh-GAY mahng-HAI
What is your name?	Nei gin mat yeh meng ah?	nay GEE-yoo maht YAY mahng-AH?

I am pleased to meet you	Ngo hou gouhlm	gwoh HOE GOH HANG
May I Introduce you to	Ngo hoyih m hoyih gaaisnh nei bei	gwoh HOE-yee mm HOE-yee GAI-SEE-yoo nay BAY
How are you?	Nei hou ma?	NAY-HOE-MAH?
Fine, thank you.	Ho ho	hoh-hoh
You are welcome	Msai haakei	mm-SAI HAHK-HAI
Excuse me	Mgoi	mm-GOY
Please	Cheng	TSHENG
Thank you	Do Jeh; m goi	DO-DJEH or mm-GOY
Yes	Haih	HAI
No	Mhaih	mm-HAI
Mr./Mrs./Miss	Sinsaang/taaitaai/siuje	SIN-sahng/TAI-rai/SHEE-YOO-dzhey
Goodbye	Joigin	DZHOY-GEEN

DUTCH (NETHERLANDS)

Good morning	Goedemorgen	KHOO-duh MOR-khen
Good afternoon	Goedemiddag	KHOO-duh MEE-dakh
Good evening	Goedenavond	KHOO-duhn AH-vont
My name is	Mijn naam is	meyn NAHM iss
What is your name?	Wat is uw naam?	VAHT iss ehoo NAHM?
I am pleased to meet you	Aangenaam	AHN-khuh-NAHM
May I Introduce you to	Mag ik u voorstellen aan	MAKH-eek ü VOR-stehlen ahn
How are you?	Hoe maakt u het?	hoo MAHKT ü heht?
Fine, thank you.	Heel goed, dank u.	Hehl-KHOOT DANK u.
How are you?	En u?	Ehn U?
You are welcome	Zonder dank	Zon-der DAHNK
Excuse me	Pardon	PAHR-don
Please	Alstublieft	AHL-stuh-bleeft
Thank you	Dank u	DAHNK-ü
Yes	Ja	YAH
No	Neen	NAYN
Mr./Mrs./Miss	Mijnheer/Mevrouw/Juffrouw	muh-NAYR/muh-VRAO/yuh-VRAO
Goodbye	Dag	DAKH

FRENCH

Good morning (hello)	Bonjour	bon-ZHOOR
Good afternoon	Bonjour	bon-ZHOOR
Good evening	Bonsoir	bon-SWAHR
My name is	Je m'appelle	zhuh-mah-PEHL
What is your name?	Comment vouz appelez-vous?	KO-Man-voo-zap-leh-VOO?
I am pleased to meet you	Enchanté(e)	an-shan-TEH

May I introduce you to	Puis-je vous présenter	PWEEZH-voo-preh-*zan*-TEH
How are you?	Comment allez-vouz?	KO-*man*-tah-leh-VOO?
Fine, thank you.	Bien, merci.	BY*IN* mehr-SEE.
How are you?	Et vous?	eh-VOO?
You are welcome	Je vous en prie	zhuh-voo-*zan*-PREE
	De rien	duh-RY*IN*
Excuse me	Pardon	pahr-D*ON*
	Excusez-moi	EKH-skü-zeh-MWAH
Please	S'il vous plaît	SEEL-voo-pleh
Thank you	Merci	mehr-SEE
Yes	Oui	Wee
No	Non	N*ON*
Mr./Mrs./Miss	Monsieur/Madame/ Mademoiselle	muh-SYUH/mah-DAM/ mad-mwah-ZEHL
Goodbye	Au revoir	o-ruh-VWAR

GERMAN

Good morning	Guten Morgen	GOO-tun MOR-gun
Good afternoon	Guten Tag	GOO-tun TAHK
Good evening	Guten Abend	GOO-tun AH-bunt
My name is	Ich heisse	eeshj HAI-suh
What is your name?	Wie heissen Sie?	vee HAI-sun-ZEE?
I am pleased to meet you	Ich freue mich Sie kennenzulernen	eeshj FROY-uh meeshj zee KEHN-n-tsoo-LEHR-nun
May I introduce you to	Darf ich Sie mit . . . bekanntmachen	dahrf-eeshj ZEE meet . . . beh-KAHNT-makhun
How are you?	Wie geht es Ihnen	vee GAYT-ehs EE-nun?
Fine, thank you.	Gut, danke.	Goot DAHNK-uh.
You are welcome	Bitte (sehr)	BIT-uh (ZEHR)
Excuse me	Verzeihung	fehr-TSA-yoong
Please	Bitte	BIT-uh
Thank you	DANKE (sehr)	DAHNK-uh (ZEHR)
Yes	Ja	YAH
No	Nein	NAIN
Mr./Mrs./Miss	Herr/Frau/Fräulein	HEHR/FRAO/FROY-lain
Goodbye	Auf Wiedersehen	aof-VEE-duhr-zehn

HINDI

Good morning	Namaste or Pranam	nah-MAHSS-TEH or prah-NAHM
Good afternoon	Namaste or Pranam	nah-MAHSS-TEH or prah-NAHM
Good evening	Namaste or Pranam	nah-MAHSS-TEH or prah-NAHM
My name is	Mera nam . . . hai	MEE-rah NAHM . . . HEH
What is your name?	Apka nam kya hai?	AHP-kah NAHM kee-yah HEH?

I am pleased to meet you	Apse milkar khushi hui	AHP-seh MEEL-kahr KHU-shee HOO-ee
May I introduce you to	Mai . . . se Apka parichay kara du	MAY . . . seh AHP-kah pahr-EE-rshey kahrah-doo
How are you?	Ap kaise hai?	AHP KAH-see HEH?
Fine, thank you.	Theek hoon	TEEK-hoon
You are welcome	Koi bat nahi	KO-ee BAHT nah-HEE
Excuse me	Kshama Kijiye	KSHAY-mah kee-gee-YEH
Please	Kripa kar (ke)	KRE-pah KAHR (keh)
Thank you	Dhanyavad	DHANN-yeh-VAHD
Yes	(Ji) Ha	(dzhee) HAH
No	(Ji) Nahi	(dzhee) ney-HEE
Mr./Mrs./Miss	Shri or Shriman/Shrimati/ Kumari or Sushri	SHREE or SHREE-mahn/ SHREE-mah-tee/koo-MAH-ree or soo-SHRE
Goodbye	Namaste or Pranam	nah-MAHSS-TEH or prah-NAHM

ITALIAN

Good morning	Buon giorno	bwohn DZHOR-noh
Good afternoon	Buon giorno/Buona sera	bwoh-nah SEH-rah
Good evening	Buona sera	bwoh-nah SEH-rah
My name is	Mi chiamo	mee KYAH-moh
What is your name?	Come se chiama?	KO-me see KYAH-mah?
I am pleased to meet you	Piacere di conoscerla	pyah-TSHEH-reh dee ko-NO-shehr-lah
May I introduce you to	Posso presentarvi al (Signore X)/alla (Signora, Signorina X)	POH-ssoh preh-sehn-TAHR-vee ahl/ahllah
How are you?	Come sta?	ko-meh STAH?
Fine, thank you.	Bene, grazie.	BEH-neh GRAH-tsay
How are you?	E lei?	eh LAY?
You are welcome	Prego	PREH-goh
Excuse me	Scusi	SKOO-zee
Please	Per favore/Per piacere	PEHR fah-VO-reh/PEHR pyah-TSHEH-reh
Thank you	Grazie	GRAH-tsyeh
Yes	Si	SEE
No	No	NOH
Mr./Mrs./Miss	Signor/Signora/Signorina	see-NYOR/see-NYO-rah/ see-nyo-REE-nah
Goodbye	Arrivederci	ahr-ree-veh-DEHR-rshee

JAPANESE

Good morning	ohayo-gozaimasu	o-HAIo-o go-zai-MAHSS
Good afternoon	kon nichi wa	KON-nee-rshee-WAH
Good evening	konban wa	KOM-bahn-WAH

My name is	watakushi wa . . . desu	WAH-tah-kshee-WAH . . . DEHSS
What is your name?	onamae wa nan desu ka?	o-NAH-MAEH-WAH NAN dehss-KAH?
I am pleased to meet you	oai dekite koei desu	o-AI DEH-kreh KO-EHEE DEHSS
May I introduce you to	. . . san wo shōkai shitai no desu ga	. . . sahn-WO SHO-OKAI shee-TAI no dehss GAH
How are you?	1. ogenki desu ka?	o-GEHN-keedehss-KAH?
	2. ikaga desu ka?	EE-kahn-gah dehss-KAH?
Fine, thank you.	genki desu	GEHN-kee DEHSS
You are welcome	dō itashimashite	DO-O eetah-sheemah-SHTEH
Excuse me (I'm sorry, pardon me)	1. sumimasen	SU-meemahsehn
Excuse me (I have to leave now)	2. shitsurei shimasu	SHEE-tsürey shee-MAHSS
Excuse me (I'm sorry to bother you)	3. gomen kudasai	GO-mehn küdah-SAI
Please (give me)	1. . . . kudasai	. . . küdah-SAI
Please (do it [for me], when requesting)	2. onegai shimasu	. . . o-neh-gah ee-shee-MAHSS
Thank you	1. dōmo (casual)	Do-omo
	2. arigatō gozaimasu	ah- REE-ngah-TO-o go-zai-MAHSS
Yes	hai	HAI
No	iie	EE-ee EH
Mr./Mrs./Miss	. . . san (suffixed to name)	. . . SAHN
Goodbye	sayōnara	sah-YO-onahrah

KOREAN

Good morning Good afternoon Good evening	Ahn nyong, ha ship nee ka?	ah-nee-yong hah-sim-NEE- kah
My name is_____	Nah eui, eeh room eun, _____eep nee da	NAH-oo-wee-eerum- oon _____eem-NEE-da
What is your name?	Song ham ee, noo koo ship nee ka?	song-ham-ee noo-goo shim-NEE-kah
I am pleased to meet you.	Boep keh doe suh, pan kap soop nee da.	BIP-geh-tway-nyee PAN-gahp-soom-NEE-dah
May I introduce you to_____.	_____see reul, soh keh ha ke soop nee da	_____see-rool SO-gah ha-GEH soom-NEE-dah
How are you?	Ahn nyong, ha ship nee ka?	ah-nee-yong hah-sim-NEE-kah
You are welcome (answer to ''Thank you'').	Chun man yeh, mal soom jep nee da	chun-MUN-ai mal-soom ee-soom NEE-dah

Excuse me (allow me to violate some etiquette).	Sheel yeh hap nee da	SHIL-yeh ham-NEE-dah
Please.	(no direct counterpart)	——
Thank you (I appreciate).	Kahm sah hap nee da	kumh-sah ham-NEE-dah
Yes	Neh	nay
No	Ah nym nee da	ah-nyim-NEE-dah
Mr./Mrs./Miss____	____See/ ____Boon/ ____yang	____see/____pooh-YIN/____yahng
Good-bye	Ahn nyung hee	ah-nyong-HEE

MANDARIN

Good morning	Zǎo ān	tsao AHN
Good afternoon	Wǔ ān	woo AHN
Good evening/night.	Wǎn ān	wahn AHN
My name is	Wǒ de míng zì jiào	WAH-duh MING-tsuh DZHIAO
What is your name?	Nín Jiào Shèn me míng zì?	neen-DZHIAO SHEM-muh MING-tsuh?
I am pleased to meet you	Xìng Huì	shing KHWEH
May I introduce you to	Wǒ géi nǐ jiè shào	wo GAY nee-TSHYEI SHAO
How are you	Ní hǎo ma?	NEE-HAO-MAH?
Fine, thank you.	Hén hǎo, xiè xiè.	HEHN-HAO SHYEH-shyeh.
How are you?	nín ne?	NEEN-neh?
You are welcome	Bú kè qì	boo-KUH-tshee
Excuse me	Duì bù qǐ	dweh-BOO-tshee
Please	Qǐng	TSHING
Thank you	Xiè xiè	SHYEH-SHYEH
Yes	Shì	SHUH
No	Bú	BOO
Mr./Mrs./Miss	Xiān shēng/tài tai/xiǎo jiě	SHEN-shung/TAI-tai/SHIAO-dzhay
Goodbye	Zài jiàn	ZAI-DZHEHN

PORTUGUESE

Good morning/Good day	Bom dia	boong DZHEE-ah
Good afternoon	Boa tarde	boah TAR-dee
Good evening	Boa noite	boah NOY-tshee
My name is	Meu nome é	meh-oo NOH-mee eh
What is your name?	Come se chama você?	KO-moo seh SHAH-mah vo-SEH?
I am happy to meet you	Muito prazer	MWEEN-too prah-ZEHR
May I introduce you to	Permita-me apresentar-lhe(s)	pehr-MEE-tah-meh apreh-zehn-TAHR-leh
How are you?	Como está?	KO-moo eesh-TAH?
Fine, thank you.	Muito bem. Obrigado/a.	MWEEN-too baing. oh-

		bree-GAH-doh. oh-bree-GAD-dah.
How are you?	E você?	eh voh-SEI
You are welcome	De nada	duh NAH-dah
Excuse me (I'm sorry)	Desculpe	deh-SKOOL-pee
(May I pass)	Com licença	kong lee-SEHN-sah
Please	Por favor	por fah-VOR
Thank you (by man)	Obrigado	obree-GAH-do
(by woman)	Obrigada	obree-GAH-dah
Yes	Sim	SEENG
No	Não	NA*ON*
Mr./Mrs./Miss	Senhor/Senhora/ Senhorita	seh-NYOR/seh-NYO-ruh/ seh-nyo-REE-tah
See you again/See you later	Até logo	ahteh LOH-goo
Goodbye (farewell)	Adeus	ah-DAY-ooss

RUSSIAN

Good morning	dobroje utro	DOH-bree OO-trah
Good afternoon	dobryj den	DOH-bree DYEHN
Good evening	dobryj vecher	DOH-bree VYEH-tshehr
My name is	menja zovut	myeh-nyah zah-VOOT
What is your name?	kak vashe imja?	KAK VAH-sheh EE-myah?
I am pleased to meet you	rad poznakomit'sja s vami	RAD (RADah) paz-nah-KOM-eetsyah s-VAH-mee
	rada poznakomit'sja s vami	
May I introduce you to	pozvol'ta poznakomit' vas s	pah-ZVOL-tah paz-nah-KOM-eet vahss s
How are you?	kok vy pozhivojete?	KAK vee pah-zhee-VAH-yetsyeh
Fine, thank you.	khorosho, spacibo.	kha-rah-SHOH spah-SEE-bah.
How are you?	A kak vi?	ah kak VEE?
You are welcome	dobro pozhalovar'	do-BROH pah-ZHA-lo-vahr
Excuse me	izvinite menja	eez-vee-NEE-tyeh myeh-NYAH
Please	pozhalujsta	pah-ZHAL-stah
Thank you	spacibo	spah-SEE-bah
Yes	da	DAH
No	net	NYET
Mr./Mrs./Miss	gaspadin/gaspaja	gass-pah-DEEN/gass-pah-ZHAH
Goodbye	do svidanija	doh-svee-DAH-nyah

SPANISH

Good morning	Buenos días	BWEH-noss DEE-ahss
Good afternoon	Buenas tardes	BWEH-nahss TAR-dehss

Good evening	Buenas noches	BWEH-nahss NOT-shehss
My name is	Me llamo	meh YAH-moh
What is your name?	Cómo se llama usted?	KO-moh seh YAH-mah oos-TEH?
I am pleased to meet you (man to man)	Encantado de conocerle	ehn-kan-TAH-doh deh ko-noh-SEHR-leh
(woman to woman)	Encantada de conocerla	ehn-kan-TAH-dah deh ko-noh-SEHR-lah
May I introduce you to	Tengo el gusto de presentarle a	Tehn-goh ehl GOOS-toh deh preh-sehn-TAR-leh a
How are you	Cómo está usted?	ko-moh ehs-TAH oos-TEH?
Fine, thank you.	Muy bien, gracias.	NWEE-byehn GRAH-syahss.
How are you?	Y usted?	ee oos-TEH?
You are welcome	De nada	deh NAH-dah
Excuse me	Perdón	pehr-DON
Please	Por favor	por fah-VOR
Thank you	Muchas gracias	MOO-tshahss GRAH-syahss
Yes	Sí	SEE
No	No	Noh
Mr./Mrs./Miss	Señor/Señora/Señorita	seh-NYOR/seh-NYO-rah/ seh-nyo-REE-tah
Goodbye	Adiós	ah-DYOSS
See you again	Hasta luego/hasta la vista	ahss-tah LWEH-goh/ahss-tah lah VEESS-tah

ACKNOWLEDGMENTS

I am sincerely grateful to the following people for their cooperation, knowledgeable advice and assistance:

Robert Agosti, Citibank; Irene Antipa; Betsy Barley; John Bertram, InterMarketing Inc.; Becky Boyd, U.S. State Department; Ambassador Antonio Cantuaria, Consul General of Brazil; Joseph Canzeri, Canzeri & Company; Pierre Casse, World Bank; Wendy Chen; Hon. Joan Margaret Clark, U.S. State Department; Harry Coburn, U.S. State Department; Marie-Jo Coclet, Council on Religion and International Affairs; Michel Coclet, Uramerica; David Cohn, specialist in Soviet studies; Kevin Corrigan, Chase Manhattan Bank; Charles Crawford, Grey & Company; Charlotte Crystal, specialist in Soviet studies; Hon. True Davis, former ambassador to Switzerland; Diane Dillard, U.S. State Department; Walter C. Douglas, Rockefeller Center Management Corporation; Lewis Eslinger, Esq.; Betty A. Evans, mother; Frank Feather, Global Management, Inc.; James Feland, Chase Manhattan Bank; John Fredenburg, U.S. State Department; Tom Furey, U.S. State Department; Ronald Gahn, U.S. State Department; Charles Gonzales, Central/South American specialist; Lundy Gordon, Shearson Lehman/American Express; Cedric Grant, Citibank (Switzerland); Arnold and Harriet Greenberg, Complete Traveller Bookstore; James Hammond, Citibank; David Hobbs, U.S. State Department; David Holmes, Bank of America; Stephen K. Iwai, Bishop of Yokohama; Sir Asher Joel, Australia; C. J. M. Kramers, Consul-General of the Netherlands; Laurie Law, Soviet specialist; Nelson Lees; Dr. Edward Leigh, China specialist; Maria Leiti, Brazilian Mission to the United Nations; W. R. Grace & Company; Jeffrey T. Long, AIA; Cornelius J. Lynch, World Trade Center; Christine McKenna; Thorrun Mathias, travel advisor; Pierre Mellinger, French Embassy; Jacqueline A. Mengone; Dilip-Kumar Mirchandani, Bhairava Productions; Mrs. Mitra, Consul of Commerce for India; Robert Moran, Ph.D., Scottsdale, Ariz.; Dr. Theodore Moran, Georgetown University School of Foreign Service, Washington, D.C.; Sir James Murray, KCMG, Hanson Industries; Alex Nader, Middle East specialist; John B. Noss, Consul, Invest in Britain Bureau; Martin Novar, research assistant; Konstantin Pio-Ulosky; Frank Rakas, Italian Trade Commission; Paul Raniolo, Gintel & Company; Dr. Kathleen Reardon, Professor of Communication Sciences; Marcia Rosenkrantz; Bette Saunders, Editor/Publisher, *The African Letter;* Dr. Werner Schwebback, Director of Training, UNITAR; Franchon Silverstein, U.S. State Department; Lawrence Smith, National Commercial Bank of Saudi Arabia; Patricia Snowden, Canada specialist; Ron Somerville, U.S. State Department; Tina Starkie, Inc., translation and interpreting services; Percy Steinhart, Citibank; Marjabelle Young Stewart, etiquette expert; Timothy P. Sullivan; Arthur R. Taylor; Mary Tierney, World Trade Center; Charles Wardell, Shearson Lehman/American Express; Ruthe Winkler; James M. Ziede, security consultant, League of Arab States.

In addition, I wish to acknowledge the many consuls and representatives of the foreign embassies and trade offices in New York, Washington, and globally, as well as the good offices of the U.S. State Department, U.S. Department of Commerce, and World Trade Center Association, and the many people devoted to expanding world trade who contributed to this book.

INDEX

We welcome your participation to join us as an Associate of the
International Protocol Officers Association.

YOUR INVITATION TO JOIN
WITH THE MOST PRESTIGIOUS GLOBAL BUSINESS PROFESSIONALS
PROMOTING DIPLOMACY IN INTERNATIONAL COMMERCE

Executive Board

Ambassador Angier Biddle Duke

Ambassador Lloyd N. Hand

Ambassador James W. Symington

Sir James Murray, KCMG

Guy F. Tozzoli, President, World Trade Association

INTERNATIONAL PROTOCOL OFFICERS ASSOCIATION

PLEASE COMPLETE AND RETURN ALONG WITH YOUR CHECK FOR $500.00 REPRE-
SENTING THE ANNUAL ASSOCIATE FEE:

Name _____

Title _____

Company _____

Address _____

City _____ State _____ Zip Code _____

Major Interests and Responsibilities:

_____

_____

_____

_____

IPOA—ONE WORLD TRADE CENTER—SUITE 7967—NEW YORK, N.Y. 10048
PHONE: (212) 524-7716
A SNOWDON INTERNATIONAL CORPORATION